The Coturnix Quail
Anatomy and Histology

The
Coturnix
Quail

Anatomy and Histology

Theodore C. Fitzgerald

The Iowa State University Press, AMES, IOWA

The late DR. THEODORE C. FITZGERALD was Head Professor and Research Professor, Department of Anatomy and Histology, School of Veterinary Medicine, Auburn University, Auburn, Alabama. He received the M.S. and D.V.M. degrees from Ohio State University which also honored him with its Distinguished Alumnus Award. He served as president of the Alabama Veterinary Medical Association and was the author of numerous journal articles.

Composed and printed by
The Iowa State University Press

First edition, 1969

Standard Book Number: 8138–0356-X
Library of Congress Catalog Card Number: 74–88001

Note of Acknowledgment

SPECIAL RECOGNITION is due Mrs. Judith Guenther, Research Associate in the Department of Anatomy and Histology at Auburn University, who drew some illustrations and reworked all of them, organized and completed the original manuscript, and accepted the responsibility of seeing it through to publication.

A Fitting Memorial . . .

THIS BOOK is Dr. Theodore C. Fitzgerald's last fine contribution to veterinary medicine. His enthusiasm for investigating and describing the anatomy of the coturnix quail remained undiminished by ill health, and his valiant fight to finish the manuscript resulted in its being essentially completed at the time of his death in 1967.

We wish to thank Mrs. Frances Bailey Fitzgerald for entrusting to us the completion of the manuscript. We hope that the book will be a fitting memorial to Dr. Fitzgerald.

THE STAFF

Department of Anatomy and Histology
School of Veterinary Medicine
Auburn University

Preface

THE COTURNIX QUAIL originates from Europe, Africa, and Asia as a migratory game bird. For several centuries in Japan a semidomesticated strain has been raised as a pet, for meat and eggs, and as a singing bird. This small, fast-maturing bird is used mainly in this country as a laboratory animal and is becoming increasingly important in research using large populations.

In recognition of the popularity of coturnix for this purpose, studies of its basic anatomy and histology are extremely desirable for the rapid advancement of research projects in many fields. These include embryological, physiological, nutritional, genetic, endocrinological, germfree, and cancer studies. Approximately 100 laboratories already are using this bird in some capacity. The adaptation of this book to the needs of current research involves more than an anatomical description; variations from the accepted anatomy of the common fowl and mammals have been emphasized and illustrated. Since coturnix research is still at a very early stage, it cannot be hoped that this endeavor will prove to be as complete a coverage of anatomy and histology as will be needed. Broader adaptations of coturnix to serve future research is certain to come. Problems constantly arise calling for the development of new ideas and techniques, all of which will place more specific demands on the depth of the basic science of anatomy.

The oldest established lines of supply for coturnix in the United States are those maintained by the Department of Poultry Science, Auburn University, Auburn, Alabama, and the University of California at Davis.

While this book is specifically designed for use in research, it is the hope of the author that it will also be useful as a reference for those who have an interest in laboratory animal medicine, veterinary medicine, poultry science, and ornithology.

The author is indebted to the veterinary students who dissected the birds; the art students who did the first drawings; Mrs. Farrys Hillestad, laboratory technician, who was responsible for the histological preparations; and Mrs. Marianne Dennis, who assisted with the typing and proofreading of the original descriptions. Dr. George Stott wrote the section on the female reproductive system and did the dissections of the cranial nerves.

This project was carried on as a cooperative effort with the Poultry Department of the School of Agriculture, Auburn University, from which all the specimens of the Auburn strain of coturnix were obtained. Dr. S. A. Edgar, Dr. W. D. Ivey, and Dr. J. R. Howes, who were also conducting research on the quail, were most helpful and in large measure responsible for the original idea for the book. Germfree quail were obtained from the Germfree Life Research Center at Tampa, Florida, through the assistance of Dr. Cavett O. Prickett, Assistant Chief of Research at that center.

The proper nomenclature to be used in the preparation of the text created somewhat of a problem. However, as far as possible the avian nomenclature used is based upon the format established by the International Anatomical Nomenclature Commission.

Contents

Illustrations

The Coturnix Quail

Anatomy and Histology

CHAPTER ONE

Osteology

THE *skeleton* (Fig. 1.1) of coturnix quail is composed of supporting and protecting structures of the body. In descriptive anatomy the ligaments which bind supporting structures together may be included as skeletal structures. This description, however, will be limited to bones and cartilages.

The description of the skeleton is divided into three classifications: axial, appendicular, and visceral. The *axial skeleton* is made up of those bones which support the linear structures of the body and include the skull, vertebral column, ribs, and sternum. The *appendicular skeleton* includes the bones of the pectoral and pelvic limbs. The *splanchnic, or visceral, skeleton* is composed of the bones found in the viscera, that is, the entoglossal and hyoid bones.

Although it may not be possible to classify the bones of coturnix according to shape, the following five general divisions will be recognized: *long bones, short bones, sesamoid bones, flat bones,* and *irregular bones.* Flat and irregular bones are found in the axial skeleton; and long, short, and sesamoid bones are characteristic of the limbs. Bones

3

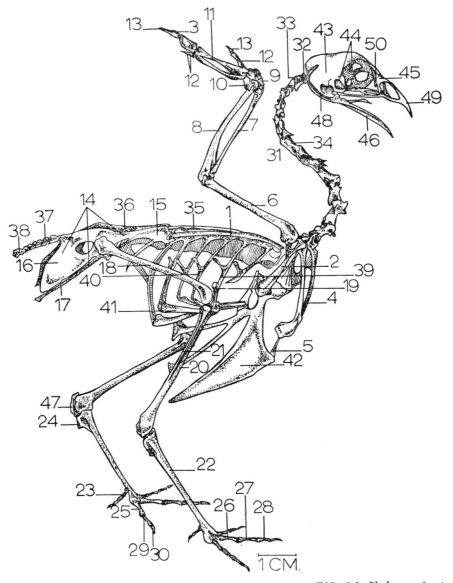

FIG. 1.1—Skeleton of coturnix.

1. Scapula	18. Femur	35. Thoracic vertebrae
2. Coracoid	19. Patella	36. Synsacrum
3. Second phalanx, 3rd digit	20. Tibiotarsus	37. Coccygeal vertebrae
4. Ramus of clavicle	21. Fibula	38. Urostilus
5. Sternoclavicular ligament	22. Metatarsus (2nd, 3rd and 4th)	39. Second rib
6. Humerus	23. First metatarsal	40. Vertebral rib
7. Radius	24. Hypotarsal ridge	41. Sternal rib
8. Ulna	25. First phalanx, 2nd digit	42. Sternum
9. Radial carpal	26. First phalanx, 3rd digit	43. Vertebral cranium (lateral parietal crest)
10. Ulnar carpal	27. Second phalanx, 3rd digit	44. Orbital fossa
11. Third carpometacarpal	28. Third phalanx, 3rd digit	45. Visceral cranium (lateral ramus of nasal bone)
12. First phalanges	29. Second phalanx, 2nd digit	46. Mandible
13. Distal phalanges	30. Distal phalanx, 2nd digit	47. Hypotarsal sesamoid
14. Os innominatum	31. Region of ligamentum nuchae	48. Hyoid
15. Ilium	32. Atlas	49. Premaxilla
16. Ischium	33. Axis	50. Lacrimal bone
17. Pubis	34. Cervical vertebrae	

may be further classified as to origin and designated as membrane or cartilage bones. Membrane bones are found primarily among those that form the face and dorsal regions of the cranium. Most of the remainder are of endochondral origin.

SKULL AS A WHOLE

Descriptions of the anatomy of the *skull* usually include the form and structure of all the bones of the head (Figs. 1.2–1.7). It is convenient in coturnix, as in mammals, to divide the bones into two regions: those which make up the structure of the cranium and those which are included in the face. The *cranial bones* enclose the brain and the organ of hearing and form parts of the orbital and nasal cavities. The *bones of the face* include those which enclose the oral and nasal cavities and part of the orbital cavity. They also form the boundaries for and help to support the pharynx, larynx, and tongue. Most of the bones of the skull are flat bones which have

their embryological development in membrane. Others of the basal region may be classified as irregular bones, since they are median in position and are unpaired. The irregular bones have their embryological development in cartilage.

The skull as a whole has the form of a four-sided pyramid, the apex of which is formed by the curved beak; the base, which is somewhat rounded off, is caudal in position. The division between the cranium and the face may be located by a plane, partly transverse and partly frontal, which passes through the caudal limits of the orbits.

Frontal Surface

The *frontal surface* (Fig. 1.2) is formed by the squamous part of the occipital, parietal, frontal, nasal, and premaxillary bones. The squamous part of the occipital bone forms only a very limited part of the caudal margin of the frontal surface. A very faint external occipital crest, which is most prominent medially, extends laterally and is continuous with the temporal crest at a distinct angle. This angle represents the widest part of the skull of coturnix. The

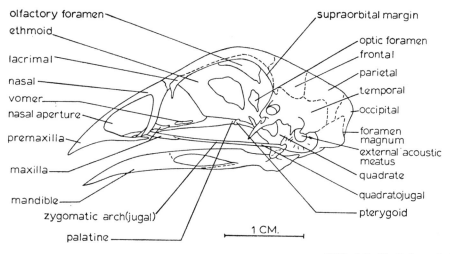

FIG. 1.2–Skull, lateral view.

temporal crest curves forward and inward to the root of the supraorbital process which forms a boundary here between the frontal and lateral surfaces of the skull. The angle of junction continues forward and inward as the margin of the supraorbital process. The parietal region extends from the external occipital crest to the parietofrontal suture. This surface is convex in all directions, with a faint transverse groove that is in the position of the frontal parietal suture.

Nasal and Premaxillary Regions

The *nasal and premaxillary regions* (Fig. 1.2) continue rostrad as a rather imperfect osseous triangle. The ventrolateral margins of the nasal and lacrimal bones are continued by the membranous wall of the infratemporal sinus. This membrane continues downward to join the maxilla and zygomatic arch, or jugal bone. The cranial nasal aperture presents the second osseous imperfection. A dorsal view through this aperture presents the nasal surface of the palatine process of the maxilla; the palatine and maxillary processes of the premaxilla; and centrally, the rostral extension of the vomer. The body of the premaxilla completes the apex of the triangle. It is convex in both longitudinal and transverse planes and is roughened by numerous vascular grooves of the corium of the beak in which the bone is encased.

LATERAL SURFACE

The *lateral surface* (Fig. 1.2) of the skull may be divided into the cranial, orbital, and preorbital regions. The cranial region presents the temporal fossa, the very large acoustic meatus, and the zygomatic process. The temporal fossa is bounded dorsally by the parietal and temporal crests, rostrally by the margin of the orbit and the supraorbital

process, caudally by the occipitotemporal suture, and ventrally by the caudal extremities of the mandible and quadratojugal bones as well as the large cornua (Fig. 1.7) of the hyoid bones. The upper portion of the fossa is smooth and concave; the lower portion is rough and gives rise to the zygomatic process which is in the form of a three-sided pyramid extending downward, forward, and inward. The base of the zygomatic process is separated from the temporal process by a large oval foramen. Situated ventral to the process is the quadrate bone, dorsal to which are two foramina which together make up the foramen lacerum. Located caudal to the condyle of the quadrate bone (Fig. 1.3) is the large oval external acoustic meatus surrounded by the external auditory process. This process is formed by parts of the occipital, temporal, and sphenoid bones. The caudal portion is perforated by the caudal carotid and jugular foramina. The extensive tympanic cavity is readily visible in the macerated specimen and presents rostroventrally the wide aperture of the eustachian tube (Fig. 1.3). Centrally in the cavity are found the fenestra ovalis and rotunda. In addition there are numerous pneumatic spaces in the base of the skull. These spaces may be considered as modified paranasal sinuses or, perhaps more specifically, as a modification of the mastoid, ethmoid, and sphenoid sinuses.

Orbital Fossa

The *orbital fossa* (Fig. 1.3) is very large in coturnix; it houses the eye and its accessory structures. The total area of both orbits exceeds that of the cranial cavity. The interorbital septum, which is incomplete in young birds, is formed primarily by the perpendicular part of the ethmoid bone and the upper surface of the rostrum of the sphenoid bone. The roof of the cavity is formed chiefly

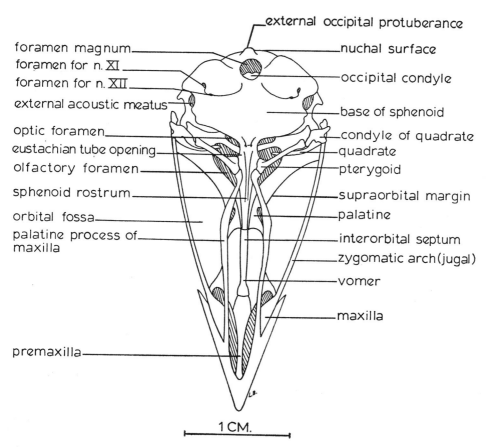

foramen magnum
foramen for n. XI
foramen for n. XII
external acoustic meatus
optic foramen
eustachian tube opening
olfactory foramen
sphenoid rostrum
orbital fossa
palatine process of maxilla
premaxilla

external occipital protuberance
nuchal surface
occipital condyle
base of sphenoid
condyle of quadrate
quadrate
pterygoid
supraorbital margin
palatine
interorbital septum
zygomatic arch(jugal)
vomer
maxilla

1 CM.

FIG. 1.3—Skull, ventral view.

by the orbital portion of the frontal bone and by the smaller lacrimal bone. The caudal region of the orbit is formed by the temporal bone above and the pterygoid and quadrate bones below. The lateral boundary is formed by the zygomatic processes of the maxilla. The floor of the cavity is incomplete and is separated from the nasal cavity and infraorbital sinuses by membrane. A lateral view of the orbital fossa and infratemporal sinus reveals part of the lacrimal and frontal bones. The optic foramen is situated in the caudoventral region. The two optic foramina are separated by a very thin median plate of bone that gives the impression of a single

foramen when viewed from a caudal position.

Preorbital Region

The *preorbital region* (Fig. 1.2) of the lateral surface presents a profile that is comparable to that of the beak and mouth. The rather large triangular nasal aperture is enclosed by the rami of the nasal bones and the premaxilla. The center of the external nares is situated midway between the eye and the point of the beak. Numerous small foramina are seen on the roughened dorsal surface of the apex of the premaxilla. The straight line is formed by the quadratojugal and jugal bones and the maxilla and premaxilla, with a slight ventral deviation at the apex of the beak.

Ventral, or Basal, Surface

The *ventral, or basal, surface* (Fig. 1.3) forms an angle with the nuchal surface of about 45°. Therefore a ventral view will present mainly the nuchal surface of the basal part of the sphenoid and the lower part of the occipital bone. The basal part of the sphenoid is wider than it is long and presents a median eminence. The lateral areas are convex in all directions. Caudal to the rostrum of the sphenoid are the rostral apertures of the osseous eustachian tube. Additional foramina which lie between the eustachian apertures lead directly to the cranial cavity. The sphenoid rostrum is continued in front by the vomer bone, which is median in position. The vomer is grooved on its upper surface to accommodate the lower margin of the nasal septa and the perpendicular plate of the ethmoid bone. The large orbital fossae which occupy a position just rostral to the cranial area of the basal surface are equal in extent to one-fourth of the total length of the skull. Each is triangular in outline and is bounded caudally by the quadrate and pterygoid bones, medially by the vomer and palatine bones, and laterally by the maxilla and the quadratojugal bones. The preorbital region of the basal surface is triangular in outline, and its apex forms the point of the upper beak. It is formed by the rostral process of the palatine bones, the palatine process of the maxilla, and the body of the premaxilla. Numerous foramina pierce the bone and perforate freely to form a corresponding row on the nasal surface.

Nuchal Surface

The occipital bone forms most of the *nuchal surface* (Fig. 1.3) of the skull. In young coturnix, as in mammals, the bone is divided into four parts which form the boundaries of the foramen magnum. The lateral parts form a portion of the tympanic cavity, and the basal part is covered largely by the sphenoid bone ventrally. Dorsally, the surface is completed by the small nuchal surfaces of the parietal bones centrally and the temporal bones laterally. No special features are apparent. Of the foramina the foramen magnum is most significant. It is roughly triangular, and at its base it presents the rounded articular surface (occipital condyle) for articulation with the condyle of the atlas and presents a central facet for the odontoid process of the axis. Foramina for the spinal accessory nerves are located just below the level of this articulation. Lateral to these are found the foramina for the vagus and hypoglossal nerves. At the ventrolateral angle of the nuchal surface the exits of the jugular and carotid foramina are found. Medially positioned and midway between the foramen magnum and the external occipital crest is found the external occipital protuberance. A fontanelle appears as a small opening at the junction of the occipital and parietal bones in young coturnix.

BONES OF THE CRANIUM

The *bones of the cranium* (ossa cranii) are the occipital, sphenoid, ethmoid, parietal, frontal, and temporal (Figs. 1.2–1.4). The first three are single and are derived from cartilage; the others are paired and have a membranous origin.

Occipital Bone

The *occipital bone* (Figs. 1.2–1.4) fuses early into a solid mass that forms the greater part of the nuchal surface of the skull. The day-old skull will demonstrate the usual four embryological

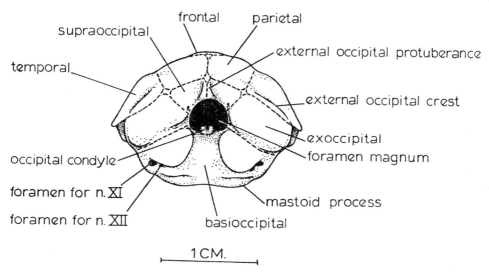

FIG. 1.4—Bones of the cranium, caudal view.

parts. They consist of the basal (basioccipital), or body, part; two lateral parts (exoccipital); and a dorsal squamosal (supraoccipital), part. All of these contribute to the formation of the margins of the foramen magnum. The supraoccipital part articulates with the parietal bone dorsally and with the temporal bone laterally. The basioccipital part is covered largely by the sphenoid. The bone is quite thick and quadrilateral in shape. Its lower part contributes to the formation of part of the tympanic cavity. The occipital bone forms a small portion of the vertex of the skull; its limits are marked by a faint external occipital crest.

Sphenoid Bone

The *sphenoid bone* (Fig. 1.3) is a median unpaired bone which makes up the greater part of the ventral surface of the cranium. It articulates caudally with the occipital and temporal bones, rostrally with the ethmoid and palatine bones, and laterally with the pterygoid and quadrate bones. It presents a wide caudal portion that is bounded caudally by the sphenoid occipital suture, laterally by the lower extent of the temporal fossa, and rostrally by the rostral extent of the temporal fossa and eustachian foramen. The bone in this region is very thick and contains part of the tympanic cavity and internal ear structures. The narrower rostral extension, called the rostrum, continues forward to join the vomer. The area of this junction is not perceptible, as these two bones fuse early in the development of coturnix. Medially, and below the rostrum is the entrance to the eustachian tubes. Further laterad are seen the external carotid foramina, and somewhat rostral to these the oval foramina are located. The deep hypophyseal fossa is medially located and extends for some distance into the body of the rostrum.

Ethmoid Bone

The *ethmoid bone* (Fig. 1.2) is composed chiefly of a perpendicular plate. However, small horizontal and cribriform plates are present. The extensive perpendicular plate forms the greater part of the interorbital septum and is continued on the median plane into the nasal cavity as a rostral part of the nasal septum. The ventral border fits into a groove in the upper portion of the sphenoid bone. The horizontal plates, which articulate with the frontal bones, are found caudoventrally. The cribriform plate areas flank the upper caudal margin of the perpendicular plate and complete the caudal wall of the orbit. The olfactory and maxillary nerves penetrate the dorsomedial area of this plate. The nasal surface of the plate is complemented by the bulbous structure of the caudal and middle turbinates. Much of the structure of the cribriform and horizontal plates of the ethmoid remains cartilaginous and is easily removed by maceration.

Parietal Bones

The paired *parietal bones* (Figs. 1.2, 1.4) are thick and form the caudal half of the cranial roof. The parietal surface is convex and smooth; the cranial surface is concave and presents numerous impressions and vascular grooves. The parietal bones present four borders and two surfaces. The borders join the occipital, frontal, and temporal bones. Meeting medially, they form no external parietal crest. Laterally, they articulate with the temporal bones at a rather extensive squamous suture.

Frontal Bones

The *frontal bones* (Figs. 1.2, 1.4) are thin, roughly four-sided plates which form most of the rostral half of the roof of the cranial vault and a small part of the orbit. They present for description two surfaces and four borders. The dorsal surface is smooth and convex in all directions. The cranial surface presents a few grooves and ridges but for the most part is smooth. Caudally, they join the temporal bones at the frontotemporal suture. The fused, narrow, rostral parts may be classified as part

of the facial bones; with the latter these parts form the greater part of the upper margin of the orbital fossa.

Temporal Bones

In coturnix the *temporal bones* (Fig. 1.2) are not separable into squamous and petrous parts, as they are in mammals. In lower vertebrates most of the temporal bones are replaced by the squamosal bones, and this term is still often used in referring to birds. It is significant that temporal bones form part of the wall of the cranial and tympanic cavities and also a part of the orbital fossa. They articulate with the parietal, occipital, sphenoid, frontal, quadrate, pterygoid, and ethmoid bones. The supraorbital margin is continued downward and forward on the very prominent triangular zygomatic process. Cranially, it presents the internal acoustic meatus. The external acoustic meatus is located caudodorsally in the lowest region of the temporal fossa. Among the foramina presented are the foramen lacerum and those of the tympanic cavity.

BONES OF THE FACE

The *bones of the face* (ossa facici) are the maxilla, premaxilla, palatine, pterygoid, nasal, lacrimal, vomer, mandible, and hyoid (Figs. 1.2–1.7).

Maxilla

The *maxilla* (Figs. 1.2, 1.3, 1.5) of coturnix is small and forms a very incomplete boundary of the nasal cavity and infraorbital sinus. It presents a somewhat triangular plate that articulates with the palatine bone. The caudomedial angle of the plate may meet its fellow at a median junction; however, the cleft palate structure present in coturnix prevents the apposition of the remainder of the bone. The oral

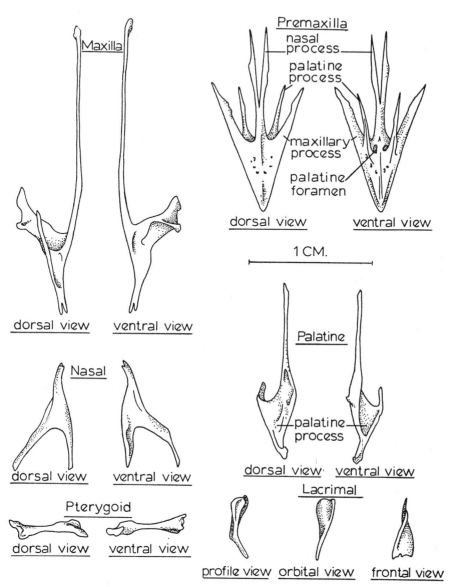

FIG. 1.5—Bones of the face.

surface is smooth; the lateral border is convex and thin and may be considered to be the caudal extremity of the hard palate. Two processes are present: the palatine and the zygomatic, or jugal.

Premaxilla

The *premaxilla* (Figs. 1.2, 1.3, 1.5)

arises from two centers but fuses early into a single unit. The fused bone is composed of a body and three pairs of processes: the nasal, palatine, and maxillary. The nasal processes are long and extend upward and backward between the nasal bones. The palatine processes are the shortest of the three, are flat, and extend caudally to form the rostral half of the incomplete portion of the hard palate. The maxillary processes extend caudally from the lateral borders of the body and form the ventral margin of the nasal aperture. The body is encased in the upper beak, to which it conforms in shape. The paired palatine foramina pierce the palatine surface of the body at the junction of the roots of the palatine and nasal processes. The dorsal surface of the body is rough and presents numerous vascular foramina for the corium of the beak.

Palatine Bones

The *palatine bones* (Figs. 1.2, 1.3, 1.5) form part of the incomplete palate of coturnix and are composed of a flat, triangular, caudal plate and a rather long, tapering, palatine process that extends to the caudal extremity of the palatine process of the premaxilla. The two processes are separated medially and form the lateral osseous borders of the caudal nares. The flat, triangular plates meet caudally and articulate with the pterygoid, sphenoid, ethmoid, and vomer bones. The palatine processes articulate with the maxilla and premaxilla.

Pterygoid Bones

The *pterygoid bones* (Figs. 1.2, 1.3, 1.5) extend caudolaterally from the rostrum of the sphenoid bones and the caudal angle of the palatine bones to the quadrate bones. They are in the form of flattened rods, being concave in length and convex in width. Medially, they bear two angles; the caudolateral angle presents two facets for articulation with the temporal bones. The rostromedial angles lie lateral to and above the pterygoids. The rostrolateral extremity bears a condyle for an articulation with the mandible.

Nasal Bones

The *nasal bones* (Fig. 1.5) are triangular, flat bones situated caudal to the nostril whose caudal extremities form a squamous suture with an extensive area of the frontal and lacrimal bones. These articulations are capable of considerable movement in the live bird. Medial and lateral rami extend forward and form the caudal border of the nostril. The medial ramus articulates with the nasal process of the maxilla, and the lateral ramus with a portion of the premaxilla.

Lacrimal Bones

The *lacrimal bones* (Fig. 1.5) are flat, oval plates which articulate with the nasal and frontal bones. The plate is curved in a spiral fashion, so that it continues the rostral margin of the orbit for a short distance. These bones are relatively small in the quail and, therefore, do not form as much of the roof of the orbit as they do in domestic fowl.

Vomer Bone

The *vomer* (Figs. 1.2, 1.3) is a median bone that assists in forming part of the nasal septum and interorbital septum. It is fusiform in shape, having the appearance of being composed of a thin lamina that is bent to form a narrow groove in which the lower part of the perpendicular plate of the ethmoid bone and the septal cartilage are received. It articulates with the ethmoid rostrum caudally, the pterygoids and the broad median process of the palatine bone laterally, and with the maxillary processes of the maxilla rostrally. The vomer in coturnix appears to be a single bone; however, in mammals it ossifies from two centers, one on either side of the membrane covering the nasal septum.

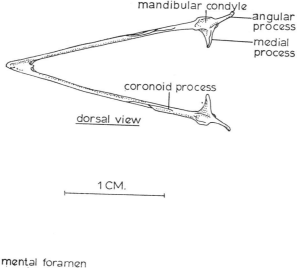

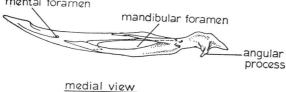

FIG. 1.6—Mandible, medial and dorsal views.

Mandible

The *mandible* (Fig. 1.6) is a strong **V**-shaped bone of the lower jaw. It consists of a body and two rami. The body narrows in front to a round, flat point. The lingual surface is deeply concave from side to side and convex longitudinally. There are numerous small foramina near the border. The mental surface is convex transversely and concave longitudinally. The mental foramina appear near the middle of the surface. The rami are two long plates which extend to the articular extremity. They are compressed laterally and imperfections occur in the center above a strong rodlike ventral border. The rami diverge from the body to produce a shallow mandibular space. The mandibular foramen is in the form of a long slit caudally. The aperture continues forward for a variable distance before forming a canal that ends at the mental foramen. The caudal or articular extremity, which is comparable to the malleus bone of mammals, is flattened dorsoventrally and presents two pointed processes, one extending medially as the medial condyloid process and the other as the caudal or angular process, which curves upward and outward. Both processes furnish attachments for ligaments. The dorsal surface of the articular angle presents a wide glenoid cavity for articulation with the quadrate bone. A small coronoid process is found a short distance in front of the articular area; it represents the widest part of the ramus. Each half of the ramus of the mandible of coturnix may be said to

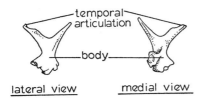

Quadrate

1 CM.

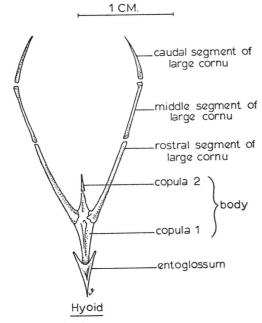

caudal segment of
large cornu

middle segment of
large cornu

rostral segment of
large cornu

copula 2 }
}body
copula 1 }

entoglossum

Hyoid

FIG. 1.7—Bones of the face.

consist of four parts: articulare, supra-articulare, angulare, and dentary. They are fused early into a single structure.

Hyoid Bone

The *hyoid bone* (Fig. 1.7) of coturnix is rather long and does not articulate with the basal surface of the skull, as it does in mammals. Instead, it encircles the nuchal surface of the skull caudally and extends to the region of the parieto-frontal surface dorsally. The rostral or entoglossal part is shaped like a spur, the point of which is cartilaginous and is buried in the base of the tongue. The body articulates with the entoglossum

rostrally and with the large cornua caudally. It lies on a median plane and is composed of two parts, or copulae. For the most part the body is shaped like a four-sided bar somewhat constricted in its center, and the second copula forms a ural process which extends caudally to the ventral region of the cranial larynx. The large cornua are long round bars which encircle the contour of the base of the skull. They terminate by joining a continuing middle segment which is of the same shape, with slightly enlarged extremities. A caudal segment is attached to the membranous structures of the dorsolateral region of the cranium. The hyoid apparatus is thus composed of nine parts.

Quadrate Bone

The *quadrate bone* (Figs. 1.3, 1.7) is so named because of its irregular four-sided outline. It is located in the space between the mandible, temporal, and pterygoid bones. It may be described as having a central thick part, called a body, that articulates with the glenoid cavity of the mandible. From the rostromedial angle of the body a muscular process projects into the temporal fossa. The extremity of a rostrally extending process articulates with the temporal bone. The presence of the quadrate bone helps to make up a compound articulation which, together with the mobility of the bones of the face, permits the opening of the mouth at a wide angle.

VERTEBRAE

The axial supporting bones of coturnix comprise the vertebral column as it is found in reptiles and mammals (Figs. 1.1, 1.8–1.12). Each vertebra helps to form a continuous chain of irregular bones that extends from the skull to the caudal termination of the column. In

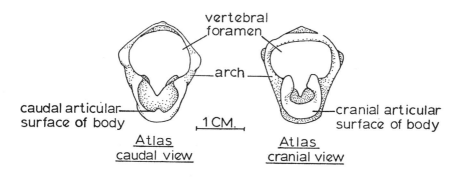

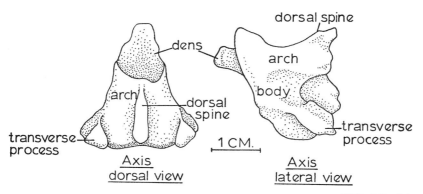

FIG. 1.8—Atlas and axis.

the adult certain vertebrae become fused to form single bony masses. Vertebrae fused in such a manner are termed "fixed" or "false." Because of the area characteristics the vertebral column of birds has been divided into five regions: cervical (C) (neck); thoracic (T) (chest); lumbar (loin) and sacral (hip) (LS, lumbosacral); and coccygeal (CY), or caudal (tail). The number of vertebrae is fairly constant in a given region in coturnix, so that the vertebral formula may be written as follows: C 14, T 7, LS 12, CY 7.

Cervical Vertebrae

In adaptation to the many uses of the head, particularly the beak, as a tool, the *vertebrae of the cervical region* (Figs. 1.8, 1.9) exceed the usual number of

seven found in mammals. This provides for more flexibility of the neck and increased motility of the head. Of the usual 14 bones, those in the center of the column are the most typical of the series. The length of the cervical vertebrae is approximately one-half the length of the entire vertebral column. When viewed from the side, the cervical column is curved to form a gentle S-shaped flexure. The succession of vertebral foramina forms the spinal canal of the region, the width of which is the greatest in vertebrae 13 and 14.

The 1st cervical vertebra (atlas) is atypical and very short. The 2nd cervical vertebra (axis) is also atypical, although it more nearly conforms to the others in size and configuration. It has a long median process, the dens, that ar-

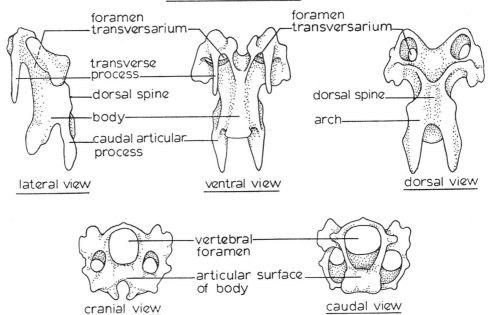

FIG. 1.9—Sixth cervical vertebra.

ticulates with the atlas and gives it added stability. The length of the succeeding vertebrae increases up to the 8th of the series, which is the longest, and then the length gradually decreases throughout the remainder. The transverse foramen is rather large and runs in a longitudinal direction. It is found at the junction of the roots of the transverse processes of all the cervical vertebrae except the 1st. The confluence of the successive foramina forms the transverse canal, which transmits the vertebral vessels and the transverse nerve of the sympathetic trunk.

The features of the cervical vertebrae, which are typical of the bones of the center of the series, may be described as follows:

The body, or centrum, is long compared to those of other regions and is in the form of a cylindrical bar that is enlarged at its extremities, slightly concave in its length ventrally, and flattened on the dorsal surface.

The dorsal surface offers attachment to the dorsal longitudinal ligament, which is not complete but fills out the osseous imperfection of the canal ventrally. Longitudinal grooves and foramina may be found on this surface.

The cranial articular surface of the body is recessed between the cranial extensions of the transverse process and arch; they are concave transversely and convex vertically. A protruding convex head like that of the mammalian cranial articular process is lacking.

The caudal articular surface is more extensive than the cranial surface, and the transverse processes are short and extend downward and forward along the body. They are thick angular structures in the forepart of the series, and those of the 13th and 14th vertebrae are flattened plates extending forward as far as the center of the body of the preceding vertebrae. From the lower part of the transverse process, short tapering projections occur, which have been considered as remnants of cervical ribs.

A ventral spine is found only on the 2nd and 3rd vertebrae cranially and on the caudal vertebrae from the 11th to the 14th. From the 5th to the 10th consecutive vertebrae the vertebral spine is replaced by a hemal process. These become quite deep in the middle of the series, and they may be found to form a complete canal at the 10th vertebra. The deep grooves and canals thus formed by the hemal arches and body are occupied by the common carotid arteries.

The neural arches are long in the longer vertebrae and are correspondingly short in the shorter ones. They give rise to the articular processes; the cranial ones, which extend downward, are confluent with the transverse processes. The caudal pair of articular processes extend upward and backward and diverge greatly, producing a large **V**-shaped opening in the osseous spinal canal. In vertebrae 3 and 4 the articular processes are connected by a thin, horizontal plate of bone which is perforated by a small foramen in the center. The dorsal spines are faint cranially, absent in the center of the series, and present as a prominent quadrilateral structure on the last cervical vertebra.

Thoracic Vertebrae

The most constant number of *thoracic vertebrae* (Figs. 1.10, 1.11) found in coturnix is seven. Vertebrae 1 and 6 are free; 2 through 5 are fused into a solid mass; and 7 is fused to the lumbosacral bone. The 1st thoracic vertebra is quite similar to the preceding cervical vertebra with the following exceptions: The dorsal spine is large, quadrilateral in shape, and presents a

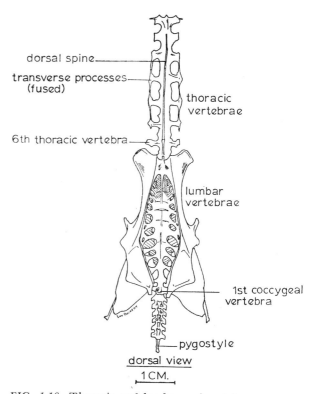

FIG. 1.10—*Thoracic and lumbosacral vertebrae, dorsal view.*

thick, rough summit. The vertebral notch in the spine is very large and extends as far forward as the center of the body. There is a strong transverse process that has a triangular tuberous extremity. Just dorsal and caudal to the root of the transverse process there is a spherical facet that articulates with the head of the 1st rib.

Thoracic vertebrae 2, 3, 4, **and 5,** which are fused, present the following features: The dorsal spine of the 2nd vertebra is the longest of the group and ends in a bifurcating plate which when viewed from above is heart shaped. It is tall and extensive enough to partly cover the dorsal spine of the last cervical vertebra. It continues back and forms caudally a rather sharp spine that is continuous throughout the length of

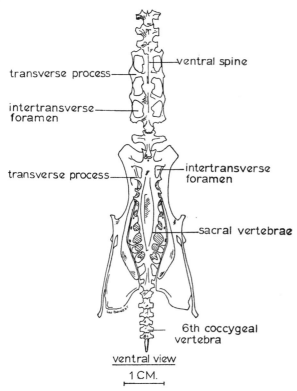

transverse process

ventral spine

intertransverse foramen

transverse process

intertransverse foramen

sacral vertebrae

6th coccygeal vertebra

ventral view

1 CM.

FIG. 1.11—Thoracic and lumbosacral verte-brae, ventral view.

the fused vertebrae. Slight elevations occur on the sides of the arches which represent vestiges of the fused articular processes. The ventral spines are long and are fused as well. The transverse processes are short, flat plates, the extremities of which are joined by a thin, flat bar of bone that is incomplete between the 2nd, 3rd, 4th, and 5th segments.

Lumbosacral Bone (Synsacrum)

The *lumbosacral bone* (Figs. 1.10, 1.11) is composed of fused vertebrae of four regions: the last, or 7th, thoracic vertebra; 12 successive segments of the lumbar and sacral regions; and the 1st coccygeal vertebra. The fused bony mass is situated dorsally between the two os coxae forming part of the roof of

the pelvis. The transverse processes of the first four segments fuse with the ventral surface of the wing of the ilium. The bodies of the fused vertebral segments are larger in the middle of the lumbosacrum and continue caudally to diminish in size to the region of the fused 1st coccygeal vertebrae. The axis of the fused bodies forms a gentle convexity dorsally. A prominent dorsal spine is formed by the fusion of the dorsal spinous processes. It has a rounded free border, is highest cranially, and gradually decreases in height to the middle of the column, where it fades out completely. The ventral spinous processes are low and rounded. The transverse processes are longest in the middle of the column and their extremities are connected by a continuous thin plate of bone which almost fills the interosseous space between the two ischii. There are, however, intertransverse foramina between the processes. Some of the roots of the caudal transverse processes are double. The intervertebral foramen between the last thoracic and 1st lumbar segments is very large. The remainder are small and are divided for separate exits of the dorsal and ventral spinal nerve branches. The 7th thoracic vertebra, which is fused with the lumbosacrum, presents an extensive articular surface on the cranial extremity of the body that extends downward and forward and resembles the appearance of a sacral promontory. The articulation is convex vertically and deeply concave horizontally. The extremities of the transverse processes fuse at the ventral surface of the ilium, and the dorsal spine extends upward and forward, forming the highest part of the fused lumbosacral spinous process.

Coccygeal Vertebrae

Seven *coccygeal vertebrae* (Figs. 1.10–1.12) are present. The 1st is fused with the lumbosacrum. Vertebrae 2 to

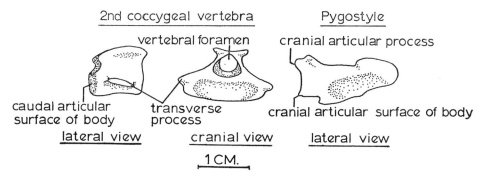

FIG. 1.12—Coccygeal vertebra and pygostyle.

6 are freely movable and are responsible for the extensive motility of the tail. The last segment, or pygostyle, appears to be formed by the fusion of at least two vertebrae. The coccygeal vertebrae are somewhat rudimentary, in that no articular processes are found. The centrum or body diminishes in length from the first to the last of the movable segments. The freely movable articulations between them are united by fibrous tissue. The transverse processes are short and blunt and form a flat plane with the ventral surface of the centrum. The dorsal spines are complete and their extremities are bifid. The vertebral canal is continuous throughout the first six vertebrae. The pygostyle is a thin plate, slightly curved, with a dorsal concave border and a ventral convex border. Each lateral surface is concave centrally, the bone terminating in a rounded point. The coccygeal vertebrae support the tail and the uropygeal gland and provide attachment for numerous muscles.

RIBS AND STERNUM

The ribs of coturnix (Figs. 1.1, 1.13) may be classified as long bones and are of two groups. They form the lateral wall of the thorax and are arranged in pairs. The dorsal group articulates with the thoracic vertebrae and thus are designed as vertebral ribs. The ventral group are designated as sternal ribs,

which may be considered as a replacement of the costal cartilages of mammals. Some of this group do not join at the sternum and articulate with the ventral segment of the preceding rib. Thus they may be classified as asternal ribs. Those vertebral ribs which are not accompanied by a sternal segment are free and are called floating ribs.

Seven vertebral pairs of ribs are usu-

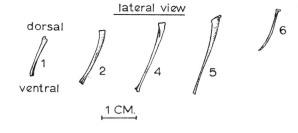

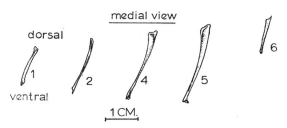

FIG. 1.13—Sternal ribs, lateral and medial views.

ally present; the first two pairs of these are floating and the next four pairs are sternal. Occasionally eight pairs are present; when this occurs, the first three and the last of the series are floating. The 7th rib is complemented by a sternal segment that articulates only with the preceding rib and therefore is considered to be an asternal rib. The sternal ribs extend outward, backward, and downward; their bodies are flattened and arched in conformity with the thoracic wall. The 1st rib is sometimes curved the least, with a convexity at the sternal extremity. The head of each rib articulates just dorsal and cranial to the root of the transverse processes of the vertebrae of the same number serially. The extensive tuberosity is articulated with the transverse processes of the same numbered vertebrae.

The head and transverse process of the 1st rib are very close together; the distance between these two structures in each succeeding rib becomes progressively greater. The sternal segments which are attached to the caudal four pairs of vertebral ribs extend forward and converge to the lateral border of the sternum, with which only the first three pairs articulate. An uncinate process extends upward and backward from the middle of the caudal border of each of the ribs except the first and the last. They are composed of flattened plates of bone which run from the caudal border of the ribs backward and upward, overlapping the surface of the succeeding rib. They are bound tightly in place by ligaments and thus strengthen the osseous thoracic wall.

Variations in Vertebral and Sternal Ribs

There is a variation in the number of pairs of vertebral and sternal ribs in the coturnix quail. Usually there are 7 vertebral and 5 sternal ribs, the 1st and 2nd

not having sternal connections. The 5th sternal rib, which articulates with the 7th vertebral rib, does not articulate with the sternum, but is closely bound to the 4th sternal rib by fibrous tissue along its cranial border. In rare instances an 8th vertebral rib may arise from the 1st lumbar vertebra. This lumbar rib does not articulate with a sternal rib and may be long on one side, extending along the cranial border of the thigh, and short on the other. In one case the short extra rib was curved caudally and ran along the ventral surface of the wing of the ilium.

Sternum

The *sternum,* or breast bone (Fig. 1.14), is a single flat bone forming the ventral floor of the thoracic cavity and part of that of the abdominal cavity. It is a bilaterally symmetrical, flat bone which may be considered the most extensive of the skeleton. It is not segmented as it is in mammals. It articulates with the coracoid bones and with the ventral extremities of the sternal ribs and is attached to the clavicle by the hypocleidial ligament. It presents two surfaces, two borders, and two extremities for description. The dorsal surface is smooth and concave. Cranially, near the median plane, bilateral pneumatic foramina are found. Two nutrient foramina also are located on this surface at the junction of the root of the lateral cranial processes with the body. The ventral surface is convex in all directions in conformity with the shape of the oval thoracic cavity and the curved profile of the ventral body wall.

Due to the well-developed pectoral muscles a prominent median keel-like crest is formed. This crest is highest cranially where it forms a rather sharp point. Caudally, the crest diminishes until it fades out at the caudal border of the body. The ventral margin of the

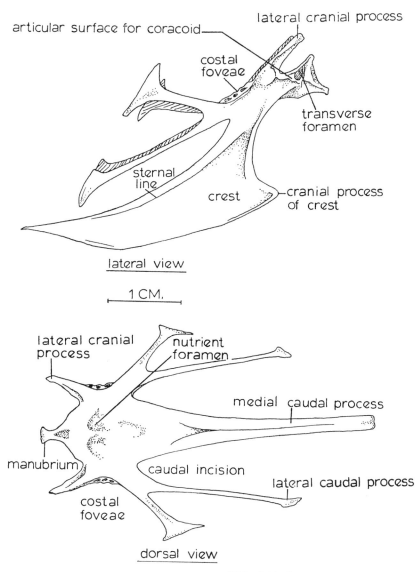

articular surface for coracoid

lateral cranial process

costal foveae

transverse foramen

sternal line

crest

cranial process of crest

lateral view

1 CM.

lateral cranial process

nutrient foramen

medial caudal process

manubrium

caudal incision

lateral caudal process

costal foveae

dorsal view

FIG. 1.14—Sternum, lateral and dorsal views.

crest is convex in its length and rather thick and rounded. A sternal line running parallel with and near the root of the crest is found, indicating the divisions of the areas of origin of the superficial and deep pectoral muscles.

The lateral border of the bone runs from the manubrium to the caudal ex-

tremity of the lateral caudal sternal process. On its cranial extremity it bears the lateral cranial sternal process, a blunt-pointed prismatic bar which extends upward, parallel to the ventral extremity of the coracoid bone. Just caudal to the root of this process the border is studded with fovea-like costal articular surfaces. These are shallow transverse facets for articulation with the sternal extremities of the 2nd, 3rd, and 4th ribs. A deep triangular notch (caudal incision) is present in the lateral border caudal to the lateral process, which is a flattened bar with a widened extremity. The caudal border is incomplete, as a deep caudal notch extends cranially between the lateral caudal process to occupy two-thirds of the length of the sternum. The width of each of the two bilaterally positioned notches is greater than that of the medial caudal process. All these flattened processes extend caudally in conformity to the curvature of the abdominal floor. The osseous imperfections produced by these notches are completed by ligaments in the freshly dissected specimen. The cranial border presents centrally a blunt-pointed cranial process, the manubrium. The articular surface for the coracoid bones is located on the border lateral to the transverse foramen.

PECTORAL LIMB

As in mammals the *pectoral limb* (Figs. 1.1, 1.15–1.18) may be divided into four segments: the pectoral girdle, the arm, the forearm, and the manus. The pectoral girdle is composed of the scapula, the coracoid, and the clavicular bones.

Scapula

The *scapula*, or shoulder blade (Fig. 1.15), is the longest bone of the shoulder girdle. It is situated along the back and extends from the shoulder to approximately the cranial limit of the lumbar portion of the synsacrum. This long, flat bone has a saber-shaped body and a rather thick, modified articular extremity. In cross section the body presents a costal and a dorsolateral surface. The costal surface is convex, and the lateral surface is concave. The dor-

sal border is thin and convex along its length, and the ventral border is rounded and concave. Just caudal to the articular angle it presents a rather small scapular tubercle. The dorsolateral portion of the articular extremity presents an oval concavity which forms approximately one-third of the glenoid cavity formed by the scapular and coracoid bones. The glenoid cavity articulates with the head of the humerus. The medial portion of the articular extremity of the scapula is developed into the tuberosity of the scapula. The lateral portion of this tuberosity presents a concave surface which forms the medial border of the foramen triosseum. The scapula of coturnix articulates with the humerus and coracoid but does not touch the clavicle at the shoulder girdle.

Coracoid Bone

The *coracoid bone* (Fig. 1.15) is the shortest but strongest of the bones of the pectoral girdle. It articulates with

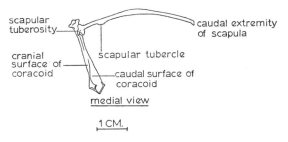

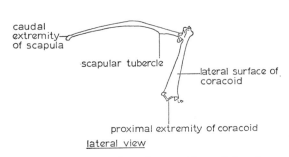

FIG. 1.15—*Scapula and coracoid, medial and lateral views.*

the sternum at the sternocoracoid articulation and with the scapula, clavicle, and humerus at the shoulder. It extends upward, forward, and outward from the sternum and forms the lateral boundary of the osseous thoracic inlet. It has been suggested that this bone is positioned to counteract the powerful forces exerted by the pectoral muscles during flight. The shaft of the bone is oval in the center but broadens considerably at its extremities. The sternal articular surface is wide and concave transversely and is convex vertically. The shape of this articulation eliminates almost all movement except extension and flexion. The proximal extremity presents a hemispherical articular surface for the clavicle. It becomes concave caudally and forms the cranial and lateral borders of the foramen triosseum. A short distance from the extremity on the lateral border a convex facet is developed for articulation with the articcular angle of the scapula.

Clavicle

The *clavicle* (Fig. 1.16) is a forklike bone fused ventrally to form a body.

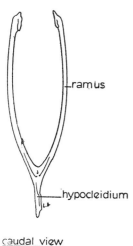

caudal view

1 CM.

FIG. 1.16—Clavicle, caudal view.

It is the homologue of the paired clavicular bones in mammals. It articulates with the sternum ventrally, by way of the sternoclavicular ligament, and dorsally with the coracoid of the shoulder girdle. It may be suggested that this bone serves as a springlike apparatus to keep the shoulder joints at their proper distance from the vertebral column. The two forklike rami are round and smooth with the exception of the upper extremities, which become flattened transversely and develop concave articular surfaces that are much smaller than the rounded articular areas of the coracoid with which they articulate. The lower extremities of the rami fuse into a single bar that in turn flattens in a transverse direction to form an ovalshaped extremity. This structure is termed the hypocleidium. When viewed from the side, the clavicle is curved along its length in conformity with the curved profile of the breast.

Humerus

The *humerus* (Figs. 1.17, 1.18) is the only bone of the upper arm. It is classified as a long bone, extending from the shoulder to the elbow. It articulates with the scapula and the coracoid bones of the shoulder girdle and with the ulna and radius at the elbow. For description it presents the shaft and two extremities. The shaft, or diaphysis, is slightly curved along its length and is cylindrical in shape. The surface is smooth except for a few faint lines and a nutrient foramen on the lateral surface. The proximal extremity is large and broad; two tuberosities accentuate its width. The lateral tuberosity overhangs a large pneumatic foramen. The articular head is oval in outline and is larger than the glenoid cavity with which it articulates. The medial tuberosity is smaller than the lateral one and overhangs a correspondingly smaller fossa. Each of the pneumatic fossae communicates with

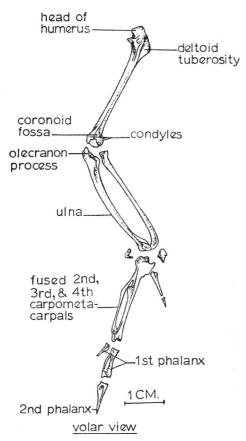

FIG. 1.17—*Pectoral limb, volar view.*

Radius and Ulna

The *radius and ulna* (Figs. 1.17, 1.18) are the long bones of the forearm. The ulna is the larger and slightly longer of the two. It is gently curved in its length, the convexity being lateral with the wing in the folded position. In addition to the articulations of each extremity with the radius, it articulates proximally with the humerus and distally with the fused metacarpus and the ulnocarpal and radiocarpal bones. The head has a small olecranon process that fits into the olecranon fossa of the humerus. The shaft is larger and somewhat flattened at the proximal extremity. It is slightly twisted in a clockwise direction, so that the axis of its articular surface is slightly rotated at the carpus. On the

the hollow medullary cavity of this bone. The medial tuberosity continues distad as a rather sharp crest which becomes thickened to form the deltoid tuberosity. The distal extremity is also broadened in a transverse direction and presents a condyloid articular surface that articulates with the radius and ulna. Epicondyles surmount the condyles and accentuate the width of the bone. A small coronoid fossa lies adjacent to the medial condyle. The olecranon fossa is present but is very shallow. In the resting position the elbow lies just lateral to the cranial extremity of the ilium.

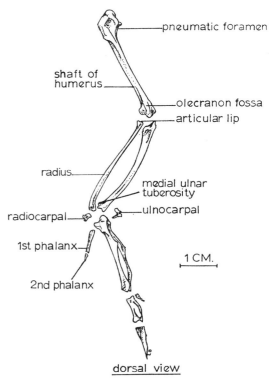

FIG. 1.18—*Pectoral limb, dorsal view.*

flattened ventral surface of the shaft near the proximal extremity, there is a nutrient foramen. The proximal extremity is quite large and presents two oval glenoid cavities, separated by a ridge, for articulation with the condyles of the humerus. Medial and lateral tuberosities are faint but recognizable. The distal extremity is somewhat larger than the shaft and bears an extensive trochlear surface. The trochlea is composed of two prominent ridges running from the medial to the lateral border. The lateral ridge is more extensive and continues on to the lateral aspect of the shaft. The medial ridge is smaller but also runs from the medial to the lateral areas of the articulation. Medial and lateral tuberosities are present, the medial one being the larger.

The radius is the smaller of the two long bones of the forearm. It lies medial to the ulna and somewhat lateral to the humerus with the wing in the folded position. It is slightly curved at its distal extremity and with the ulna forms a long, oval, interosseous space. Its shaft is cylindrical and smooth; the distal extremity is enlarged and presents an oval articular surface that caps over the trochlear articular surface of the distal extremity of the ulna. It also presents a rounded facet that articulates with a concave articular area of the radiocarpal bone. The proximal extremity presents a glenoid cavity that articulates with the lateral condyle of the humerus. At each extremity are found narrow facets which articulate with corresponding areas at the extremities of the ulna. Ligaments firmly bind the radius and ulna together at these articular areas.

Manus

The *manus* segment, or hand (Figs. 1.17, 1.18), in coturnix is made up of the carpus, metacarpus, and digits in the mature bird. The carpus is represented by only two bones of the proximal row, which may be described as individual short bones of the thoracic limb. The radiocarpal bone is in the form of a flattened rectangular disc. The proximal surface is divided into two concavities, the smaller of which articulates with the convex articular surface of the distal extremity of the radius. The larger concave surface articulates with the smaller trochlear ridge of the distal extremity of the ulna. The distal articular surface is an oval concavity that articulates with the rather prominent convex articular surface of the carpometacarpus. The ulnocarpal bone lies lateral to the radiocarpal bone and is a **V**-shaped, short bone which articulates with the ulna and carpometacarpus. No articulation appears between the ulnocarpal and the radiocarpal bones. The articular surface for the carpometacarpus is located in the incisural area of the **V**-shaped bone, and the articular area for the ulna is on the side of the thickest ramus of the ulnocarpal bone.

The carpometacarpus is composed of the distal row of the carpal bones, which are fused into a single bony mass with the 2nd, 3rd, and 4th metacarpal bones. The largest in the group is the 3rd metacarpal, the shaft of which is flattened laterally and is rounded medially. It becomes slightly twisted distally, so that the long axis of the flattened distal extremity is oblique. A flattened tubercle is present in the upper third of the interosseous space. The proximal extremity is fused with the 2nd metacarpal bone, which presents a rounded tubercle and a concave facet with the 1st phalanx of the 2nd digit. The shaft of the 4th metacarpal curves caudally from the axis of the 3rd and is flattened in a transverse direction. The distal extremity of the large 4th metacarpal bone presents a wide articular surface for the proximal extremity of the 1st phalanx of the 4th digit. The proximal extremity of the carpometacarpus, which is composed of the fused distal row of carpal bones, and the 2nd, 3rd, and 4th metacarpal bones presents a large condyle for articulation with the ulnocarpal and a small facet for articulation with the radiocarpal bone.

Phalanges

The *phalanges* (Figs. 1.17, 1.18) of coturnix are somewhat reduced in number. The 1st phalanx of the 2nd digit is a long, tapering, three-sided bone which articulates proximally with the distal extremity of the 2nd metacarpal bone. It is succeeded by a small, pointed, 2nd phalanx. The 1st phalanx of the 3rd digit is the largest of the phalanges. The body is flattened caudally and terminates in a rounded, thin border. The medial and lateral surfaces are concave centrally. The 2nd phalanx of the 3rd digit is a rather long, three-sided, prismatic bone that terminates in a sharp point. The 1st phalanx of the 4th digit is in the shape of a flattened cone that terminates in a blunt point. In coturnix there are 5 phalanges. The 1st and 2nd are present in the 2nd and 3rd digits, and only the 1st is represented in the 4th digit. The last phalanx represented in either the manus or pes of birds is called the terminal phalanx.

PELVIC LIMB

As in mammals, the *pelvic limb* (Figs. 1.1, 1.19–1.21) is made up of four segments or regions: the pelvic girdle; the thigh; the crus, or leg; and the pes, or foot. The pelvic girdle which is made up of the os coxae (hip bone), or os innominatum, is fused into a single mass; but in the fetus or very young bird it may be found to be composed of the

ilium, ischium, and pubis. The thigh contains a single bone, the femur. The crus, or leg, is made up of the tibiotarsus and the fibula and patella. The pes, or foot, is comprised of the remainder of the bones, which are the tarsometatarsus and the digits. Due to the fact that there is an absence of the symphysis pubis, birds are able to lay unusually large eggs. For rigidity of the back the pelvis is exceptionally long and expansive and is fused to the lumbosacral bone. All the bones of the os coxae are very thin and are modified with numerous convexities and concavities which produce rigidity and strength. The length of the pelvis equals half the length of the trunk of the body.

Ilium

The *ilium* (Fig. 1.19) is a flat bone and is the most extensive of the pelvic group. It joins the ischium and pubis to form the acetabulum. The craniodorsal surface is deeply concave and the wing is rather short, so that a tuber coxae is not present. The caudal part of the dorsal surface is convex and is separated from the cranial concave portion by a diverging ridge. This ridge begins at the cranial medial angle, where the two wings are fused to the dorsal spine of the

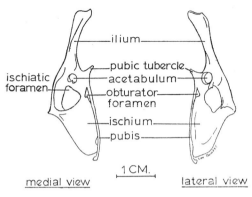

FIG. 1.19—*Pelvic girdle, medial and lateral views.*

lumbosacral bone, and extends outward and backward to terminate just caudal to the acetabulum. The caudal convex portion of the ilium is fused with the transverse processes of the sacrum and is subcutaneous. The pelvic surface is very irregular; the cranial or wing portion is convex and is fused with the transverse processes of the last thoracic and lumbar vertebrae. The caudal part of the pelvic surface presents an extensive fossa which houses the kidneys and adrenal glands. The lateral border begins at the wing and is concave and thin as it extends toward the acetabulum. The caudal part of the lateral border extends caudally above the ischiatic foramen and joins the caudal border at a rather sharp angle. It joins the medial border opposite the 2nd coccygeal vertebra and continues craniad at the margin of the transverse processes of the lumbar and sacral segments to terminate finally at the fused area of the wing with the spine of the lumbar segments. The cranial border is thin, bordering the round cranial extent of the wing. The ischium joins the pubis and ilium at the acetabulum, to which the ilium contributes about two-thirds of its circumference.

Ischium

The *ischium* (Fig. 1.19) is a roughly triangular, flat bone which forms the greater part of the caudal region of the upper and lateral pelvic wall. The plate extends downward and outward and is widely separated from its fellow ventrally. It forms the caudoventral part of the acetabulum and a large ischiatic foramen which is more than twice the size of the acetabulum. The caudal portion of the ilium overhangs its cranial medial border. The ventral and caudal borders are convex and thin. The ventral border is attached to the caudal extremity of the pubis by a liga-mentous membrane (the ischiopubic membrane).

Pubis

The *pubis* (Fig. 1.19) is the smallest bone of the os coxae. It is a narrow bone which extends caudally from the acetabulum along the ventral border of the ischium to a point slightly beyond the caudal extent of the ischium. The pubis contributes very little to the acetabulum and presents a rather prominent process (pubic tubercle) that extends downward and forward from the acetabulum. Just caudoventral to the acetabulum a notch in the ventral border of the ilium is transformed into an interosseous space, a narrow opening between the ischium and the pubis (obturator foramen).

Femur

The *femur* (Figs. 1.20, 1.21) is the long bone of the thigh and extends downward and forward from the acetabulum to the stifle joint, where it articulates with the patella, tibia, and fibula. The shaft, or diaphysis, is cylindrical and curved along its length, with the convexity being dorsal. The medial surface is slightly concave in its length.

The caudal surface presents a faint linea aspera. From the center of the shaft the line is divided, one continuing upward as the medial surface and the other extending upward and laterally to the trochanter major. From the center the line continues distad and forms a rather sharp crest joining the summit of the medial condyle. The cranial surface is convex and smooth in the center. Distally, it widens and flattens and presents a shallow trochlea, the median ridge of which is the most prominent; but it does not extend as far proximally as does the lateral one. The cranial surface widens above and presents a rather

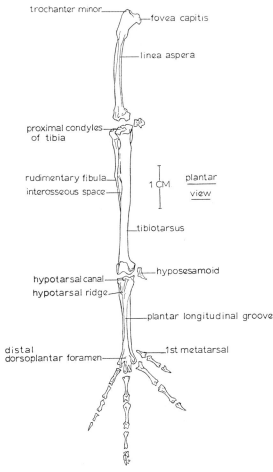

FIG. 1.20—*Pelvic limb, plantar view.*

ispherically shaped articular head which presents a small fovea capitis medially. The neck of the head is very short and thick. The long axis of the neck forms an angle of about 90° with the axis of the shaft. Distal to the root of the neck on the median surface there is a small trochanter minor. The trochanter ma-

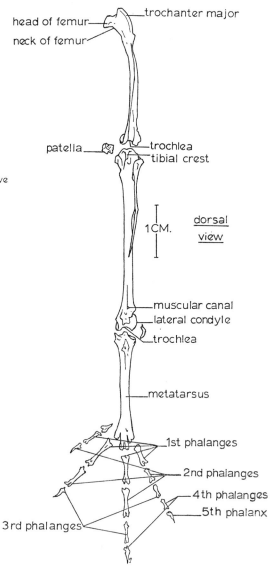

FIG. 1.21—*Pelvic limb, dorsal view.*

sharp crest that extends proximally to the lateral limit of the trochanter major.

The lateral surface of the shaft is smooth and convex, and its center becomes quite narrow just above the lateral epicondyle. The proximal extent of the surface is encroached upon by the distal extension of the trochanter major, which is roughened for muscular attachment. The medial surface is smooth and convex in a transverse direction and is somewhat concave in its length when viewed from a cranial position.

The proximal extremity has a hem-

jor extends above the level of the head and presents a rounded protuberance which is convex laterally and concave medially. The cranial portion of the trochanter major is the largest and most extensive part. Little or no trochanteric ridge or fossa is perceptible below the level of the head. The distal extremity is larger than the proximal extremity and presents the trochlea for articulation with the patella. Medial and lateral condyles, both of which articulate with the tibia, are separated by a rather wide groove. The caudolateral region of the lateral condyle articulates with the proximal extremity of the fibula.

Centrally positioned in the intercondyloid groove is a rather extensive fossa, part of which is synovial, and the remainder offers an area of attachment for the meniscal and cruciate ligaments. The medial condyle is the largest and is continuous with the medial ridge of the trochlea. A distinct notch appears at the proximal extent of the medial trochlear ridge where it ends abruptly on the shaft. The ridge of the lateral condyle is not continuous with the lateral trochlear ridge. A rather prominent lateral epicondyle is found, but there is no supracondyloid fossa. The medial condyle is very faint.

Patella

The *patella* (Figs. 1.20, 1.21) is a small sesamoid bone that articulates with the trochlea of the femur. It presents two borders, two surfaces, a base, and an apex. The cranial, or free, surface is convex in both directions and presents an oblique groove across its middle. The articular surface presents two uneven concave facets that articulate with the ridges of the trochlea. The medial facet is the larger. The base is oval in outline and is concave craniodorsally. It is roughened for muscular attachment. The apex forms a blunt point

extending distally. The borders, medial and lateral, converge toward the apex. The medial border is attached to a complementary fibrocartilage.

Tibiotarsus

The *tibiotarsus* (Figs. 1.20, 1.21) is a long bone that extends distally and caudally and somewhat medially from the stifle, or knee, to the hock, or tibiotarsal joint. In coturnix the tibiotarsus is a compound bone composed of the tibia and a fused bony nodule of the distal tarsal bones, which represent a fetal remnant of the distal row of the tarsal bones. This remnant is present in young birds in the form of an epiphysis.

The leg segment of the limb of coturnix is 25% longer than the thigh. The bones are correspondingly of the same length in proportion. The body, or shaft, of the bone is slightly curved along its length, the convexity being dorsal. In cross section the shaft is cylindrical, but at the proximal extremity it becomes three-sided. Distally, it is somewhat flattened in a sagittal direction. The medial surface of the shaft becomes wide above and is roughened for the attachment of the medial ligament. This surface winds around dorsally to become confluent with the medial portion of the crest and is smooth and subcutaneous below. The lateral surface is wide above and curves around distally to join the plantar surface. Just below the proximal extremity the lateral surface presents a well-formed fibular crest to which the fibula is attached. Above and below the crest the tibia and fibula are free, thus forming the proximal and distal interosseous spaces. The lower fourth of the surface is roughened for muscular attachments.

THE PLANTAR SURFACE

The upper one-fifth of the plantar surface is roughened for muscular attachments. Below this a faint popliteal line runs upward from the medial border and outward to end at the proximal interosseous space. Below the line the surface is smooth and convex transversely. The proximal extremity is large and somewhat quadrilateral in shape. It presents two proximal condyles which articulate with the fibrocartilage menisci and the condyles of the distal extremity of the femur. The medial and lateral condyles are separated by a ridge and a not too prominent tibial spine. The convexities of the condyles are uneven; the medial one is much the larger of the two, is oval in outline, and is separated from the medial convexity by a shallow popliteal notch. The lateral border of the convexity presents a facet for articulation with the head of the fibula. The convexities of the condyles with the menisci offer an extensive undulated area which permits a certain amount of rotation in addition to flexion and extension of the stifle. The cranial border of the articular surface forms a transverse ridge for attachment of the broad patellar ligament. Centrally from the ridge a prominent tibial crest extends downward and medially to fade out on the dorsal surface of the shaft. Between the lateral extremity of the transverse ridge and the head of the fibula there is a rather deep muscular canal.

THE DISTAL EXTREMITY

The distal extremity is large and is a compound articular area. It is formed not only by the distal extremity of the tibia but also by the embryological remnant of the tibiotarsal bone and perhaps by part of the fibulotarsal bone. The extensive cranial portion presents two large condyles which are separated by intercondyloid fossa. The condyles are continuous distally and caudally by a wide, grooved trochlea. The lateral condyle is wide and convex; the medial

one is much thinner but higher. The extensive articular surface of the condyles and trochlea permit a great deal of movement of the tibiotarsal-metatarsal articulation. Where the tendons of the digital flexor play over the trochlea, a tarsal sesamoid, the hyposesamoid, is embedded. It appears that the tarsal sesamoid is a fetal remnant of at least part of the fibulotarsal bone. The tarsal sesamoid is crescent-shaped; the articular surface, which articulates with the groove of the tibial trochlea, is concave in its length and convex transversely. The distal extremity is round and blunt; the proximal extremity is pointed.

Fibula

The *fibula* (Figs. 1.20, 1.21) is a reduced long bone situated lateral to the tibia. It presents a head and a rudimentary shaft which terminates in a free point about in the middle of the shaft of the tibia. It is somewhat curved, so that its caudal angle extends distally as far as the medial condyle of the tibia. It articulates proximally with the femur and medially with the lateral condyle. About one-half the length of its shaft is fused with the fibular crest of the tibia. The proximal interosseous space is about one-half the size of the distal one. A fibrous ligament complements its distal extremity and runs to the distal extremity as it does in some mammals.

Metatarsus

The length of the *metatarsus* (Figs. 1.20, 1.21) is approximately one-half that of the tibia. The shaft is somewhat flattened and presents a dorsal and a plantar surface. It is straight in length and oval in cross section. The upper portion of the proximal surface is somewhat wider and presents a depression, in the bottom of which is a perforating foramen connecting the dorsal and plantar surfaces. This foramen indicates the junction area between the 2nd and 3rd metatarsal bones. There is no spur projection extending from the lower portion of the medial border, as seen in the chicken.

The proximal extremity is roughly triangular in shape and presents two articular grooves which receive the condyles of the tibia. The two grooves are separated by a sagittal ridge, upon which is a small synovial fossa. Caudal and distal to the articular grooves is a rectangular mass, the hypotarsus. A longitudinal hypotarsal canal courses through the structures slightly medial to its center. The plantar surface of the hypotarsus presents two longitudinally directed grooves. The grooves and the canal of the hypotarsus accommodate the flexor tendons of the digit.

The 1st metatarsal and its digit are attached by a ligamentous articulation a short distance from the distal extremity on the medial border of the large, or 3rd, metatarsus. The distal extremity presents three partially separated articular areas for the 2nd, 3rd, and 4th digits. The second process is the shortest and is very faintly grooved on its caudomedial area. The articular extremity of the third segment is the longest and presents a sagittally grooved trochlea which extends well up on the dorsal and plantar surfaces of the extremity. The grooved trochlea of the 4th digit is not so extensive, and the groove is directed obliquely forward and outward. In the mature coturnix a histological section of the distal extremity shows that the three medullary cavities of the second, third, and fourth extremities converge to form a single cavity in the center of the diaphysis.

Digits

The 1st, 2nd, 3rd, and 4th *digits* are present in coturnix (Figs. 1.20, 1.21). The 1st digit extends caudomedially and is used primarily for balance. The 2nd, 3rd, and 4th digits radiate forward from the distal extremity of the metatarsus. The 1st digit has two phalanges, the 2nd has three, the 3rd has four, and the 4th has five. The digit of the 3rd metatarsus is the longest of the group, and its length is comparable to that of the metatarsus. It is composed of four phalanges. The 4th digit, extending laterally, is somewhat shorter than the 3rd and longer than the 2nd. Its five phalanges are the smallest of the representative groups of the forward-directed digits. The 2nd digit arises from the short 2nd metatarsal segment and extends forward and medially.

Each of the phalanges except the last in each toe has a common structural form. They are classified as a long bone with a shaft and two extremities. The shaft is slightly curved, the convexity being dorsal. The dorsal and mediolateral surfaces are convex and smooth. The plantar surface is flattened and concave in its length. The bone tapers slightly from the proximal to the distal extremity. The proximal articular surface is rather large and presents two concave facets. Medial and lateral tubercles are present for attachment of the collateral ligaments. The distal extremity is not quite as large as the proximal extremity and presents two condyles separated by a groove. These condyles are quite extensive, which permits a great deal of movement of the phalangeal joints.

The size of the phalanges decreases progressively in the succeeding digits. The terminal, or ungual, phalanx presents the following differential characteristics: The basal portion has the usual concave articular surface which is continued at its plantar border by a tubercle. The claw-shaped cranial projection is called the ungual process. It is a curved, conical projection terminating in a curved point. The surface of the process is slightly roughened to accommodate the corium of the claw.

CHAPTER TWO

Arthrology

THE study of the articulations of coturnix has been pursued with the following generally accepted plan in mind: The descriptions are brief but comprehensive enough to emphasize the proper nomenclature or name of each joint, its classification, anatomical location, osteology, ligaments, and action. Special details and characteristics of highly modified articulations have been elaborated upon.

THE AXIAL SKELETON: MEMBRANES AND ASSOCIATED LIGAMENTS

In addition to the ligaments and flat aponeuroses there are a number of thin, fibrous, connective tissue membranes that partially fill in the skeletal imperfections. These membranes not only assist in supporting and binding together the bones of the skeleton but also support the weight and help to fix the viscera in their normal positions.

Pectoral Membrane

The *pectoral membrane* (Fig. 2.1) attaches to the cranial process, the cranial border of the crest, and the craniolateral process of the manubrium of the sternum. It continues craniodorsad to attach to the medial surface of the shaft of the coracoid and the ramus and hypocleidium of the clavicle. It helps to

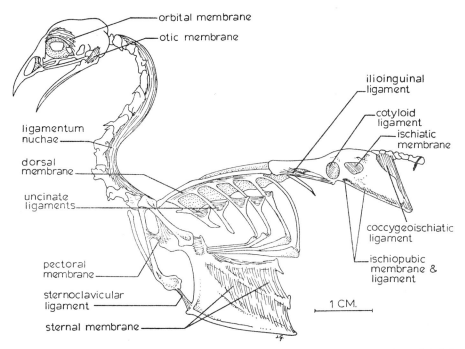

FIG. 2.1—Ligaments and membranes of the axial skeleton.

form a portion of the lateral wall of the thorax and also surrounds the structures passing through the thoracic inlet. Its fibers run parallel to and become confluent with those of the sternoclavicular ligament.

Sternal Membrane

The *sternal membrane* (Fig. 2.1) completes the osseous imperfections of the sternum and is attached to the lateral border of the caudomedial process and the lateral border of the lateral caudal process of the sternum. It also continues dorsolaterad to fill in the space between the caudolateral process and the costal process of the sternum and the costal arch formed by the last two sternal ribs. It is related on the right side to the liver and cranial flexures of the duodenum and on the left side to the left lobe of the liver, the proventriculus, and the ventriculus.

Ischiatic Membrane

The *ischiatic membrane* (Fig. 2.1) covers the ischiatic foramen, which is situated caudoventrally to the acetabulum. It helps to complete the lateral wall of the pelvis and is pierced by the ischiatic vessels and nerves.

Ischiopubic Membrane and Ligament

Cranially, the *ischiopubic membrane* and *ligament* (Fig. 2.1) take the form of a thin membrane covering the obturator foramen. This structure becomes ligamentous caudally as it extends between the rami of the pubis and the borders of the ischium.

Orbital Membrane

The *orbital membrane* (Fig. 2.1) of the quail is more complete than that of the chicken. It occupies the entire circumference of the orbit, is thick and dense dorsally, but thins out ventrally to become attached to the jugal, or zygomatic, arch. The lacrimale supraorbitale and lacrimale maxillary ligaments of the chicken are absent in the quail.

Dorsal Longitudinal Membranes

The *dorsal longitudinal membranes* (Fig. 2.3) lie in the floor of the spinal canal and extend between the dorsal surfaces of the cranial and caudal ends of adjacent vertebrae. They are not continuous. Ventral longitudinal ligaments have not been found. Intervertebral discs are inconstant and are represented by the suspensory ligament of the nucleus pulposus.

Cotyloid Ligament

The *cotyloid ligament* (Figs. 2.1, 2.11) attaches to the borders of the acetabulum and closes the bony imperfections of the socket. Free passageways for the ligamentum teres and blood vessels are provided by intervening fascia.

Dorsal Membranes

The *dorsal membranes* (Fig. 2.1) are bilateral sheets of fibrous tissue which run along the lateral borders of the fused vertebrae. They complement the width of the solid roof of the thoracic and abdominal cavities and fuse with the costotransverse ligaments, thus binding the proximal extremities of the ribs together.

In addition to the skeletal membranes there are a number of ligaments that serve to bind bony segments of the axial skeleton together. They will be described as a group, since some of them are multiple and others have specific functions to perform. Most of them are bilateral in position.

Uncinate Ligaments

The *uncinate ligaments* (Fig. 2.1) are triangular bands which extend from the overlapping uncinate processes of all the ribs, except the first and last, of the series to the lateral surface and caudal border of the same rib and to the lateral surfaces of the succeeding rib. They aid in strengthening the costal thoracic wall.

Ilioinguinal Ligament

The *ilioinguinal ligament* (Fig. 2.1) is a triangular band of fibrous tissue extending from the ventral surface and border of the lateral angle of the ilium to the pubic tubercle. It gives attachment to the oblique and transverse abdominal muscles and forms the craniolateral border of the femoral canal.

Ligamentum Nuchae

The *ligamentum nuchae* (Fig. 2.1) in the quail does not form the wide tendinous sheet found in mammals. However, the muscles biventer cervicis and semispinalis capitis in the craniodorsal part of the neck bear rather strong tendons that take its place. The deep interspinous ligaments are narrow elastic bands that extend from the dorsal spines of successive cervical vertebrae. The superficial ones lie on the dorsal surface of the dorsal membrane and are larger than the deep ones. All of them diminish in size as they proceed craniad.

THE AXIAL SKELETON: ARTICULATIONS OF THE SKULL

Articulations of the bones of the head are in general classed as synarthrosis. The bones of the cranium fuse very early in coturnix and their articulations are hard to find. Those of the face display unions only during their growing period. The permanent movable articulations are as follows:

Nasofrontal Articulation

CLASSIFICATION: Amphiarthrosis. The classification of this joint is difficult since it has all the characteristics of

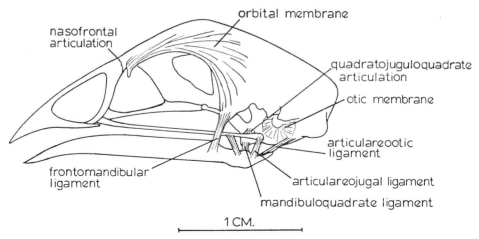

FIG. 2.2—Articulations of the skull.

a synarthrosis (squamosa) with a great deal of gliding movement.

LOCATION: At the base of the beak.

OSTEOLOGY: The caudal border of the nasal bones, the rostral border of the frontal bones, and the rostromedial border of the lacrimal bones are involved in this articulation (Fig. 2.2).

LIGAMENTS: An extensive union by fibrous tissue is present.

MOVEMENT: Through the gliding movement of the articulations, accompanied by a rostral movement of the premaxilla, palatine, malar, and quadrate bones, the mouth can be opened much wider than is possible in mammals.

Mandibuloquadrate Articulation

CLASSIFICATION: Diarthrosis, ginglymus.

LOCATION: Just below the lateral canthus of the eye and the quadratojugal bone.

OSTEOLOGY: The anatomical parts involved are the condyle on the distal extremity of the quadrate bone and the correspondingly concave articular surface on the caudal aspect of the mandible. The joint capsule is complete with fibrous and synovial

layers. It is very roomy and facilitates the displacement of the articulation when swallowing large insects, worms, and the like. When this occurs, the caudal part of the mandible drops down and the esophageal opening is very wide.

LIGAMENTS: The *mandibuloquadrate ligament* (Fig. 2.2) corresponds to a collateral ligament and extends from the medial border of the articular surface of the mandible to the medial surface of the quadrate bone just above its medial condyle.

The *frontomandibular ligament* (Fig. 2.2) extends from the lateral extremity of the supraorbital process of the frontal bone to the lateral surface of the mandible just rostral to its articular surface. Its fibers are not continuous with those of the supraorbital membrane as they are in the chicken.

The *articulareojugal ligament* (Fig. 2.2) extends from the lateral surface of the jugal bone to the base of the caudal border of the medial process of the mandible.

The *articulareootic ligament* (Fig. 2.2) extends from the caudal border of the external auditory process and otic membrane to the caudal border of the medial process of the articular area of the mandible.

The *mandibuloparasphenoid ligament* extends from the middle of the caudal surface of the medial mandibular process caudally to the rostrolateral border of the parasphenoid bone.

MOVEMENT: Flexion and extension of this hinge articulation occur as the mouth is opened and closed. It is of importance in the prehension of food.

Quadratojuguloquadrate Articulation

CLASSIFICATION: Diarthrosis, arthrodia.

LOCATION: Just above and lateral to the mandibuloquadrate articulation.

OSTEOLOGY: Involved are the medial surface of the quadratojugal process of the zygomatic (jugal) bone and the lateral process of the quadrate bone. The joint capsule is present with fibrous and synovial layers. The capsule is not extensive.

LIGAMENTS: There are no distinct ligaments as such, but the fibrous connective layer of the capsule extends about the circumference of this articulation to bind the bony parts together (Fig. 2.2).

MOVEMENT: Movement occurs by the gliding of the articular surfaces over one another. An insignificant movement of the maxilla is accomplished when food is taken.

The *otic membrane* (Figs. 2.1, 2.2) is a very dense connective tissue structure that assists in closing the caudal and ventral portion of the external auditory canal and is quite expansive along the rostral border of the external ear. It lies close to the lateral side of the cranium,

blending with the subcutaneous tissues and musculature.

Basihyoentoglossal Articulation

CLASSIFICATION: Diarthrosis, arthrodia.

LOCATION: Actually inside the base of the tongue.

OSTEOLOGY: Involved are the laterally concave articular surface on the rostral extremity of the 1st (rostral) copula of the basohyoid bone and the reciprocal articular surfaces on the caudal aspect of the entoglossum and adjacent articular facets on the bases of the median surfaces of the caudal processes of the entoglossum. The joint capsule is complete with synovia and both fibrous and synovial layers.

LIGAMENTS: No real ligaments are present.

MOVEMENT: This articulation is not extensively movable, the bones gliding on one another as the tongue is moved.

Interbasihyocornual Articulation

CLASSIFICATION: Diarthrosis, arthrodia.

LOCATION: Caudal to and partly incorporated in the base of the tongue.

OSTEOLOGY: Involved are the four wedge-shaped articular surfaces, one on each proximal articular extremity of the large cornua. One each on the caudal extremity of copula 2 which fit closely together, each occupying an angular area of the square articulation. The joint capsule is complete with both fibrous and synovial layers. Synovia are present.

LIGAMENTS: There are no distinct ligaments as such, but dense connective tissue binds the articular surfaces together around the borders of this articulation.

MOVEMENT: Gliding movements facilitate the use of the tongue. The caudal cornu is joined to the rostral cornu by a rather loose connective tissue cornu, but little actual movement of the articular surfaces is present. The cartilaginous extensions of the caudal extremities of the caudal cornu are noted; these extend to the caudodorsal surface of the cranium. When the tongue is strongly retracted, the tips of these processes almost meet on the mid-caudal aspect of the skull.

THE AXIAL SKELETON: ARTICULATIONS OF THE VERTEBRAL COLUMN

Occipitoatlantal Articulation

CLASSIFICATION: Enarthrosis.

LOCATION: This articulation is the union of the head to the neck and is situated just beneath the caudoventral aspect of the cranium.

OSTEOLOGY: The following bony structures are involved: the convex condyle of the occipital bone, the cotyloid cavity on the cranial extremity of the atlas, and the dens of the axis.

LIGAMENTS: The *atlas* (Fig. 2.3) is in the form of an intercartilaginous disc which is oval in shape and is found between the occipital condyle and the cranial extremity of the axis. It is attached dorsally to the ventral surface of the dens ligament.

The *dorsal occipitoatlantal membrane* (Fig. 2.3) is wide and expansive to allow great movability of this articulation. It extends from the cranial surface of the arch of the atlas to the bony rim about the dorsal and lateral aspects of the foramen magnum.

The *ventral occipitoatlantal membrane* (Fig. 2.3) represents the continuation of the dorsal occipitoatlantal membrane and extends from the ventral surface of the body (articular part) of the atlas to an area just beneath and adjacent to the occipital condyle. A joint capsule exists with both fibrous and synovial layers. It is extensive and may communicate with that of the occipitoaxial articulation.

MOVEMENT: This articulation allows the head to pivot and glide on the atlas.

Atlantoaxial Articulation

CLASSIFICATION: Diarthrosis, arthrodia, trochoides.

LOCATION: Partly within, by means of the dens, and partly behind the occipitoatlantal articulation.

OSTEOLOGY: The involved bony parts are the convex articular surface on the caudal border of the ventral arch of the atlas which articulates with the cranially projecting dens of the atlas and the cranial articular surface of the atlas. Both articular areas of the atlas form the boundaries of the longitudinal groove which houses the dens.

LIGAMENTS: The *dorsal atlantoaxial membrane* (Fig. 2.3) extends from the caudal edge of the arch of the atlas to the cranial edge of the arch of the axis.

The *dens ligament* (Fig. 2.3) is a broad bandlike ligament that forms part of the floor of the spinal canal. It is attached to the dorsal surface of the dens process and passes craniad across the atlas, where it attaches to the transverse atlantal ligament and the dorsal surface of the occipital condyle. The joint capsule is extensive with fibrous and synovial layers. Synovia are present.

MOVEMENT: The head may pivot by the rotating action of the dens in the longitudinal groove. A slight gliding action also occurs.

Occipitoaxial Articulation

CLASSIFICATION: Diarthrosis, trochoides.

LOCATION: This articulation is located

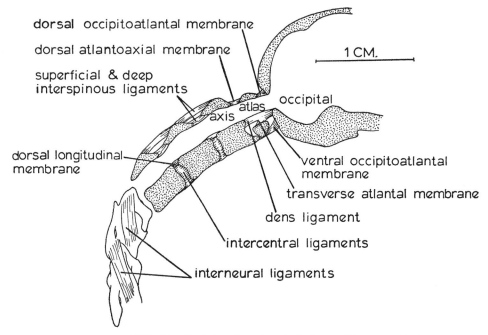

FIG. 2.3—Occipitoatlantal articulation and intervertebral articulations.

at the ventral border of the foramen magnum on the mid-dorsal aspect of the occipital condyle.

OSTEOLOGY: Involved are the midventral part of the articular surface of the occipital condyle and the odontoid process of the dens of the axis.

LIGAMENTS: The fibrous synovial coverings of the dens ligament and the *transverse atlantal membrane* (Fig. 2.3) lie dorsal to the dens process and are united to the dorsal region of the occipital condyle. This thick ligament is the immediate dorsal association of the occipitoaxial articulation. It alone binds the dens in its proper position in the longitudinal groove of the atlas. The odontoid process terminates in a small **V**-shaped articular fovea in the dorsal part of the articular surface of the occipital condyle.

MOVEMENT: The dens process pivots on the skull for movements of the neck, and the skull rotates on the dens when the neck is stationary.

Vertebral Intercentral Articulations

CLASSIFICATION: Amphiarthrosis.

LOCATION: The limited movement of the intercentral articulations is that of the bodies of all the cervical series except the first two and those of the free thoracic vertebrae.

OSTEOLOGY: Involved are the caudal articular surfaces, which are concave transversely and convex vertically, and the cranial articular surfaces of successive vertebrae, which are convex transversely and concave vertically. The structure of these articular surfaces composes a horizontally placed hinge between these vertebrae, and gliding surfaces exist in the vertical plane to allow for lesser lateral movements than those of the hinge, which are median in position and considerably freer.

LIGAMENTS: Joint capsules, or *intercentral ligaments* (Fig. 2.3), present in each of these articulations are composed of fibrous and synovial layers.

MOVEMENT: The hinge and gliding movements of these articulations are the basic movements of the vertebral column.

Interneural Articulations

CLASSIFICATION: Diarthrosis, arthrodia.

LOCATION: These are the bony unions of the articular processes of the vertebrae.

OSTEOLOGY: Involved are the articular processes, which are designated as cranial and caudal. They are paired, and the articular surfaces are variable from flatly oval to slightly concave or convex. As a rule the articular surfaces of the caudal articular processes will be concave, and those of the cranial process convex. Caudal articular processes exist on cervical vertebrae 2 through 14; on thoracic vertebrae 1, 2, 5, 6, and 7; and on the 1st lumbar vertebra. **Note:** The articular processes which occur on the fused lumbar and thoracic vertebrae are also fused.

LIGAMENTS: The *capsular ligament,* or *interneural ligament* (Fig. 2.3), occurs as a thin ring of connective tissue that extends about the circumference of each interneural articulation of the cervical region, attaching to the rim about the articular surfaces. The capsular ligaments bind together the margins of the articular processes of all the successive movable cervical and thoracic vertebrae.

The *lateral interneural ligament* (Fig. 2.3) extends from the caudolateral surface of the cranial articular process to the lateral surface of the neural arch of each cervical vertebra near the origin of the caudal articular process.

Superficial and *deep interspinous ligaments* (Fig. 2.3) extend between the dorsal spines.

MOVEMENT: Gliding movements occur between these processes.

THE ABAXIAL SKELETON: ARTICULATIONS OF THE PECTORAL LIMB

Sternoclavicular Articulation

CLASSIFICATION: Synarthrosis, syndesmosis.

LOCATION: Cranial portion of the breast at the midline.

OSTEOLOGY: This articulation is formed by the hypocleidium of the clavicle and the cranial process of the sternal crest.

LIGAMENTS: The *sternoclavicular ligament* (Fig. 2.1, 2.4) extends from the cranial process of the crest of the sternum to the sides and ventral border of the hypocleidium of the clavicle. This strong, wide ligament assists in stabilizing the chest wall

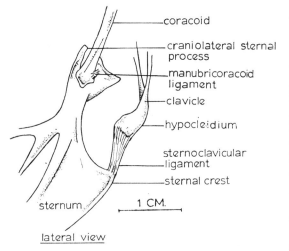

FIG. 2.4—Sternoclavicular articulation, lateral view.

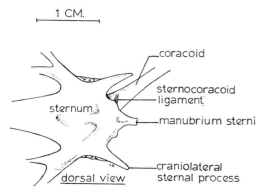

1 CM.

coracoid

sternocoracoid
ligament

sternum

manubrium sterni

craniolateral
sternal process

dorsal view

FIG. 2.5--Sternocoracoid articulation,
dorsal view.

and shoulder girdle during the powerful contractions of the pectoral muscles during flight.

MOVEMENT: Has only a stabilizing function of the shoulder.

Sternocoracoid Articulation

CLASSIFICATION: Diarthrosis, arthrodia, ginglymus.

LOCATION: Between the manubrium sterni and the craniolateral sternal process and cartilage. The joint capsule is complete with an articular cavity.

OSTEOLOGY: The condyles of the proximal extremity of the coracoid bone articulate with an oval glenoid cavity on the craniolateral border of the sternum between the manubrium and the craniolateral process.

LIGAMENTS: The *medial sternocoracoid ligament* (Fig. 2.5) is a short, flat ligament that extends from the caudomedial surface of the proximal extremity of the coracoid bone to the lateral margin of the manubrium sterni.

The *manubricoracoid ligament* (Fig. 2.4) extends from the lateral surface of the manubrium to the cranial aspect of the proximal extremity of the coracoid bone.

MOVEMENT: A gliding and hinge movement when the shoulder is moving, as in flight. Motion is craniocaudal in direction and provides dorsal and ventral movements during respiration.

Scapulocoracoid Articulation

CLASSIFICATION: Synarthrosis, syndesmosis.

LOCATION: Medial articulation of the shoulder girdle.

OSTEOLOGY: Joint is formed by the articulation of the medial distal extremity of the coracoid bone and the proximal lateral extremity of the scapula.

LIGAMENTS: The *medial interfibrous ligament* (Figs. 2.6, 2.7) extends from the dorsal proximal border of the scapula to the large dorsal tuberosity on the mediodistal surface of the coracoid bone. This ligament completes the foramen triosseum medially and lies cranial and lateral to the clavicle.

The *lateral interfibrous ligament* (Figs. 2.6, 2.7) is the lateral connection of the scapula and coracoid. It lies medial to the head of the humerus which may make contact with it.

The *ventral interfibrous ligament* (Fig. 2.7) lies at the base of the foramen triosseum and connects the proximal lateral surface of the scapula with the ventral tuberosity on the medial surface of the distal extremity of the coracoid.

MOVEMENT: These bones are united by ligaments in such a manner that only slight movement occurs.

Coracoclavicular and Scapuloclavicular Articulation

CLASSIFICATION: Synarthrosis, syndesmosis.

LOCATION: Shoulder girdle.

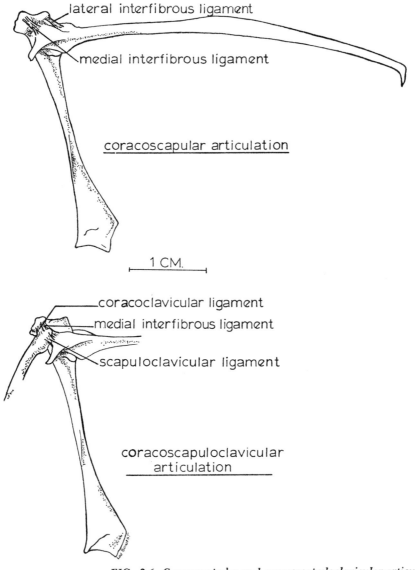

lateral interfibrous ligament

medial interfibrous ligament

coracoscapular articulation

1 CM.

coracoclavicular ligament

medial interfibrous ligament

scapuloclavicular ligament

coracoscapuloclavicular
articulation

FIG. 2.6—Coracoscapular and coracoscapuloclavicular articulations.

OSTEOLOGY: This articulation, as the name implies, is an area of junction of the coracoid, scapular, and clavicular bones at the shoulder joint. The craniomedial area of the distal extremity of the coracoid bone articulates with the lateral aspect of the flattened distal extremity of the clavicular bone. The caudal margin of the flattened extremity of the clavicle forms an articulation with the mediocranial extremity of the head of the scapula and the caudomedial region of the coracoid bone. Lateral to this junction the coracoid and scapula form a rather imperfect

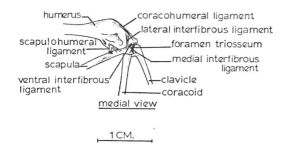

1 CM.

proximal radioulnar ligament — ulna

— radius

lateral view

*FIG. 2.7–Shoulder articulation, medial and
lateral views.*

glenoid cavity that articulates with
the large head of the humerus.

LIGAMENTS: The *coracoclavicular ligament* (Fig. 2.6) extends from the
dorsomedial extremity of the clavicle to a large dorsal tuberosity on
the distomedial surface of the coracoid.

The *scapuloclavicular ligament*
(Fig. 2.6) extends from the ventral
border of the distal extremity of the
clavicle to the dorsal border of the
proximal extremity of the scapula.
This is a short, wide ligament
which makes contact extensively
along the borders of the bones. Both
of the above ligaments lie in contact
with the interfibrous ligament of
the coracoscapular joint on its
medial surface.

MOVEMENT: There is no specific action
because the ligamentous connections
prevent any perceptible movement.

Costosternal Articulation

CLASSIFICATION: Ball and socket.

LOCATION: The head of each of the
sternal ribs articulates with the lateral border of the sternum.

OSTEOLOGY: The ribs and sternum are
the bones involved.

LIGAMENTS: There is only a capsular
costosternal ligament around the
head of each rib.

MOVEMENT: Extremely slight rotation
may take place with deep respiration.

Humeroscapulocoracoid Articulation (Shoulder Joint)

CLASSIFICATION: Diarthrosis, enarthrosis,
ball and socket.

LOCATION: Most proximal joint of the
pectoral limb, which serves to connect the limb with the trunk.

OSTEOLOGY: The distal extremity of the
coracoid and the proximal extremity
of the scapula form a glenoid cavity
laterally that makes contact with a
small portion of the head of the
humerus. The head of the humerus
is oval in outline and much larger
than the glenoid cavity. The articular cavity and articular cartilages are
present. The joint capsule is large
and complete, consisting of synovial
and fibrous layers.

LIGAMENTS: The *coracohumeral ligament* (Fig. 2.7) is a large, wide, triangular ligament with its base attaching on the lateral surface of the
neck of the humerus and its apex attaching on the dorsal aspect of the
distal extremity of the coracoid
bone. A ramus extends deep to the
main portion of the ligament from
its cranial attachment on the humerus and continues to the dorsal
portion of the ridge which surrounds the glenoid cavity.

The *scapulohumeral ligament*
(medial ligament) (Fig. 2.7) extends
from the medial aspect of the proximal extremity of the humerus to the

lateral surface of the proximal extremity of the scapula.

MOVEMENT: There are several movements which are possible from the shoulder joint, but the main ones are adduction and abduction. Other movements such as flexion, extension, rotation, and circumduction occur.

Humeroradioulnar Articulation (Elbow)

CLASSIFICATION: Diarthrosis, ginglymus.

LOCATION: Approximately 2¼ inches from the tip of the wing when it is extended. When the wing is folded, this joint makes an acute angle that is located near the region of the ilium and the caudal extremity of the scapula.

OSTEOLOGY: The skeletal parts are the two condyles on the distal extremity of the humerus and the concave glenoid cavities of the proximal extremities of the radius and ulna.

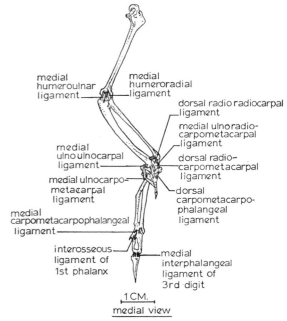

FIG. 2.9–Articulations of the pectoral limb, medial view.

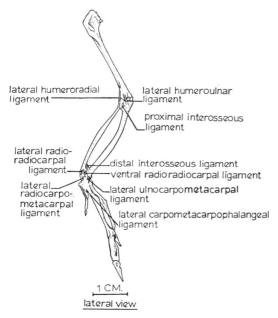

FIG. 2.8–Articulations of the pectoral limb, lateral view.

Articular cartilages are present. The joint capsule is complete with both layers of the capsule represented.

LIGAMENTS: The *lateral humeroradial ligament* (Fig. 2.8) (dorsal collateral of Chamberlain) extends from the lateral epicondyle of the humerus to the craniolateral aspect of the proximal extremity of the radius.

The *lateral humeroulnar ligament* (Fig. 2.8) (ventral collateral of Chamberlain), the longer of the two lateral ligaments, extends from a point proximal to the lateral epicondyle of the humerus to the lateral epicondyle of the humerus to the lateral aspect of the proximal extremity of the ulna.

The *medial humeroradial ligament* (Fig. 2.9) extends from the coronoid fossa of the humerus to the medial surface of the proximal extremity of the radius.

The *medial humeroulnar liga-ment* (Fig. 2.9) extends from the medial epicondyle of the humerus to the medial aspect of the proximal extremity of the ulna. The two medial ligaments are in close prox-imity at their attachment on the humerus and may be considered as continuous humeral attachment.

MOVEMENT: The main action is flexion and extension.

Proximal Radioulnar Articulation

CLASSIFICATION: Diarthrosis, trochoides.

LOCATION: Distal to the humeroradial ulnar joint. This is considered to be a part of the elbow joint.

OSTEOLOGY: The facets on the ventral aspect (caudal aspect when the wing is extended) of the proximal ex-tremity of the radius and the corre-sponding facet on the dorsal aspect (cranial when wing is extended) of the proximal extremity of the ulna. An articular cartilage is present and the joint capsule is complete.

LIGAMENTS: The *proximal interosseous ligament* (Fig. 2.8) surrounds the articulation.

The *proximal radioulnar liga-ment* (Fig. 2.7) extends from the lateral aspect of the neck of the radius to an area on the ulna just lateral to the condyloid cavity and just caudal to the facet for articula-tion with the radius.

MOVEMENT: Very little movement except for limited rotation of the forearm.

Distal Radioulnar Articulation

CLASSIFICATION: Synarthrosis, syndesmo-sis.

LOCATION: Just proximal to the wrist joint.

OSTEOLOGY: Skeletal parts include the ventral aspect of the distal extremity of the radius (caudal aspect when the wing is extended) and the dorsal

aspect of the distal extremity of the ulna (cranial aspect when the wing is extended).

LIGAMENTS: The *distal interosseous liga-ment* (Fig. 2.8) extends from the respective surfaces of the ulna and radius and binds these bones to-gether at their distal extremity.

MOVEMENT: A slightly sliding motion of the radius and ulna as the carpus is extended and flexed.

Carpal Articulation

CLASSIFICATION: Diarthrosis, arthrodia, ginglymus.

LOCATION: Between the radius and ulna and the manus.

OSTEOLOGY: The carpal joint is made up of several articulations which will be discussed individually below.

Radiocarpal Articulation

CLASSIFICATION: Arthrodia.

OSTEOLOGY: The distal extremity of the radius articulates with the dorso-proximal articular surface of the radiocarpal bone. These bones are bound closely together by ligaments.

LIGAMENTS: The *dorsal radioradiocarpal ligament* (Fig. 2.9) is a short, strong ligament that extends from the dorsomedial aspect on the distal ex-tremity of the radius to the medial surface of the proximal extremity of the radiocarpal bone.

The *ventral radioradiocarpal ligament* (Fig. 2.8) is a narrow, short ligament that extends from the ventrolateral surface of the distal extremity of the radius to the ven-trolateral aspect of the proximal ex-tremity of the radiocarpal bone.

The *lateral radioradiocarpal ligament* (Fig. 2.8) extends from the lateral aspect of the proximal ex-tremity of the radiocarpal bone. This ligament is the most superfi-cial of the three ligaments of this articulation, and it does not aid in binding these bones together as do the other two. The ligament branches just proximal to its attachment on the radiocarpal bone into superficial and deep rami which go over and under the tendons of the extensor carpi radialis muscle and attach on the lateral aspect of the radius. In surrounding this tendon, it keeps the muscle bound on the dorsolateral aspect of the wing.

MOVEMENT: Limited gliding movement between the bones.

Ulnocarpal Articulation

CLASSIFICATION: Arthrodia.

OSTEOLOGY: The dorsal part of the articular surface of the ulna articulates with the ventral articular surface of the radiocarpal bone.

LIGAMENTS: The *dorsal ulnoradiocarpal ligament* extends from a point just distal to the attachment of the distal interosseous ligament on the dorsal surface of the distal extremity of the ulna to a crest formed between the articular surface for the radius and ulna on the radiocarpal bone.

The *distal ulnocarpal ligament* extends from a point in the intercondyloid groove just distal to the dorsal ulnoradiocarpal ligament and attaches to the middle of the ulnar articular surface on the radiocarpal bone.

The *medial ulnoradiocarpal ligament* extends from the medial condyle of the articular surface for the ulna on the radiocarpal bone. It runs deep to the ulnoradiocarpometacarpal ligament.

OSTEOLOGY: The ventral articular surface of the ulna articulates with the dorsal surface of the ulnocarpal bone.

LIGAMENTS: The *medial ulnoulnocarpal ligament* (Fig. 2.9) is a large, rather wide ligament that extends from the medial aspect of the distal extremity of the ulna to the dorsomedial aspect of the distal extremity of the ulnocarpal bone.

The *lateral radiocarpometacarpal ligament* (Fig. 2.8) extends from the dorsal surface of the distal extremity of the ulnocarpal bone and attaches to the small lateral tubercle on the proximal extremity of the metacarpus.

The *dorsal radiocarpometacarpal ligament* (Fig. 2.9) extends from the dorsal surface of the distal extremity of the radiocarpal bone to the distal extremity of the 2nd metacarpus.

MOVEMENT: Limited gliding motion.

Ulnocarpometacarpal Articulation

CLASSIFICATION: Arthrodia.

OSTEOLOGY: The incisural surface of the ulnocarpal bone and the ridge on the ventral surface of the proximal extremity of the metacarpus are the anatomical parts involved.

LIGAMENTS: The main portion of the *medial ulnocarpometacarpal ligament* (Fig. 2.9) extends from the distal extremity of the medial horn of the ulnocarpal bone to the medial surface of the 4th digit at its proximal fusion with the 3rd metacarpus. A ramus branches off the main portion and extends dorsally to the ventral surface of the 1st phalanx of the 2nd digit. Another ramus extends from the ulnocarpal bone and attaches to the medial tubercle on the proximal extremity of the metacarpus. Both rami bind tendons of muscles to the metacarpus between their points of attachment.

The *lateral ulnocarpometa-*

carpal ligament (Fig. 2.8) extends from the dorsal surface of the distal extremity of the ulnocarpal bone and attaches to the small lateral tubercle on the proximal extremity of the metacarpus.

MOVEMENT: Limited gliding movement.

Intercarpal Articulation

CLASSIFICATION: Arthrodia.

OSTEOLOGY: The articular surfaces of the carpal bones are involved.

LIGAMENTS: The *intercarpal ligament* extends from the lateral part of the crest on the radiocarpal bone to the dorsal surface on the distal extremity of the lateral horn of the ulnocarpal bone.

MOVEMENT: Extremely little gliding movement is possible.

Ulnometacarpal Articulation

CLASSIFICATION: Diarthrosis, ginglymus.

OSTEOLOGY: The articular surface of the distal extremity of the ulna and the proximal extremity of the metacarpus articulate between the two carpal bones.

LIGAMENTS: The *medial ulnoradiocarpometacarpal ligament* (Fig. 2.9) is the only ligament that has fibers running directly from the ulna to the carpometacarpus. It offers fibers extending from the ulna to the carpal bones and from the carpal bones to the carpometacarpus.

MOVEMENT: Allows the manus to move back and forth.

Carpometacarpophalangeal Articulation (2nd Digit)

CLASSIFICATION: Diarthrosis, ginglymus.

LOCATION: Just distal to the wrist joint on the dorsal surface of the carpometacarpus.

OSTEOLOGY: Involved are the distal articular surfaces of the 2nd metacarpus and the reciprocal articular

surface of the 1st phalanx of the 2nd digit. The joint capsule is complete.

LIGAMENTS: The *dorsal carpometacarpophalangeal ligament* (Fig. 2.9) extends from the dorsal aspect of the proximal extremity of the 1st phalanx of the 2nd digit. This ligament is the largest of the three ligaments connecting these bones and does not attach directly to the distal extremity of the 2nd metacarpus, but extends a short distance proximally and attaches to the distal surface of the large dorsal process of the carpometacarpus.

The *medial carpometacarpophalangeal ligament* (Fig. 2.9) extends from the medial aspect of the proximal extremity of the 1st phalanx.

The *lateral carpometacarpophalangeal ligament* (Fig. 2.8) is a short ligament that extends from the dorsolateral aspect of the 3rd metacarpus at the level of the distal extremity of the 2nd metacarpus to the lateral aspect of the proximal extremity of the 1st phalanx.

MOVEMENT: Movement is limited.

Interphalangeal Articulation (2nd Digit)

CLASSIFICATION: Diarthrosis, ginglymus.

LOCATION: On the distal extremity of the 1st phalanx of the 2nd digit.

OSTEOLOGY: This joint is formed by the articular surface of the distal extremity of the 1st phalanx and the reciprocal articular surface of the 2nd phalanx of the 2nd digit. The 2nd phalanx is very small and pointed. Articular cartilage and cavity are present and the joint capsule is complete. The fibrous layer of the joint capsule serves to bind the two phalanges together.

LIGAMENTS: There are no ligaments in this articulation.

MOVEMENT: None.

Carpometacarpophalangeal Articulation (3rd Digit)

CLASSIFICATION: Diarthrosis, ginglymus.

LOCATION: Approximately ⅜ inch from the distal extremity of the wing.

OSTEOLOGY: The condyles on the distal extremity of the 3rd metacarpus articulate with the reciprocal articular surface of the 1st phalanx of the 2nd digit to form this joint. Articular cartilage and cavity are present; the joint capsule is complete.

LIGAMENTS: The *medial carpometacarpophalangeal ligament* (Fig. 2.9) of the 3rd digit is a medial collateral ligament that extends from the medial surface of the distal extremity of the 3rd metacarpus to the medial aspect of the proximal extremity of the 1st phalanx of the 3rd digit. There are no ligaments laterally.

MOVEMENT: Movement is limited.

Interphalangeal Articulation (3rd Digit)

CLASSIFICATION: Diarthrosis, ginglymus.

LOCATION: The distal articulation of the wing, approximately ⅜ inch from the extremity of the wing.

OSTEOLOGY: The anatomical parts involved are the condyles on the distal articular surface of the 1st phalanx and the reciprocal articular surface of the proximal extremity of the 2nd phalanx. Articular cartilage and cavity are present, and the joint capsule is complete.

LIGAMENTS: The *medial interphalangeal ligament of the 3rd digit* (Fig. 2.9) is the only ligament of this joint. It extends from the medial aspect of the distal extremity of the 1st pha-

lanx to the medial aspect of the proximal extremity of the 2nd phalanx.

MOVEMENT: None.

Carpometacarpophalangeal Articulation (4th Digit)

CLASSIFICATION: Diarthrosis, ginglymus.

LOCATION: Approximately ⅜ inch from the distal extremity of the wing on the ventral aspect of the distal extremity of the carpometacarpus.

OSTEOLOGY: Involved are the articular surfaces of the distal extremity of the 4th metacarpus and the reciprocal articular surfaces on the proximal extremity of the 1st phalanx of the 4th digit. Articular cartilage and cavity are present and the joint capsule is complete with synovial and fibrous layers.

LIGAMENTS: The *lateral carpometacarpophalangeal ligament* (Fig. 2.8) extends from the lateral aspect of the distal extremity of the 4th metacarpus to the lateral surface of the proximal extremity of the 1st phalanx of the 4th digit.

The *medial carpometacarpophalangeal ligament* (Fig. 2.9) extends from the medial aspect of the distal extremity of the 4th metacarpus to the entire distal extremity on the medial aspect of the 1st phalanx of the 4th digit.

MOVEMENT: The joint has limited motion. This region of the wing is made for stability rather than motility. There is an interphalangeal joint of the 4th digit, since the 2nd digit is either absent or fused.

Interdigital Articulation

CLASSIFICATION: Synarthrosis, syndesmosis.

LOCATION: Along the proximal ventral border of the 1st phalanx of the 3rd digit.

OSTEOLOGY AND LIGAMENTS: The 1st phalanx of the 4th digit is attached along its entire dorsal border to the ventral border of the 1st phalanx of the 3rd digit by the *interosseous ligament* (Fig. 2.9). There is no joint cavity or articular cartilage.

MOVEMENT: None.

THE ABAXIAL SKELETON: ARTICULATIONS OF THE COCCYX AND THE PELVIC LIMB

Costocoxal Articulation

CLASSIFICATION: Amphiarthrosis, diarthrosis. The head of the last rib unites with the body of the last vertebra and the tubercle of the same rib with the ventral surface of the cranial extremity of the ilium (syndesmosis).

LOCATION: Bilateral, opposite the last thoracic vertebra and the ilium.

OSTEOLOGY: The last rib, the last thoracic vertebra, and the ilium make up this joint.

LIGAMENTS: The *costoiliac ligament* (Fig. 2.10) extends over the ventral surface of the tubercle of the last rib to the ilium just cranial and caudal to the tubercle. The joint capsules of both articulations are incomplete.

MOVEMENT: Action is slight and movement occurs during respiration.

Lumbosacral Articulation

CLASSIFICATION: Diarthrosis and synarthrosis. The latter is joined by fibrous tissue and a ligament (syndesmosis).

LOCATION: Bilateral, adjacent to the lumbosacral bone.

OSTEOLOGY AND LIGAMENTS: The united bones are the os coxae and the lumbosacral bone medially (some-

times movable and sometimes fixed).

A: Diarthrosis: A small gliding (arthrodia) joint exists between a projection of the medial and caudal border of the ilium and the transverse process of the adjacent vertebra. The occurrence of a capsule and synovial membrane is inconstant, and when present it is slight.

B: Suture: The entire lateral border of the lumbosacral bone is closely united to the medial border of the os coxae by fibrous tissue composing the *sutural ligament*.

C: Syndesmosis, synarthrosis: The *dorsal sacroiliac ligament* (Fig. 2.10) extends from the dorsal spines of the four cranial lumbar vertebrae to the dorsal border of the cranial part of the ilium on each side. There is no ventral lumbosacral ligament. The *coccygeoischiatic ligament* (Figs. 2.1, 2.10) extends from the transverse processes of the first three coccygeal vertebrae to the caudal extremity of the pubis. The medial connective tissue is present as the linea alba and extends from the mediocaudal process of the ster-

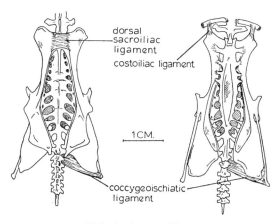

FIG. 2.10—Sacroiliac articulation.

num to the anal area near the coccygeoischiatic ligament.

MOVEMENT: Slight and perhaps important in egg laying. The eggs are surprisingly large when compared to the size of the body.

Coxofemoral Articulation

CLASSIFICATION: Diarthrosis, true joint; enarthrosis, ball and socket.

LOCATION: This joint is the junction of the head of the femur and the acetabulum, joining the thigh to the pelvis.

OSTEOLOGY: The head of the femur inserts into the acetabulum of the os coxae. The joint capsule is complete, loose, and intact with synovia.

LIGAMENTS: The *cotyloid ligament* (Figs. 2.1, 2.11) complements the bony and cartilaginous rim of the acetabulum and deepens its cavity.

The *transverse acetabular ligament* is a very slight acetabular notch, and strands of ligamentous fibers traverse it to complete the cotyloid ligament. These form a continuous ring around the circumference of the articular cavity.

The *round ligament* extends from the border of the acetabular ligament to the fovea capitis.

The *cranial collateral ligament* (Fig. 2.11) extends from the iliac part of the acetabulum to the cra-

nial surface of the neck of the femur.

Note: Ligaments *cranial collateral* and *pubiofemoral* (Fig. 2.11) are fused at their cranial borders, and both accommodate the fibrous layers of the joint capsule throughout their expanse. They extend around the entire articulation except at the caudolateral aspect where the joint capsule may be clearly seen.

MOVEMENT: Chiefly flexion and extension of walking. Almost any angular movement may be accomplished (rotation, adduction, abduction, and circumduction).

Stifle Articulation (Knee)

The stifle is a compound articulation composed of the femoropatellar, femorotibial, and fibular joints. It is the largest and most complicated articulation of the body and therefore will be described in two parts.

Femoropatellar Articulation

CLASSIFICATION: Diarthrosis, arthrosis.

LOCATION: At the distal extremity of the thigh the patella, or knee cap, articulates with the femur.

OSTEOLOGY: The trochlea of the distal extremity of the femur and the articular surface of the patella are involved. The capsule is extensive and pouches upward; it is covered ventrally by the broad tibiopatellar ligament. The cavity communicates with that of the femorotibial capsule.

LIGAMENTS: The *medial femoropatellar ligament* (Fig. 2.12) extends from the medial border of the patella to the medial epicondyle of the femur. A lateral femoropatellar ligament has not been found.

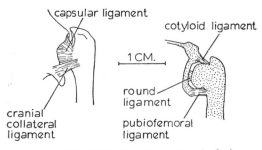

FIG. 2.11—*Coxofemoral articulation.*

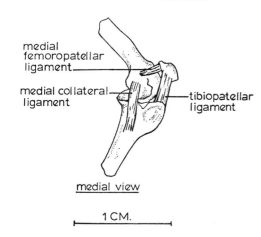

medial view

1 CM.

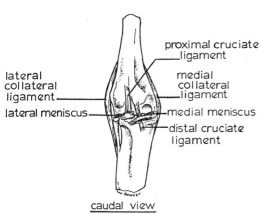

caudal view

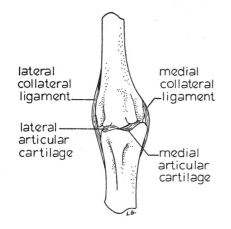

cranial view

FIG. 2.12—*Stifle articulation, medial, caudal, and cranial views.*

The *tibiopatellar ligament* (Fig. 2.12) is broad and extensive. It is attached to the distal border of the patella above and extends to the broad transverse crest on the dorsal border of the proximal articular surface of the tibia.

MOVEMENT: The movement is gliding, as the patella is in reality a sesamoid bone incorporated in the tendon of insertion of the quadriceps femoris and biceps femoris muscles.

Femorotibial and Fibular Articulation

CLASSIFICATION: Diarthrosis, ginglymus.

LOCATION: This articulation is commonly called the knee joint. It is quite large and is situated at the junction of the thigh with the leg.

OSTEOLOGY: This joint is made up of the femoral and tibial condyles, the tibial spine and the proximal articular extremity of the fibula. The joint capsule is continuous over both the femoropatellar and femorotibiofibular joints. The fibrous layer is variable in thickness and is supplemented by ligaments and tendons. The synovial membrane is expansive and continuous with the synovial membrane of the tendon sheath of the cranial tibial muscle.

LIGAMENTS: The *medial collateral ligament* (Figs. 2.12, 2.13) extends from the medial surface of the medial condyle of the femur to a small ridge on the medial surface of the proximal extremity of the tibia.

The *femorofibular ligament* (Fig. 2.14) occupies a trochlear area on the caudal part of the lateral femoral condyle and extends from a depression behind the trochlea to the medial side of the head of the fibula.

The two *cruciate ligaments* (Fig. 2.12) are situated chiefly in the

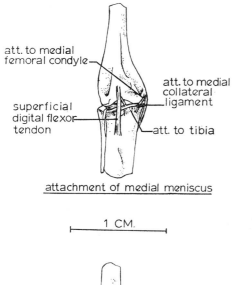

att. to medial femoral condyle

att. to medial collateral ligament

superficial digital flexor tendon

att. to tibia

attachment of medial meniscus

1 CM.

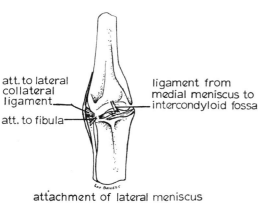

att. to lateral collateral ligament

att. to fibula

ligament from medial meniscus to intercondyloid fossa

attachment of lateral meniscus

FIG. 2.13—*Stifle articulation, attachment of the menisci.*

intercondyloid fossa between the two synovial sacs. They are strong, rounded bands and cross each other in the form of an **X**. They are named according to their tibial attachments: The *proximal cruciate ligament* (Fig. 2.12), the smaller of the two, arises from a fossa on the tibial spine and ends on the caudal aspect of the lateral wall of the intercondyloid fossa. The *distal cruciate ligament* (Fig. 2.12), medial to the preceding one, extends from the popliteal notch of the tibia to the

distal part of the intercondyloid fossa of the femur.

MENISCI: There are two menisci of fibrocartilaginous tissue interposed between the greater part of the articular surfaces of the femur and tibia: The *medial meniscus* (Figs. 2.12, 2.13) is attached to the caudal part of the articular ridge on the caudomedial aspect of the proximal extremity of the tibia and to the medial side of the medial femoral condyle. It also attaches to the tendon of origin of the superficial digital flexor muscle, which originates in a depression behind the intercondyloid fossa. The medial meniscus has a strong ligament that extends from its caudolateral border to insert in the intercondyloid fossa adjacent to the femoral attachment of the distal cruciate ligament. The *lateral meniscus* (Figs. 2.12–2.14) is attached caudally to the medial surface of the head of the fibula and to the entire medial border of the femorofibular ligament. A strong ligament extends from the craniomedial border of the lateral meniscus across the articular surface of the tibia to the midpoint of the medial

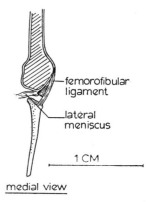

femorofibular ligament

lateral meniscus

1 CM

medial view

FIG. 2.14—*Femorofibular articulation, medial view.*

articular ridge of the proximal extremity of the tibia. Both menisci are attached to the collateral ligaments of their respective sides and cranially to the broad tibiopatellar ligament.

MOVEMENT: Flexion and extension of the knee.

Tibiofibular Articulation

CLASSIFICATION: Synarthrosis, syndesmosis.

LOCATION: The distal extent of the knee on the lateral side of the leg.

OSTEOLOGY: The lateral border of the proximal extremity of the tibia and the medial side of the head of the fibula form this joint.

LIGAMENTS: The *interosseous ligament* (Fig. 2.15) extends from the proximal one-third of the lateral border of the tibia to the corresponding medial surface of the fibula.

The *proximal tibiofibular ligament* (Fig. 2.15) extends from a depression behind the lateral edge of the tibial crest to the cranial angle of the head of the fibula.

The *caudal tibiofibular ligament* (Fig. 2.15) extends from the caudal angle of the fibular head to attach just beneath the lateral proximal tibial condyle. The joint capsule is complete and is fused with the joint capsule of the knee.

MOVEMENT: Slight, if any. The caudal part of the fibula may deviate medially or laterally with movement of the leg.

Tibiotarsal-tarsometatarsal Articulation (Hock Joint)

CLASSIFICATION: Diarthrosis, ginglymus.

LOCATION: The tibiotarsal-tarsometatarsal (hock) articulation joins the leg and pes segments of the pelvic limb.

OSTEOLOGY: This articulation is compound in nature and represents the

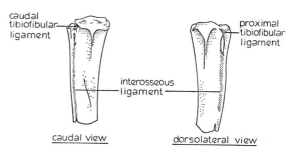

FIG. 2.15—Tibiofibular articulation, caudal and dorsolateral views.

tibiotarsal, intertarsal, and tarsometatarsal articulations of mammals. In coturnix the tibiotarsal bone is formed by the fusion of the distal extremity of the tibia to the fibula and remnants of the proximal row of tarsal bones. It appears that the condyles of the distal extremity of the tibiotarsal bone are in reality the modified tibial tarsal bone and that the tarsal sesamoid bone is a modified remnant of the fibular tarsal bone. Numerous articular areas are formed: They are the two sagittal ridges of the condyle of the distal extremity of the tibiotarsal bone, the concave sagittal grooves of the proximal extremity of the tarsometatarsus, and the concave articular surface of the tarsal sesamoid (hyposesamoid) bone, which articulates with the plantar extension of the tibiotarsal bone. The joint capsule is quite extensive and incorporates all the distal extremity of the tibiotarsus and articular areas of the proximal extremity of the tarsometatarsus. The synovial membrane is complete. The fibrous layer is thin on the dorsal surface and thick on the plantar surface of the articulation.

LIGAMENTS: The *medial collateral ligament* (Figs. 2.12, 2.13) of the articulation extends from a slight elevation on the medial side above the articular surface of the tibiotarsal bone to a medial eminence just below the articular margin of the tarsometatarsal bone.

The *lateral collateral ligament* (Figs. 2.12, 2.13) extends from the concave depression on the lateral aspect of the tibiotarsal condyle below which the ligament divides into two parts. The lateral part extends distally to a roughened triangular area just below the lateral margin of the sagittal articular groove. The deeper medial part extends downward and medially to the summit of the hypotarsus.

The *dorsal tibiometatarsal ligament* extends from the distal extremity of the dorsal surface of the shaft of the tibiotarsal bone distally between the medial and lateral condyles to attach to a somewhat pointed area at the midcentral region of the articular margin of the tarsometatarsal bone. This ligament prevents overextension of the hock joint.

The *hypotarsotibiotarsal ligament* extends from the caudal surface of the medial articular ridge of the tibiotarsus to the medial margin of the hypotarsal bone. The hypotarsal bone is incorporated in the plantar portion of the joint capsule and is attached to the Achilles tendon. Distally it articulates with the tarsometatarsus and the medial portion of the distal articular surface of the tibiotarsus.

MOVEMENT: Extension and flexion.

Intertarsometatarsal Articulation

CLASSIFICATION: Diarthrosis, arthrodia.
LOCATION: This joint is situated between the distal extremity of the tarsometatarsus and the 1st metatarsal bone of the 1st digit. It corresponds in position to the dewclaw of the pelvic limb of the dog and is similarly located, quite proximal to the remaining digits of the foot.

OSTEOLOGY: A very slight concave articular cavity on the medioplantar area of the tarsometatarsus and correspondingly concave surface on the proximal extremity of the 1st phalanx.

LIGAMENTS: Two intermetatarsal ligaments support this articulation: The *distal intermetatarsal ligament* (Fig. 2.16) extends from the proximal extremity of the 1st metatarsal bone to the medial surface of the distal extremity of the 2nd metatarsal bone. The *proximal intermetatarsal ligament* (Fig. 2.16) extends from the proximal extremity of the 1st metatarsal bone dorsally to attach to the medial surface of the tarsometatarsus just above this articulation. The presence of a joint capsule and articular cartilages is questionable and is not confirmed because of the small size and character of this articulation.

MOVEMENT: Almost unlimited for an arthrodial joint; movement of the digit is possible in almost any direction. Digits are used as a brace in standing.

Tarsometatarsophalangeal Articulation

CLASSIFICATION: Diarthrosis, ginglymus.
LOCATION: The distal articular extremity of the tarsometatarsal bone and the proximal extremity of the 1st phalanx.
OSTEOLOGY: Involved are the condyles of the distal extremities of metatarsal bones 1, 2, 3, and 4 and the double concave surfaces of the 1st phalanx of the corresponding digits. The joint capsule is complete with fibrous and synovial layers.

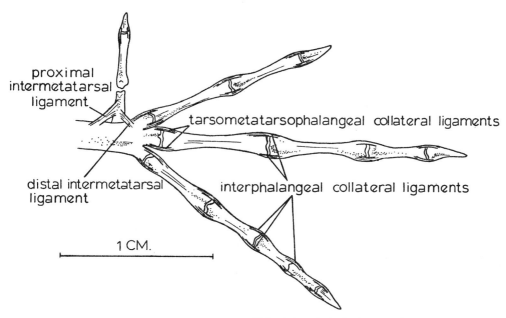

proximal intermetatarsal ligament

tarsometatarsophalangeal collateral ligaments

distal intermetatarsal ligament

interphalangeal collateral ligaments

1 CM.

FIG. 2.16—Articulations of the foot, dorsal view.

LIGAMENTS: The *tarsometatarsophalangeal collateral ligament* (Fig. 2.16) extends from the respective surfaces of the distal extremities of the metatarsal bones to the corresponding surfaces of the proximal extremities of the phalanges. The medial collateral ligament is slightly larger than the lateral one on digit 4, and those on digits 1, 2, and 3 are approximately the same size.

MOVEMENT: Flexion and extension.

Interphalangeal Articulations

CLASSIFICATION: Diarthrosis, ginglymus.

LOCATION: These ten articulations are those in the toes or digits of the quail.

OSTEOLOGY: Involved are the paired condyles on the distal extremities of the phalanges, and the receptive concave articular surfaces on the proximal extremities of succeeding phalanges. The numbers of the phalanges involved are listed for each digit:

Digit 1: phalanges 1 and 2

Digit 2: phalanges 1 and 2, 2 and 3

Digit 3: phalanges 1 and 2, 2 and 3, 3 and 4

Digit 4: phalanges 1 and 2, 2 and 3, 3 and 4, 4 and 5

LIGAMENTS: The ligaments are the *interphalangeal collateral* (Fig. 2.16) of which the medial is slightly larger except for the 3rd digit. They extend from the respective surfaces of the distal extremities of the above phalanges to the corresponding medial or lateral surfaces of the succeeding phalanges. The joint capsule is thin with fibrous and synovial layers.

MOVEMENT: Flexion and extension.

CHAPTER THREE

Angiology

THE blood vascular system consists of the heart and the arteries and veins. This chapter will also deal briefly with the lymphatic system and with the cell types found in blood and lymph.

HEART

The *heart* (Figs. 3.1–3.5) is the muscular pump which maintains the circulation of the blood throughout the cardiovascular system. The cone-shaped organ of coturnix occupies the caudoventral portion of the thoracic cavity from the level of the 1st rib to the 3rd intercostal space. Enclosed by the pericardium, the heart lies ventral to the esophagus, bronchi, and lungs and rests on the cranial portion of the sternum. The long axis passes forward less than 45° from the vertical plane and lies almost in the median plane of the body. The base (basis cordis), or hilus, faces dorsocranially and lies opposite the lateral thoracic wall from the 1st to the 3rd rib. It is formed by the atria and the great vessels entering and leaving the heart and lies in contact with the bronchi, esophagus, and lungs. The apex (apex cordis) points caudoventrally and lies in the cardiac groove between the right and left lobes of the liver. This caudoventral portion of the heart is formed by the mesocardium of the left ventricle and is usually bent slightly to the right of the median plane.

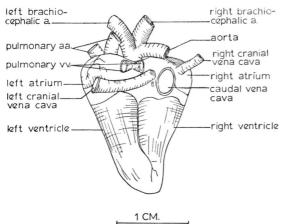

left brachio-cephalic a.

pulmonary aa.

pulmonary vv.

left atrium

left cranial vena cava

left ventricle

right brachio-cephalic a.

aorta

right cranial vena cava

right atrium

caudal vena cava

right ventricle

1 CM.

FIG. 3.1—Heart, dorsal view.

There are two faces, or surfaces, of the heart of coturnix, the sternocostal and the diaphragmatic. The sternocostal surface (cranial surface, facies cranialis) of the heart is convex, curving caudoventrally. It lies in contact with the sternum and its processes. The diaphragmatic surface (caudal surface, facies caudalis) is concave and shorter than the cranial surface. It lies almost in a vertical plane between the lobes of the liver. The thoracoabdominal diaphragm lies between the heart (pericardium) and the liver. The right margin (margo dextra) and the left margin (margo sinister) are ill-defined borders of the heart. Both are convex in shape and are located at the junction of the sternocostal and diaphragmatic surfaces of the organ.

The size of the heart of the quail varies and represents on an average about .74% to 1% of the body weight. The heart in the female is usually about .1% of the body weight larger than that of the male.

Like that of mammals the heart of the quail is divided into 4 chambers: 2 atria and 2 ventricles, the limits of which are marked on the surface by the coronary groove. Coronary vessels and fat oc-cupy this groove, which encircles the base of the heart with the exception of the area of the conus arteriosus. The cranial and caudal longitudinal grooves mark the location of the interventricular septum and have been referred to by some authors as the interventricular grooves. These grooves are indistinct and poorly outlined in the quail and are not occupied by fat as in mammals.

The cranial longitudinal groove (cranial interventricular groove, left longitudinal groove, sulcus longitudinalis sinister) is less noticeable than the caudal longitudinal groove. It begins at the coronary groove to the left of the conus arteriosus and descends obliquely along the left cranioventral border of the heart toward the apex. The left coronary vein passes in this groove to the base of the heart.

The caudal longitudinal groove (caudal interventricular groove, sulcus longitudinalis dexter) arises from the coronary groove ventral to the caudal vena cava and passes toward the apex. The right caudal (small) coronary vein passes in this groove to the junction of the postcava and right atrium.

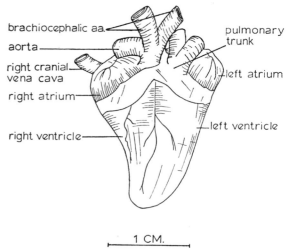

brachiocephalic aa.

aorta

right cranial vena cava

right atrium

right ventricle

pulmonary trunk

left atrium

left ventricle

1 CM.

FIG. 3.2—Heart, ventral view.

Pericardium

The *pericardium* of coturnix is a very thin but strong fibroserous sac which conforms in general to the shape of the heart which it encloses. It is composed of an outer fibrous layer and an inner serous layer. The inner layer is the parietal reflection of the serous epicardium. The serous layer of the thoracic pleura is reflected on the free surface of the fibrous pericardium to which it is firmly attached. The base of the pericardium continues for a variable distance on the great vessels entering and leaving the heart. Its apex is attached to the sternum, the falciform ligament of the liver, and the thoracoabdominal diaphragm.

The serous pericardium forms a closed sac invaginated by the heart and surrounded by the fibrous pericardium. The invaginated portion covering the heart is the visceral layer. The uninvaginated portion lining the fibrous pericardium is the parietal layer.

The pericardial cavity is the space between the visceral and parietal layers of the serous pericardium. It contains a small amount of serous fluid which serves as a lubricant.

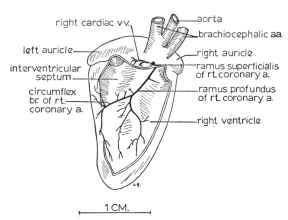

FIG. 3.4—Heart, right lateral view.

Atria and Ventricles

The *atria* of the heart are the blood-receiving chambers, and the *ventricles* are the blood-pumping chambers (Figs. 3.1–3.5). Arterial (oxygenated) blood from the lungs is received by the left atrium from the pulmonary veins and passes to the left ventricle. Contraction of the left ventricle forces the blood through the aorta and into the systemic circulation. Venous (unoxygenated) blood is received by the right atrium from the postcava (caudal vena cava) and the right and left precava (cranial vena cava). The right ventricle receives blood from the right atrium and pumps it to the lungs through the pulmonary artery.

The *right atrium* (atrium dextrum) (Figs. 3.1, 3.2, 3.5) forms the right portion of the base of the heart and lies over the right ventricle. It is divided into two portions, the sinus venarum cavarum and the auricle. The sinus venarum cavarum is the main portion of the atrium and receives the veins. The auricle (Figs. 3.3, 3.4), or appendage, is small in the quail and forms a blind pouch that projects over the ventricle and lies cranial and to the right of the aortic trunk.

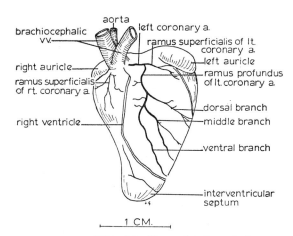

FIG. 3.3—Heart, left lateral view.

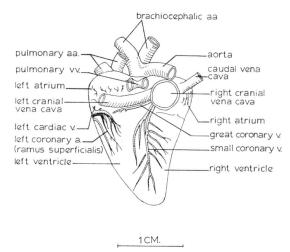

FIG. 3.5—Heart, caudal view.

There are four major openings in the right atrium. The *caudal vena cava* (Figs. 3.1, 3.5) opens into the caudal portion of the atrium. It presents the largest opening into the atrium and drains blood from the abdominal and pelvic regions or caudal area of the body. The *right cranial vena cava* (Figs. 3.1, 3.2, 3.5) enters the dorsolateral aspect of the cranial portion of the atrium. It drains blood from the right cranial half of the head and neck. The *left cranial vena cava* (Figs. 3.1, 3.5) enters the caudal portion of the atrium. It opens near the interatrial septum dorsal and to the left of the caudal vena cava. The veins corresponding to the *great coronary vein* and right cardiac vein (Fig. 3.4) of the mammal open into the right atrium below the caudal vena cava. This opening corresponds to the coronary sinus in mammals but no distinct sinus is present in the quail. The left cardiac vein (Fig. 3.5) enters the right atrium caudal to the aortic trunk. The middle cardiac vein opens into the lateral aspect of the atrium.

In common with the other chambers of the heart, the inner wall of the right atrium is lined with a thin glistening membrane, the endocardium.

The atrial wall does not possess a crista terminalis, or pectinate, muscle, but instead is traversed by several thick muscular bands or ridges. These muscular ridges are referred to as columnae carneae (trabeculae carneae) by Kaupp (1918) and Chamberlain (1943). Between these columnae carneae the interatrial septum is thin and tendinous; in its caudal portion lies the fossa ovalis.

The *right ventricle* (Figs. 3.1–3.5) (ventralis dextra) forms the right and cranial portion of the ventricular mass. Its external surface area is greater than that of the left ventricle, but it does not reach the apex of the heart. In outline it resembles to some extent an oblique triangle, and in cross section it is crescent shaped. The wall of the right atrium is about one-third as thick as the left. The right atrioventricular orifice is an obliquely rounded opening or slit between the atrium and the ventricle. Its opening is controlled by the right atrioventricular valve. Unlike the tricuspid valve in mammals, the right atrioventricular valve in the quail is a comparatively thick muscular band. The peripheral edge of the band is attached to the ventricular border of the opening, and its ends are attached cranially and caudally to the interventricular septum. When the orifice is opened, the free margin of the valve lies in the ventricle and faces toward the apex of the heart. There are no chordae tendinae or papillary muscles to control the valve. The lower wall of the ventricle is marked by several muscular ridges or columns, the columnae carneae. Some of these columnae carneae extend for a short distance from the interventricular septum to the wall of the ventricle. These muscular ridges are as numerous as those of the mammalian heart.

Blood leaves the right ventricle

through the pulmonary orifice and passes to the lungs through the pulmonary arteries (Figs. 3.1, 3.5). The funnel-shaped conus arteriosus is that portion of the right ventricle which joins the pulmonary trunk (Fig. 3.2). It represents the dorsocranial portion of the ventricle and lies between the aortic trunk and the left atrium. The pulmonary orifice is situated at the dorsal part of the conus arteriosus and is guarded by a valve.

The pulmonary valve consists of three cusps, right, left, and caudal, which are formed by fibrous connective tissue, lined on each surface with endothelium and having their convexities toward the ventricle. The peripheral border of each cusp has a semilunar attachment to the pulmonary fibrous ring which is located at the junction of the conus arteriosus and pulmonary trunk. These cusps are very thin and show no distinct central nodule or lunula. Behind each cusp on the arterial side is a sinus that collects blood. This collection of blood prevents the valve from closing completely against the wall of the artery when the ventricle contracts.

The *left atrium* (Figs. 3.1, 3.2, 3.5) forms the left portion of the base of the heart. It lies over the left ventricle and is not as large as the right atrium. The pulmonary trunk lies to the right and cranial to the atrium, and the left cranial vena cava lies caudal to the atrium. Like the right atrium it consists of an auricle and a sinus venarum cavarum.

The left auricle (Figs. 3.3, 3.4) is more distinct than the right and lies to the left of the pulmonary trunk and conus arteriosus. The sinus venarum cavarum receives the opening of the pulmonary veins. This venous opening is in the right dorsocaudal part of the atrium near the interatrial septum. The wall of the left atrium, like that of the right, is traversed by several columnae carneae. Between these muscular ridges

the wall is thin and appears to be pitted. The fossa ovalis appears on the left side of the interatrial septum just cranial to the pulmonary opening.

The *left ventricle* (Figs. 3.1, 3.2, 3.5) forms the left caudal portion of the ventricular mass. It is more conical in shape and longer than the right. In cross section its cavity is circular in outline, and its walls are about three times as thick as the right ventricle. It receives the oxygenated blood from the left atrium through the atrioventricular orifice. The left atrioventricular orifice is oval in shape and is guarded by the left atrioventricular valve (bicuspid or mitral). The left atrioventricular valve very much resembles that of mammals. It is composed of two cusps, a ventral (cranial or aortic) and a dorsal (caudal) cusp that attach peripherally to the left atrioventricular fibrous ring and extend into the ventricle. Chordae tendinae attach to the ventricular surface of the valves and to the papillary muscles. Both cusps are formed by fibrous connective tissue with an endothelial covering on each surface. The wall of the left ventricle presents many of the features of the ventricular wall in mammals.

The chordae tendinae are dense cords of fibrous connective tissue covered with endothelium. They extend from the papillary muscles to the ventricular surfaces of the valve cusps. Upon contraction of the ventricle, the chordae tendinae prevent the valve cusp from being forced into the atrium by the pressurized blood. Each cusp receives about 20 chordae tendinae from each of the two papillary muscles.

The columnae carneae are more numerous and distinct in the left ventricle, particularly toward the apex. Below the junction of the valve cusp the columnae carneae appear as two small mounds of muscles, the papillary muscles. These muscles provide attachment for the chordae tendinae and aid in controlling the atrioventricular valve.

The aortic orifice is a circular opening located cranial to and to the right of the ventral atrioventricular cusp. This opening to the systemic circulation is guarded by the aortic valve. The aortic semilunar valve consists of three cusps which resemble those of the mammalian heart more closely than do those of the pulmonary valve. These cusps are thick and strong and attach to the aortic fibrous ring. Their free margin presents a central nodule and lunula. The aortic sinuses are present behind each cusp on the arterial side. The cusps are formed by a center of fibrous tissue with a covering of endothelium.

Coronary Arteries

The left and right coronary arteries arise from the aortic trunk at the base of the heart and furnish the organ with its main blood supply.

The *left coronary artery* (Fig. 3.3) arises from the aortic sinus of the left valve cusp. At its origin on the left side of the aorta a small artery arises and enters the left atrium, which it supplies. It then passes with the ventral (left or cranial) coronary vein to the pulmonary trunk, where it divides into a ramus profundus and a ramus superficialis. The *ramus superficialis* (Figs. 3.3, 3.5) continues in company with the coronary vein. It passes between the pulmonary trunk and the left auricle to the left coronary groove. In the coronary groove it passes caudad and supplies a branch to the left atrium and numerous small branches to the left ventricular wall. The artery terminates after entering the caudolateral wall of the ventricle. The *ramus profundus* (septal branch) (Fig. 3.3) passes deep to the pulmonary trunk in the cranial portion of the interventricular septum toward the apex of the heart. It divides into dorsal, middle,

and ventral branches which pass obliquely in the respective portions of the septum to the lateral wall of the left ventricle. These branches join the circumflex branch of the right coronary artery in supplying the tissue in this region.

The *right coronary artery* (Figs. 3.3, 3.4) arises from the aortic sinus of the right valve cusp and divides at its origin into a ramus superficialis and a ramus profundus. The *ramus superficialis* (Figs. 3.3, 3.4) passes between the right auricle and the conus arteriosus and divides into three branches. These three branches supply the lateral wall of the right ventricle. The *ramus profundus* (Fig. 3.4) descends in the interventricular septum at the level of the aortic trunk toward the apex of the heart. About halfway down the septum it gives off a large circumflex branch before dividing into two terminal branches which continue to the apex. The circumflex branch passes in the caudal portion of the interventricular septum to the lateral wall of the left ventricle. Before leaving the septum, it gives off numerous branches to supply the left ventricular wall and the caudal portion of the right atrium.

Cardiac, or Coronary, Veins

The heart is supplied with four main veins, all of which empty into the right atrium.

The *left cardiac vein* (Fig. 3.5) arises in the cranial longitudinal groove and continues in the coronary groove to receive tributaries from the right and left ventricular wall and from the left atrium. In the groove it is accompanied by the left coronary artery, and at the conus arteriosus it passes caudad between the pulmonary trunk and the left auricle. It then enters the right atrium caudal to the aortic trunk.

Some of the *right cardiac veins* (Fig.

3.4) are satellites of the branches of the right coronary artery on the cranial portion of the right ventricle. They vary in number and size. In the right coronary groove they join to form a short trunk that passes directly into the cranioventral portion of the right ventricle.

The *middle cardiac vein* is the homologue of the middle coronary vein of mammals and is the largest and most extensive vein in the quail heart. It arises in the caudal longitudinal groove near the apex of the heart and passes toward the base. It enters the right atrium below the caudal vena cava in conjunction with the great coronary vein and receives large tributaries from the left and right ventricular walls.

The *great coronary vein* (Fig. 3.5) corresponds in location to the very large coronary vein of the mammalian heart. It is not, however, the largest or most extensive vein of the heart of the quail. It arises near the cranial longitudinal groove in the dorsal portion of the left ventricular wall and continues caudad in the coronary groove. It enters the right atrium below the caudal vena cava in conjunction with the middle cardiac vein.

Pulmonary Arteries and Veins

The *pulmonary trunk* (Fig. 3.2) arises from the base of the right ventricle to the left of the aortic trunk. It passes through the pericardium and fat at the base of the heart before dividing into left and right pulmonary arteries. The pulmonary trunk and arteries carry unoxygenated blood. No ligamentum arteriosum was observed in the adult quail heart.

The *left pulmonary artery* (Figs. 3.1, 3.5) passes caudal to the left brachiocephalic artery and into the left lobe of the lung cranial to the entrance of the bronchus.

The *right pulmonary artery* (Figs. 3.1, 3.5) passes between the aortic arch and heart to the lung. It enters the right lobe cranial to the entrance of the bronchus.

The *right and left pulmonary veins* (Figs. 3.1, 3.5) arise from the lung caudal to the entrance of the bronchi. They pass to the base of the heart and fuse just before entering the left atrium.

BRANCHES OF THE AORTA

The *aorta* (Figs. 3.1–3.7) arises from the left ventricle of the heart and immediately gives origin to a ventral right and a dorsal left coronary artery. The right coronary and the left coronary course caudoventrad to furnish the major blood supply to their respective sides of the heart wall. The aorta courses craniodorsad for .5–1 mm and gives origin to the *left and right brachiocephalic arteries* (Figs. 3.1, 3.2, 3.4, 3.5, 3.7).

At the level of the 2nd or 3rd vertebral rib, following the origin of the right brachiocephalic artery, the aorta courses dorsad to the right of the midline and turns to continue its caudal course. It passes dorsal to the proventriculus and the right lobe of the liver. At the level of the origin of the 5th vertebral rib, the aorta gives rise to a very small unpaired *caudal esophageal artery* that courses craniodorsad to supply the dorsal portion of the caudal extremity of the esophagus.

The unpaired *celiac artery* (Figs. 3.6, 3.7) arises approximately 1 mm further caudad. It courses caudoventrad cranial to the right testicle in the male or the ovary in the female and dorsal to the proventriculus. The first branch of the celiac artery, the *proventricular artery* (Fig. 3.6), passes craniad for 1 mm and enters the dorsomedial wall of the proventriculus.

The succeeding branches of the celiac, the dorsal and the left gastric ar-

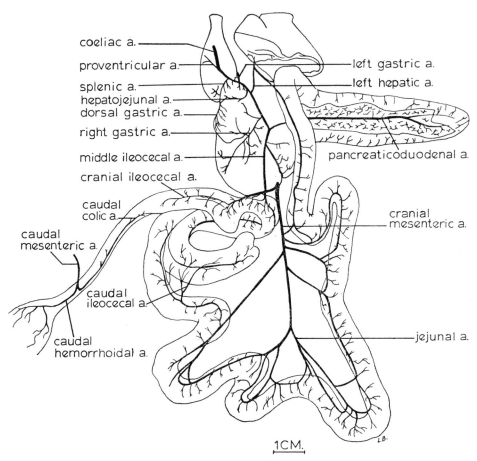

coeliac a.
proventricular a.
splenic a.
hepatojejunal a.
dorsal gastric a.
right gastric a.
middle ileocecal a.
cranial ileocecal a.
caudal colic a.
caudal mesenteric a.
caudal ileocecal a.
caudal hemorrhoidal a.

left gastric a.
left hepatic a.
pancreaticoduodenal a.
cranial mesenteric a.
jejunal a.

1CM.

FIG. 3.6—Arteries of the abdominal digestive tract.

teries, may arise by a common trunk or close to each other. The *dorsal gastric artery* (Fig. 3.6) courses dorsad to the junction of the ventriculus and proventriculus, bifurcates, and sends branches to the cranial portion of the former and to the caudal portion of the latter. The *left gastric artery* (Fig. 3.6) courses to the left of the midline ventral to the caudal end of the proventriculus, turns caudad, and gives origin to the left hepatic artery. The left gastric artery also sends a small cranial branch to the caudoventral portion of the proventriculus.

The *left hepatic artery* (Fig. 3.6) courses craniad to enter and supply the

left lobes of the liver. The *splenic arteries* (Fig. 3.6), three to four in number, enter the sphere-shaped spleen. The *hepatojejunal artery* (Fig. 3.6) arises from the celiac at the level of the caudal tip of the spleen. It courses to the right of the midline for 2 mm and splits at the junction of the duodenum and jejunum into the right hepatic arteries and the jejunal artery.

The *right hepatic arteries,* two in number, course craniad and enter the large right lobe of the liver. The *jejunal artery* (Fig. 3.6) courses dorsolaterad to supply about the first inch of the jejunum and then anastomoses with the

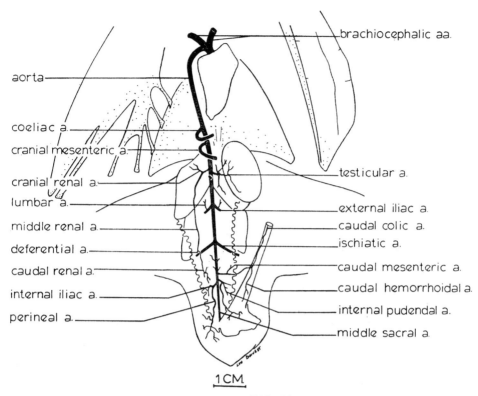

aorta

coeliac a.

cranial mesenteric a.

cranial renal a.

lumbar a.

middle renal a.

deferential a.

caudal renal a.

internal iliac a.

perineal a.

brachiocephalic aa.

testicular a.

external iliac a.

caudal colic a.

ischiatic a.

caudal mesenteric a.

caudal hemorrhoidal a.

internal pudendal a.

middle sacral a.

1 CM

FIG. 3.7—Branches of the aorta, ventral view.

second branch of the cranial mesenteric artery. The occurrence of this anastomosis may vary considerably, as the jejunal artery may divide into many small branches, some of which supply the caudal portion of the duodenum.

The celiac turns to course directly caudad for 3 to 4 mm before it gives off the large *right gastric artery* (Fig. 3.6) This artery courses mediad to branch and to supply the entire right side of the ventriculus.

The celiac then turns ventrad and after 2 or 3 mm terminates by giving rise to many branches. The *pancreatico-duodenal artery* (Fig. 3.6) is one of the terminal branches. It courses ventrad between the dorsal and ventral lobes of the pancreas medial to the ascending and descending portions of the duo-

denum. It supplies the pancreas and duodenum with a rich blood supply. The other terminal branch of the celiac, the *middle ileocecal artery* (Fig. 3.6), passes in a caudal direction, adjacent to the middle of the right side of the ventriculus, and becomes related ventrally to the ileum and left cecum. Its branches supply the middle portion of the ileum and the two ceca and anastomose with branches of the cranial and caudal ileocecal arteries.

The *cranial mesenteric artery* (Figs. 3.6, 3.7) arises from the aorta about 1 mm caudal to the origin of the celiac artery. This unpaired large branch of the aorta courses ventrolaterad in relation to the cranioventral portion of the right testicle in the male or to the large ovarian follicle in the female. Its first branch, the *cranial ileocecal artery,* (Fig. 3.6) courses dorsomediad to supply the cranial portion of the two ceca and the ileum.

The artery anastomoses with the *caudal colic artery* (Figs. 3.6, 3.7) on the ventral surface of the descending colon. The second branch of the cranial mesenteric artery courses craniad to supply the cranial portion of the jejunum and anastomoses with the jejunal artery. The cranial mesenteric artery then gives rise to many mesenteric arteries which supply the major portion of the small intestines. These arteries anastomose freely with each other and form four to five mesenteric arches. The cranial mesenteric artery terminates by giving origin to a *caudal ilocecal artery* (Fig. 3.6) that supplies the distal portion of the ceca and the proximal portion of the ileum.

The paired *6th intercostal artery* is the next branch of the aorta. It arises from the dorsal surface and courses dorsolaterad adjacent to the body of the 6th thoracic vertebra and reaches the caudal surface of the 6th rib. In this area the intercostal artery gives origin to a dorsal branch that supplies the skin and muscles of the back, sends a small twig into the intervertebral foramen, and joins the ventral spinal artery. The intercostal then gives origin to the main artery supplying the 6th intercostal space. It courses near to or under the caudal border of the 6th rib and to the lower intercostal space, where it anastomoses with a small ventral intercostal artery arising from the internal thoracic artery.

After supplying the 6th intercostal artery, the main trunk then passes craniad dorsal to the articulation of the 6th rib to anastomose with the caudal vertebral artery which gives rise to the *1st to the 5th intercostal arteries.* There is much variation in the 5th intercostal artery. In a few specimens its origin was by way of the aorta. In such cases it had anastomosed with the caudal vertebral artery at the level of the 5th rib.

The *lumbar and sacral arteries* (Fig. 3.7) are dorsal branches of the aorta. They are small paired vessels supplying the skin and the muscles of the back in this region and are 10 to 11 in number. The first lumbar artery gives origin to a small cranial 7th costal artery that courses adjacent to the caudal border of the 7th rib. These lumbar and sacral arteries send small branches to the ventral spinal artery.

The *cranial renal artery* (Fig. 3.7) arises from the aorta at the level of the thoracolumbovertebral junction. This artery courses caudolaterad ventral to the kidney and supplies its cranial lobe. It anastomoses with the *middle renal artery* as it proceeds caudad dorsal to the ureter.

The *testicular arteries* (Fig. 3.7) originate from the aorta in close relation to the cranial renal artery. Each testicle is supplied by two, sometimes three, arteries. One of these consistently originates from the cranial renal artery. The arteries course ventrolaterad for a very short distance through the mesorchium, branch, and then pass toward the free border of the testicle in a circular manner. The homologue of the spermatic arteries is the *ovarian arteries.* Normally they are two in number and appear only on the left side, for the right ovary does not develop in the quail. The cranial ovarian artery arises consistently from the cranial renal artery. About 1 mm further caudad the caudal ovarian artery arises from the aorta. The ovarian artery, or arteries as the case may be, bifurcates into three to five spiralling branches as it enters the ovarian hilus and subdivides as it extends out into the cortex of the ovary. Branches from these cortical vessels supply the follicles.

The paired *external iliac artery* (Fig. 3.7) arises from the aorta in the region of the 4th to 5th synsacral segment. It courses caudolaterad in the cranial one-third of the middle lobe of the kidney to supply the kidney and then continues on to the pelvic limb.

The *ischiatic artery* (Fig. 3.7), which is also paired, arises from the aorta about 7–9 mm caudal to the external iliac artery. It is the largest branch of the aorta in the abdominal and pelvic regions. It courses caudolaterad ventral to the junction of the caudal and middle lobes of the kidney. In addition to supplying the kidney, it also furnishes blood to the uterus, oviduct, and the pelvic limb. The continuations of the external iliac and ischiatic arteries will be described in detail in the description of the arteries to the pelvic limb.

The aorta continues caudad ventral to the spinal vertebrae in the median plane. The unpaired *caudal mesenteric artery* (Figs. 3.6, 3.7) arises from the ventral surface of the aorta in the region of the 12th to 13th synsacral segment. It courses caudoventrad in the mesentery to the dorsal surface of the colon. Here it gives rise to a cranial branch, the caudal colic artery, that anastomoses in the mesentery with a branch of the cranial ileocecal artery. The caudal branch of the caudal mesenteric artery is the *cranial hemorrhoidal artery*, which courses caudad on the dorsal surface of the colon and supplies the colon and the cranial portion of the cloaca.

The *internal iliac artery* (paired) (Fig. 3.7) arises at the termination of the aorta in the region of the last synsacral segment or 1st coccygeal vertebra. Its origin is 2–3 mm caudal to the origin of the caudal mesenteric artery. In some cases the internal iliac arteries arise from a short common trunk of the aorta. After a short course of 1–2 mm in a caudoventral direction the internal iliac

bifurcates into the perineal and internal pudendal arteries.

The *internal pudendal artery* (Fig. 3.7) courses ventrolaterad medial to the cranial portion of the semimembranosus muscle and dorsal to its satellite vein and the accompanying nerve. After a course of 8 to 9 mm it gives off two branches which supply the obturator internus, semimembranosus, caudofemoralis, retractor ani, coccygeus, and other muscles of this region. The main continuation of the internal pudendal artery courses caudodorsad in relation to the caudal portion of the cranial part of the semimembranosus muscle and the caudal border of the ischium. It terminates after a short course by branching into two cutaneous arteries which supply the skin and tissue of the dorsolateral vent region. The final branching of the internal pudendal artery demonstrates several minor variations. The perineal branch of the internal iliac artery courses ventrocaudad medial to the ureter and ductus deferens and dorsal to the caudal portion of the colon in the male. In the female it is related dorsally to the colon, medial to the oviduct on the left side, and lateral to the dorsal ligament on the left side.

The *perineal artery* (Fig. 3.7) continues to the dorsal portion of the cloaca, where it branches into four to five small arteries. These branches show many variations; the most constant ones are: the *caudal hemorrhoidal artery* (Figs. 3.6, 3.7), which supplies the short rectum and part of the cloaca; the *caudal renal artery* (Fig. 3.7); the small *caudal deferential artery* (Fig. 3.7) in the male, which supplies the caudal portion of the ductus deferens or its homologue, the *caudal artery of the oviduct* in the female (only present on the left side), which supplies part of the uterus, the vagina, and a portion of the cloaca; additional ones to the skin and tissue in the perineal region, and one to supply the bursa of Fabricius are found.

The *middle sacral artery* (Fig. 3.7) is the continuation of the aorta beyond the origin of the internal iliac arteries. It should be called the middle coccygeal artery because it arises ventral to the coccygeal vertebrae and terminates by giving rise to the dorsolateral branches to the coccygeus muscles, uropygial gland, and the large follicles of the tail feathers.

CRANIAL VENA CAVA

The *cranial vena cava* (Figs. 3.1, 3.2, 3.5, 3.10) is a paired vessel in the quail. It lies dorsal to the brachiocephalic artery and caudal to the pulmonary artery and vein. The longer left vena cava lies in contact with the esophagus near the heart. The cranial vena cava is formed by the convergence of the jugular and subclavian veins and drains the cranial part of the body, head, neck, wing, and breast and the greater part of the thoracic wall. It passes through the pericardium and opens into the right atrium. The right vena cava enters the cranial portion of the right atrium. The left vena cava circles and enters the caudal portion of the right atrium. There is no distinct line of demarcation between the atrium and the vena cava. The tributaries of the cranial vena cava are described below.

The *ventral proventricular vein* arises over the entire surface of the proventriculus and courses mediad to enter the left surface of the most caudal portion of the cranial vena cava.

The *internal thoracic vein* corresponds to the dorsal branch of the artery. It receives intercostal veins and joins the cranial vena cava at the junction of the jugular and subclavian vein. The peripheral portion of the vein is a satellite of the dorsal branch of the internal thoracic artery.

The *vertebral vein* (Fig. 3.21) consists of a cervical and a thoracic portion and is formed by the cranial vertebral and the caudal vertebral veins. The cranial vertebral vein arises at the foramen magnum and is a continuation of the mid-dorsal head sinus or the straight sinus. It anastomoses with the occipital vein and passes through the transverse foramen, with the *vertebral artery* (Figs. 3.8, 3.20, 3.21) and the sympathetic nerve trunk, to the 14th cervical vertebra. At this vertebra it joins the caudal vertebral vein and passes through the cranial wall of the cranial vena cava at the junction of the jugular and subclavian veins. The vertebral veins drain the muscles of the neck and back, the intercostal muscles, and the spinal cord. The right vertebral vein of the quail is larger than the left.

The *subclavian vein* (Fig. 3.10) is the continuation of the *axillary vein* (Fig. 3.10) through the thoracic wall and into the thoracic cavity. It passes dorsal to the subclavian artery and joins with the jugular vein to form the cranial vena cava. It drains the pectoral muscles, the wing, and part of the thoracic wall.

The tributaries of the subclavian vein are: The *coracoid vein* (Fig. 3.10) is a satellite of the artery and drains the muscles it supplies. In addition it receives a satellite vein of the ventral branch of the internal thoracic artery a short distance from the subclavian vein. The coracoid vein joins the subclavian vein medial to its junction with the external thoracic veins. The *cranial external thoracic, caudal external thoracic,* and *dorsal thoracic veins* (Fig. 3.10) are satellites of the arteries of the same name and drain mainly the superficial pectoral muscle and the skin of this region. They join the subclavian vein on the lateral thoracic wall between the first rib and the coracoid bone. Unlike the arteries, these veins do not form a common trunk.

ARTERIES OF THE THORAX

The *right and left brachiocephalic* arteries (Figs. 3.1, 3.2, 3.4, 3.5, 3.7, 3.8, 3.21) arise from the aortic trunk near the base of the heart and are directed laterally toward the 1st ribs of their respective sides. A short distance from the heart these vessels give rise to the *common carotid arteries* (Fig. 3.8) which are directed cranially at the base of the neck. After giving off the carotids, the brachiocephalic artery is continued as the subclavian at the level of the 1st rib. In the region between the 1st rib and the coracoid bone the subclavian branches and supplies arteries to the pectoral and shoulder muscles and is continued to the shoulder joint as the axillary artery. From the shoulder on into the brachium the axillary becomes the brachial artery. There are discrepancies in the various descriptions used by different authors as to the regions in which each of the above mentioned arteries are located in other birds.

The *bronchoesophageal artery* (Fig. 3.8) is small and arises from the subclavian just lateral to the origin of the common carotid. The artery is bilateral, but not symmetrical in its branching or course. Both right and left arteries are directed craniomesially and pass ventral to the common carotid and onto the thyroid gland, which they supply with a branch. At the trachea they branch to supply the sternothyrohyoideus and sternotrachealis muscles. Each sends a small caudal tracheal artery up the trachea to anastomose with the cranial tracheal artery formed by the descending esophageal and superior laryngeal arteries. The course of the right and left

bronchoesophageal arteries from the trachea is not the same. The right bronchoesophageal artery passes craniad for a short distance along the caudal esophagus to the ventral surface of the crop. It terminates by giving rise to numerous branches in the fascia on the ventral surface of the crop. The left bronchoesophageal artery passes dorsal to the trachea and to the dorsal portion of the crop, which it supplies by many branches. It does not terminate at this point, but continues up the dorsolateral aspect of the esophagus as the left ascending esophageal artery.

Both right and left *ascending esophageal arteries* (Fig. 3.8) are symmetrical in their course along the esophagus. The right ascending esophageal artery arises from the right *caudal cervical artery* (Fig. 3.8) dorsal to the crop. In most instances the left ascending esophageal artery arises from the broncho-

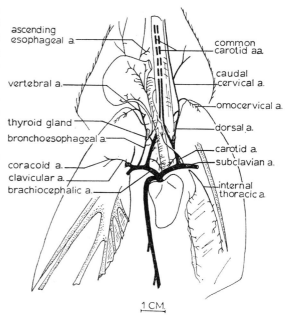

FIG. 3.8—Arteries of the cervical and thoracic region.

esophageal artery at the junction of the crop and esophagus; however, it may arise from the left common carotid artery. The ascending esophageal arteries pass up the dorsolateral surface of the esophagus and anastomose with the descending esophageal artery from the superior laryngeal artery. Throughout its course the ascending esophageal artery supplies many branches to the esophagus.

The *coracoid artery* (Fig. 3.8) arises on the ventral surface of the subclavian artery between the pectoral trunk and the axillary artery. It courses ventrad over the medial surface of the distal extremity of the coracoid bone into the pectoral muscle. Near its origin from the subclavian this artery gives off a branch that courses laterad to the coracobrachialis ventralis muscle and then turns and runs along the coracoid bone to the shoulder joint, where it terminates. Throughout its course to the shoulder this branch of the coracoid artery supplies small arteries to the sternocoracoid, coracobrachialis ventralis, and deep pectoral muscles. The sternal artery arises from the coracoid artery on the dorsomedial surface of the distal extremity of the coracoid bone and passes caudoventrad over the coracosternal articulation and sternocoracoid muscle. Numerous minute branches arise from the artery along the medial aspect of the sternum. On the ventral surface of the distal extremity of the coracoid bone, two minute arteries arise from the coracoid artery and course craniad into the supracoracoideus muscle. These two arteries are very small and may not be seen unless a good injection is obtained. After giving rise to the supracoracoideus arteries the coracoid passes over the coracoid bone medial to the manubrium of the sternum and into the deep pectoral muscle. From this point it continues caudad and terminates.

The *clavicular artery* (Fig. 3.8) is the first branch of the coracoid artery to arise in the deep pectoral muscle. Near its origin this artery gives rise to a comparatively large branch that is directed craniodorsally in the deep pectoral muscle parallel to the coracoid bone. This branch, which commonly arises from the clavicular artery, may also originate from the coracoid artery. The clavicular artery continues craniad for a short distance toward the middle of the clavicular bone. Near the lateral extent of the deep pectoral muscle the clavicular artery turns and courses craniodorsad parallel to the clavicle and toward the shoulder joint. Throughout its course the clavicular artery supplies numerous small branches to the cranial region of the deep pectoral muscles. There are variations in its pattern of distribution.

The *subclavian artery* (Fig. 3.8) is the continuation of the brachiocephalic artery laterally to the thoracic wall between the coracoid bones and the 1st rib. It gives rise to the pectoral trunk and coracoid artery before becoming the axillary artery.

The *pectoral artery* (Fig. 3.9) is the largest of the arteries arising from the subclavian, and some authors consider it the continuation of the subclavian instead of the axillary artery. The pectoral trunk is short and extends only to the lateral surface of the thoracic cavity before dividing into three large branches: the cranial external thoracic, the caudal external thoracic, and the dorsal thoracic arteries. These three arteries furnish the superficial pectoral muscle with its blood supply. In addition, the smaller internal thoracic artery arises from the pectoral trunk near its origin from the subclavian.

The *cranial external thoracic artery* (Fig. 3.9) supplies the cranial half of the superficial pectoral muscle. Ventral to the shoulder joint it divides into two

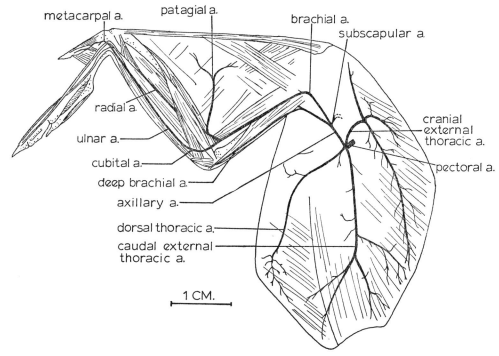

FIG. 3.9—Arteries of the pectoral limb, ventrolateral view.

large branches, which in turn give off many smaller branches. Near the middle of the course of the caudal one of these two branches, an artery arises that passes to the superficial surface of the pectoral muscle and courses caudoventrad.

The *caudal external thoracic artery* (Fig. 3.9) is a large branch of the pectoral muscle. Near its origin a small branch arises which runs ventrad into the coracobrachialis ventralis muscle. Throughout the continuing course of the caudal external thoracic artery, numerous branches are given off which supply the caudal half of the superficial pectoral muscle.

The *dorsal thoracic artery* (Fig. 3.9) is the smallest of the three arteries arising from the pectoral trunk. It continues caudodorsad and becomes subcutaneous over the caudal half of the dorsal thoracic region. It gives rise to

two branches, one near its origin, a small artery which passes caudad into the dorsal portion of the superficial pectoral muscle, and another further dorsad which supplies the teres major muscle. As the dorsal thoracic artery continues its course, it supplies the superficial pectoral muscle and the skin and feather follicles over the caudodorsal region of the thorax.

The *internal thoracic artery* (Fig. 3.8) arises from the caudal surface of the pectoral trunk at its origin from the subclavian artery. It continues only a short distance on the inner thoracic wall before it divides into a dorsal and a ventral branch. The bifurcation occurs near the cranial extremity of the costosternalis muscle. As the dorsal branch from the bifurcation passes caudad, it gives off small branches to the costosternalis muscle and other small muscles between the sternal ribs, where it terminates. The ventral branch passes caudo-ventrad to the costosternalis muscle at the costosternalis articulation where the trunk disseminates into many branches.

ARTERIES OF THE PECTORAL LIMB

The *axillary artery* (Fig. 3.9) is the continuation of the subclavian artery from the first rib to the tendon of the teres major muscle at the shoulder joint. The *subscapular* artery (Fig. 3.9) arises from the axillary artery a short distance from its origin. It is small and supplies the coracobrachialis ventralis, supracora-coideus, and subscapularis muscles.

The *deep brachial artery* (Fig. 3.9) arises from the axillary artery near the tendon of the teres major. The axillary artery is then continued down the brachium as the brachial artery. Just lateral to the tendon of the teres major the deep brachial divides giving rise to two arteries. The cranial branch passes caudodorsad and supplies the latissimus dorsi. The caudal branch, the *cranial circumflex humeral artery,* courses dor-sad between the long head of the triceps and the deltoideus muscles. It supplies small branches to both of these muscles and to the teres minor. Over the head of the humerus the cranial circumflex humeral artery divides and supplies branches to the patagialis brevis muscle, the cranial patagium, and the skin and feather follicles of this region. The deep brachial artery continues distad along the medial surface of the long head of the triceps to the elbow. Throughout its course it supplies numerous small branches to the triceps brachii muscle and, at the middle of the humerus, gives off the *caudal circumflex humeral artery.* The caudal circumflex humeral courses obliquely between the long head of the triceps and the deltoideus muscles to the dorsal surface of the humerus, where it gives off in turn a large branch to the cranial patagium, continues on the humerus to the dorsal surface of the elbow, and terminates. At the caudal aspect of the elbow the deep brachial artery terminates by supplying the fascia and feather follicles of the area.

The *brachial artery* (Fig. 3.9) is the distal continuation of the axillary. It passes over the neck of the humerus and into the medial portion of the biceps brachii muscle, which it supplies. It then continues distad to the elbow, where it bifurcates into the ulnar and the radial arteries.

The *ulnar artery* (Fig. 3.9) is the most medial of the two terminal branches of the brachial artery. It courses subcutaneously along the cranial border of the flexor carpi radialis muscle to the carpus. At its origin a small artery arises and passes into the brachialis muscle. After supplying the brachialis muscle, this same branch turns and runs craniodorsad to supply the cranial portion of the extensor carpi radialis. As the ulnar artery passes distal to the carpus, it gives off the cubital artery and continues distad across the medial surface of the carpus just cranial to the ulnocarpal bone, from which point it continues as the metacarpal artery.

After the *cubital artery* (Fig. 3.9) takes its origin from the ulnar artery at the elbow, it supplies the flexor carpi radialis, anconeus medialis, extensor and adductor of digits 2 and 3, and flexor metacarpi muscles. It then runs caudad under the tendinous band covering the flexor carpi radialis muscle to the caudal aspect of the elbow joint. Here it supplies the expansor secundariorum muscle and feather follicles of this region.

The *metacarpal artery* (Fig. 3.9) gives rise to a small artery to the 2nd digit at the proximal extremity of the carpometacarpal bone. This artery branches and supplies the adductor and abductor muscles of the 2nd digit. At the junction of the 3rd and 4th metacarpal bones, small arteries arise from the metacarpal and run along the dorsomedial surface of the 3rd metacarpus to supply the abductor of the 2nd digit and the flexor metacarpi. The metacarpal artery then passes deep between the interosseous volaris and interosseous dorsalis muscles, which it supplies, and emerges on the dorsal aspect of the distal extremity of the metacarpus.

The *radial artery* (Fig. 3.9) is the deep terminating branch of the brachial artery. It passes between the pronator muscles and the radius into the interosseous space at the carpus. At the elbow it supplies a small branch to the brachialis muscle.

Just distal to the elbow two large caudal branches and a single large cranial branch arise from the radial artery. The proximal caudal branch supplies the brachialis muscle and then passes over the dorsoproximal extremity of the ulna, supplying the anconeus medialis muscle and feather follicles on the proximal end of the forearm.

The *patagial artery* (Fig. 3.9) arises from the cranial surface of the radial artery just distal to the elbow. It courses craniad and supplies the supinator medialis and extensor carpi radialis muscles. It then passes distad along the cranial surface of the extensor carpi radialis for about 1 cm before sending a branch into the cranial patagium. The patagial artery branches and supplies small distal and proximal branches to the patagium.

The *nutrient artery* is the second of the caudal branches of the radial artery. It passes caudolaterad for a short distance before entering the cranial surface of the ulna. This nutrient artery may arise in common with the first branch. The large dorsal branch of the radial

artery passes dorsad through the extensor of digit 3, which it supplies. In its distal course it branches and supplies the common digital extensor, the extensor carpi ulnaris, and the extensor pollicis longus muscles. The main trunk of the radial artery continues caudad between the anconeus medialis muscle, which it supplies, and the extensor carpi ulnaris to the feather follicles along the caudal aspect of the middle of the forearm. Continuing distad in the interosseous space to the carpus, the radial artery gives rise to numerous branches which supply the muscles on the dorsal extensor surface of the forearm and the feather follicles along the caudal aspect of the humerus. The radial artery terminates as minute branches at the distal radioulnar articulation.

Summary of the Arteries of the Thorax and Pectoral Limb

The paired brachiocephalic arteries arise from the aortic trunk at the base of the heart and are directed laterally toward the 1st rib of their respective sides. After giving off the common carotids, they are continued as the subclavian arteries. The subclavian branches into the coracoid artery which supplies the large deep pectoral and other muscles around the coracoid bone. It also gives off the pectoral artery which supplies the superficial pectoral muscle. The subclavian is continued to the shoulder joint as the axillary artery. The axillary gives rise to the subscapular and the deep brachial arteries and is continued down the arm as the brachial artery. The subscapular artery supplies the triceps brachii, deltoideus, and latissimus dorsi muscles and the cranial patagium. The brachial artery continues down the medial aspect of the arm in the biceps brachii muscle. At the elbow the brachial artery bifurcates into a radial and an ulnar artery. The median and subcutaneous ulnar artery passes to the carpus along the flexor carpi ulnaris and supplies the flexor group of muscles. The ulnar artery is continued across the carpus.

VEINS OF THE PECTORAL LIMB

The *axillary vein* (Fig. 3.10) is formed at the medial surface of the shoulder joint by the confluence of three veins: the median, the deep brachial, and the brachial. It passes along the caudal surface of the corresponding artery for a very short distance before joining the cranial external thoracic veins and becoming the subclavian vein. It drains the entire wing and a portion of the dorsal thoracic wall.

The *median vein* (Fig. 3.10) is the largest vein in the brachium. It is formed proximal to the elbow on the medial surface of the brachium by the junction of the radial and ulnar veins. It passes along the medial surface of the triceps brachii muscle to the axillary vein and drains the major portion of the wing. Near and proximal to the elbow it receives two anastomotic veins, both of which connect the median vein with the deep brachial vein.

The *ulnar vein* (Fig. 3.10) is a continuation of the dorsal metacarpal vein into the forearm. At the caudal aspect of the carpus it receives a tributary from the primary feather follicles and anastomotic veins from the vena comitans. Just proximal to the carpus the ulnar vein receives another anastomotic vein which connects it and the palmar metacarpal vein. The ulnar vein passes along the caudal aspect of the ulna and receives small tributaries from the flexor carpi ulnaris and the secondary feather follicles. Approaching the elbow, it passes across its medial surface to the forearm and joins with the radial vein to form the median vein. Near its junction with the radial it receives two additional anastomotic veins from the vena comitans.

The *dorsal digital vein* for digit 3 (Fig. 3.10) receives tributaries from the dorsal surface of the 3rd digit and the primary feather follicles in this region. It passes along the craniodorsal border of the 3rd digit and over the metacarpus, where it becomes the dorsal metacarpal vein.

The *dorsal metacarpal vein* (Fig. 3.10) is the continuation of the dorsal digital vein for digit 3. It passes along the craniodorsal border of the metacarpus and at the 2nd digit turns and runs

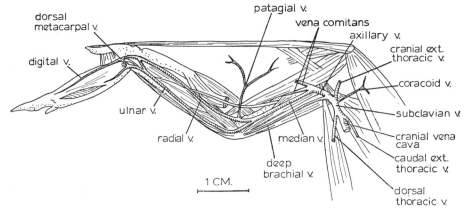

FIG. 3.10—Veins of the pectoral limb, ventrolateral view.

across the dorsal surface of the metacarpus to the caudal aspect of the carpus, where it becomes the ulnar vein. Crossing the metacarpus, it receives a small tributary from the 2nd digit and a large tributary from the primary feather follicles.

The *radial vein* (Fig. 3.10) is the deepest vein of the forearm and drains the greater portion of the musculature in this region. It is formed by the convergence of two veins on the medial aspect of the proximal end of the radius. The cranial vein arises from a tributary of the vena comitans at the end of the radius. It passes along the caudal border of the radius for the entire length of this bone and enters the radial vein. This cranial tributary of the radial vein forms a venous loop between the vena comitans and the radial vein and receives many small tributaries from the surrounding flexor and extensor muscles. The caudal tributary of the radial vein arises in the distal portion of the interosseous space and courses on the cranial surface of the ulna. Approaching the elbow, it passes craniad over the interosseous space, where it receives a large tributary from the deep muscles of the forearm. At the

radius it joins with the cranial branch to form the radial vein. The radial vein passes with the artery and receives a large tributary, the patagial vein (Fig. 3.10), which drains the patagium, extensor carpi radialis, and superficial muscles on the dorsal surface of the forearm. Proximal to the elbow and on the medial surface of the humerus it converges with the ulnar vein to form the median vein.

The *vena comitans* (v. brachialis, v. satellite) (Fig. 3.10) is a satellite vein of the brachial and ulnar arteries. It is the continuation of the palmar metacarpal vein of the forearm. Proximal to the carpus an anastomotic vein connects it to the ulnar vein. At this point it receives from the distal portion of the interosseous space a tributary that forms the venous loop with the radial vein. It then divides into a paired vein on the cranial and caudal surface of the artery. Throughout their courses to the axillary vein these paired vessels anastomose with each other many times. At the elbow the vena comitans is connected to the ulnar vein by two short anastomotic veins.

The *deep brachial vein* (deep humeral) (Fig. 3.10) is a satellite of the ar-

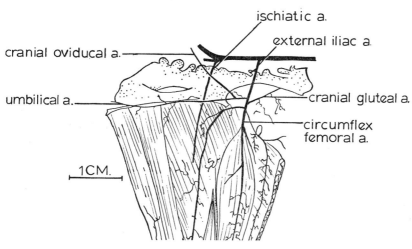

FIG. 3.11—Arteries of the pelvic region, medial view.

tery of the same name. It primarily drains the triceps brachii muscle. In addition it receives venous tributaries which accompany the caudal circumflex humeral artery. The deep brachial joins the median and vena comitans veins to form the axillary vein.

ARTERIES OF THE PELVIC LIMB

The nomenclature used in this description is mainly in accordance with that used for the chicken by Nishida (1963). (See Figs. 3.7, 3.11–3.14, 3.26, 3.27.)

The large arteries arise from the aorta and supply the pelvic limb: the external iliac and the ischiatic arteries. The external iliac supplies only muscles in the cranial crural region, while the larger ischiatic artery supplies muscles of the leg in general.

The *external iliac artery* (Figs. 3.7, 3.11, 3.26, 3.27) arises from the aorta in the region of the 4th or 5th synsacral vertebra and courses caudolaterad through the middle lobe of the kidney. Near the lateral wall of the pelvic cavity it gives rise to the umbilical artery and the cranial gluteal artery. At the lateral pelvic wall, just cranial to the femoral notch formed by the pelvic tubercle, it terminates as such and gives rise to the circumflex femoral artery and the femoral artery.

The *lumbar artery* (Fig. 3.7) arises from the external iliac at the lateral border of the vertebral bodies. This artery is small and courses dorsad to supply a spinal artery and branches to the lumbar muscles.

The *umbilical artery* (Fig. 3.11) is a large branch of the external iliac near its termination. It is directed caudoventrally along the entire length of the medial surface of the pubis. Throughout its course it supplies branches to the abdominal musculature and internal obturator and caudofemoralis muscles. In

female birds the *cranial oviducal artery* (Fig. 3.11) arises from the left umbilical artery a short distance from its origin. It passes to the ventral surface of the oviduct on the dorsal ligament, where it bifurcates and supplies branches to the cranial and caudal portions of this organ. No corresponding artery to the one supplying the oviduct in the female has been observed in the male.

The *cranial gluteal artery* (Fig. 3.11) arises from the cranial surface of the external iliac lateral to the origin of the umbilical artery. It passes craniodorsad into the gluteal muscles and supplies the cranial head of the gluteus superficialis, gluteus medius, and gluteus profundus muscles.

The *femoral artery* (Fig. 3.14) is the smaller of the terminal branches of the external iliac. It passes caudoventrad through the femoral notch, which is formed by the pubic tubercle, ischium, and ilium, and on into the pelvic limb. In this region it lies deep to the pectineus muscle and branches before reaching the intramuscular groove formed by the vastus medialis and adductor muscles. These branches supply the gluteal muscles, the iliacus, the gemellus, the cranial portion of the adductor and rectus femoris muscles, and the pectineus muscle. Caudomedial to the femur the artery passes distad between the vastus medialis and adductor muscles, which it also supplies. On the medial surface of the knee the femoral artery anastomoses with the genu suprema artery.

The *circumflex femoral artery* (Fig. 3.11) is the largest of the terminal branches of the external iliac. It passes from the pelvic cavity into the muscles of the cranial crural region. At the proximal extremity of the quadriceps femoris muscle the artery divides into three branches. The cranial branch enters the proximal portion of the sartorius muscle and gives off branches extending proximally and distally to it. The branches running proximad supply the proximal portion of the sartorius and tensor fasciae latae muscles and the skin. The branches running distad in the sartorius fuse with branches from the genu suprema artery in the distal portion of this muscle. The middle branch from the circumflex femoral passes along the deep surface of the quadriceps femoris for a short distance before entering this

muscle. In addition to supplying the quadriceps femoris, it gives off a few small branches to the tensor fasciae latae and sartorius muscles. The large caudal branch passes directly into the medial surface of the quadriceps femoris and continues in this muscle to the patella.

The *ischiatic artery* (Figs. 3.7, 3.12) is the largest artery to arise from the aorta. It passes laterad over the ventral

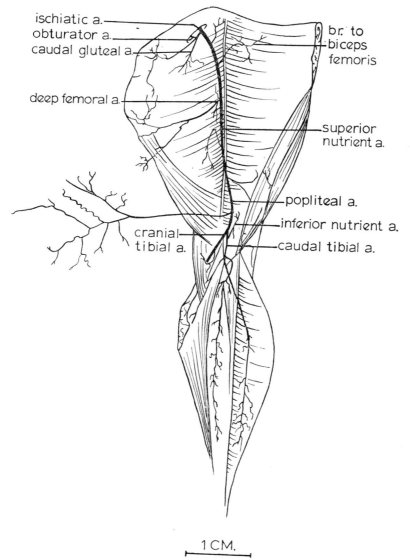

1 CM.

FIG. 3.12—Arteries of the pelvic region, caudal view.

surface of the kidney and emerges through the ischiatic foramen with the ischiatic nerve. As it crosses the kidney, the ischiatic artery gives off a common trunk for the middle and caudal renal arteries and the middle artery of the oviduct in the female, or deferential artery in the male. At the ischiatic foramen it gives rise to the large caudal gluteal artery and passes into the pelvic limb. As the ischiatic artery passes distad in the thigh, it lies deep to the biceps femoris, lateral to the quadriceps femoris and adductor muscles, and caudal to the femur. It gives rise to the deep femoral artery, the superior nutrient artery, the caudal femoral artery, and several small-

er arteries which are unnamed. At the caudomedial aspect of the knee the ischiatic artery gives rise to the caudofemoral artery and terminates by becoming the popliteal artery.

The *middle and caudal renal arteries* (Fig. 3.7) are small and arise from the ischiatic artery from a common trunk with the deferential artery. They pass into their respective lobes of the kidney.

The *middle artery of the oviduct* (Fig. 3.27) supplies the wall of the oviduct and uterus in the female and is present only on the left side. It courses through the dorsal ligament to the oviduct and gives off branches which anastomose with the cranial and caudal arteries of this organ.

The *deferential artery* (Fig. 3.7) is a small paired artery in the male. It bifurcates and runs craniad and caudad on the dorsal surface of the ductus deferens, which it supplies.

The *caudal gluteal artery* (Fig. 3.12) is comparatively large and is the first of a number of branches of the ischiatic after it emerges through the ischiatic foramen. It gives rise to a caudal and a distal branch. The branch directed distally enters the semitendinosus muscle and gives off branches to the biceps femoris muscle. The branch directed caudally supplies the external obturator muscle, quadratus femoris, and the cranial portion of the semitendinosus and semimembranosus muscles.

The *obturator artery* (Fig. 3.12) arises from the caudal gluteal artery at its bifurcation. It passes distad through the pubioischiatic foramen and supplies the internal obturator muscle.

The *deep femoral artery* (Fig. 3.12) arises from the ischiatic artery at about the middle of the thigh. It courses caudad and branches to supply the adductor, semimembranosus, semitendinosus, gracilis, and caudofemoralis muscles and the skin of the region.

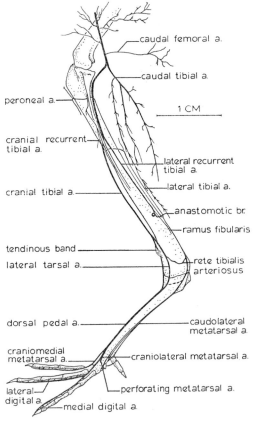

FIG. 3.13—*Arteries of the pelvic limb, lateral view.*

The *superior nutrient artery* to the femur (Fig. 3.12) arises from the cranial surface of the ischiatic artery a short distance distal to the deep femoral artery. It passes craniad into the nutrient foramen on the caudolateral aspect of the femur and branches to supply the biceps femoris, vastus lateralis, adductor, and semimembranosus muscles.

The *caudal femoral artery* (Figs. 3.13, 3.14) arises from the caudal aspect of the distal portion of the ischiatic artery. It passes caudad between the semitendinosus and biceps femoris muscles and becomes cutaneous at the junction of the thigh and leg.

The *popliteal artery* (Fig. 3.12) is the distal continuation of the ischiatic artery. The change of the name of the artery begins just below the origin of the caudal femoral artery. It courses caudomediad in the region of the stifle articulation.

The *caudal tibial artery* (Figs. 3.12–3.14) arises from the popliteal artery proximal to the femorotibial articulation. It divides into three branches which supply the gastrocnemius; the distal portion of the semimembranosus, semitendinosus, and gracilis muscles; and the following flexor muscles: superficial flexor of digit 2, superficial flexor of digit 3, superficial flexor of digit 4, median intermediate digital flexor, and intermediate digital flexor. In addition to supplying these muscles, it gives rise to a cutaneous artery for the region.

The *cranial tibial artery* (Figs. 3.12–3.14) is the larger of the two terminal branches of the popliteal artery. It passes craniodistad through the interosseous space, obliquely down the peroneus brevis muscle between the extensor digitus longus muscle, and deep to the peroneus longus muscle to the cranial surface of the distal portion of the tibia. Near the hock it gives off many collateral arteries to form the rete tibialis

arteriosus. At the hock it divides into the medial and lateral tarsal arteries.

The *inferior nutrient artery* of the femur (Fig. 3.12) arises from the cranial surface of the cranial tibial artery at the distal end of the femur. Muscular branches arise from this artery and pass to the semimembranosus muscle and fascia in this region.

The *medial tibial artery* (Fig. 3.14) is large and arises from the cranial tibial artery on the caudal surface of the proximal extremity of the tibia. It passes craniad to the cranial edge of the medial head of the gastrocnemius, where it gives rise to the genu suprema. The medial tibial artery branches to supply the cau-

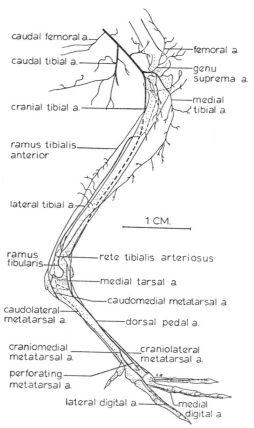

FIG. 3.14—Arteries of the pelvic limb, medial view.

dal tibial muscle and passes distad in the cranial edge of the medial head of the gastrocnemius for its entire length. It supplies this muscle and also the peroneus longus and plantaris muscles.

The *genu suprema artery* (Fig. 3.14) has its origin from the medial tibial artery. It passes proximad to anastomose with the femoral artery. This anastomosis forms a collateral circulation between the cranial tibial and the femoral arteries. After anastomosing, the genu suprema passes craniad on the proximal surface of the knee to the sartorius muscle. It supplies branches to the vastus medialis, rectus femoris, and medial head of the gastrocnemius and the knee joint. In the sartorius muscle its branches anastomose with those from the circumflex femoral artery.

The *peroneal artery* (Fig. 3.13) arises from the cranial surface of the cranial tibial artery at the neck of the tibia. It passes craniad through the interosseous space between the tibia and fibula and branches to supply the tibialis cranialis, the extensor digitus longus, the lateral head of the gastrocnemius, the superficial flexor of digit 2, and the superficial flexor of digit 3. In addition it anastomoses with a branch from the cranial recurrent tibial artery and sends a branch proximally into the femorotibial articulation.

The *ramus tibialis* (Fig. 3.14) arises from the cranial tibial artery on the caudal surface of the proximal extremity of the tibia and passes distad to the hock. It lies deep to the plantaris muscle and branches to supply the medial head of the gastrocnemius, the flexor hallucis longus, and the caudal tibial muscles. Muscular branches in the distal extremity of the gastrocnemius anastomose with those from the medial tibial artery. On the caudomedial surface of the hock small terminal branches of the ramus

tibialis anastomose with the caudomedial metatarsal artery.

The *ramus fibularis* (Figs. 3.13, 3.14, 3.16) has its origin from the cranial tibial artery as it passes through the interosseous space. It courses distad along the caudal surface of the fibula to its extremity, where it passes obliquely across the plantar surface of the tibia, deep to the tendons in this area, and on the medial surface of the distal extremity of the tibia. It supplies branches to the peroneus and the flexor digitus longus muscles. On the medial surface of the distal extremity of the tibia the medial tibial artery joins the ramus fibularis, and from this junction a small branch arises which in turn anastomoses with the caudomedial metatarsal artery.

The *cranial recurrent tibial artery* (Fig. 3.13) arises just after the cranial tibial artery passes through the interosseous space to the craniolateral surface of the tibia. It passes into the cranial tibial muscle, to which it distributes branches. Other muscular branches are supplied to the peroneus longus and the extensor digitus longus muscles. A small branch from the cranial recurrent tibial artery passes proximad to anastomose along the fibula with a small branch from the peroneal artery.

The *lateral tibial artery* (Figs. 3.13, 3.14) arises from the cranial tibial artery a short distance from the origin of the cranial recurrent tibial artery. It passes caudad for a short distance and then distad at the junction of the peroneus longus muscle and the lateral head of the gastrocnemius. It continues distad along the tendon of the intermediate digital flexor to the distal end of the tibia, where it anastomoses with the lateral recurrent tibial artery. Throughout its course it supplies muscular branches to the gastrocnemius, peroneus longus, and flexor digitus longus muscles.

The *rete tibialis arteriosus* (Figs. 3.13, 3.14) results from a formation of a complex network from the cranial tibial artery on the cranial surface of the distal extremity of the tibia. Some authorities have proposed that the function of this network in other birds is to warm the venous blood at this level. At the proximal end of the hock the main trunk (cranial tibial artery) bifurcates into the medial and lateral tarsal arteries.

The *lateral tarsal artery* (Fig. 3.13) gives off the lateral recurrent tibial artery and passes distad to the hock. The *medial tarsal artery* (Fig. 3.14) is larger and passes deep to the cranial tibial tendon and an annular ligament on the tibia. It continues distad on the medial side of the cranial surface of the hock; and on the cranial surface of the proximal extremity of the metatarsus, the medial and lateral tarsal arteries converge to form the dorsal pedal artery. Just before uniting, the medial tarsal artery gives rise to the caudolateral metatarsal and the caudomedial metatarsal arteries.

The *lateral recurrent tibial artery* (Fig. 3.13) arises from the lateral tarsal artery, which is a branch of the main trunk of the rete tibialis. It passes to the lateral surface of the distal end of the tibia. Proximally, it anastomoses with the lateral tibial artery and distally with the caudolateral metatarsal artery. In addition it supplies minute arteries to the lateral surface of the hock.

The *caudolateral metatarsal artery* (Figs. 3.13, 3.14) arises from the medial tarsal artery of the rete tibialis in close association with the caudomedial metatarsal artery. It passes laterad through the proximal lateral foramen of the metatarsus, anastomoses with the lateral recurrent tibial artery on the lateral surface of the metatarsus, and continues distad deep to the flexor tendons. On the

volar surface of the distal extremity of the metatarsus it joins the perforating artery and a branch to the medial plantar metatarsal artery.

The *caudomedial metatarsal artery* (Fig. 3.14) passes through the medial foramen of the metatarsus and the medial surface of the hock. It anastomoses with the ramus tibialis proximally and with the caudolateral metarsal artery distally.

The *dorsal pedal artery* (Figs. 3.13, 3.14) is formed by the confluence of the medial and lateral branches of the rete tibialis. It courses distad deep to the tendon of the extensor digitus longus muscle, and on the distal half of the metatarsus it divides into a large craniolateral metatarsal artery and a smaller cranial metatarsal artery.

The *craniolateral metatarsal artery* (dorsal metatarsal artery 3) (Figs. 3.13, 3.14) passes distad and joins the lateral plantar metatarsal artery between the digits to supply the medial digital artery for the 4th digit and the lateral digital artery for the 3rd digit. On the distal end of the metatarsus the craniolateral metatarsal artery gives rise to the large perforating metatarsal artery.

The *craniomedial metatarsal artery* (Figs. 3.13, 3.14) is small and passes distad to join the middle plantar metatarsal artery in supplying the medial digital artery for the 3rd digit and the lateral and medial digital arteries for the 2nd digit (Figs. 3.13, 3.14).

The *perforating metatarsal artery* (Figs. 3.13, 3.14) arises from the plantar surface of the craniolateral metatarsal artery and passes through the distal metatarsal foramen. As it emerges from the foramen on the plantar surface, the large artery anastomoses with the caudolateral metatarsal artery and branches into the medial, lateral, and middle plantar metatarsal arteries. The lateral plantar metatarsal joins with the lateral dorsal artery, and the middle plantar metatarsal joins with the medial dorsal metatarsal to give off digital arteries.

VEINS OF THE PELVIC LIMB

The pelvic limb is drained by two veins, the external iliac vein and the ischiatic vein (Figs. 3.15–3.17, 3.25). The external iliac is the larger and drains the major portion of the leg.

The *external iliac vein* (Fig. 3.15) is

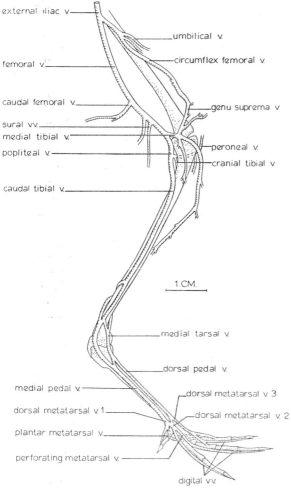

external iliac v.

umbilical v.

femoral v.

circumflex femoral v.

caudal femoral v.

genu suprema v

sural vv.
medial tibial v.
popliteal v.

peroneal v.

cranial tibial v.

caudal tibial v.

1 CM.

medial tarsal v.

dorsal pedal v.

medial pedal v.

dorsal metatarsal v. 3

dorsal metatarsal v. 1

dorsal metatarsal v. 2

plantar metatarsal v.

perforating metatarsal v.

digital vv.

FIG. 3.15—Veins of the pelvic limb, medial view.

the continuation of the femoral vein into the pelvic cavity, where it receives the umbilical vein and in a few instances the circumflex femoral vein ventrolateral to the cranial part of the middle lobe of the kidney. The external iliac is joined by the internal iliac to form the common iliac vein.

The *ischiatic vein* (Fig. 3.25) arises in the distal portion of the thigh by tributaries from the muscles in this region. It passes with the artery and nerve through the ischiatic foramen and enters the afferent renal vein near the middle lobe of the kidney.

The *umbilical vein* and the *circumflex femoral vein* (Fig. 3.15) are satellites of the arteries and drain the muscles supplied by the artery; however, the circumflex femoral usually enters the common iliac vein cranial to the junction of the internal and external iliac veins.

The *femoral vein* (Figs. 3.15, 3.16) is the continuation of the popliteal vein. Its first tributary is the *caudal femoral vein* (Figs. 3.15, 3.16). The junction of this tributary marks the beginning of the femoral vein. It passes caudal to the femur between the adductor and biceps femoris muscles in company with the ischiatic artery and vein to the neck of the femur. At the neck of the femur the femoral vein receives a venous satellite of the femoral artery and passes across the femur and into the pelvic cavity, where it becomes the external iliac vein. Throughout its course the femoral vein receives muscular tributaries which accompany the various branches of the ischiatic artery in the distal three-fourths of the thigh.

The *popliteal vein* (Figs. 3.15, 3.16) is formed by the junction of the cranial and caudal tibial veins on the caudal surface of the neck of the tibia, deep to and between the lateral and medial heads of the gastrocnemius muscle. It receives the peroneal, medial tibial, and

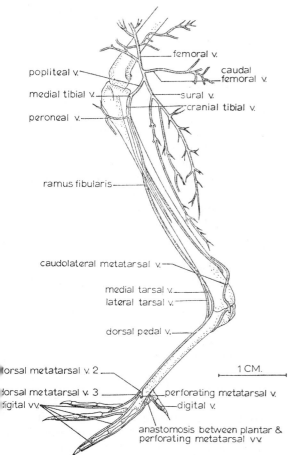

FIG. 3.16—Veins of the pelvic limb, lateral view.

The *medial tibial vein* (Figs. 3.15, 3.16) accompanies the medial tibial artery and receives a satellite vein of the genu suprema artery (genu suprema vein, Fig. 3.15) that anastomoses with the satellite vein of the femoral artery.

The *sural vein* (Figs. 3.15, 3.16) accompanies the caudal tibial artery into the gastrocnemius muscle, which it drains. It enters the popliteal vein at the origin of the caudal tibial artery.

The *caudal tibial vein* (Figs. 3.15, 3.17) is a continuation of the medial pedal vein of the leg. It passes from the cranial surface of the tarsus to the caudomedial aspect of the tibia, where it runs proximad in company with the ramus tibialis. It joins the cranial tibial

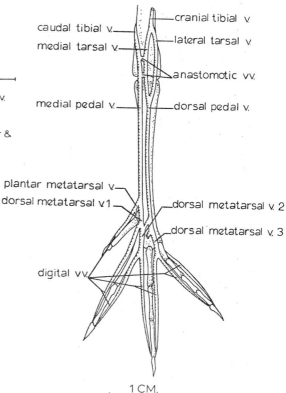

FIG. 3.17—Veins of the lower pelvic limb, dorsal view.

sural veins as it passes over the caudal surface of the knee. At this region it is accompanied by the cranial tibial artery. It enters the thigh lateral to the adductor and semimembranosus muscles and medial to the biceps femoris muscle. Just distal to the caudal femoral vein the popliteal becomes the femoral vein.

The *peroneal vein* (Figs. 3.15, 3.16) is a satellite of the artery of the same name. It passes caudad between the tibia and fibula with the artery, and joins the popliteal vein about 2 mm from its origin.

vein to form the popliteal vein. Proximal to the tarsus the caudal tibial vein receives venous tributaries which accompany the caudolateral metatarsal and the caudomedial metatarsal arteries.

The *medial pedal vein* (Figs. 3.15, 3.17) (considered the medial metatarsal by Gadow and Selenka; Chamberlain) is formed on the medial surface of the distal extremity of the metatarsus by the confluence of the palmar metatarsal vein and the *dorsal metatarsal vein 1* (Figs. 3.15, 3.17). It follows the medial aspect of the metatarsus to its proximal extremity, where it passes to the dorsal surface of the tarsus. On the tarsus it is connected with the medial tarsal vein by two short *anastomotic veins* (Fig. 3.17). Cranial to the tarsus the medial pedal vein becomes the caudal tibial vein.

The *cranial tibial vein* (Figs. 3.15–3.17) is formed proximal to the tarsus on the dorsal surface of the tibia by the confluence of the medial and lateral tarsal veins. It courses laterad with the artery and passes between the tibia and fibula to join with the caudal tibial vein at the neck of the tibia. On the lateral surface of the tibia it receives satellite veins of the ramus fibularis and the lateral recurrent tibial and lateral tibial arteries.

The *medial and lateral tarsal veins* (Figs. 3.15–3.17) are formed at the tarsus by the branching of the dorsal pedal vein. They are satellites of the arteries and join proximal to the tarsus, forming the cranial tibial vein. The medial tarsal vein receives satellites of the caudomedial metatarsal and caudolateral metatarsal arteries.

The *dorsal pedal vein* (Figs. 3.15–3.17) is a satellite of the corresponding artery and is formed at the distal one-fourth of the metatarsus by the junction of the dorsal metatarsal veins 2 and 3.

The *lateral digital vein 4* (Figs. 3.15–3.17) passes across the plantar surface of the metatarsus as the *plantar metatarsal vein* (Figs. 3.15, 3.17). It is superficial to the flexor tendons and receives the digital vein 1. It converges with the dorsal metatarsal vein 1 to form the medial pedal vein. The *medial digital vein 4* (Figs. 3.15–3.17) joins the lateral digital vein 3 at the distal end of the metatarsus and passes over the dorsal surface of the metatarsus as the dorsal metatarsal vein 3.

The *dorsal metatarsal vein 3* (Figs. 3.15–3.17) courses with the artery of the same name. It receives the perforating metatarsal vein and joins the dorsal metatarsal vein 2 to form the dorsal pedal vein.

The *medial digital vein 2* and the *lateral digital vein 3* converge and divide over the digital extremity of the metatarsus into the *dorsal metatarsal vein 2* and the *dorsal metatarsal vein 1* (Figs. 3.15–3.17).

The *perforating metatarsal vein* (Figs. 3.15, 3.16) accompanies the artery through the distal metatarsal foramen to the plantar surface of this bone. Deep to the flexor tendons it connects with the plantar metatarsal vein and dorsal metatarsal vein 1 by two anastomotic tributaries.

ARTERIES OF THE HEAD

The main blood supply to the head is by way of the *common carotid arteries* (Figs. 3.18, 3.19). They arise as the cranial termination of the brachiocephalic artery, lateral to the trachea at its bifurcation into the primary bronchi. The two arteries reach the median plane dorsal to the trachea at about the level of the 12th to 14th vertebrae. At this point they enter a canal formed by the ventral processes of the cervical vertebrae dorsally and accompanying longus colli muscle ventrally. After coursing craniodorsad with the contour of the neck, the arteries emerge from the canal at the level of the 3rd or 4th cervical vertebra, separate from each other, and pass to the ventrolateral part of the caudal border of the base of the skull, where each artery terminates by dividing into the internal and external carotid arteries.

The *external carotid artery* (Figs.

3.18, 3.19) begins its ventrolateral course at the level of and medial to the glossopharyngeal ganglion. It promptly gives rise to the occipital artery and then continues rostrad for 1–2 mm before it terminates by dividing into the hyoid and external and internal maxillary arteries.

The *occipital artery* (Fig. 3.19) is

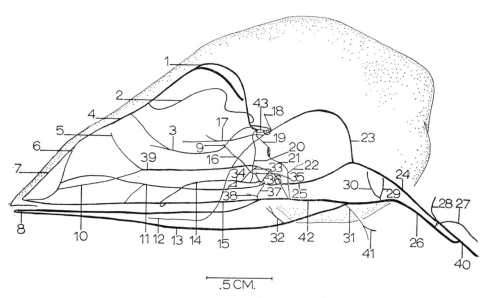

.5 CM.

FIG. 3.18–Arteries of the head, lateral view.

1. Supraorbital artery
2. Dorsal palpebral artery
3. Ophthalmic branch of rete temporalis
4. Ethmoidal artery
5. Dorsal cutaneous branch of facial artery
6. Internal ethmoidal artery
7. External ethmoidal artery
8. Lower internal maxillary artery
9. Central retinal artery
10. Ventral branch of facial artery, anastomotic with internal ethmoidal artery
11. Palatine artery
12. Inferior alveolar artery
13. External maxillary artery
14. Sphenomaxillary artery
15. Middle internal maxillary artery
16. Internal ophthalmic artery
17. Infraorbital artery
18. Meningeal artery
19. Muscular branch of rete temporalis
20. Anastomotic branch from rete to sphenomaxillary artery
21. Branch of cranial auricular artery to join muscular branch from rete temporalis
22. Cranial auricular artery
23. Stapedial artery
24. Internal carotid artery
25. Carotid canal
26. External carotid artery
27. Cranial cervical artery
28. Cranial auricular artery
29. Caudal auricular artery
30. Hyoid artery
31. Superior laryngeal artery
32. Lingual artery
33. Sphenomaxillary facial anastomotic artery
34. Sphenomaxillary palatine anastomatic artery
35. Internal carotid artery (to brain)
36. Palatinofacial anastomotic artery
37. Anastomosis between a branch of upper internal maxillary artery and palatinofacial anastomotic artery
38. Upper internal maxillary artery
39. Facial artery
40. Common carotid artery
41. Descending esophageal artery
42. Internal maxillary artery
43. Rete temporalis

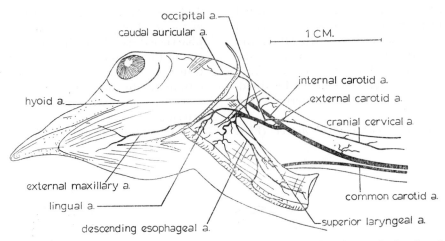

FIG. 3.19—Superficial arteries of the cranioventral region of the head and neck.

the first branch of the external carotid. It initially courses dorsolaterad medial to the vagus and lateral to the hypoglossal nerves. It gives off branches which supply the cranial portions of the dorsal cervical muscles, and just rostral to the first spinal ganglion it gives off a small medial branch that enters the transverse canal in company with the cervical sympathetic nerve.

The *cranial cervical artery* (Figs. 3.18, 3.19) arises near the base of the occipital artery and courses caudad in conjunction with the jugular vein and vagus nerve. It supplies cutaneous and muscular branches to the ventral cervical muscles before anastomosing with the caudal cervical artery.

The *hyoid artery* (Figs. 3.18, 3.19) is the smallest terminal branch of the external carotid artery. It courses rostrodorsad for 2 mm, where it divides into two branches of almost equal size. The short rostral branch courses laterad lateral to the vagus to supply the caudal portion of the hyomandibularis muscle which surrounds the caudal cornu of the hyoid apparatus. The caudal branch, the *caudal auricular artery* (Figs. 3.18,

3.19), runs dorsad medial to the caudal cornu and crosses the lateral surface of the occipitomandibularis muscle, supplying it and the temporalis muscle. It continues rostrodorsad to supply the cutaneous muscle, fascia, and skin of the region.

The *external maxillary artery* (Figs. 3.18, 3.19) is the ventrolateral terminal branch of the external carotid artery. It courses ventrorostrad medial to the attachment of the hyomandibularis muscle to the cornu of the hyoid bone. It continues rostrad and passes dorsal to the hyoid bone, ventral to the sublingual gland, and terminates by supplying the corium of the beak. Along its course it gives rise to the superior laryngeal artery, the lingual artery, and several muscular branches to the hyomandibularis muscle.

The *superior laryngeal artery* (Figs. 3.18, 3.19) arises from the external maxillary approximately 1–2 mm from its origin. It accompanies the laryngeal vein and the laryngeal branch of the glossopharyngeal nerve. A small branch is given off that supplies the caudoventral surface of the larynx. The superior laryngeal artery then courses caudad over the dorsal surface of the caudal portion of the pharynx, where it gives off the *descending esophageal artery* (Figs. 3.18, 3.19), which courses along the dorsal surface of the esophagus. The main continuation of the superior laryngeal courses laterad and supplies the caudal portion of the larynx and the trachea.

The *lingual artery* (Figs. 3.18, 3.19) arises from the external maxillary artery 5–6 mm rostral to the origin of the superior laryngeal artery. It courses rostrolaterad adjacent to the lateral surface of the pharynx. About 2 mm caudal to the hyoideus transversus muscle it gives off numerous small branches which supply the rostral hyoid muscles. Its main portion, however, courses dorsad to enter and supply the tongue.

The *internal maxillary artery* (Fig. 3.18) is the ventromedial branch and the largest of the terminal branches of the external carotid artery. It courses rostrad dorsal to the pharynx and ventral to the cranial portion of the rectus capitis ventralis medialis muscle and the caudal portion of the mandibulomaxillaris medialis and lateralis muscles. After first giving off the cranial auricular artery, then the external facial artery, it terminates by dividing into the lower, middle, and upper internal maxillary arteries.

The *cranial auricular artery* (Fig. 3.18) arises from the internal maxillary artery 3–4 mm rostral to the origin of the external maxillary artery. This distance is subject to much variation. It courses dorsolaterad medial to the temporalis muscle, caudal to the medial process of the mandible, and caudal to the pterygoid and quadrate bones. After reaching the ventral surface of the external auditory process, the cranial auricular artery divides into several small

branches to supply the ear region. One or two branches form a small plexus that passes over the masseter muscle, supplying it. It then anastomoses with a muscular branch of the rete temporalis.

The *external facial artery* (Fig. 3.18) arises from the internal maxillary 1–2 mm rostral to the origin of the cranial auricular artery. Initially, it courses caudodorsad for 2–3 mm. As it passes between the dorsal surface of the medial process of the mandible and the ventral surface of the pterygoid bone, it receives the *palatinofacial anastomotic artery* (Fig. 3.18). The latter artery courses mesiad ventral to the mandibulomaxillaris lateralis muscle, then turns dorsad for 1–2 mm, and anastomoses with the palatine branch of the internal carotid artery. Small muscular branches to the muscles in this region arise from the anastomotic artery. The external facial artery then passes between the two bones mentioned above and turns dorsad on the caudal surface of the distal and lateral extremity of the pterygoid bone. Here it receives another anastomotic artery, the *sphenomaxillary facial* (Fig. 3.18). The latter artery courses caudomesiad caudal to the pterygoid bone, dorsal to the pterygoquadrato-mandibulomaxillaris muscle, and ventral to the quadratomandibularis lateralis muscle to which it sends a small branch. After a course of 4 mm it makes a 90° turn to course directly rostrad for 1–2 mm before joining the sphenomaxillary branch of the internal carotid artery. After receiving the latter anastomotic artery, the external facial artery courses dorsolaterad and becomes related to the caudal border of the masseter muscle. It sends a small branch to the latter muscle as well as to the supraorbitomandibularis muscle, then continues rostrad to the frontal region and bifurcates into a dorsal and a ventral branch. The ventral branch courses rostrad to anastomose with the internal ethmoid artery. The dorsal branch supplies the frontal region and sends cutaneous branches to the skin.

The *lower internal maxillary artery* (Fig. 3.18) is the lateral terminal branch of the internal maxillary artery. It courses rostrolaterad ventral to the lateral pharyngeal region and medial to the mandible. It supplies small branches to the lateral pharyngeal region in its course. At the caudal extremity of the sublingual salivary gland, the artery gives rise to a branch that courses along the dorsal surface of the gland, which it supplies. The main continuation of the lower internal maxillary progresses rostrad to anastomose with the external maxillary artery.

The *middle internal maxillary artery* (Fig. 3.18) is the largest of the terminal branches of the internal maxillary artery. It courses rostrad over the pharynx ventral to the mandibulomaxillaris lateralis muscle for 4–5 mm, where it receives the sphenomaxillary branch of the internal carotid artery. It then becomes related to the dorsal surface of the palate, which it supplies. It continues rostrad to terminate by supplying the palatine and maxillary glands and the corium of the beak, anastomosing with the *internal ethmoidal artery* (Fig. 3.18).

The *upper internal maxillary artery* (Fig. 3.18) courses mesiad ventral to the mandibulomaxillaris medialis muscle, where it sends a small branch that anastomoses with the palatinofacial artery. The upper internal maxillary terminates by dividing into numerous small branches which supply the muscles of this region and the rostral portion of the pharynx.

The medial termination of the common carotid artery is the *internal carotid artery* (Figs. 3.18, 3.19). It

courses craniad for 5–6 mm ventral to the rectus capitis ventralis medialis muscle. Just before it enters the carotid canal in the temporal bone, it gives rise to the stapedial artery. The internal carotid enters the bony canal which courses mediodorsad. After a course of 6 mm in the canal it gives off a palatine artery. The sphenomaxillary artery arises ½–1 mm further rostrad. Just after they are given off, the latter two arteries leave the carotid canal by way of the foramen lacerum. Rostral to the sphenomaxillary artery the internal carotid enters the pituitary fossa and anastomoses with its fellow. It then gives off the internal opthalmic artery which runs through a foramen in the wall of the pituitary fossa. After giving off the ophthalmic artery, the internal carotid enters the brain cavity and divides into cranial and caudal rami of the circle of Willis.

The *palatine artery* (Fig. 3.18) arises from the internal carotid in the bony canal just caudal to the origin of the sphenomaxillary artery. The palatine artery leaves the diploë of the basitemporal region of the skull by way of the foramen lacerum. It courses rostrad ventral to the sphenomaxillary artery for 1–2 mm, where it receives the external anastomotic artery from the external facial artery. After coursing ventrad to the pterygoquadratosphenoideus muscle, medial to the pterygoquadratomandibulomaxillaris muscle and lateral to the sphenoid bone, it passes through a small foramen in the pterygoid bone near the articulation of the latter with the palatine process of the maxilla. The palatine artery then continues rostrad ventral to the ventral rectus muscle of the eye and dorsal to the cartilage and oral mucosa of the nasal septum. It bifurcates just caudal to the choanae, or caudal nares. The medial branch courses ventrodorsad along the medial nasal septum to anastomose with the middle internal maxillary artery. The lateral branch courses laterad giving off small branches to the lateral portion of the choanae. It then continues rostro-laterad to anastomose with the internal ethmoidal artery.

The *sphenomaxillary artery* (Fig. 3.18) arises from the internal carotid .5 mm rostral to the origin of the palatine artery and leaves the cranium by way of the foramen lacerum. After coursing for 1 mm, it gives off an anastomotic branch that courses caudolaterad for 5–6 mm before joining the rete temporalis near the origin of the inferior alveolar artery. The sphenomaxillary artery then passes dorsal to the pterygoid bone. Along its course it gives off small muscular branches to the pterygoquadratosphe-noideus muscle. Rostral to the pterygoid bone it receives the anastomotic branch from the external facial artery. At a point ventral to the center of the eyeball the sphenomaxillary artery gives off a small branch that courses rostrad on the dorsal surface of the palatine bone to anastomose with the palatine artery which aids in supplying the circulation to the hard palate. The main continua-tion of the artery turns to course rostrolaterad, giving off small muscular branches before anastomosing with the middle internal maxillary artery.

The *internal ophthalmic artery* (Fig. 3.18) arises from the internal carot-id, after it anastomoses with its fellow in the pituitary fossa. It leaves the fossa through a small foramen. The internal ophthalmic courses rostrodorsad around the ciliary ganglion and gives off two or three branches which help to supply the circulation to the lateral rectus and dorsal rectus eye muscles. The main continuation of the artery courses 1–2 mm further rostrad along the lateral sur-face of the short optic nerve, where it terminates by anastomosing with the

ophthalmic branch of the stapedial ar-tery. After giving off the short rostral branch, the ophthalmic courses ventrad under the optic nerve, then turns ros-trad to course between the sclera and the ventral rectus and medial rectus muscles. It terminates by branching into four to five twigs which supply the medial rectus, ventral rectus, and the ventral oblique muscles of the eye. The most dorsal twig courses dorsad medial to the eye to anastomose with the eth-moidal artery. The ethmoidal artery will be discussed in the arteries of the brain since its origin is from the cranial ramus of the internal carotid artery.

The *stapedial artery* (Fig. 3.18) arises from the internal carotid a short distance before the latter enters the ca-rotid canal. It courses dorsad for a short distance, then pierces the tympanic por-tion of the ear and becomes related to the caudal wall of the tympanic cavity. It courses rostrodorsad over this cavity and passes mesiad to the otic process of the quadrate bone, then through the cranioquadrate opening to form the rete temporalis. After forming the rete, the stapedial artery continues to the region of the lacrimal gland and follows the contour of the supraorbital margin. Several cutaneous branches are dis-tributed to the skin and fascia of the dorsal region of the head.

The *rete temporalis* (Fig. 3.18) is a plexus of arteries which lies medial to the masseter and supraorbitomandibu-laris muscles and caudomedial to the supraorbital process. This rete is formed from the termination of the stapedial artery, and from it originate seven ar-teries. They are from caudal to rostral: the small meningeal artery, the inferior alveolar artery, the infraorbital artery, a muscular branch, the ophthalmic branch, the supraorbital branch, and an anastomotic branch.

The *meningeal artery* (Fig. 3.18) is

a small artery that arises from the caudo-dorsal portion of the rete temporalis. It passes mesiad through a small foramen and enters the cranial cavity near the caudolateral portion of the cerebral hemisphere just cranial to the optic lobe of the brain. It then pierces the dura mater and ramifies into three or four branches which supply the dura.

The *inferior alveolar artery* (Fig. 3.18) arises from the caudoventral portion of the rete temporalis. It courses rostroventrad, with the nerve of the same name, between the masseter and quadratomandibularis lateralis muscle and caudal to the supraorbitomandibularis muscle, giving off a small muscular branch to each. Upon reaching the dorsal surface of the mandible, it enters a slitlike opening in the bone from the medial side. It then turns rostrad to course forward in the mandible and becomes the mental artery. The latter terminates by supplying the corium of the ventral beak.

The *infraorbital artery* (Fig. 3.18) arises from the middle rostral portion of the rete and courses rostrolaterad lateral to the ventral portion of the eye. It sends a small dorsal branch to the lower eyelid before passing medial to the depressor palpebrarum ventralis muscle. While medial to the latter muscle, the infraorbital artery bifurcates; its dorsal branch courses dorsad with the muscle and terminates by ramifying over the lower eyelid near the insertion of the muscle. The ventral branch continues further rostrad until it reaches the medial canthus of the eye, where it terminates by branching into three or four small arteries which enter the sclera and choroid layers of the eye.

A *muscular branch of the rete temporalis* (Fig. 3.18) arises from the rostrodorsal portion of the plexus and courses dorsolaterad in the dorsal portion of the masseter muscle. It then turns ventrad

to course down the lateral side of the muscle a short distance before anastomosing with a branch of the cranial auricular artery. It helps to supply the masseter and supraorbitomandibularis muscles.

The *ophthalmic branch of the rete temporalis* (Fig. 3.18) arises from the rostrodorsal portion of the rete temporalis. Initially, it courses mediad for 2–3 mm, then turns ventrad, and passes between the sclera of the caudal portion of the eye and the lateral rectus muscle lateral to the dorsal rectus muscle. Both of the above mentioned muscles receive one or two branches from the ophthalmic artery. Just before passing ventral to the optic nerve, the ophthalmic artery gives rise to a short rostral branch that is joined by the internal ophthalmic artery. This branch then passes into the eye with the optic nerve. A *central retinal artery* (Fig. 3.18) is not constantly present; but when it is, it appears to be formed by the joining of the small arteries of the choroid fissure and the internal ophthalmic artery.

The *supraorbital artery* (Fig. 3.18) arises from the rostrodorsal portion of the rete medial to the ventral portion of the lacrimal gland. It courses rostrodorsad caudal to the sclera and medial to the lacrimal gland. Numerous small lacrimal arteries are given off by the supraorbital artery as it courses in relation to the lacrimal gland. At approximately the middle of the gland the supraorbital gives rise to the prominent *dorsal palpebral artery* (Fig. 3.18), which in turn courses rostrodorsad caudal to the lateral canthus of the eye. From this point it passes into the upper eyelid, forming a small plexus. It turns to course rostroventromesiad to anastomose with the ethmoidal artery.

The *anastomotic branch* (Fig. 3.18) connecting the sphenomaxillary artery and the rete temporalis joins the latter near the origin of the inferior alveolar artery. It courses mesiad and is described in more detail in the description of the sphenomaxillary artery.

ARTERIES OF THE NECK

The *common carotid arteries* (Figs. 3.8, 3.18–3.21) arise as a terminal branch of the *brachiocephalic arteries* (Fig. 3.21). They lie laterally in the base of the neck and pass craniad about 5 mm before reaching the thyroid gland. Caudal to the thyroid gland they give off a small artery which passes caudomediad and branches to supply the primary bronchi and the caudal portion of the esophagus (esophageal artery) (Fig. 3.21). Craniodorsal to the thyroid gland each common carotid gives off a large lateral branch, the dorsal artery. It then courses craniomesiad to meet the artery of the opposite side on the midline of the neck, dorsal to the esophagus, and at about the level of the 12th cervical vertebra. It passes craniad with its fellow in the canal formed by the ventral processes of the cervical vertebrae and the longus colli muscle. At the 3rd cervical vertebra the two carotids begin to separate and pass toward the caudoventral surface of the mandible. At the level of the atlas they terminate by dividing into internal and external carotid arteries.

From the 10th to the 5th cervical vertebral articulation on the right and from the 9th to the 5th vertebral articulation on the left, the carotid arteries give off the *intervertebral arteries.* These arteries promptly divide into a small *ventral cervical artery* (Fig. 3.20) and a large *dorsal cervical artery* (Fig. 3.20). The paired ventral cervical arteries pass into and supply the ventral cervical muscles. The paired dorsal cervical arteries pass to the transverse foramen and anastomose with the vertebral artery which is formed in this region by small anastomotic arteries between the dorsal

cervical arteries. After anastomosing, the dorsal cervical artery passes dorsocraniad through the transverse foramen and supplies small twigs to the vertebrae and spinal cord at the intervertebral foramen and continues dorsad to supply the dorsal and lateral cervical muscles. These intervertebral arteries of the quail take the place of the large vertebral artery in the region of the 10th to the 5th vertebrae in mammals.

The *dorsal artery* (Fig. 3.8) arises from the common carotid and is related at its origin to the craniodorsal portion of the thyroid gland. Just after arising, it gives off a small artery to the thyroid gland and continues craniolaterad on its course. At the level of the 14th cervical vertebra the dorsal artery terminates by dividing into the caudal cervical artery, the vertebral artery, and the omocervical artery.

The paired *caudal cervical arteries* (Fig. 3.8) pass craniad with the jugular veins on the lateral sides of the neck and anastomose with the cranial cervical arteries. They supply branches to the cutaneous muscles of the neck, the skin, and the esophagus. The right caudal cervical artery supplies a large branch to the crop and gives off the caudal esophageal artery.

The *omocervical artery* (Fig. 3.8) is the smallest of the three terminal branches of the dorsal artery. It arises between the caudal cervical artery and the vertebral artery and passes laterad to the medial shoulder region. It branches to supply the cranial portion of the superficial pectoral muscles.

From its origin on the dorsal artery the *vertebral artery* (Figs. 3.20, 3.21) passes craniomesiad to a point between the 10th and 11th cervical vertebrae. It divides into cranial and caudal vertebral arteries.

The *caudal vertebral artery* (subcostal) (Fig. 3.20) is paired and passes

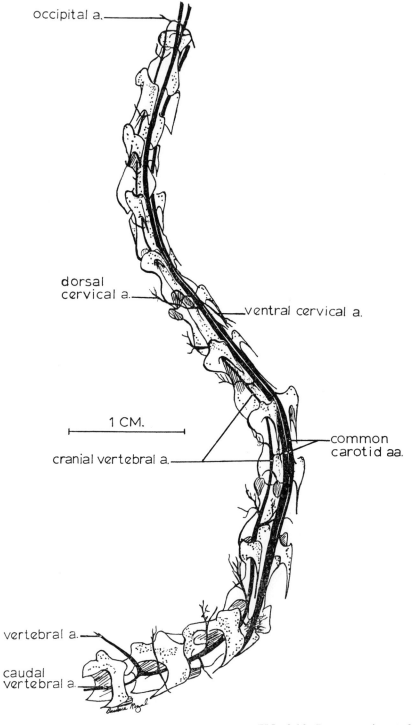

occipital a.

dorsal
cervical a.

ventral cervical a.

1 CM.

common
carotid aa.

cranial vertebral a.

vertebral a.

caudal
vertebral a.

FIG. 3.20—Deep arteries of the neck.

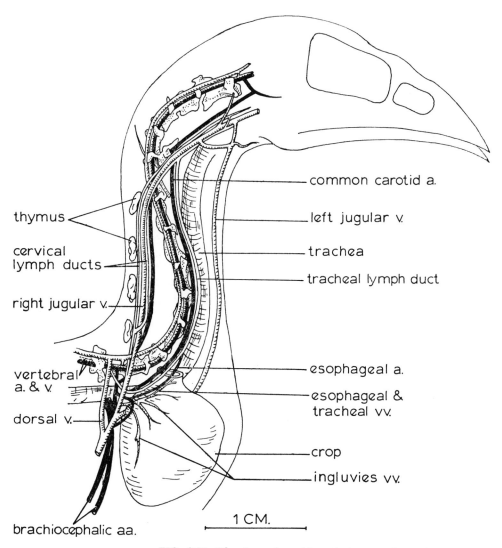

thymus

cervical
lymph ducts

right jugular v.

vertebral
a. & v.

dorsal v.

brachiocephalic aa.

common carotid a.

left jugular v.

trachea

tracheal lymph duct

esophageal a.

esophageal &
tracheal vv.

crop

ingluvies vv.

1 CM.

FIG. 3.21—Blood vessels and lymph ducts of the neck, lateral view.

caudad through the transverse foramen to the 5th or 6th intercostal space, where it anastomoses with an intercostal artery from the aorta. Throughout its course it supplies intercostal arteries and small twigs to the vertebrae and to the spinal canal.

The paired *cranial vertebral artery* (Fig. 3.20) is larger than the caudal vertebral artery and lies along the lateral surface of the neck in the foramen of the

transverse processes of the cervical vertebrae. It is accompanied by the cranial vertebral vein and the sympathetic nerve trunk to the cranium, where it anastomoses with the *occipital artery* (Figs. 3.19, 3.20). From the 10th cervical vertebra on the right and the 9th on the left to the 5th cervical vertebra, the cranial vertebral artery anastomoses with the dorsal cervical arteries and becomes very small. In this region of the neck it appears that the vertebral artery is formed by small anastomotic arteries between the dorsal cervical arteries. At the 5th cervical vertebra the cranial cervical artery resumes its large size and is confluent with the dorsal cervical arteries which are given off from the common carotids at this point. From the 13th to the 10th cervical vertebrae and from the 5th cervical vertebra to the cranium the artery branches to supply the cervical muscles, vertebrae, and spinal cord. However, in the region of the 10th to the 5th cervical vertebrae the function of this artery is assumed by the dorsal and ventral cervical arteries.

VEINS OF THE HEAD AND NECK

Most of the veins are paired and will be described as they appear on one side. Those which are unpaired will be so designated.

The *jugular vein* (Figs. 3.21, 3.22) returns blood from the head and neck region to the heart. It arises as a result of the joining of the cranial and caudal cephalic veins, which occurs ventromedial to the bifurcation of the common carotid artery. The right jugular vein follows a more ventral course in the cranial cervical region. It runs caudoventrad with the cervical artery and vagosympathetic trunk lateral to the ventrolateral neck muscles and dorsal to the esophagus. It is related dorsally to the crop and thyroid gland and ventrally to the thymus and brachial nerve plexus. It terminates by joining with the subclavian vein to form the cranial vena cava. The left jugular vein follows a course similar to the right, but is more dorsal in the cranial cervical region and is not related to the crop and the esophagus, as is the right jugular. In the neck both jugular veins are covered by skin, fascia, thymus gland in the young, and cutaneous muscles. Each jugular receives the following tributaries:

1. The *lateral occipital vein* (Fig. 3.22) enters the dorsal surface of the jugular 2 mm caudal to the origin of the latter. It is a small vein formed by a main tributary from the cranial cervical muscles and one from the vertebral vein.

2. The *dorsal vein* (Fig. 3.21) is unpaired and is a tributary from the vertebral vein.

3. The *esophageal and tracheal veins* (Fig. 3.21) are very numerous, with the majority entering the right jugular vein. Coursing with the esophageal arteries are two larger veins which drain most of the blood from the trachea and ventral surface of the esophagus. The smaller vessels drain the dorsal region of the esophagus into the right jugular.

4. The *ingluvies veins* (Fig. 3.21) are four to five in number. They arise over the entire surface of the crop and converge to form four to five small vessels, most of which enter the right jugular.

5. The *vertebral veins* (Fig. 3.21) may occasionally drain into the jugular veins, but they usually drain into the subclavian or precava. They are discussed in detail in the description of the tributaries to the precava (cranial vena cava). When a vertebral vein does join the jugular, it is very short. The vein will pass out of the transverse foramen at the point where the vertebral artery enters and will course caudolaterad for 4–5 mm before it joins the jugular.

6. The *muscular tributaries* draining the cervical muscles are very numerous and inconsistent; the majority of these veins join the jugular.

7. The *cutaneous veins* of the neck

course with the cutaneous branches of the cervical spinal nerves. There are 13–14 on each side. They drain blood from the skin, feather follicles, and cutaneous muscles. A small cutaneous vein from the ventral ingluvies region joins the left jugular as it enters the thoracic cavity. This vein arises from the fat, fascia, and skin covering the ingluvies. A small thyroid vein enters each jugular.

8. The *caudal cephalic vein* (Fig. 3.22) receives tributaries from the sinuses of the cranium, brain, carotid vein, external occipital vein, and the auris interna vein. The latter three veins converge to form the caudal cephalic at a point caudomedial to the tem-

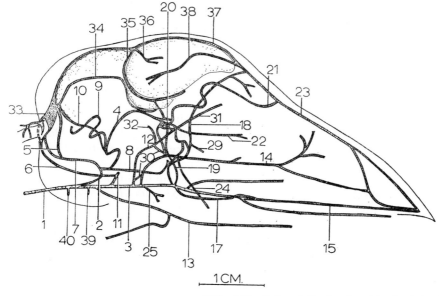

FIG. 3.22—Veins of the head and brain, lateral view.

1. Jugular vein
2. Caudal cephalic vein
3. Cranial cephalic vein
4. Auris interna vein
5. Caudal anastomotic vein
6. Median occipital vein
7. External occipital vein
8. Carotid vein
9. Auris interna vein
10. Floccular vein
11. Transverse vein
12. Temporal vein
13. Laryngeal vein
14. External facial vein
15. Maxillary vein
17. Infrapalatine vein
18. Ophthalmic vein
19. Rete mirabilis temporalis vein
20. Venous rete temporalis

21. Supraorbital vein
22. Infraorbital vein
23. Ethmoidal vein
24. Inferior alveolar vein
25. Superior pharyngeal vein
29. Vein coursing with optic nerve
30. Anastomotic veins joining temporal and external facial veins
31. Palpebral vein
32. Auricular vein
33. Mid-dorsal head sinus
34. Middle cerebral vein
35. Cranial cerebral vein
36. Cranial choroid plexus vein
37. Cranial portion of mid-dorsal head sinus
38. Prolongation of cranial cerebral vein
39. Hyoid vein
40. Lateral occipital vein

poralis muscle, medial to the caudo-dorsal portion of the cornu, and lateral to the origin of the rectus capitis ventralis medialis muscle. The vein then courses caudoventrad for 1.5–2 mm before joining with the cranial cephalic vein to form the jugular vein.

The *external occipital vein* (Fig. 3.22) is the largest tributary of the caudal cephalic vein. It arises from the mid-lateral portion of the mid-dorsal head sinus near the foramen magnum. It courses ventrolaterad around the caudal portion of the skull related ventrally to the external occipital crest to join with the other two veins in the formation of the caudal cephalic vein. Near its origin the external occipital vein receives the *caudal anastomotic vein* (Fig. 3.22). The latter arises in the cranium from the mid-dorsal sinus near the junction of the middle cerebral vein with the external occipital vein. It courses caudo-laterad through the cranium to join the rostrodorsal portion of the external occipital vein. A small vein from the median occipital joins the external occipital vein on its ventral surface near the junction of the caudal anastomotic vein.

The *auris interna vein* (Fig. 3.22) originates from the venous rete temporalis. It courses in a similar manner to that of the stapedial artery and drains the internal ear region. It receives the connection from the sinus semicircularis along its course. Before joining in the formation of the caudal cephalic, it receives the *floccular vein* (Fig. 3.22), which is related to the floccular lobe of the cerebellum and the cerebellar artery. The latter vein runs laterad in the wall of the auditory capsule, turns ventrad, and crosses the floor of the capsule to join the auris interna vein.

The *carotid vein* (Fig. 3.22) accom-panies the carotid artery in the carotid canal of the temporal bone. It originates from the cavernous sinuses of the sella turcica and courses caudolaterad in the canal to join with the external occipital and auris interna veins in the formation of the caudal cephalic vein.

The *cranial cephalic vein* (Fig. 3.22) is formed by the confluence of the maxil-lary, ophthalmic, and rete mirabilis temporalis veins. This joining occurs medial to the division of the internal maxillary artery into upper, middle, and lower branches, dorsal to the roof of the pharynx, and caudoventral to the ptery-goid bone. This large vein then courses caudad ventral to the rectus capitis ven-tralis medialis muscle for 7–8 mm before joining with the caudal cephalic vein to form the jugular vein. Along its course it receives the external facial, temporal, superior pharyngeal, transverse laryn-geal, and hyoid veins.

The *maxillary vein* (Fig. 3.22) arises in the region of the upper beak. (It could be called the palatine in this region.) It courses caudad dorsal to the hard palate and medial to the jugal, or zygomatic, arch. It then passes dorsal to the muscles of this region and becomes related to the midventral portion of the eyeball, where it receives a branch from the lower beak and tongue region. It then continues caudad to join in the formation of the cranial cephalic vein. Near its termination the maxillary vein receives a small *infrapalatine vein* (Fig. 3.22) that arises in the region of the commissure of the mouth from a small plexus of veins at the caudal portion of the hard palate. It courses ventrad to the mandibulomaxillaris lateralis muscle for 5–6 mm before joining the maxillary vein. A suprapalatine vein from the dorsal palatine region also joins the maxillary vein.

The *ophthalmic vein* (Fig. 3.22) arises from the ethmoidal vein just before the latter enters the cranial cavity. Initially, it courses caudoventrad directly toward the optic nerve. After approximately 1 mm it receives a small vein from the dorsal portion of the orbital fundus which drains the dorsal muscles of the eye. The ophthalmic vein then continues on for about 2 mm, passes between the eyeball and the medial rectus muscle, and becomes related to the rostrodorsal portion of the optic nerve. Here it receives a lateral vein from the venous rete temporalis; a very small vein arises from this branch and courses caudoventrad through the pituitary fossa with the internal ophthalmic artery to join the sinus of the sella turcica. The ophthalmic vein then passes medial to the optic nerve and receives a small vein of the choroid fissure; the latter courses with the optic nerve into the eye. After a course of 1 mm further caudoventrad the ophthalmic vein joins in the formation of the cranial cephalic vein.

The *rete mirabilis temporalis* (Fig. 3.22) arises from the ventral portion of the venous rete temporalis and courses rostrocaudad over the pterygoid bone and around the ventral rectus and ventral oblique muscles to join with the maxillary and ophthalmic veins in the formation of the cranial cephalic vein.

The *venous rete temporalis* (Fig. 3.22) is a plexus of veins very similar to and located in the same position as the arterial rete temporalis. The *supraorbital and infraorbital veins* (Fig. 3.22), satellites of the arteries of the same name, drain blood from the orbital region supplied by the supraorbital and infraorbital arteries. These two veins terminate by joining the venous rete temporalis.

The *external facial vein* (Fig. 3.22) is a satellite of the external facial artery. Many small vessels of the cranial facial region, just dorsal to the cranial portion of the jugal arch and caudal to the termination of the corium of the beak, converge to form the beginning of the external facial vein. Once formed, it courses caudad adjacent dorsally to the jugal arch. Near the middle of the jugal arch the vein receives a muscular tributary from the muscles of this region. It then passes lateral to the masseter muscle and continues caudad to the end of the jugal arch. Here the external facial vein receives the *inferior alveolar vein* (Fig. 3.22) from the mandible. It then turns mediad around the otic process of the pterygoid bone and courses ventromesiad over the pterygoid bone to enter the cranial cephalic vein near its origin. Two small anastomotic veins connect it with the closely running temporal vein.

The *temporal vein* (Fig. 3.22) is formed by the junction of the palpebral and auricular veins. The *palpebral vein* (Fig. 3.22) arises by tributaries from the eyelids and courses caudoventrad over the masseter muscle to a point very close to the tip of the caudal articular process of the mandible. Here it is joined by the *auricular vein* (Fig. 3.22) from the ear to form the temporal vein. An anastomotic vein from the external facial vein also joins the temporal vein in this region. The temporal vein then passes between the two processes of the mandible medial to the temporalis muscle to enter the cranial cephalic vein. The latter veins are joined by an anastomotic vein just before they enter the cephalic vein.

The *superior pharyngeal vein* (Fig. 3.22) arises from many small tributaries from the dorsal surface of the pharynx. They all converge to form this main vein, which enters the ventral surface of the cranial cephalic vein near the entry of the external facial vein. Many of the small tributaries anastomose with fellow tributaries of the opposite side.

The single *transverse vein* (Fig. 3.22)

connects the two cranial cephalic veins. It originates from the left cephalic vein ventral to the rectus capitis ventralis medialis muscle and courses caudomesiad at a slight angle, crosses the midline, and joins the right cranial cephalic vein. From this anastomotic vein some of the blood from the left cranial cephalic vein crosses to the right, thereby making the right jugular the larger of the two. The vein is 4–5 mm in length and receives small tributaries from the dorsal pharyngeal region and the cranioventral cervical muscles. Near its middle the transverse vein receives the large *median occipital vein* (Fig. 3.22) which arises from the ventral portion of the mid-dorsal head sinus, passes downward in the cranial cervical muscles, and joins the transverse vein in such a manner that the flow of its blood is directed toward the lumen of the right cranial cephalic vein.

The *laryngeal vein* (Fig. 3.22) originates from many small tributaries on the ventral surface of the tongue and larynx in the region of the hyoideus transversus muscle. It is a very distinct vein and courses caudolaterad medial to the hyoid bone and enters the ventral surface of the cranial cephalic vein approximately 1 mm before becoming the jugular vein.

The *hyoid vein* (Fig. 3.22) arises from tributaries of the hyomandibularis and tongue muscles. It is a very small vein which enters the cranial cephalic vein about .25 mm before the latter joins with the caudal cephalic to form the jugular vein.

The *ethmoidal vein* (Fig. 3.22) arises in the nasal region as a satellite of the ethmoidal artery. It continues as such up to the point where it passes through the olfactory foramen into the cranium. It courses caudodorsad with the olfactory nerve and ethmoidal artery along the medial wall of the orbital fundus. After passing through the olfactory fora-

men, it joins with its fellow to form the cranial prolongation of the mid-dorsal head sinus.

ARTERIES OF THE BRAIN

The main blood supply to the brain is by way of the *internal carotid artery* (Figs. 3.18, 3.19) which enters the cranial cavity through the pituitary fossa. As it enters the cavity, it divides into the cranial and caudal rami or communicating branches. This division takes place at a point ventral to where the transverse fissure, separating the optic lobe and the cerebellum, originates from the midline.

The *cranial ramus,* or cranial communicating artery, courses dorsolaterad around the optic chiasma forming an almost complete circle. It is incomplete, however, since the two rami do not join. Instead each ramus gives off the caudal and cranial cerebral arteries and then divides into the ethmoidal and middle cerebral arteries. This division takes place at a point where the cranial portion of the optic lobe meets the caudal portion of the cerebral hemisphere. These structures are separated by a transverse fissure through which the caudal cerebral artery courses.

Each of the *caudal rami* or caudal communicating arteries, courses caudomesiad for .5–1 mm, giving off the bigeminal artery before joining with its fellow to form the closed circle of Willis. At this point the basilar artery arises and gives off the cerebellar and medullary arteries. The right caudal ramus, caudal to the origin of the bigeminal artery, however, is much larger than the left caudal ramus in most specimens. On the left side the bigeminal artery is the main continuation of the caudal ramus, with a small branch coursing to the midline to meet its fellow. Out of eight coturnix specimens examined, five showed a larger right caudal ramus, while three had larger left rami. In gallus it has been reported that about four out of five had a larger left caudal ramus.

The *ethmoidal artery* (Figs. 3.18, 3.23) arises from the cranial ramus of the circle of Willis at its termination, craniolateral to the optic chiasma. It courses rostrodorsad ventral to the cranial portion of the cerebrum, giving off approximately four small branches to this region. It then passes through the olfactory (ethmoidal) foramen and becomes related dorsomedially to the orbital fundus. Near a point where the supraorbital artery anastomoses with the ethmoidal artery, two to three small branches are given off to the dorsal rectus and dorsal oblique muscles of the eye. The ethmoidal artery continues rostrad, gives off two small branches to the medial rectus muscle, receives an anastomotic branch from the termination of the ophthalmic branch of the stapedial artery, and then passes out of the orbital fundus in relation to the olfactory nerve. In an area rostral to the

medial canthus of the eye and caudal to the external nares, the ethmoidal artery bifurcates into the *internal and external ethmoidal arteries* (Fig. 3.18). The external ethmoidal artery courses over the membranous wall of the nasal cavity and supplies the dorsal nasal region. The internal ethmoidal artery turns ventrad, caudal to the membranous wall of the nasal cavity, and continues to the ventral portion of the external nares. At this point it receives the anastomosis of the external facial artery and then turns to course rostrad to supply the ventral nasal region.

The *middle cerebral artery* (Fig. 3.23) is another terminal branch of the cranial ramus of the circle of Willis. Shortly after its origin it enters the ventromedial portion of the cerebral hemisphere. It ramifies into numerous branches which supply the middle portion of the cerebrum and the choroid plexus of the lateral ventricles.

The *cranial cerebral artery* (Figs. 3.23, 3.24), proceeding caudad, is the succeeding branch of the cranial ramus of the circle of Willis. It arises .5 mm

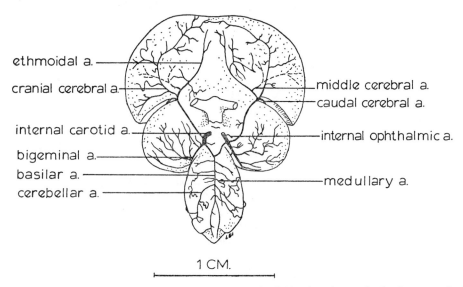

ethmoidal a.

cranial cerebral a.

internal carotid a.

bigeminal a.

basilar a.

cerebellar a.

middle cerebral a.

caudal cerebral a.

internal ophthalmic a.

medullary a.

1 CM.

FIG. 3.23—Arteries of the brain, ventral view.

caudal to the termination of the cranial ramus and courses craniodorsad lateral to the ethmoidal artery. It divides into cranial and caudal branches which ramify out in the cranioventral portion of the cerebral hemisphere. The artery terminates at the most cranial portion of the cerebrum.

The *caudal cerebral artery* (Figs. 3.23, 3.24) arises from the cranial ramus just opposite the origin of the cranial cerebral artery. It passes caudolaterad between the optic lobe caudally and the cerebral hemisphere cranially and is covered by these two structures, to which it supplies a number of small branches. As it reaches the dorsal surface of the brain, the caudal cerebral artery bifurcates into caudal and cranial branches (Fig. 3.24). The course of these two branches is asymmetrical and subject to variation. The cranial branch of one side courses craniad between the two cerebral hemispheres, giving off numerous branches to this area, while the cranial branch of the opposite side ramifies in the caudal portion of the hemisphere of its respective side. In the examination of six specimens, three cranial

branches from the left were found to form the main artery between the cerebral hemispheres, and in three cases the artery was found to be formed by three branches from the right. In those instances where the cranial branch of the caudal cerebral artery courses craniad to supply both cerebral hemispheres, the caudal branch of the caudal cerebral artery will ramify out over the craniodorsal portion of the optic lobe of the brain. In other instances, where the cranial branch terminates in the caudal portion of the hemisphere, the caudal branch of the same side will send numerous branches to the optic lobe, exactly like its fellow artery, and will continue caudad to supply the craniodorsal portion of the cerebellum.

The *bigeminal artery* (tectal) (Figs. 3.23, 3.24) arises from the caudal ramus of the circle of Willis. It courses caudolaterad caudal to the optic lobe and cranial to the cerebellum. It is distributed over the ventrolateral portion of the optic lobe and sends to the cerebellum several small branches which anastomose with the caudal branch of the caudal cerebral artery.

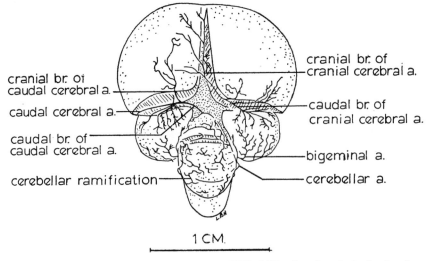

cranial br. of
caudal cerebral a.

caudal cerebral a.

caudal br. of
caudal cerebral a.

cerebellar ramification

cranial br. of
cranial cerebral a.

caudal br. of
cranial cerebral a.

bigeminal a.

cerebellar a.

1 CM.

FIG. 3.24—Arteries of the brain, dorsal view.

The *basilar artery* (Fig. 3.23) is formed by the joining of the larger right and the smaller left caudal rami. It is an unpaired artery which courses caudad as a median vessel along the ventral surface of the medulla oblongata and the spinal cord. At the caudal portion of the medulla, 1–2 mm after giving origin to the cerebellar artery, the basilar tends to divide for 2 mm and then rejoins to form one artery at the beginning of the spinal cord. This is termed the ventral spinal artery. The latter artery courses with the spinal cord to its termination.

The *medullary arteries* (Fig. 3.23) are paired, usually symmetrical branches of the basilar artery. They course laterodorsad to supply the ventrolateral portion of the medulla. There are three or four pair originating cranial to the origin of the cerebellar artery, and six or seven smaller pair caudal to its origin.

The *cerebellar artery* (Figs. 3.23, 3.24) arises from the basilar artery .5 mm cranial to the origin of the abducens nerve. It courses laterodorsad around the medulla and gives off a small artery that supplies the choroid plexus of the fourth ventricle. A small artery to the restiform body and one to the internal ear accompanying the acoustic nerve arise from the cerebellar artery just before it makes a loop around the lateral portion of the flocculus. The cerebellar artery terminates by ramifying over the dorsal portion of the cerebellum.

VEINS OF THE BRAIN

Due to the lack of specific details and the characteristics of the veins of the brain cavity the task of differentiating the regions of the veins into sinuses was not undertaken.

In one way or another the *mid-dorsal head sinus* (Fig. 3.22) is joined by every vein of the brain cavity. It is formed caudoventrally by the median occipital vein which connects to the sinus near the foramen magnum, just ventral to the spinal cord. The sinus bifurcates and encircles the region between the occipital bone and the atlas and then rejoins dorsally. The external occipital vein joins the sinus as its bifurcation passes lateral to the spinal cord. The mid-dorsal sinus of the spinal cord joins the mid-dorsal head sinus near the dorsal portion of the foramen magnum. In this region the head sinus is very large, approximately 2 mm wide. (This larger portion is called the sinus foraminis occipitalis by some authors.) The sinus receives the middle cerebral vein and the caudal anastomotic vein (from the external occipital vein) at its most lateral portion, which is adjacent to the caudolateral portion of the cerebellum. The mid-dorsal head sinus then courses craniodorsad up and over the (middle portion) midline of the cerebellum. As it reaches the caudodorsal portion of the cerebrum, it receives the cranial cerebral and cranial choroid plexus veins. The sinus then continues craniad in the dorsal portion of the longitudinal fissure between the cerebral hemispheres to join its cranial prolongation near the most cranial portion of the cerebrum. The caudal cerebral vein degenerates in embryological development of the quail.

The *middle cerebral vein* (Fig. 3.22) joins the mid-dorsal head sinus at its most lateral portion near the foramen magnum. It courses cranioventrad over the lateral surface of the cerebellum related dorsally to the flocculus. It then reaches the caudodorsal region of the optic lobe of the brain, passes between the latter lobe and the cranial part of the medulla oblongata, turns mediad and continues forward to join the sinus venosus annularis basilaris which surrounds the pituitary gland in the sella turcica. It runs a similar course to the bigeminal artery.

The *cranial cerebral vein* (Fig. 3.22) joins the mid-dorsal head sinus at the point where the dorsal portions of the cerebrum and cerebellum meet. It courses craniolaterad in the transverse fissure between the latter two portions of the brain for approximately 2 mm before it gives off a small vein to the venous rete temporalis which courses with the meningeal artery. It then continues in the transverse fissure between the optic lobe and the cerebral hemisphere until it reaches the cranial portion of the former, where it turns ventromediad to course and join the ophthalmic branch to the sinus annulus basilaris. It runs a similar course to that of the caudal cerebral artery.

The *cranial choroid plexus vein* (Fig. 3.22) (unpaired) joins the ventral surface of the mid-dorsal head sinus at the same point where the cranial cerebral vein joins. It courses cranioventrad between the two cerebral hemispheres to join with and supply the choroid plexus of the lateral ventricles.

The *prolongation of the cranial cerebral vein* (Fig. 3.22) joins the mid-dorsal head sinus near the junction of the ethmoidal veins at the most cranial portion of the cerebrum. It passes caudolaterad to ramify over the dorsal surface of the cerebrum.

TRIBUTARIES TO THE CAUDAL VENA CAVA

The caudal vena cava returns most of the blood from the abdomen, pelvis, and pelvic limb to the heart (Figs. 3.25–3.27). Two portal systems complicate the system. The caudal vena cava is formed by the confluence of the right and left *common iliac veins* (Figs. 3.25–3.27) ventromedial to the cranial lobe of the kidney and chiefly to the right of the median

plane. It courses cranioventrad for 7–9 mm and enters a groove in the dorsal portion of the right lobe of the liver. After receiving four to six hepatic veins, the caudal vena cava leaves the liver and courses craniad for 1–3 mm to enter the caudal surface of the right atrium of the heart. The portion extending from the liver to the heart is 2–3 mm in diameter and is much larger than the portion caudal to the liver. The caudal vena cava receives the following direct tributaries: the ventral mesenteric vein, the hepatic veins, the lumbar veins, and the testicular or the ovarian veins.

The *ventral mesenteric vein* (Fig. 3.25) is formed in the mesentery of the ventral abdominal region. It courses craniodorsad ventral to the pancreas and duodenum, then passes between the dorsal portion of the right and left medial lobes of the liver and enters the ventral surface of the caudal vena cava just caudal to the heart at the craniomedial border of the liver.

The *hepatic veins* open into the caudal vena cava as it lies in the groove in the liver and drains blood from this organ. There are two to three large veins and two to three smaller veins opening into the vena cava as it passes through the groove in the liver.

The *lumbar veins* are very small and usually correspond to the arteries.

The *testicular veins* (Figs. 3.25, 3.26) are generally two in number for each testicle. The most cranial testicular vein consistently opens into the caudal vena cava 1–2 mm cranial to its origin from the joining of the common iliac veins. The caudal testicular vein may open either into the extreme caudal end of the vena cava or into the cranial portion of the common iliac vein, in common with the cranial renal vein.

The *ovarian veins* (Fig. 3.25) are three to four in number and are found only on the left side. Two of these veins

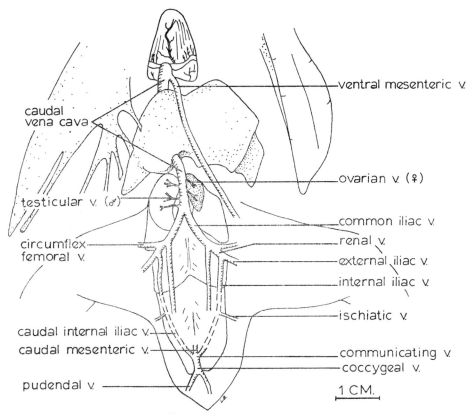

FIG. 3.25—Caudal vena cava, ventral view.

open into the vena cava, and generally the other two caudal ones open into the left common iliac vein.

RENAL PORTAL SYSTEM

Due to the presence of the hepatic and renal portal systems of coturnix (Figs. 3.26, 3.27), the venous pattern of the kidney region is somewhat complicated and entirely different from that of mammals. The hepatic portal system corresponds reasonably well to the mammalian system in that it returns venous blood from the abdominal viscera to the liver; however, the venous blood from the terminal portion of the intestinal tract flows to the kidney, rather than to the liver, by way of the caudal

mesenteric vein. A network of afferent and efferent veins make up the renal portal system which filters the blood through the kidneys from the pelvic limbs, pelvic viscera, and tail region.

Blood is conveyed from the caudal portion of the body to the renal portal system by the following veins: the external iliac, ischiatic, communicating, hypogastric (internal iliac), and the the caudal mesenteric (coccygeomesenteric).

Distal to the origin of the prominent afferent renal vein the *external iliac* (Figs. 3.25–3.27) is called the common iliac, as the veins from the testicles (ovaries) and the kidney all join this vessel on its way to the caudal vena cava. The terminology of this vessel as

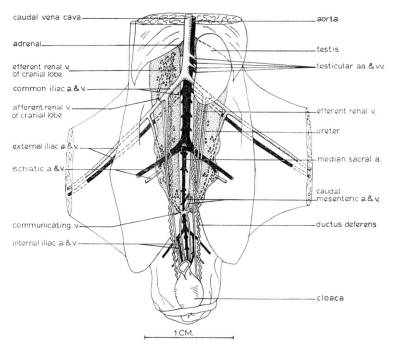

caudal vena cava
adrenal
efferent renal v.
of cranial lobe
common iliac a. & v.
afferent renal v.
of cranial lobe
external iliac a & v.
ischiatic a. & v.
communicating v.
internal iliac a. & v.

aorta
testis
testicular aa. & vv.
efferent renal v.
ureter
median sacral a.
caudal
mesenteric a. & v.
ductus deferens
cloaca

1 CM.

FIG. 3.26—Renal portal system of the male, ventral view.

the *common iliac* (Figs. 3.25–3.27) coin-
cides with the description of the veins
of the pelvic limbs. It lies ventrolateral
to the cranial part of the middle lobe of
the kidney just cranial to the pectineal
process of the pubis and continues craniomesiad ventral to the external iliac
artery and the cranial lobe of the kidney to join its fellow to the right of the
median plane. The larger afferent renal
vein which comes from the external iliac
is joined by the *ischiatic vein* (Figs. 3.25–
3.27) and conveys all of its blood through
the middle lobe of the kidney before it
is returned to the common iliac vein by
way of the efferent renal vein.

The *communicating vein* (Figs. 3.25,
3.26) is a short trunk, approximately 1
mm in length and situated at the caudal
extremity of the kidney, that forms a
junction between the caudal extremity
of the caudal mesenteric vein and the
cranial extremity of the paired hypogastric (internal iliac) veins and the origin

of the afferent renal vein to the caudal
lobe of the kidney.

The *hypogastric vein (internal iliac)*
(Figs. 3.25–3.27) is short and corresponds
closely to the internal iliac artery (Figs.
3.25–3.27) in that it is only 2–3 mm long.
It drains the area of the vent and the
tail region supplied by the artery of the
same name. The *caudal hemorrhoidal*
and the cutaneous veins join the *perineal vein* (Fig. 3.28) in the region of
the 3rd or 4th coccygeal vertebra. After
a short cranial course the perineal joins
the *pudendal vein* (internal pudic) (Figs.
3.25, 3.28) to form the hypogastric (internal iliac) vein which continues craniad to enter the communicating vein.
In the adult female the caudal oviducal
vein draining the vagina enters the hypogastric (internal iliac) vein.

The *caudal mesenteric vein* (coccygeomesenteric) (Figs. 3.25–3.28) drains
blood from the terminal portion of the
intestinal tract toward the kidney. Along

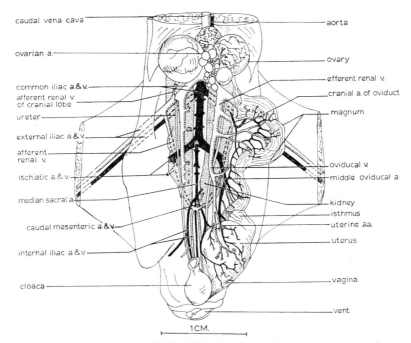

FIG. 3.27—Renal portal system of the female, ventral view.

its course ventral to the colon it receives small efferent tributaries, and near the cranial portion of the cloaca it receives the small *cranial hemorrhoidal vein*. It continues caudad to enter the communicating vein.

The afferent vessels to the three lobes of the kidney are the afferent renal of the cranial lobe from the common iliac, the afferent renal to the middle and caudal lobes from the external iliac, and the afferent renal to the middle and caudal lobes from the communicating vein.

The system of *afferent renal veins* (Figs. 3.26–3.28) is somewhat complicated, since blood enters the kidney from both ends and the middle. The middle and caudal lobes are supplied by an afferent vein which arises from the external iliac. This afferent renal vein courses caudad along the ventrolateral border of the middle lobe for 2–3 mm and then turns dorsad into the parenchyma and supplies the interlobular

veins. The caudal lobe is supplied by an afferent renal vein which is derived from a communicating vein at the caudal extremity of the kidney. It courses dorsolaterad in the parenchyma and continues craniad to anastomose with the termination of the afferent vein from the external iliac. It also receives the ischiatic vein ventral to the ischiatic artery and dorsal to the ischiatic nerve. An afferent vein to the cranial lobe of the kidney arises from the common iliac approximately 1 mm from the origin of the afferent vein to the middle lobe. It courses craniodorsad into the substance of the cranial lobe as the interlobular afferent vein.

In the adult female, five to seven *oviducal veins* (Fig. 3.27) may be considered as afferents to the renal portal system. The cranial oviducal vein is the largest and is situated near the middle lobe of the kidney. Its tributaries closely follow the arterial system and

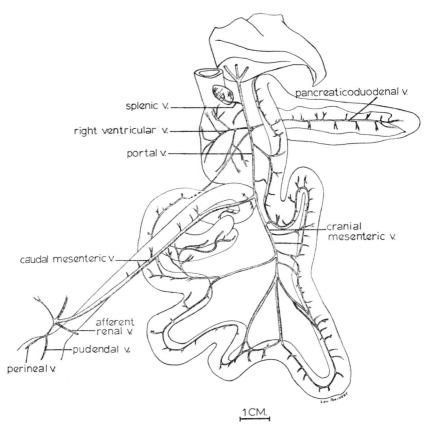

splenic v.

right ventricular v.

portal v.

pancreaticoduodenal v.

cranial mesenteric v.

caudal mesenteric v.

afferent renal v.

pudendal v.

perineal v.

1 CM.

FIG. 3.28—Veins of the abdominal digestive tract, hepatic portal system.

drain blood principally from the magnum and the isthmus. The middle oviducal vein at the caudal extremity of the kidney is also quite large and conveys blood principally from the uterus to the renal portal system. The remaining smaller three to five vessels are inconstant as to position but also assist in supplying blood to the large afferent renal portal vein. Veins from the infundibular portion of the oviduct and the ovary do not enter the renal portal system but empty into the vena cava or left common iliac vein.

The efferent vessels from the three lobes of the kidney are the efferent renal vein from the cranial lobe to the common iliac and the efferent renal vein from the middle and caudal lobes to the common iliac.

Two *efferent renal veins* (Figs. 3.26, 3.27) drain blood from the kidney to the common iliac veins. The cranial lobe is drained by a rather small efferent renal vein that has its origin from the numerous interlobular veins. A much larger efferent renal vein courses through the ventromedial areas of the middle and caudal lobes. It is related dorsomedially to the ductus deferens and the ureter. Along its course it receives blood from the interlobular veins. Both the larger and the smaller efferent renal veins enter the common iliac vein.

Hepatic Portal System

The hepatic portal system (Fig. 3.28) and its tributaries drain the blood carried to the viscera via the celiac artery and the cranial mesenteric artery. It is formed mainly by the confluence of the intestinal veins and the *cranial mesenteric vein,* which is a satellite of the corresponding artery. This confluence takes place in an area ventral to the postcava near the caudal border of the right lobe of the liver and to the right of the cranial portion of the cecum. From this point the *portal vein* (Fig. 3.28) passes forward toward the hilus of the liver, related between the cranial portion of the jejunum on the right side and the ventriculus and spleen on the left side. Before it reaches the liver it receives two to three jejunal tributaries, the *splenic vein* (Fig. 3.28) and the *pancreaticoduodenal vein* (Fig. 3.28). The latter receives branches from the pancreas, duodenum, right ventricular region, and the area supplied by the middle ileocecal artery. The portal vein then enters the right lobe of the liver by way of the portal fissure. Here it divides into branches which ramify in the parenchyma of the gland. From the lobules the blood passes into the hepatic vein which channels the blood to the postcava. The veins from the left and the ventral ventricular and caudoventral proventricular regions converge at the cranial border of the ventriculus to enter the left lobe of the liver.

LYMPHATIC SYSTEM

In coturnix the lymphatic system (Fig. 3.29) appears not to have developed to a stage comparable to that of mammals. No lymph nodes with a capsule, trabeculae, or afferent lymphatics are found. The system may be considered to be more like lymphatic infiltrations,

subepithelial aggregations of lymphatics, and nodules that are well developed in the digestive and respiratory tracts. They appear very much as do the tonsils and Peyer's patches of mammals. Condensed infiltrations and nodules also appear in the thymus, spleen, and bursa of Fabricius. Germinal and reaction centers are seen in the nodular developments, but in no instance have organized nodular efferent and afferent lymphatics been found. The blind-end lymphatic capillaries appear very much as they do in mammals and converge to form larger vessels and ducts.

A search for the so-called "lymphat-

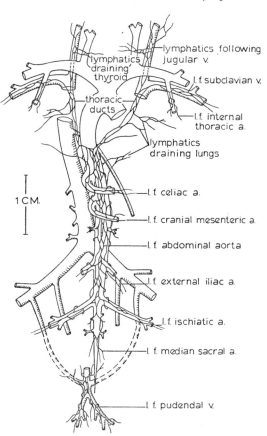

FIG. 3.29—*Lymphatics of the abdomen and thorax, ventral view.*

ic heart" in day-old coturnix revealed nothing more than dilatations of the lymphatic vessels, forming a plexus in the region of the middle sacral artery at the junction of the sacral and coccygeal regions. With the type of injection method used, no lymphatic vessels or plexuses were found other than those which followed the veins of the head and neck, appendages, and the main arteries of the trunk. The arrangement of these lymphatic vessels about the arteries and veins was always in the form of a well-anastomosed plexus around the vessel. The names of the lymphatics as they appear in the legend of the drawing will thus be listed by the names of the arteries or veins which they accompany. Due to the variations of the plexuses that are formed no description will be attempted for any but the larger trunks or ducts. The right and left thoracic ducts, one on either side of the vertebral column, run toward the neck and terminate by entering the left cranial vena cava, rather than the right jugular as is frequently reported in other birds.

The *lymphatics of the head and neck* principally follow the course of the jugular vein. They are usually two in number on each side, one dorsal and the other ventral to the jugular vein. The more condensed lymphatic plexuses are found in those areas of the head and neck where one would normally find lymph nodes in mammals, for example, in the mandibular spaces and between the esophagus and larynx. The main lymphatics from the head and neck pass through the thoracic inlet and join the jugular veins just rostral to the subclavian-jugular junction.

The *lymphatics of the pectoral region and limb* may well be considered as a single group. Those veins which are followed by the main trunks in the forearm and manus are the tributaries to the median, ulnar, and radial veins—in the upper region of the forearm and arm the median, axillary, deep brachial, and brachial veins; in the region of the shoulder and breast the cranial external thoracic, caudal external thoracic, cutaneous abdominal, internal thoracic, axillary, and subclavian veins.

The *lymphatics of the pelvic limb* begin in company with the digital veins which traverse either side of the digital bones and, upon reaching the metatarsus, convey their lymph to the tributaries of the dorsal and plantar metatarsal veins and the dorsal and medial pedal veins of the metatarsal region. Lymphatics of the leg region are satellites of the popliteal and cranial and caudal tibial veins. Between the heads of the gastrocnemius muscle there is a noticeable thickening of the lymphatic plexus that may be suggestive of the position of the popliteal lymph nodes in mammals. In the region of the thigh the lymphatics follow the course of the tributaries of the femoral, circumflex femoral, and caudal femoral veins. In addition to the femoral tributaries some of the lymphatics of the thigh follow the course of the ischiatic vein. The lymphatic tributaries arise in the external and internal obturator, gemellus, and adductor muscles and pass through the ischiatic foramen to the pelvis, where they join the tributaries to the aortic plexuses at the level of the 9th or 10th synsacral vertebra.

The *lymphatics of the abdomen and thorax* (Fig. 3.29) follow the aorta, receiving drainage from the plexuses along the blood vessels as they ascend. About the level of the heart they separate into right and left thoracic ducts, which empty into the left cranial vena cava.

HEMATOLOGY: THE BLOOD AS A TISSUE

The embryonic connective tissue, the mesenchyme, gives rise to the blood,

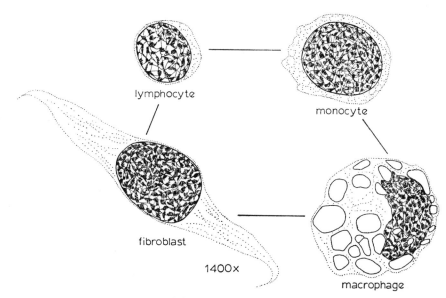

FIG. 3.30—Nongranular leucocytes and their differentiation.

the blood vessels, and the various types of connective tissue. Blood and lymph may be considered a type of connective tissue, since, like other types, it is characterized by an abundance of the intercellular material, which in this case is a fluid. The other types of connective tissue—bone, cartilage, and connective tissue proper—are characterized by intercellular material which ranges from a solid in bone to a semisolid in cartilage or to that with an abundance of fibers, as found in connective tissue proper. In blood the liquid fraction of the tissue is known as blood plasma. The cells and solid substances are known as the formed elements. Blood plasma minus the fibrin is known as blood serum. The cellular elements of the blood of coturnix are the erythrocytes (rubricytes or red corpuscles) and the leucocytes (white blood cells) which are divided into the nongranular leucocytes (the lymphocytes and monocytes) (Fig. 3.30) or the granular leucocytes (the eosinophils, basophils, and heterophils) (Fig. 3.31). In

the bird true thrombocytes replace the blood platelets of mammals.

Probably one of the most confusing situations is brought about by the fact that the normal peripheral blood of birds is not only made up of the mature elements but also includes most of the developmental forms which are released as immature cells to the circulating blood. An attempt, therefore, will not be made to illustrate all the developmental stages of a specific cell, but rather to illustrate a differential picture of the mature forms and those most common developmental forms, as they present themselves in the peripheral circulating blood. The morphology of the mature formed elements revealed the differential characteristics discussed below.

A normal mature erythrocyte of coturnix conforms very favorably with the structure of the erythrocyte of the domestic fowl as reported by Lucas and Jamroz (1961). The nucleated mature cell is generally found to be convex in

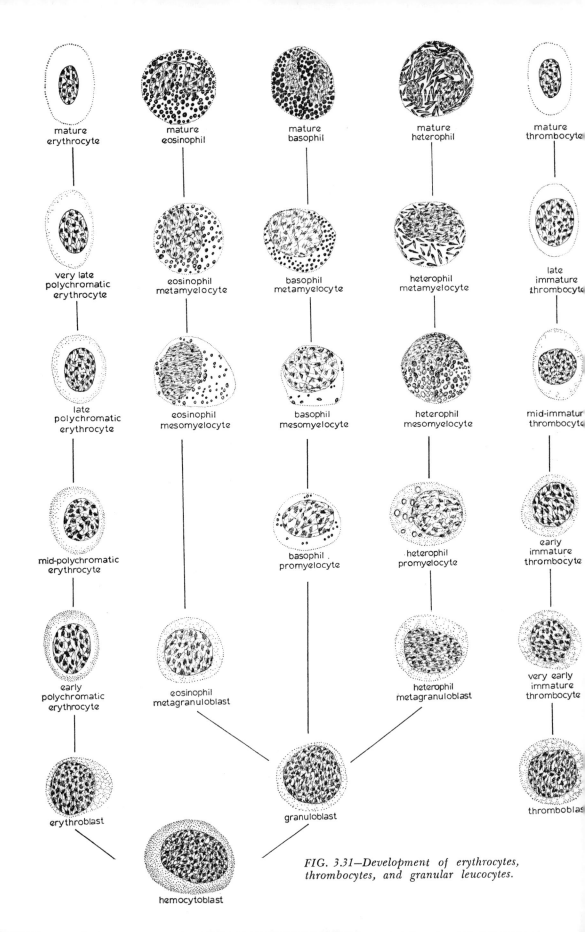

mature
erythrocyte

mature
eosinophil

mature
basophil

mature
heterophil

mature
thrombocyte

very late
polychromatic
erythrocyte

eosinophil
metamyelocyte

basophil
metamyelocyte

heterophil
metamyelocyte

late
immature
thrombocyte

late
polychromatic
erythrocyte

eosinophil
mesomyelocyte

basophil
mesomyelocyte

heterophil
mesomyelocyte

mid-immature
thrombocyte

mid-polychromatic
erythrocyte

basophil
promyelocyte

heterophil
promyelocyte

early
immature
thrombocyte

early
polychromatic
erythrocyte

eosinophil
metagranuloblast

heterophil
metagranuloblast

very early
immature
thrombocyte

erythroblast

granuloblast

thromboblast

hemocytoblast

FIG. 3.31—Development of erythrocytes,
thrombocytes, and granular leucocytes.

length and breadth, but it is subject to many deviations from its regular outline because of its extreme softness and flexibility. The slightest mechanical influence distorts it. If the osmotic pressure of the plasma is increased, the erythrocyte gives up water to the plasma and becomes irregular in outline, or crenated. If the osmotic pressure of the plasma is decreased, water is absorbed and the cell membrane ruptures, thus releasing the hemoglobin. The blood in which the hemoglobin has been released to the plasma is said to be hemolyzed. The marked tendency of the mammalian erythrocytes to adhere to one another in rouleaux formation is not found in birds. Agglutination of erythrocytes, as it occurs in mammals, does occur. The recognition of artifacts and atypical cells is an art that requires the ability to differentiate such things as cytoplasmic granules superimposed over the nucleus, the presence of stain or dirt granules, and false vacuolization. The nucleus of the erythrocyte stains intensely and presents a well-defined nuclear membrane, beneath which chromatin granules are suspended in a chromatin reticulum. The cytoplasm adjacent to the nucleus does not stain as intensely as that just beneath the cell membrane. This characteristic is not apparent in erythrocytes stained in fixed tissue where smears have not been made.

Lucas and Jamroz (1961) report that the formation of erythrocytes of birds parallels the process of mammals, in that the first yolk-sac generation of embryonic erythrocytes is primarily in round form, whereas the latter embryonic forms are ellipsoidal. The development of the hemopoietic areas also parallels that of mammals, in that the first embryonic erythrocytes are formed in the blood islands of the yolk sac. These are successively followed by the vascular endothelium, liver, spleen, and finally the red bone marrow.

According to Welty (1962) the number of corpuscles per cu mm of blood of the different avian species varies from 1.5–6.6 million, the number of erythrocytes for the 100-gm quail being 5 million. Male birds have a higher erythrocyte count than do females. Other factors such as the time of day, season of the year, and altitude will have a varying effect on the number. Avian blood generally has a slightly lower hemoglobin content than does the blood of mammals. Chicken erythrocytes are thought to remain alive only for about 20 days as compared to 28–100 days in mammals, according to Sturkie (1965). As in mammals, mature erythrocytes are formed mainly in the red bone marrow, but surprisingly the main areas of leucocyte hemopoiesis are in the spleen and ceca in the adult. Sturkie (1965) lists the erythrocyte count of a number of investigations of both domestic and wild birds. The figure of 3.4 million per cu mm for the quail corresponds more closely to the count made on the Auburn strain of coturnix. The corpuscular volume (hematocrit) of the strain was found to be 38 with no sex difference. Reticulocytes present a stage of red-cell maturation between the normoblast and the mature red cell. Lucas (1959) discussed the nomenclature applied to cells of this series in avian and mammalian blood, and has proposed terminology applicable to all vertebrates.[1] See Table 3.1.

Blood platelets of mammals having their origin from the fragmentation of the megakaryocytes of the lungs and bone marrow are not found in avian blood. Lucas and Jamroz (1961) describe the thrombocytic hemopoiesis

---

[1] P. D. Sturkie, *Avian Physiology* (Ithaca, New York: Comstock Publishing Co., 1965), p. 8.

TABLE 3.1

AVIAN	MAMMALIAN	PROPOSED VERTEBRATE TERMINOLOGY
Early erythroblast	Rubriblast	Early rubriblast
Late erythroblast	Prorubricyte	Late rubriblast
Early polychromatic erythrocyte	Rubricyte	Prorubricyte
Mid-polychromatic erythrocyte	Metarubricyte	Mesorubricyte
Late polychromatic erythrocyte		Metarubricyte
Reticulocyte	Reticulocyte	Reticulocyte
Mature erythrocyte	Erythrocyte	Erythrocyte

from the blastic cells to the mononucleated thromboblast of the bone marrow. Blount (1939) reports that they belong to the erythrocyte series and that all of the stages of the erythrocyte-thrombocyte hemopoiesis can be demonstrated from smears of avian bone marrow. Thrombocytes of coturnix are characterized by their clear cytoplasm in which a deeply staining round nucleus is centrally located. The chromatin granules are arranged in large clumped masses surrounded by the parachromatin. The most characteristic feature is the rather constant occurrence of one or more bright-red–staining granules at the poles of the cell. Their size and shape vary considerably. Most of them, however, are round or oval and approximately two-thirds the size of the neighboring erythrocytes. According to Sturkie (1965) one of the important steps in clotting of avian blood is the transformation of the soluble protein fibrinogen into the insoluble fibrin by the activity of thrombin. Thrombin is a protein derived from prothrombin by the proteolitic breakdown of the prothrombin molecules; and the reaction is catalyzed by thromboplastin, calcium ions, and several accessory factors. One probable source of thromboplastin is from the thrombocytes or platelets.

The differential characteristics of the leucocytes, as described by Olson (1937), of the blood of the fowl were checked for conformity with the cells of coturnix; those features which were applicable to coturnix blood are listed. The heterophil leucocytes possess cytoplasmic granules which are not neutral staining, but are acid in reaction. The cells are usually round and have a diameter of about 10–15μ. Brilliant red rod- or spindle-shaped granules in a colorless cytoplasm characterize the cell. The nucleus is polymorphic and will present various numbers of lobules according to the age of the cell. The eosinophils of coturnix are almost as large as the average heterophil. The cytoplasmic granules are spherical and most of them are relatively large and compact in the mature cell. Their dull red color as compared to the brilliant red color of the heterophil may be used as a differential characteristic of the eosinophil when stained with Wright's stain. The cytoplasm stains darker than that of the basophil or the heterophil and is of a grey-blue shade. The nucleus stains a deep blue; and the lobes, of which there are rarely more than two, are not so widely separated as they appear in the heterophil. The percentage of eosinophils in the leucocytes of coturnix, as well as in most birds, is quite low; therefore, one should be cautious in naming a questionable cell as an eosinophil. The basophil is best characterized by its clear cytoplasm in which the deep blue granules are suspended. The number, size, and plan of distribution of the granules vary a great deal from cell to cell. The spherical or oval nucleus stains a much lighter blue than do the cytoplasmic granules.

The size and shape of avian lymphocytes vary considerably and, therefore, the classification of them into small, medium-sized, and large types is very difficult. Lucas and Jamroz (1961) state that the large ones are for the most part hemocytoblasts and, therefore, only the small- and medium-sized ones should be recognized. Lymphocytes as a type are the most numerous of the avian leucocytes in the peripheral blood. They have their origin chiefly from the germinal centers of the widely distributed lymphatic nodules of the body. They are ameboid and, therefore, may be found as infiltrations of transient proliferating nodules throughout the body. Their close linkage to other connective tissue cells is exemplified by their inherent developmental potentialities to act as stem cells for the production of many of the types of connective tissue cells. Lympho-

cytes from the circulating blood of coturnix reveal a wide range of shapes and sizes. The cytoplasm of the smaller cell is weakly basophilic and is usually confined to one side of the nucleus, which may be round or slightly indented. In the larger lymphocytes the cytoplasm may contain a few azurophilic granules, particularly in the area of the nuclear indentation.

Generally monocytes are large cells with relatively more cytoplasm than the large lymphocytes. The nucleus is larger and more irregular than in the lymphocyte. The nuclear architecture is usually of a more delicate composition than that of the lymphocyte and appears in the form of strands rather than thick masses. The cytoplasm usually stains lighter than the cytoplasm of the lymphocytes. There is some evidence that monocytes under the proper stimulus may transform into ameboid phagocytic inflammatory elements. The monocyte is probably capable of further differentiation into a fibroblast.

CHAPTER FOUR

Myology

FOR the sake of brevity the description of the myology of coturnix will be presented in outline form and will include only the skeletal muscles and accessory structures that are large enough to be seen with the unaided eye.

An attempt has been made to include those muscles which present the specific characteristics of configuration of the family of coturnix and which are most often described in avian myology. The nomenclature used is considered to be current, meaningful, and most applicable to the purpose for which the book was written. The terminology used by present-day students of avian myology tends to be characteristic of the educational background of the individual and his opinion of of how names of muscles should be made. Some names exemplify the form, structure, function, or position of the muscle; others perpetuate the nomenclature of the bird's reptilian ancestors.

Smooth and cardiac muscle structures will be described in the section on splanchnology and angiology.

115

CUTANEOUS MUSCLES

The cutaneous muscles of coturnix are a thin, incomplete layer of striated muscle fibers developed in the superficial fascia. Because of the incomplete development it is not possible to name and to give the anatomical locations or action of all the cutaneous muscles.

Cutaneous Colli Lateralis

LOCATION: From the lateral region of the skull to the lateral cervical region.

ORIGIN: Supraorbital process and the area over the petrous temporal bone and the caudal half of the otic membrane.

INSERTION: Dorsal, lateral, and ventral cervical pterylae.

ACTION: Raises or erects the feathers of the cervical pterylae.

RELATIONS: Superficially the dermis; deeply the skull and the muscles and viscera of the head and neck.

BLOOD SUPPLY: Branches of the vertebral artery.

NERVE SUPPLY: Cervical spinal nerves, facial nerve.

Cutaneous Nuchalis

LOCATION: Composed of four to six fasciculi in the center of the nuchal area of the neck.

ORIGIN: Muscular fasciculi originate from the transverse processes of the 4th to the 10th cervical vertebrae.

INSERTION: Dorsal cervical pterylae.

ACTION: Erects the feathers of the nuchal area of the neck.

RELATIONS: Superficially the dermis of the cervical skin; deeply the dorsal and lateral muscles of the neck.

BLOOD SUPPLY: Vertebral and deep cervical artery.

NERVE SUPPLY: Dorsal branches of the cervical spinal nerves.

Cutaneous Cleidodorsalis

LOCATION: From the distal extremity of the clavicle transversely to the dorsal spinal pterylae.

ORIGIN: Craniomedial surface of the distal extremity of the clavicle.

INSERTION: Dorsal spinal pterylae.

ACTION: Erects the feathers of the dorsal spinal pterylae.

RELATIONS: Superficially the skin, except near the midline where the cutaneous spinalis dorsalis runs dorsad; deeply the muscles of the humerus, scapula, and spine.

BLOOD SUPPLY: Dorsal and deep cervical arteries.

NERVE SUPPLY: Dorsal branches of the cervical and thoracic spinal nerves.

Cutaneous Aucheniatria (Fig. 4.4)

LOCATION: Ventral region of the neck below the ear.

ORIGIN: Ventrolateral area of the temporal bone, caudal to the external acoustic meatus.

INSERTION: Ventral cervical pterylae and the median raphe.

ACTION: Tenses the skin and elevates the feathers of the mandible and throat.

RELATIONS: Superficially the skin; deeply the lateral and ventral muscles and viscera of the region of the throat.

BLOOD SUPPLY: Occipital and common carotid arteries.

NERVE SUPPLY: Ventral branches of cervical spinal nerves 1, 2, and 3.

Cutaneous Trunciventralis

LOCATION: In the ventrolateral region of the abdomen fibers run downward and forward, an extensive muscle.

ORIGIN: Pubic fascia, ventral to the pubis and acetabulum.

INSERTION: Subcutis of the ventrolateral abdominal area.

ACTION: Erects the feathers of the ventrolateral pterylae of the abdomen.
RELATIONS: Superficially the skin; deeply the external oblique muscle.
BLOOD SUPPLY: Cutaneous branch of the caudal gluteal artery.
NERVE SUPPLY: Caudal gluteal nerve.

Cutaneous Cleidoventralis

LOCATION: Ventrolateral region of the breast.
ORIGIN: Ventral border of the hypocleidium and the sternoclavicular ligament.
INSERTION: Craniomedial surface of the shoulder joint and the caudal region of the ventral cervical pterylae.

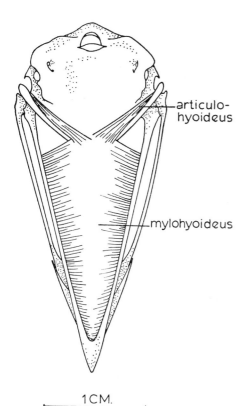

1 CM.

FIG. 4.1—Hyoid muscles, superficial dissection.

ACTION: Erects the feathers in the cervical pterylae.
RELATIONS: Superficially the skin; deeply the pectoral muscles, crop, and trachea.
BLOOD SUPPLY: Ventral cervical artery.
NERVE SUPPLY: Ventral branches of the cervical spinal nerves.

Metapatagialis

LOCATION: Dorsolateral region of the thorax below the arm.
ORIGIN: Transverse processes of the 5th to 7th thoracic spines.
INSERTION: Humeral and caudal patagiae.
ACTION: Immobilizes the humeral pterylae and tenses the caudal patagium.
RELATIONS: Superficially the skin; deeply the muscles of the shoulder girdle and back.
BLOOD SUPPLY: Costocervical and intercostal arteries.
NERVE SUPPLY: Dorsal branches of the thoracic spinal nerves.

MUSCLES OF THE HEAD

Mylohyoideus (Fig. 4.1)

LOCATION: In the mandibular space, forming a suspensory apparatus for the tongue and glottis.
ORIGIN: The medial surface of the rami of the mandible.
INSERTION: A median fibrous raphe extending from the body of the mandible to the hyoid bone.
ACTION: Elevates or raises the floor of the mouth, the hyoid bones, and the tongue.
RELATIONS: Superficially the skin and fascia; deeply the hyoid apparatus and the hyoideus transversus.
BLOOD SUPPLY: Lingual artery, external maxillary artery.
NERVE SUPPLY: Mylohyoid branch of the mandibular nerve.

Hyomandibularis (Fig. 4.2)
(Stylohyoideus)

LOCATION: In the intermandibular region between the rostral cornu of the hyoid and the mandible.

ORIGIN: Middle portion of the larger rostral cornu of the hyoid.

INSERTION: Caudal one-fourth of the lateral surface of the mandible and the rostral portion of the medial surface of the mandible.

ACTION: Moves the tongue and hyoid rostrally; also pulls the cornu laterally.

RELATIONS: Superficially the skin and fascia and the sublingual salivary gland, the mylohyoideus, and articulohyoideus muscles; deeply the oral mucosa and the pharynx.

BLOOD SUPPLY: Lingual, hyoid, and external maxillary arteries.

NERVE SUPPLY: Facial nerve.

Hyoideus Transversus (Fig. 4.2)

LOCATION: A thin, triangular muscle lying in the intermandibular region ventral to the larynx.

ORIGIN: Large cornu of the hyoid bone at its most rostral portion.

INSERTION: Median raphe and the spur process of copula 2.

ACTION: Elevates the tongue.

RELATIONS: Superficially the skin and fascia; deeply the oral mucosa and pharynx.

BLOOD SUPPLY: Lingual artery.

NERVE SUPPLY: Facial and hypoglossal nerves.

Styloentoglossum (Fig. 4.2)

LOCATION: In the intermandibular region between the cornu of the hyoid and the mandible.

ORIGIN: Lateral side of the terminal portion of the rostral cornu.

INSERTION: By a very thin tendon on the caudoventral portion of the entoglossum.

ACTION: Retracts the tongue caudally and dorsally.

RELATIONS: Superficially the hyomandibularis and mylohyoideus muscles; deeply the larynx and the oral mucosa.

BLOOD SUPPLY: Lingual artery.

NERVE SUPPLY: Hypoglossal nerve.

Copuloentoglossum (Fig. 4.2)

LOCATION: A very short, thin muscle in the intermandibular area adjacent to copula 1.

ORIGIN: Ventrolateral surface of the caudal extremity of copula 1.

INSERTION: Caudoventral surface of the entoglossum.

ACTION: Retracts the tongue caudally and laterally.

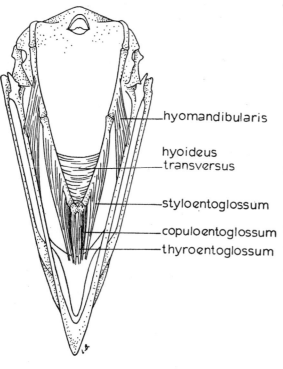

hyomandibularis

hyoideus transversus

styloentoglossum

copuloentoglossum

thyroentoglossum

1 CM.

FIG. 4.2—Hyoid muscles, deep dissection.

RELATIONS: Superficially the sublingual salivary gland and the mylohyoideus muscle; deeply copula 1 and the hyomandibularis muscle.

BLOOD SUPPLY: Lingual artery.

NERVE SUPPLY: Hypoglossal nerve.

Thyroentoglossum (Fig. 4.2)

LOCATION: In the intermandibular region adjacent dorsally to the cranial one-fourth of the rostral cornu and copula 1.

ORIGIN: Lateral cartilage of the larynx and from tendinous fibers of the sternothyroideus muscle.

INSERTION: Caudodorsal surface of the entoglossum.

ACTION: Draws the tongue caudally on the larynx and mandible.

RELATIONS: Superficially the cranial portion of the rostral cornu, copula 1, and the styloentoglossum and hyomandibularis muscles; deeply the oral mucosa and the lingual glands.

BLOOD SUPPLY: Lingual artery.

NERVE SUPPLY: Hypoglossal nerve.

Occipitomandibularis (Fig. 4.3)

LOCATION: A thin, wide, curved muscle in the gutteral region caudal to the external acoustic process.

ORIGIN: External occipital crest, the frontal fascia, and the base of the temporal bones.

INSERTION: Midventral surface of the caudal (angular) process of the mandible.

ACTION: Raises the caudal end of the mandible, thereby assisting in the opening of the oral aperture.

RELATIONS: Superficially the skin and fascia and the cutaneous aucheniatria; deeply the temporalis muscle.

BLOOD SUPPLY: Occipital, hyoid, and caudal auricular arteries.

NERVE SUPPLY: Facial nerve.

Masseter (Fig. 4.4)
(Buccinator)

LOCATION: This very distinct muscle, with careful dissection, can be divided into a large rostral portion and a smaller caudal portion. It is located in the buccal region just caudal to the supraorbital process. Located in the caudal portion of the rostral part there is a thin tendon that extends the entire length of the muscle.

ORIGIN: Caudal surface of the supraorbital process, the temporal fossa area of the frontal, parietal, and temporal bones.

INSERTION: Lateral surface of the mandible from the cranial edge of the slit

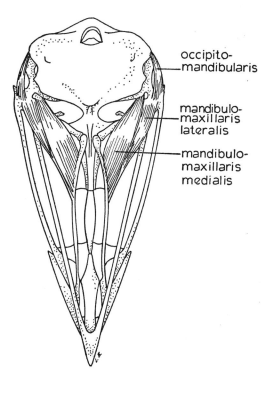

occipito-mandibularis

mandibulo-maxillaris lateralis

mandibulo-maxillaris medialis

1CM.

FIG. 4.3—Superficial muscles of the mandibular articulation, ventral view.

of the mandibular canal caudal to the angular process.

ACTION: Depresses the oral cavity.

RELATIONS: Superficially the frontomandibular ligament and the jugal arch, skin, and fascia; deeply the quadratomandibularis lateralis and medialis muscles and the supraorbitomandibularis muscles.

BLOOD SUPPLY: Cranial auricular, external facial, and inferior alveolar arteries and muscular branches from the rete temporalis.

NERVE SUPPLY: Mandibular nerve.

Temporalis (Fig. 4.4)

LOCATION: This is a wide muscle occupying the caudal portion of the temporal fossa adjacent to the external acoustic process.

ORIGIN: Convex occipitotemporal junction, the otic membrane, and the rounded mastoid process.

INSERTION: Medial and lateral surfaces of the caudal angular process of the mandible and, partially, the medial mandibular process.

ACTION: Enlarges the oral cavity.

RELATIONS: Superficially the occipitomandibularis muscle; deeply the otic membrane, temporal fossa, and the quadratomandibularis muscles.

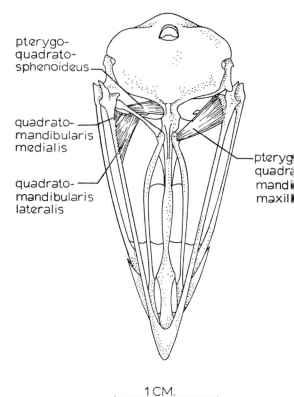

FIG. 4.5—Deep muscles of the mandibular articulation, ventral view.

BLOOD SUPPLY: Occipital, hyoid, and external facial arteries.

NERVE SUPPLY: Facial nerve.

Quadratomandibularis Lateralis (Figs. 4.4, 4.5)

LOCATION: A very short, thin muscle in the temporal region. It is situated caudal to the quadratomandibularis medialis muscle.

ORIGIN: Ventrolateral surface of the short quadrate bone.

INSERTION: Dorsolateral surface of the mandible just medial to the masseter muscle.

ACTION: Closes the oral cavity.

RELATIONS: Superficially the frontomandibular ligament, the masseter

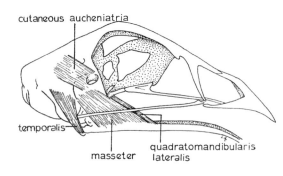

FIG. 4.4—Muscles of the mandibular articulation, lateral view.

muscle, and the jugal arch; deeply the pterygoquadratomandibulomax-illaris and the mandibulomaxillaris muscles.

BLOOD SUPPLY: Inferior alveolar artery.

NERVE SUPPLY: Mandibular nerve.

Quadratomandibularis Medialis (Fig. 4.5)

LOCATION: A short, triangular muscle situated in the dorsolateral region of the roof of the mouth.

ORIGIN: Ventral surface of the quadrate bone.

INSERTION: Dorsomedial surface of the mandible.

ACTION: Depresses or closes the oral cavity.

RELATIONS: Superficially the large masseter muscle; deeply the pharyngeal wall.

BLOOD SUPPLY: Sphenomaxillary artery.

NERVE SUPPLY: Mandibular nerve.

Supraorbitomandibularis (Fig. 4.6)

LOCATION: A very small, indistinct muscle in the buccal region.

ORIGIN: Medial surface of the supra-orbital process.

INSERTION: Caudal portion of the lateral surface of the mandible.

ACTION: Depresses the oral cavity.

RELATIONS: Superficially the rostral portion of the masseter muscle; deeply the orbital membrane and quad-ratomandibularis muscles.

BLOOD SUPPLY: External facial and inferior alveolar arteries and branches from the rete temporalis.

NERVE SUPPLY: Mandibular nerve.

Mandibulomaxillaris Lateralis (Fig. 4.3)

LOCATION: A somewhat rounded, triangular muscle in the oral region medial to the caudal end of the mandible. Fibers run craniomediad.

ORIGIN: Ventromedial surface of the mandible in the angle formed by its body and the medial mandibular process.

INSERTION: By a narrow tendon over the lateral middle portion of the palatine process of the maxilla.

ACTION: Enlarges the oral cavity.

RELATIONS: Ventrally or superficially the hard palate and rostral portion of the pharynx; dorsally or deeply the pterygoquadratomandibulomax-illaris and quadratomandibularis medialis muscles.

BLOOD SUPPLY: Upper internal maxillary and sphenomaxillary arteries.

NERVE SUPPLY: Mandibular nerve.

Mandibulomaxillaris Medialis (Fig. 4.3)

LOCATION: The most distinct muscle in the roof of the mouth region medial to the mandibulomaxillaris lateralis muscle. Its fibers run longitudinally.

ORIGIN: Dorsal extremity of the medial process of the mandible by a strong tendon.

INSERTION: A fleshy and tendinous attachment to the ventrolateral surface of the palatine process of the maxilla.

ACTION: Enlarges the oral cavity.

RELATIONS: Ventrally the hard palate and the cranial portion of the pharynx; deeply the pterygoquad-ratomandibulomaxillaris muscle.

BLOOD SUPPLY: Upper internal maxillary and sphenomaxillary arteries.

NERVE SUPPLY: Mandibular nerve.

Pterygoquadratomandibulomaxillaris (Fig. 4.5)

LOCATION: Situated in the caudal portion of the roof of the mouth, its fibers run for the most part transversely.

ORIGIN: The ventral surface of the entire pterygoid bone, the ventromedial surface of the quadrate bone, and dorsally at an angle formed by the two caudal mandibular processes.

INSERTION: Palatine process of the maxilla just rostral to the articulation of the palatine and pterygoid bones.

ACTION: Enlarges the oral cavity.

RELATIONS: Ventrally the mandibulomaxillaris lateralis and medialis muscles; dorsally the pterygoid and quadrate bones and the pterygoquadratosphenoideus muscle and the orbital membrane.

BLOOD SUPPLY: Upper internal maxillary and palatine arteries.

NERVE SUPPLY: Mandibular nerve.

Pterygoquadratosphenoideus
(Fig. 4.5)

LOCATION: A very small muscle in the dorsal oral region, situated caudoventrally to the eye and the most dorsal of all the muscles of the roof of the mouth.

ORIGIN: Middle of the lateral surface of the sphenoid bone.

INSERTION: Dorsal surface of the pterygoid bone and partially from the ventromedial surface of the quadrate bone.

ACTION: Draws the maxilla medially; aids in swallowing and opening the mouth.

RELATIONS: Superficially or ventrally the pterygoquadratomandibulomaxillaris muscle; deeply or dorsally the orbital membrane and the eye.

BLOOD SUPPLY: The palatine and sphenomaxillary arteries.

NERVE SUPPLY: Mandibular nerve.

MUSCLES OF THE EYE

Orbicularis Palpebrarum
(Fig. 4.6)

LOCATION: A thin, delicate muscle lying in the fat and fascia of the orbit. It forms a slender loop extending from the maxillary and lacrimal bones to surround the palpebral margin.

ORIGIN: From the free or ventral extremity of the lacrimal bone and the rostral extremity of the maxillary bone.

INSERTION: Around the palpebral margins of the upper and lower eyelids.

ACTION: Aids in closing the palpebral fissure and rotating the eye forward.

RELATIONS: Superficially the skin; deeply the maxillary and lacrimal bones and the palpebral conjunctiva.

BLOOD SUPPLY: The ophthalmic artery and branches from the rete temporalis.

NERVE SUPPLY: Ophthalmic nerve.

Levator Palpebrarum Dorsalis
(Fig. 4.6)

LOCATION: A wide, thin muscle lying along the dorsal roof of the orbit. The fibers are mixed with fat and fascia and are hard to distinguish. The bird opens and closes the eye with the lower eyelid; therefore, this muscle is of little use and is not as well developed as the depressor palpebrarum ventralis muscle of the lower eyelid.

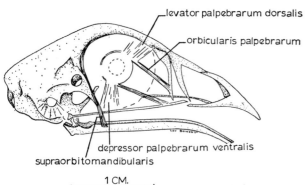

levator palpebrarum dorsalis

orbicularis palpebrarum

depressor palpebrarum ventralis
supraorbitomandibularis

1 CM.

FIG. 4.6—Muscles of the orbital cavity.

ORIGIN: Along a sagittal line near the middle of the orbital surface of the frontal bone.

INSERTION: Upper eyelid near the margin of the orbicularis palpebrarum.

ACTION: Elevates the upper eyelid.

RELATIONS: Superficially the orbital surface of the frontal bone, skin and periorbita; deeply the palpebral conjunctiva, the dorsal oblique and pyramidalis oculi muscles, and the sclera.

BLOOD SUPPLY: Dorsal palpebral artery and a small branch from the ethmoidal arteries.

NERVE SUPPLY: Ophthalmic nerve.

Depressor Palpebrarum Ventralis (Fig. 4.6)

LOCATION: This is the most distinct muscle of the eyelid. It is wide and thin, lying in the caudoventral region.

ORIGIN: Interorbital septum just ventral and rostral to the optic foramen.

INSERTION: Near the margin of the lower eyelid.

ACTION: Depresses or opens the lower eyelid.

RELATIONS: Superficially the skin and periorbita; deeply the palpebral conjunctiva, the ventral oblique muscle, the ventral rectus muscle, and the sclera.

BLOOD SUPPLY: Infraorbital artery.

NERVE SUPPLY: Ophthalmic nerve.

Dorsal Oblique (Fig. 4.7) (Obliquus Oculi Dorsalis)

LOCATION: A small, thin, fan-shaped muscle lying obliquely across the sclera between the insertions of the dorsal rectus and medial rectus muscles.

ORIGIN: From the dorsolateral border of the interorbital plate.

INSERTION: On the dorsal surface of the sclera between the insertions of the dorsal rectus and medial rectus muscles.

ACTION: Opposed to that of the ventral oblique muscle in that it rotates the eye rostrally about a longitudinal axis.

RELATIONS: Superficially the skin and periorbita and the frontal bone; deeply the sclera and quadratus oculi muscle.

BLOOD SUPPLY: Supraorbital artery and a branch from the ethmoidal artery.

NERVE SUPPLY: Trochlear nerve.

Ventral Oblique (Fig. 4.7) (Obliquus Oculi Ventralis)

LOCATION: A small, flat muscle located obliquely across the ventromedial aspect of the sclera between the insertions of the medial rectus and ventral rectus muscles.

ORIGIN: Dorsorostral region of the interorbital plate ventral and rostral to the attachment of the dorsal oblique muscle.

INSERTION: On the sclera between the insertions of the medial rectus and ventral rectus muscles.

ACTION: Rotates the eye caudally about a longitudinal axis and opposes the action of the dorsal oblique muscle.

RELATIONS: Superficially the periorbita, skin, and interorbital plate; deeply the pyramidalis oculi muscle and the sclera.

BLOOD SUPPLY: Ophthalmic artery and branches from the rete temporalis.

NERVE SUPPLY: Oculomotor nerve.

Dorsal Rectus (Fig. 4.7) (Rectus Oculi Dorsalis)

LOCATION: The smallest of the straight muscles, overlying the dorsal border of the quadratus oculi muscle.

ORIGIN: Bone forming the dorsocaudal border of the optic foramen.

INSERTION: On the dorsal region of the

sclera just lateral to the insertion of the quadratus oculi muscle.

ACTION: Rotates the eye about a transverse axis, moving the eye upward.

RELATIONS: Superficially the periorbita, levator palpebrarum dorsalis muscle, and the frontal bone; deeply the quadratus oculi and the sclera.

BLOOD SUPPLY: Supraorbital ophthalmic arteries and branches from the ethmoidal arteries.

NERVE SUPPLY: Oculomotor nerve.

Ventral Rectus (Fig. 4.7)
(Rectus Oculi Ventralis)

LOCATION: This muscle is a little larger than the dorsal rectus and is located in the ventral region of the orbit.

ORIGIN: Sphenoid bone along the ventrolateral border of the optic foramen.

INSERTION: This muscle passes over the ventrolateral edge of the pyramidalis oculi muscle and inserts on the sclera.

ACTION: Opposes that of the dorsal rectus; it rotates the eye downward about a transverse axis.

RELATIONS: Superficially the depressor palpebrarum oculi muscles and the periorbita; deeply the pyramidalis oculi muscle and the sclera.

BLOOD SUPPLY: Ophthalmic artery and branches of the rete temporalis.

NERVE SUPPLY: Oculomotor nerve.

Lateral Rectus (Fig. 4.7)
(Rectus Oculi Lateralis)

LOCATION: A bandlike muscle resembling the ventral rectus, lying on the sclera at about the same plane as the lateral canthus.

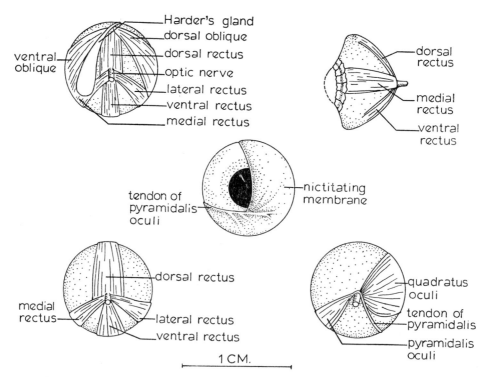

FIG. 4.7—Muscles of the eyeball.

ORIGIN: Lateral border of the optic foramen.

INSERTION: Lateral surface of the sclera.

ACTION: Rotates the eyeball about a vertical axis, pulling the eye caudally.

RELATIONS: Superficially the periorbita and frontal bone; deeply the optic nerve, the sclera, and the tendon of the pyramidalis oculi muscle.

BLOOD SUPPLY: Ophthalmic artery and branches of the stapedial and dorsal palpebral arteries.

NERVE SUPPLY: Abducens nerve.

Medial Rectus (Fig. 4.7)
(Rectus Oculi Medialis)

LOCATION: The widest of the rectus muscles, located on the medial aspect of the sclera.

ORIGIN: Craniodorsal border of the optic foramen.

INSERTION: Sclera, rostromedially.

ACTION: Rotates the eye inward about its vertical axis.

RELATIONS: Superficially the periorbital and interorbital plate; deeply the pyramidalis oculi muscle and the sclera.

BLOOD SUPPLY: Ophthalmic artery and branches of the stapedial artery.

NERVE SUPPLY: Oculomotor nerve.

Quadratus Oculi (Fig. 4.7)

LOCATION: A wide, fan-shaped muscle that widens as it passes forward on the dorsal surface of the sclera. This muscle is very thin and is considerably lighter in color than the rectus muscles.

ORIGIN: Dorsocaudal one-fourth of the sclera.

INSERTION: Dorsal aspect of the sclera near the optic nerve, where its fibers form a sling through which the tendon of the pyramidalis oculi muscle passes. The sling formed by this muscle tends to hold the tendon

away from the optic nerve, and in addition assists the pyramidalis oculi muscle in its action.

ACTION: Aids the pyramidalis oculi in drawing the nictitating membrane over the eye.

RELATIONS: Superficially the dorsal rectus and dorsal oblique muscles and the periorbita; deeply the sclera.

BLOOD SUPPLY: Supraorbital artery.

NERVE SUPPLY: Oculomotor nerve.

Pyramidalis Oculi (Fig. 4.7)

LOCATION: A thin, fan-shaped muscle, smaller than the quadratus oculi, lying on the ventromedial aspect of the sclera deep to the ventral oblique muscle. Its tendon passes dorsally over the optic nerve through the sling formed by the quadratus oculi. After passing through this sling, the tendon runs ventrolaterad and around to the palpebral surface of the sclera, where it inserts into the lower portion of the nictitating membrane, or third eyelid.

ORIGIN: Ventromedial region of the sclera.

INSERTION: By a long tendon to the nictitating membrane.

ACTION: Pulls the nictitating membrane over the eye; rotates the eye rostrally.

RELATIONS: Superficially the ventral oblique, ventral rectus, and medial rectus muscles; deeply the sclera and the deep conjunctiva of the nictitating membrane.

BLOOD SUPPLY: Ophthalmic artery and branches from the stapedial artery.

NERVE SUPPLY: Oculomotor nerve.

MUSCLES OF THE NECK

Complexus (Fig. 4.8)

LOCATION: A rather thin muscle located in the dorsomedial area of the neck.

ORIGIN: Lateral half of the occipital crest.

INSERTION: Transverse processes of the 2nd to 4th cervical vertebrae.

ACTION: Extends the head.

RELATIONS: Superficially the cutaneous temporalis muscle and skin; deeply the fused rectus capitis dorsalis major, trachelomastoideus, and rectus capitis dorsalis major muscles; medially the biventer cervicis.

BLOOD SUPPLY: Dorsal branches of the cranial portion of the common carotid artery and the vertebral and occipital arteries.

NERVE SUPPLY: Dorsal branches of cervical spinal nerves 1 through 4.

Biventer Cervicis (Fig. 4.8)

LOCATION: Laterodorsal to the midline extending from the occipital crest to the 2nd vertebral spinal process;

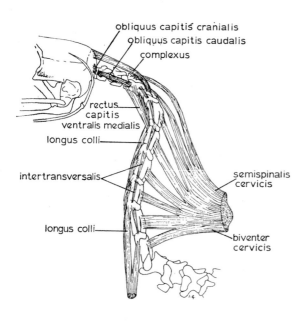

FIG. 4.8–Muscles of the neck, deep dissection.

the ligamentous section has a slight attachment to the 2nd cervical vertebra then proceeds caudad and fuses with the semispinalis cervicis.

ORIGIN: Occipital crest near the midline.

INSERTION: Attaches slightly in a ligamentous section at the 2nd vertebra and then fuses with the semispinalis cervicis. A terminal attachment is by way of a tendon to the crests of the spines of the 1st and 2nd thoracic vertebrae.

ACTION: Raises the head and neck.

RELATIONS: Superficially the skin and fascia; deeply the fused semispinalis cervicis and rectus capitis dorsalis major muscles, branches of the vertebral artery, and the cervical vertebrae.

BLOOD SUPPLY: The dorsal branches of the brachiocephalic artery and the common carotid and vertebral arteries.

NERVE SUPPLY: Dorsal branches of cervical spinal nerves 1 through 13.

Semispinalis Cervicis (Fig. 4.8)

LOCATION: This muscle is composed of numerous superficial fasciculi throughout its length.

ORIGIN: The 1st and 2nd cervical vertebrae by way of the supraspinous ligament.

INSERTION: Dorsal cervical spinous processes from the 3rd through the 13th.

ACTION: Acts with its fellow to raise the neck; one muscle alone would flex the neck to the side.

RELATIONS: Superficially the muscle is covered by the biventer cervicis and the skin caudal to it; deeply the muscle lies over the multifidus cervicis and interspinalis muscles.

BLOOD SUPPLY: Dorsal spinal and dorsal arteries.

NERVE SUPPLY: Dorsal branches of cervical spinal nerves 3 through 14.

Rectus Capitis Dorsalis Major and Rectus Capitis Ventralis Lateralis (Fig. 4.9) (Fused Muscles)

LOCATION: Dorsolateral area of the neck from the 3rd and 4th cervical vertebrae to the occipital bone.
ORIGIN: Spinal and lateral processes of the 2nd to 4th cervical vertebrae.
INSERTION: From the lateral extent of the occipital crest to near the midline.
ACTION: Raises the head when both muscles act together; singly this muscle would flex the neck laterally.
RELATIONS: Dorsally the complexus and trachelomastoideus muscles; medially the intertransversalis muscle; ventrally the vertebrae, rectus capitis ventralis medialis, and longus colli muscles.
BLOOD SUPPLY: Occipital artery.
NERVE SUPPLY: Cervical spinal nerves 1 through 4.

Rectus Capitis Ventralis Medialis (Fig. 4.8)

LOCATION: Courses from the ventrolateral occipital crest to the 2nd through the 5th cervical vertebrae ventral and deep to the biventer cervicis.
ORIGIN: Vertebral spines of the 2nd through the 5th cervical vertebrae.
INSERTION: Passes obliquely upward to insert on the ridge of the basitemporal bone.
ACTION: To flex the neck and aid in turning the head to the side.
RELATIONS: Ventrally the pharynx and carotid and jugular anastomosis; dorsally the fused rectus capitis dorsalis major and rectus capitis ventralis lateralis and the longus colli muscles.
BLOOD SUPPLY: Common carotid, vertebral, and occipital arteries.

NERVE SUPPLY: Ventral branches of the cervical spinal nerves.

Trachelomastoideus (Fig. 4.9)

LOCATION: This thick muscle extends from the lateral areas of the 3rd and 4th cervical vertebrae to the occipital area of the skull.
ORIGIN: The 3rd and 4th cervical vertebrae with the bulk of its origin from the 4th.
INSERTION: Occipital bone dorsal and lateral to the occipital condyle near the foramen magnum.
ACTION: Raises the head.
RELATIONS: Superficially the obliquus capitis cranialis and caudalis muscles and the atlas and occipital bones near the articular area; deeply the rectus capitis dorsalis major.

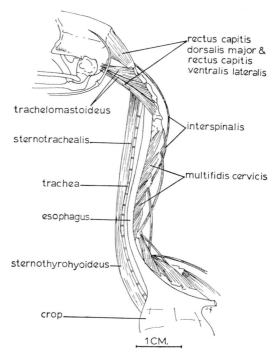

FIG. 4.9—Muscles of the neck, superficial dissection.

BLOOD SUPPLY: Common carotid and vertebral arteries.

NERVE SUPPLY: Ventral branches of the cervical spinal nerves.

Multifidus Cervicis (Fig. 4.9)

LOCATION: The muscle is composed of spindle-shaped segments lying along the arches of the cervical vertebrae.

ORIGIN: It has multiple origins and insertions to accommodate the many segments of its length. The origins begin caudally on the articular processes of the 3rd thoracic vertebra and continue successively to the 3rd cervical vertebra.

INSERTION: Insertions extend from the articular process of the 1st thoracic vertebra throughout the cervical series.

ACTION: To flex the neck downward and laterally.

RELATIONS: Superficially the skin, semispinalis cervicis, and biventer cervicis; deeply the cervical vertebrae and interspinalis muscle.

BLOOD SUPPLY: Deep cervical and vertebral arteries.

NERVE SUPPLY: Lateral branches of the 4th to the last cervical spinal nerves.

Interspinalis (Fig. 4.9)

LOCATION: This muscle is located on the spinous processes of the cervical vertebrae.

ORIGIN: The interspinalis is made up of numerous small segments connecting the spines of the cervical vertebrae. The small bundles usually pass from one spine to the succeeding spine; however, their arrangement is not strictly segmental, and the spines of some vertebrae may not bear an attachment. In a general sense the origin is the cranial surface of each spinous process.

INSERTION: Lateral surface and caudal border of each spinous process.

ACTION: Aids in elevating the head and tends to bind the vertebral segments together.

RELATIONS: The interspinalis is covered by most of the muscles and structures of the area. It is related deeply to the vertebral column from the 2nd through the 12th segments.

BLOOD SUPPLY: Cervical and vertebral arteries.

NERVE SUPPLY: Dorsal branches of cervical spinal nerves 2 through 12.

Intertransversalis (Fig. 4.8)

LOCATION: This muscle arises at the 4th vertebral rib near the vertebral column and proceeds craniad covering the ribs and lateral processes of the vertebrae encountered. It terminates at the 4th cervical vertebra.

ORIGIN: The intertransversalis begins its origin at the 4th rib near the transverse vertebral process, and continuing attachments arise from each vertebral transverse process cranial to the 5th cervical vertebra.

INSERTION: The transverse processes of the 2nd through 14th cervical vertebrae.

ACTION: Flexion of the neck laterally, with stabilization of the neck when both muscles are acting.

RELATIONS: Superficially the skin and shoulder muscles; medially the multifidus cervicis muscle; deeply the first four ribs and the transverse processes.

BLOOD SUPPLY: Intercostal and cervical arteries.

NERVE SUPPLY: The 2nd cervical to the 4th thoracic spinal nerves.

Obliquus Capitis Cranialis (Fig. 4.8)

LOCATION: A very small muscle located lateral to the dorsal spine of the axis and passing forward to the nuchal surface of the occipital bone.

ORIGIN: Dorsolateral area of the axis.

INSERTION: Nuchal surface of the occipital bone.

ACTION: Raises and rotates the head.

RELATIONS: Superficially the rectus capitis dorsalis major muscle; ventrally and laterally the trachelomastoideus muscle.

BLOOD SUPPLY: Occipital artery.

NERVE SUPPLY: Dorsal branch of the 1st cervical spinal nerve.

Obliquus Capitis Caudalis (Fig. 4.8)

LOCATION: Craniolateral region of the neck.

ORIGIN: From the craniolateral surface of the 2nd, 3rd, and 4th cervical vertebrae.

INSERTION: This segmented, flattened muscle converges on and attaches to the lateral surface of the atlas.

ACTION: Flexes the cranial part of the neck and rotates the head.

RELATIONS: Superficially the dorsal muscles which have origin in the occipital bone area; deeply the axis and the 3rd and 4th cervical vertebrae.

BLOOD SUPPLY: Occipital and vertebral arteries.

NERVE SUPPLY: Dorsal branches of cervical spinal nerves 2 through 4.

Sternothyrohyoideus (Fig. 4.9)

LOCATION: This small muscle has its origin on the manubrium of the sternum and runs forward superficially to the lateral surface of the larynx and the medial surface of the tongue.

ORIGIN: Manubrium sterni.

INSERTION: Thyroid cartilage of the larynx, the body of the hyoid bone, and the entoglossum.

ACTION: Retracts the tongue and larynx caudally.

RELATIONS: Superficially the skin and crop; deeply the larynx and trachea.

BLOOD SUPPLY: Carotid and bronchoesophageal arteries.

NERVE SUPPLY: Ventral branches of the cervical spinal nerves, the recurrent vagus nerve, and the cervical branches of the vagus and hypoglossal nerves.

Sternotrachealis (Fig. 4.9)

LOCATION: At the thoracic inlet.

ORIGIN: At the thoracic inlet, and runs craniomesiad from the craniolateral process of the sternum.

INSERTION: An area of the trachea just cranial to the syrinx, and caudal to the thyroid gland.

ACTION: Pulls the trachea caudally.

RELATIONS: Superficially the esophageal and tracheal muscles; deeply the trachea.

BLOOD SUPPLY: Common carotid and bronchoesophageal arteries.

NERVE SUPPLY: Ventral branches of the cervical spinal nerves.

Longus Colli (Fig. 4.8)

LOCATION: This muscle is located on the ventral surface of the entire length of the cervical vertebrae and is divided into a caudal portion and a cranial oblique portion.

ORIGIN: The caudal portion originates from the 10th cervical vertebra through the 1st thoracic vertebra. The cranial oblique portion originates from the diaphysis of the 3rd, 4th, and 5th cervical vertebrae.

ACTION: Flexes the neck ventrally.

INSERTION: The caudal portion is inserted by a tendon to the tubercle on the inferior portion of the atlas. Slender tendons are given off to and are inserted on the apices of the parapophysis of the 4th through the 10th cervical vertebrae. The cranial oblique portions become tendinous as they insert on the tubercle on the inferior portion of the body of the atlas.

RELATIONS: Superficially the skin; deeply the cervical vertebrae and intertransversalis muscle.

BLOOD SUPPLY: Vertebral and occipital arteries.

NERVE SUPPLY: Lateral branches of cervical spinal nerves 5 through 14.

Articulohyoideus (Fig. 4.1)

LOCATION: A small muscle that runs along the medial aspect of the cranial cornu of the hyoid bone.

ORIGIN: Articular part of the caudal mandibular process.

INSERTION: Median raphe.

ACTION: Retracts the hyoid apparatus and the tongue.

RELATIONS: Superficially the mylohyoideus muscle, skin, and fascia in the region of wattle; deeply the large cornu of the hyoid bone and the occipitomandibularis and hyomandibularis muscles.

BLOOD SUPPLY: Lingual and hyoid arteries.

NERVE SUPPLY: Hypoglossal and facial nerves.

MUSCLES OF THE SHOULDER GIRDLE: DORSAL DIVISION

The muscles of the shoulder girdle consist of those that connect the pectoral limb with the neck and trunk.

Latissimus Dorsi (Figs. 4.10, 4.17)

LOCATION: A wide muscle lying on the lateral wall of the thorax from the 1st lumbar to the 1st thoracic vertebra. This muscle consists of cranial and caudal portions joined by dense fascia. The cranial portion is very thin, and its fibers pass almost vertically over and perpendicular to the scapula. The fibers of the much

thicker caudal portion are directed cranioventrally toward the proximal extremity of the humerus.

ORIGIN: The cranial portion arises from the supraspinous ligament of the 1st through the 4th thoracic vertebrae; the caudal portion arises from the lumbodorsal fascia which attaches to the spines of the 1st lumbar and last few thoracic vertebrae.

INSERTION: The cranial portion passes between the long and lateral heads of the triceps brachii to insert by a wide, fleshy band to the caudomedial aspect of the proximal extremity of the humerus. The caudal part passes deep to the cranial part and is continued by an aponeurosis that inserts with the fleshy band of the cranial part. In addition dense connective tissue from the caudal part passes to the distal tendon of the long head of the triceps brachii to insert on the caudal aspect of the proximal extremity of the humerus.

ACTION: Adducts and flexes the humerus, drawing it upward and backward.

RELATIONS: Superficially the superficial fascia and skin, and at its attachment to the humerus, the long and lateral heads of the triceps brachii muscle; deeply the longissimus dorsi, rhomboideus, trapezius, and teres major muscles.

BLOOD SUPPLY: Subscapular, deep brachial, intercostal, and lumbar arteries.

NERVE SUPPLY: Thoracodorsal nerve.

Trapezius (Fig. 4.11)

LOCATION: A rather wide muscle located on the dorsolateral wall of the thorax between the scapula and vertebrae. The fibers run cranioventrad from vertebrae to scapula.

ORIGIN: From the supraspinous ligaments of the 1st through the 4th thoracic vertebrae deeply to that of the latissimus dorsi muscle.

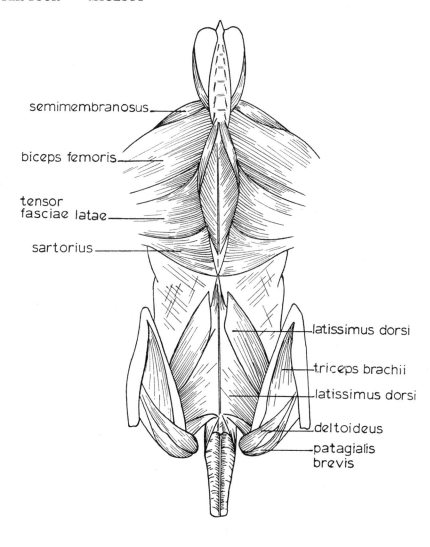

semimembranosus

biceps femoris

tensor
fasciae latae

sartorius

latissimus dorsi

triceps brachii

latissimus dorsi

deltoideus

patagialis
brevis

1CM.

FIG. 4.10—Superficial muscles of the back, dorsal view.

INSERTION: Cranial three-fourths of the vertebral border of the scapula.

ACTION: To elevate or draw the scapula and shoulder upward.

RELATIONS: Superficially the latissimus dorsi muscle and skin; deeply the rhomboideus, teres major, and infraspinatus muscles.

BLOOD SUPPLY: Dorsal and intercostal arteries.

NERVE SUPPLY: Spinal accessory, long thoracic, and dorsal branches of the spinal nerves.

Rhomboideus (Fig. 4.11)

LOCATION: A thin, wide muscle lying on

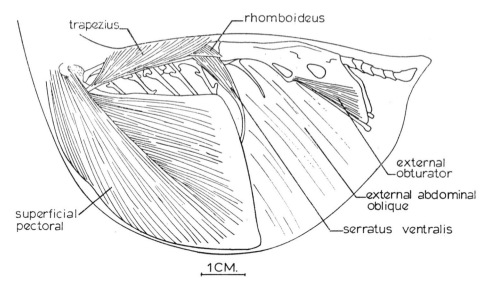

external
obturator

external abdominal
oblique

superficial
pectoral

serratus ventralis

1CM.

FIG. 4.11—Muscles of the thorax, superficial dissection.

the dorsolateral wall of the thorax between the scapula and vertebrae and deep to the trapezius muscle. Its fibers pass caudoventrad from the vertebrae to the scapula.

ORIGIN: Spines of the 1st to 5th thoracic vertebrae by way of the supraspinous ligament.

INSERTION: Caudal one-half of the dorsomedial surface of the scapula.

ACTION: To adduct and elevate or draw the scapula upward.

RELATIONS: Superficially the trapezius and latissimus dorsi muscles; deeply the longissimus dorsi muscle.

BLOOD SUPPLY: Dorsal spinal arteries.

NERVE SUPPLY: Dorsal branches of the thoracic spinal nerves.

MUSCLES OF THE SHOULDER GIRDLE: VENTRAL DIVISION

Superficial Pectoral (Fig. 4.11) (Pectoralis Superficialis)

LOCATION: The largest muscle of the quail, covering the breast completely. The muscle fibers extend

craniodorsally from their origin and converge and attach to an intramuscular fibrous raphe that divides the muscle into two fleshy parts.

ORIGIN: From the cranial, lateral, and caudal surfaces of the rami of the clavicle, the hypocleidium, the caudolateral and craniolateral processes of the sternum, the membranes closing the triangular spaces between these processes, the 3rd and 4th ribs, and the ventral (free) border of the sternal crest.

INSERTION: By a short, strong tendon to the craniolateral one-third of the proximal extremity of the humerus, lateral to the tendon of insertion of the biceps brachii muscle.

ACTION: This muscle is the exclusive depressor or adductor of the wing, and since this motion is the power stroke in flying it is especially well developed in such birds of short, rapid flight as the quail.

RELATIONS: Superficially the skin and cutaneous cleidoventralis muscle; deeply the deep pectoral, coracobrachialis medialis ventralis, and intercostal muscles and the caudolateral process of the sternum, the clavicle, and the 2nd, 3rd, and 4th ribs.

BLOOD SUPPLY: External thoracic, dorsal thoracic, and subclavian arteries.

NERVE SUPPLY: Pectoral and intercostal nerves.

Deep Pectoral (Fig. 4.12)
(Pectoralis Profundus)

LOCATION: In the pectoral region deep to the superficial pectoral muscle. Muscle fibers extend craniodorsally and converge on a median fibrous raphe which becomes the tendon. The muscle forms an oblique triangle covering the craniolateral surface of the coracoid bone and the lateral surface of the sternum except for the caudolateral processes.

ORIGIN: Keel, or lateral surfaces of the sternum; the hypocleidium of the clavicle; the sternoclavicular ligament; and the manubrium, or rostrum, of the sternum.

INSERTION: By means of a strong heavy tendon which passes through the foramen triosseum and over the proximolateral aspect of the head of the humerus, where it is bound down by a tendinous loop. The tendon continues and inserts just medial to the deltoid tuberosity and lateral to a large fossa on the proximal end of the humerus. It is surrounded by a synovial sheath in its course through the foramen triosseum.

ACTION: Elevates the wing.

RELATIONS: Superficially the superficial pectoral muscle; deeply the sternum, coracoid, and clavicular bones; in addition the cranial portion of the coracobrachialis ventralis lateralis muscle.

BLOOD SUPPLY: External thoracic, subclavian, clavicular, and coracoid arteries.

NERVE SUPPLY: Pectoral nerves.

Coracobrachialis Ventralis
(Figs. 4.12, 4.15)

LOCATION: There are two parts: medial (internal) and lateral (external). (The longus and brevis of Getty and Chamberlain, in the gallus.) Both parts are located in the deep pectoral region. The lateral part is

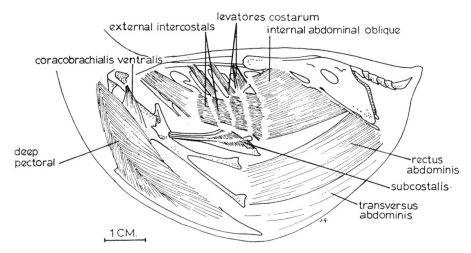

FIG. 4.12—Muscles of the body wall, lateral view.

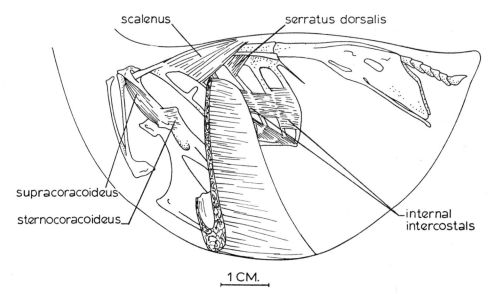

FIG. 4.13—Muscles of the body wall, lateral view.

located caudal to the deep pectoral muscle, and lies along the entire caudolateral aspect of the coracoid bone. Fibers originating from the wide base or proximal end of the coracoid run craniodorsad almost parallel with the shaft of the coracoid bone. The fibers originating more distally on the shaft run dorsad to join with the proximal fibers. The medial part is a thick muscle extending vertically along the medial surface of the coracoid bone.

ORIGIN: The lateral part arises from the the lateral and caudal surface of the coracoid bone from its wide, expanded proximal extremity to the level of the coracoscapular articulation. The medial part arises from the medial surface of the coracoid bone and the manubrium, or rostrum, of the sternum.

INSERTION: The lateral part inserts by a short tendon to the proximal margin of the pneumatic fossa on the caudal aspect of the proximal extremity of the humerus. The medial part inserts by a short tendon lying beneath the tendon of the lateral part to attach on the proximal margin of the rim of the pneumatic fossa but medial to the insertion of the lateral part.

ACTION: Depresses or adducts the wing, flexes the shoulder, and counteracts the rotating movement produced by the superficial pectoral muscle.

RELATIONS: Lateral part: cranially and superficially the deep pectoral muscle and the superficial pectoral muscle; deeply the coracoid bone and medial part of the coracobrachialis ventralis muscle. Medial part: superficially the coracoid bone and the lateral part of the coracobrachialis ventralis muscle.

BLOOD SUPPLY: Subclavian, subscapular, external thoracic, and coracoid arteries.

NERVE SUPPLY: Pectoral nerves.

Supracoracoideus (Fig. 4.13)

LOCATION: In the pectoral region cranial to the deep pectoral muscle, lying along the cranial border of the coracoid bone with its fibers directed parallel to the coracoid bone.

ORIGIN: Manubrium, or rostrum, of the sternum and the ramus of the coracoid bone.

INSERTION: By a tendon which passes through the foramen triosseum and attaches to the lateral aspect of the proximal extremity or head of the humerus between the insertions of the deep pectoral and superficial pectoral muscles.

ACTION: Aids in elevating the wing.

RELATIONS: Superficially the pectoral muscles; deeply and caudally the coracoid bone. The tendon of insertion lies between those of the triceps brachii, the teres major and infraspinatus, the coracobrachialis ventralis metialis, the subscapularis, and the coracobrachialis ventralis lateralis muscles.

BLOOD SUPPLY: Subclavian, subscapular, and coracoid arteries.

NERVE SUPPLY: Pectoral nerves.

Sternocoracoideus (Fig. 4.13) (Subclavis–Shufeldt)

LOCATION: A short, wide muscle lying on the craniolateral process of the sternum with its fibers running cranioventrad.

ORIGIN: Concave cranial border of the craniolateral process of the sternum.

INSERTION: A triangular area on the caudal surface of the coracoid bone.

ACTION: Flexes the coracosternal articulation.

RELATIONS: Superficially the external portion of the coracobrachialis ventralis lateralis and the deep pectoral muscle and sternum; deeply the coracoid and sternum.

BLOOD SUPPLY: Subclavian, subscapular, and coracoid arteries.

NERVE SUPPLY: Pectoral nerves.

Serratus Ventralis (Fig. 4.11)

LOCATION: Cranial portion: a long, narrow muscle lying on the craniolateral portion of the thorax caudal to the coracobrachialis ventralis with its fibers directed craniodorsally. Caudal portion: an oval-shaped muscle lying on the caudolateral aspect of the thorax with its fibers directed craniodorsally.

ORIGIN: Cranial portion: from the distal extremity of the 2nd rib. Caudal portion: from the middle of the 5th, 6th, and 7th thoracic ribs.

INSERTION: Cranial portion: by fibrous tissue to the scapular tuberosity. The caudal portion inserts on the ventrocostal aspect of the caudal extremity of the scapula.

ACTION: Pulls the scapula and shoulder caudally and ventrally.

RELATIONS: Cranial portion: superficially the teres major; deeply the intercostal muscles and the 1st and 2nd vertebral ribs. Caudal portion: superficially the skin; deeply the intercostal muscles and the 5th, 6th, and 7th vertebral ribs.

BLOOD SUPPLY: Intercostal artery.

NERVE SUPPLY: Intercostal nerves, long thoracic nerve.

Serratus Dorsalis (Fig. 4.13)

LOCATION: A wide, thin muscle on the lateral surface of the thorax deep to the scapula, with its fibers directed caudodorsally.

ORIGIN: Lateral surface of the proximal extremity of vertebral ribs 1 through 4.

INSERTION: Ventral surface of the scapula.

ACTION: Draws the ribs to which it attaches outward, and assists in inspiration.

RELATIONS: Superficially the scapula, rhomboideus, latissimus dorsi, and teres major muscles; deeply the intercostal muscles and the proximal extremities of vertebral ribs 1 through 4.

BLOOD SUPPLY: Intercostal arteries.

NERVE SUPPLY: Intercostal nerves, long thoracic nerve.

MUSCLES OF THE SHOULDER

Deltoideus (Figs. 4.10, 4.14)

LOCATION: In the omobrachial region on the dorsal aspect of the humerus between the long head of the triceps brachii and patagialis brevis muscles.

ORIGIN: Beside its main origin from the clavicle there are fleshy attachments to the proximal extremity of the coracoid and the distal extremity of the scapula just dorsal to the origins of the infraspinatus and coracobrachialis ventralis muscles.

INSERTION: The main insertion is on the proximolateral half and the deltoid tuberosity of the humerus; however, a strong, tapering, tendinous extremity of this muscle inserts on the lateral epicondyle. In addition some caudal deep fibers of this muscle converge with those of the distal tendon of the long head of the triceps brachii muscle.

ACTION: Flexes the shoulder and elevates or rotates the wing outward.

RELATIONS: Superficially the skin and cranial patagial muscles; deeply the teres minor and triceps brachii muscles and the humerus.

BLOOD SUPPLY: Cranial circumflex humeral artery.

NERVE SUPPLY: Axillary and subscapular nerves.

Coracobrachialis Dorsalis
(Coracobrachialis Anterior—Hudson)

LOCATION: A small, fleshy muscle located on the dorsolateral surface of the shoulder joint deep to the deltoideus muscle.

ORIGIN: Fleshy origin from the dorso-

lateral aspect of the proximal extremity of the coracoid bone and the medial scapulocoracoid ligament.

INSERTION: Fleshy insertion on the dorsolateral aspect of the head of the humerus just caudal and dorsal to the insertion of the superficial pectoral muscle.

ACTION: Elevates the humerus.

RELATIONS: Superficially the deltoideus muscle and the patagialis longus; deeply the shoulder articulation.

BLOOD SUPPLY: Cranial circumflex humeral artery.

NERVE SUPPLY: Axillary and radial nerves.

Teres Major (Fig. 4.15)
(Scapulohumeralis Posterior—Hudson)

LOCATION: A large, fleshy muscle located on the ventrolateral surface and caudal three-fourths of the scapula; the fibers are directed cranioventrally.

ORIGIN: Fleshy origin from the caudal three-fourths of the lateral surface of the scapula.

INSERTION: The medial border of the pneumatic foramen on the caudomedial aspect of the head of the humerus by a strong tendon.

ACTION: Adducts and possibly rotates the arm caudally.

RELATIONS: Superficially the skin, trapezius muscle, and the cranial and caudal parts of the latissimus dorsi muscles; deeply the scapula, subscapularis muscle, and the cranial portion of the serratus ventralis muscle.

BLOOD SUPPLY: Circumflex scapular and subscapular arteries.

NERVE SUPPLY: Axillary and subscapular nerves.

Teres Minor (Fig. 4.15)

LOCATION: A small, cylindical muscle exposed upon removal of the del-

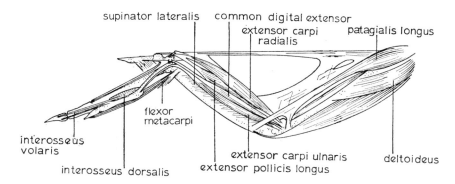

FIG. 4.14—Superficial muscles of the pectoral limb, dorsal view.

toideus, lying adjacent to the cranial part of the teres major and subscapularis muscles. The muscle is fleshy throughout, with fibers directed craniodorsally in the omobrachial region.

ORIGIN: Arises from the distal one-fourth of the lateral surface of the scapula just cranial to the origin of the subscapularis.

INSERTION: Caudomedial aspect of the head of the humerus just distal to the pneumatic foramen, after passing through the triceps brachii muscle (lateral and medial heads are fused).

ACTION: Tends to move the arm caudally and toward the body.

RELATIONS: Superficially the deltoideus, long head of the triceps brachii, and latissimus dorsi (cranial portion) muscles; deeply and caudally the subscapularis.

BLOOD SUPPLY: Axillary and cranial circumflex humeral arteries.

NERVE SUPPLY: Axillary and subscapular nerves.

Subscapularis (Fig. 4.15)

LOCATION: A small, triangular muscle located cranially and deeply to the teres major in the omobrachial region; fibers are directed cranioventrally.

ORIGIN: On the lateral aspect of the cranial one-fourth of the scapula just cranial to the teres major and caudal to the teres minor muscle.

INSERTION: Common tendon of insertion with the coracobrachialis ventralis medialis muscle on the proximal edge of the pneumatic foramen just medial to the external portion of the tendon of insertion of the coracobrachialis ventralis lateralis.

ACTION: Draws the wing caudally and rotates it upward.

RELATIONS: Superficially the teres major and the long head of the triceps brachii; deeply the serratus ventralis muscle (cranial portion).

BLOOD SUPPLY: Subscapular arteries.

NERVE SUPPLY: Subscapular nerves.

Infraspinatus

LOCATION: Found on the scapula below the spine and extending across to the humerus. At the shoulder joint a strong tendon arises from the fleshy muscle, giving it a pennate form.

ORIGIN: The infraspinous fossa, spine, and caudal border of the scapula and the tendon of the deltoideus.

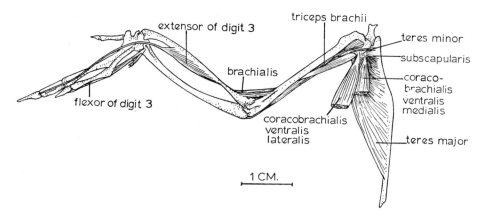

FIG. 4.15—Deep muscles of the pectoral limb, dorsal view.

INSERTION: Distal to the tubercle of the humerus.

ACTION: Abducts and rotates the humerus outward.

RELATIONS: Superficially the deltoideus, deeply the scapula.

BLOOD SUPPLY: Suprascapular artery.

NERVE SUPPLY: Suprascapular nerve.

Patagialis Longus (Fig. 4.14)

LOCATION: The largest of the three patagial muscles lying between the insertions of the superficial pectoral and the deltoideus muscles.

ORIGIN: From the cranial surface of the lateral extremity of the clavicle in common with the patagialis longus muscle.

INSERTION: Terminates by a strong, wide, thin tendon attaching to the dorsal aspect of the proximal extremity of the extensor carpi radialis muscle.

ACTION: Flexes the elbow, and extends the carpus and the cranial patagium.

RELATIONS: Superficially the skin; deeply the patagialis longus muscle.

BLOOD SUPPLY: Cranial circumflex humeral artery.

NERVE SUPPLY: Axillary nerve.

Patagialis Brevis (Figs. 4.10, 4.16) (Propatagialis Brevis—Gadow and Selenka)

LOCATION: A small muscle located in the cranial patagium with its fleshy belly lying on the biceps brachii and extending into the patagium.

ORIGIN: From the cranial aspect of the distal extremity of the clavicle and coracoid bones in common with the patagialis brevis.

INSERTION: By a wide, strong, fibroelastic tendon that attaches to the cranial aspect of the carpus. The main insertions are on the cranial aspect of the distal extremity of the radius and 2nd carpus. The wide fibroelastic tendon is divided into a cranial part that is thicker and less elastic than the adjacent wide, elastic, caudal portion. The cranial portion inserts more on the distal aspect of the carpus, the carpal bones, and the proximal extremity of the carpometacarpus, while the more elastic, caudal portion inserts on the distal extremity of the radius and the carpal bones.

ACTION: Flexes the elbow, extends the carpus, and tenses the patagium.

RELATIONS: Superficially the skin and fascia; deeply the patagialis brevis and triceps brachii muscles.

BLOOD SUPPLY: Patagial artery.

NERVE SUPPLY: Axillary nerve.

Patagialis Accessorius (Fig. 4.16)

LOCATION: A small muscle lying deep to the patagialis brevis in the cranial patagium.

ORIGIN: From the tendon and belly of the biceps brachii.

INSERTION: A short tendon to the distal end of the patagialis longus.

ACTION: Tenses the cranial patagium and ruffles the feathers on the humeral tract.

RELATIONS: Superficially the skin; deeply the biceps brachii.

BLOOD SUPPLY: Patagial artery.

NERVE SUPPLY: Musculocutaneous nerve.

MUSCLES OF THE ARM

The muscles of this group arise from the scapula and/or the humerus and their actions affect generally the elbow

and the tendons and fascia of the forearm.

Biceps Brachii (Fig. 4.16)

LOCATION: A large, fusiform muscle located on the cranial surface of the humerus in the brachial region.

ORIGIN: By two tendons, one arising from the craniolateral aspect of the dorsal or upper extremity of the coracoid bone; the other arising from the medial crest on the head of the humerus. Both tendons unite distal to the head of the humerus.

INSERTION: Near its distal extremity the tendon bifurcates into two short branches, one a little longer than the other. The longer branch inserts on the craniomedial aspect of the proximal extremity of the ulna; the shorter branch inserts on a median tubercle located on the proximal extremity of the radius.

ACTION: Flexion of the elbow in opposition to the triceps brachii; in addition it extends the shoulder joint.

RELATIONS: Superficially the skin and the patagialis accessorius and brevis

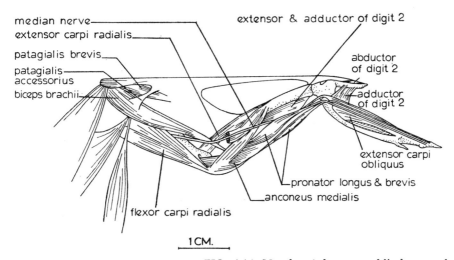

FIG. 4.16—Muscles of the pectoral limb, ventral view.

muscles; deeply the humerus and the pronator brevis muscle.

BLOOD SUPPLY: Brachial artery.

NERVE SUPPLY: Median nerve.

Brachialis (Fig. 4.15)

LOCATION: A rather short, bandlike muscle located across the medial surface of the elbow joint deep to the pronator longus and pronator brevis muscles.

ORIGIN: Cranial to the medial epicondyle and proximal to the coronoid fossa of the humerus.

INSERTION: The craniomedial aspect of the proximal extremity of the ulna.

ACTION: To assist the biceps brachii in flexing the elbow joint.

RELATIONS: Superficially the anconeus medialis, pronator teres, extensor of digits 2 and 3, and medial extensor of the extensor carpi radialis muscle.

BLOOD SUPPLY: Ulnar and radial arteries.

NERVE SUPPLY: Median nerve.

Triceps Brachii (Figs. 4.10, 4.15, 4.17) (Three Heads)

LOCATION: Along the entire lateral, caudal, and medial aspect of the humerus.

LONG HEAD
(TRICEPS SCAPULARIS—HUDSON)

ORIGIN: A fleshy origin from the lateral surface of the neck of the scapula. A tendinous origin is also present and is made up of fibers from the fleshy portion of the muscle just caudal to the glenoid cavity of the scapula and additional fibers arising near the pneumatic fossa of the humerus. The tendinous fibers continue distad and fuse into the substance of the muscle.

LATERAL AND MEDIAL HEADS
(TRICEPS HUMERALIS—HUDSON)

ORIGIN: Along the caudomedial border of the entire length of the humerus and from the pneumatic fossa and another fossa just lateral to the pneumatic fossa. The teres minor divides the proximal one-third of this muscle into lateral and medial heads, the remaining two-thirds fuse into a single belly throughout the remainder of its length.

INSERTION: The long head: tendinous insertion on the lateral or dorsal aspect of the glenoid process. The lateral and medial heads: mainly

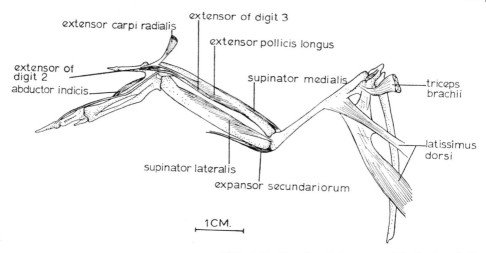

FIG. 4.17—Muscles of the pectoral limb, dorsal view.

by a strong tendon attaching to the apex of the olecranon process; in addition muscle fibers attach dorsal to the tendinous attachment.

ACTION: Extends the elbow; the long head of the triceps brachii tends to flex the shoulder or draw the arm caudally against the trunk.

RELATIONS: Superficially the skin and the deltoideus muscle superficial to the proximal extremity of the long head of the triceps brachii; the superficial pectoral and the biceps brachii conceal the proximal extent of the lateral and medial heads of the triceps brachii; deeply the humerus.

BLOOD SUPPLY: Deep brachial and cranial circumflex humeral arteries.

NERVE SUPPLY: Radial nerve.

Anconeus Medialis (Fig. 4.16)
(Entepicondyloulnaris—Hudson)

LOCATION: An oblique, triangular muscle lying along the proximal half of the ventral surface of the ulna; its base lies on the ulna, with its apex extending to the medial epicondyle of the humerus.

ORIGIN: From the medial epicondyle of the humerus in common with the pronator longus and brevis.

INSERTION: A wide, fleshy insertion along the caudomedial border of the proximal extremity of the ulna.

ACTION: Extends the elbow, assisting the pronators in depressing the distal end of the forearm.

RELATIONS: Superficially the flexor carpi radialis and extensors of digits 2 and 3; deeply the ulna and brachialis muscle.

BLOOD SUPPLY: Cubital and radial arteries.

NERVE SUPPLY: Ulnar nerve.

MUSCLES OF THE FOREARM

Extensor Carpi Radialis
(Figs. 4.14, 4.16, 4.17)
(Extensor Metacarpus Radialis)

LOCATION: A large, powerful muscle lying along the cranial surface of the radius.

ORIGIN: Fleshy and tendinous origins from the lateral epicondyle of the humerus.

INSERTION: By a tendon inserting on the cranial surface of the distal extremity of the 2nd metacarpus to its dorsal process. At the carpus this tendon fuses with the tendon of the extensor of digit 3 to have a common insertion.

ACTION: Extension of the carpus and flexion of the elbow.

RELATIONS: Superficially the skin; deeply the supinator muscle.

BLOOD SUPPLY: Ulnar artery.

NERVE SUPPLY: Radial and median nerves.

Common Digital Extensor (Fig. 4.14)
(Extensor of Digits 2 and 3—
Chamberlain; Extensor Digitorum
Communis—Hudson)

LOCATION: A large, fleshy muscle resembling the extensor carpi radialis, lying in the middle of the dorsal aspect of the forearm (antebrachium).

ORIGIN: From the lateral epicondyle of the humerus.

INSERTION: About two-thirds of its way down the forearm the muscle narrows into a tendon that branches past the carpus. The short branch inserts on the caudodorsal aspect of the proximal extremity of the 1st phalanx of the 2nd digit. The longer tendon extends down the carpometacarpus with the tendon of the extensor of digit 3 and inserts on the dorsoproximal end of the 1st phalanx of the 3rd digit.

ACTION: Primarily elevation of the 2nd (pollex) digit, extension of the 3rd digit, and flexion of the elbow.

RELATIONS: Superficially the skin; deeply the supinator lateralis, extensor of digit 3, and extensor carpi radialis muscles and the radius, carpus, and metacarpus.

BLOOD SUPPLY: Nutrient artery.

NERVE SUPPLY: Radial nerve.

Extensor Carpi Ulnaris (Fig. 4.14) (Ulnaris Lateralis—Chamberlain)

Both Hudson and Fujioka refer to this muscle as extensor carpi ulnaris. Chamberlain calls it the ulnaris lateralis and refers to the flexor carpi ulnaris as the extensor carpi ulnaris.

LOCATION: On the dorsal surface of the forearm deep to and between the common digital extensor and the supinator lateralis muscles.

ORIGIN: From the lateral epicondyle of the humerus, in common origin with the common digital extensor and the supinator lateralis muscles.

INSERTION: The belly of this muscle terminates into a tendon near the distal extremity of the forearm. An annular ligament on the distal extremity of the ulna binds the tendon in place and directs the action of the muscle. The insertion of the tendon is the caudodorsal projection of the proximal portion of the carpometacarpus.

ACTION: Flexion of the carpometacarpus when the wing is extended and elevation (abduction) of the distal extremity of the wing. Note: From Hudson this muscle belongs to the extensor group, but due to the peculiar structure of the carpus and adjacent parts in birds it has secondarily assumed a flexor function.

RELATIONS: Superficially the skin, in part the common digital extensor muscle and tendon of the extensor of digit 3.

BLOOD SUPPLY: Nutrient artery.

NERVE SUPPLY: Radical nerve.

Supinator Medialis (Fig. 4.17) (Supinator—Hudson; Supinator Brevis—Fisher, Chamberlain)

LOCATION: A small muscle located in the forearm deep to the extensor carpi radialis; it covers the cranioproximal border of the radius.

ORIGIN: By a short tendon from the lateral epicondyle of the humerus in common with the tendon of the extensor carpi ulnaris and supinator lateralis muscles.

INSERTION: Fleshy insertion on the cranial border of the proximal two-thirds of the radius.

ACTION: Flexes the elbow and supinates the manus.

RELATIONS: Superficially the extensor carpi radialis; deeply the radius.

BLOOD SUPPLY: Interosseous, radial, and patagial arteries.

NERVE SUPPLY: Median nerve.

Supinator Lateralis—Chamberlain (Figs. 4.14, 4.17) (Anconeus—Hudson)

LOCATION: A large muscle located adjacent to the extensor carpi ulnaris and common digital extensor in the dorsal forearm region. It lies along the craniodorsal border of the ulna.

ORIGIN: By a short tendon from the lateral epicondyle of the humerus along the supinator medialis and extensor carpi ulnaris.

INSERTION: Fleshy along the entire craniodorsal border of the ulna.

ACTION: Tends to elevate the distal end of the wing with a slight flexing motion.

RELATIONS: Superficially the skin, extensor carpi ulnaris, and extensor of digits 2 and 3, deeply the humerus and ulna.

BLOOD SUPPLY: Interosseous artery, radial nerve.

Extensor Pollicis Longus
(Figs. 4.14, 4.17)

LOCATION: A long, slender muscle with two heads lying in the interosseous space on the dorsal side of the forearm. (Not listed by Chamberlain and Hudson.)

ORIGIN: Radial head: arises along the caudal border of the distal two-thirds of the radius. Ulnar head: arises on the cranial aspect of the proximal extremity of the ulna, deep to the proximal interosseous ligament.

INSERTION: Ulnar head: about halfway down the radius, tapers into a narrow tendon on which the muscle fibers and tendinous connective tissue of the radial head converge and form a larger common tendon. This common tendon fuses at the region of the carpus with the tendon of the extensor carpi radialis and, after passing under an annular ligament extending from the distal end of the radius to the radiocarpal bone, it inserts on the proximal extremity of the dorsal process of the 2nd metacarpus.

ACTION: Assists the extensor carpi radialis in extending the carpometacarpus.

RELATIONS: Superficially the common digital extensor, the extensor carpi ulnaris, the anconeus, and the extensor muscles of digit 3; deeply the radius and ulna.

BLOOD SUPPLY: Nutrient artery.

NERVE SUPPLY: Radial nerve.

Extensor of Digit 3 (Figs. 4.15, 4.17)
(Extensor Digiti Tertii)
(Extensor Indicis Longus—Hudson)

Chamberlain lists cranial and caudal parts in gallus, but only the cranial parts can be found in the quail.

LOCATION: In the distal half of the interosseous space between the radius and ulna.

ORIGIN: Fleshy origin starting near the midpoint of the radius along its caudal border.

INSERTION: The tendon of this muscle passes distally between the radius and ulna. At the carpal joint it passes over the cranial surface of the ulna and continues over the dorsal side of the carpometacarpus. At the center of the bone the tendon passes along the cranial aspect of the 3rd metacarpus and the 1st phalanx of the 3rd digit to its insertion on the cranial side of the proximal extremity of the 2nd phalanx of the 3rd digit.

ACTION: Extension of the manus and 3rd digit. In addition it tends to elevate the distal end of the wing.

RELATIONS: Superficially the skin, the common digital extensor, and the extensor pollicis longus muscle.

BLOOD SUPPLY: Nutrient artery.

NERVE SUPPLY: Median nerve.

Flexor Carpi Radialis—Chamberlain
(Fig. 4.16)
(Flexor Carpi Ulnaris—Hudson)

LOCATION: A large muscle located in the forearm which makes up the caudal border of the musculature. The belly of the muscle seems to consist of two fusiform parts with a common origin and insertion.

ORIGIN: By a strong tendon from the medial epicondyle of the humerus. The expansor secundariorum lies upon the tendon of origin.

INSERTION: By a strong tendon to the caudal aspect of the proximal extremity or base of the ulnocarpal bone.

ACTION: Principal flexor of the carpus; in addition it supinates the manus, erects the secondaries, and extends the elbow.

RELATIONS: Superficially the skin and a heavy tendinous band from the medial epicondyle to the cranial aspect of the proximal extremity of the base of the ulnocarpal bone; deeply the anconeus, extensor carpi ulnaris, and the common digital extensor.

BLOOD SUPPLY: Ulnar, median, cubital, and radial arteries.

NERVE SUPPLY: Median and ulnar nerves.

Pronator Longus—Chamberlain and Fisher (Fig. 4.16) (Pronator Profundus—Hudson)

LOCATION: A rather thick muscle located on the proximal half of the ventral aspect of the forearm.

ORIGIN: Common origin on the medial epicondyle of the humerus with the anconeus. This mainly tendinous origin is between the tendon of the flexor carpi radialis and the tendon of the pronator brevis.

INSERTION: Fleshy insertion to the caudolateral aspect of the proximal half of the radius. The insertion is caudal to the insertion of the pronator.

ACTION: Pronates the forearm and manus; tends to depress or move the distal end of the forearm and manus ventrally.

RELATIONS: See the origin and insertion above.

BLOOD SUPPLY: Radial and median arteries.

NERVE SUPPLY: Median nerve.

Pronator Brevis—Fisher (Fig. 4.16)

LOCATION: The ventroproximal two-thirds of the forearm cranial to the pronator longus.

ORIGIN: By a short tendon arising from the proximal aspect of the medial epicondyle of the humerus. The tendon arises proximal to the tendon of the pronator longus and anconeus medialis.

INSERTION: The insertion is mainly fleshy along the proximal two-thirds of the cranioventral aspect of the radius. Insertion is ventral and adjacent to insertion of the anconeus.

ACTION: Same as pronator longus.

RELATIONS: Superficially the extensor muscle of digit 3, and flexor carpi radialis and extensor carpi ulnaris muscles.

BLOOD SUPPLY: Radial artery, median artery.

NERVE SUPPLY: Median nerve.

Extensor and Adductor of Digits 2 and 3 (Fig. 4.16) (Extensor et Adductor Digitorum Secundi et Tertii) (Flexor Digitorum Profundus—Hudson; Extensor and Adductor of Digit 3—Chamberlain)

LOCATION: Largest muscle of the flexor group, lying on the cranial surface of the ulna in the interosseous space of the forearm.

ORIGIN: Fleshy origin from the middle one-third of the cranioventral aspect of the ulna.

INSERTION: The muscle tapers into a tendon just proximal to the carpus. The tendon passes across the carpus and is bound down by a fibrous sheath. It branches at the cranial extremity of the 1st phalanx of the 2nd digit, giving off a narrow tendon that passes down the ventral surface of the 1st phalanx of the 2nd digit. The larger branch continues distad on the cranioventral surface of the 3rd metacarpus and 1st phalanx of the 3rd digit to its insertion on the cranioventral aspect of the proximal extremity of the 2nd phalanx of the 3rd digit.

ACTION: Extension and depression of the 3rd digit along with flexion and depression of the 2nd digit.

RELATIONS: Superficially the skin and fascia, flexor carpi radialis, and extensor indicis longus; deeply the ulna and radius.

BLOOD SUPPLY: Ulnar, metacarpal, and digital arteries.

NERVE SUPPLY: Brachial and median nerves.

Flexor Digitorum Sublimis—Hudson (Included With Flexor Carpi Ulnaris—Fisher)

LOCATION: A small muscle located on the distal half of the forearm deep to the flexor carpi radialis.

ORIGIN: Main origin is fleshy, from the caudodistal half of the ulna; in addition, some fibers arise from the distal one-third of the condyle of the humerus to the ulnar carpal bone (cranial part of the flexor carpi ulnaris—Fisher).

INSERTION: The fleshy portion of this muscle ends at the carpus; its tendon passes distad over the cranioventral surface of the ulnocarpal bone. On the ventrolateral aspect of the 2nd metacarpus it angles slightly craniad to meet the tendon of the extensor and adductor of digits 2 and 3 on the cranioventral surface at the midpoint of the 3rd metacarpus. Continuing along with and under the tendon of this muscle, it passes distad to its insertion on the cranial aspect of the distal end of the 1st phalanx and the proximal end of the 2nd phalanx of the 3rd digit. This insertion is just cranial to the insertion of the extensor and adductor of digits 2 and 3.

ACTION: Main action is depression of

the manus; in addition it tends to flex the carpus when the wing is completely extended.

RELATIONS: Superficially the flexor carpi radialis; deeply the extensor carpi obliquus.

BLOOD SUPPLY: Ulnar, cubital, and radial arteries.

NERVE SUPPLY: Median nerve.

Extensor Carpi Obliquus (Fig. 4.16) (Ulnometcarpalis Ventralis—Hudson; Flexor Carpi Brevis—Fisher)

LOCATION: This muscle is located on the caudodistal half of the forearm lying on the ventral surface of the distal half of the ulna deep to the flexor digitorum sublimis and profundus muscles. Its fibers run obliquely craniodistad toward the cranial surface of the carpus.

ORIGIN: Ventral surface of the distal one-half to one-third of the ulna.

INSERTION: Near the carpus the muscle tapers into a tendon which passes over the cranial surface of the proximal extremity of the 2nd metacarpus.

ACTION: Extends and rotates the manus inward.

RELATIONS: This muscle lies between the common digital extensor and the flexor carpi radialis; superficially it is covered by the skin and fascia; deeply it is related to the distal extremity of the radius and ulna.

BLOOD SUPPLY: Radial and median arteries.

NERVE SUPPLY: Median nerve.

Expansor Secundariorum (Fig. 4.17)

LOCATION: A small, triangular muscle located on the caudoventral surface of the forearm just distal to the elbow.

ORIGIN: Medial epicondyle of the humerus and the medial humeroulnar ligament. In addition, a long narrow tendon arises from the tendon of the teres major and passes down the caudal aspect of the brachium to the fleshy portion.

INSERTION: Insertion is mostly on the proximal two or three secondary feather follicles.

ACTION: Because of the great amount of connective tissue interwoven in the fleshy belly of this muscle, its action of contraction is limited. Its main action is expansion of the proximal secondary feathers, tending to draw them ventrally.

RELATIONS: Superficially the skin; deeply the ulna and triceps brachii muscle.

BLOOD SUPPLY: Deep brachial, cubital, and radial arteries.

NERVE SUPPLY: Radial nerve.

MUSCLES OF THE MANUS

Extensor of Digit 2 (Fig. 4.17)
(Exterior Digiti Secundi)
(Extensor Pollicis Brevis—Hudson and Fisher)

LOCATION: A small muscle lying on the craniodorsal aspect of the proximal extremity of the carpometacarpus in the manus region.

ORIGIN: Fleshy origin from the entire dorsal proximal extremity of the 2nd metacarpus; in addition a few fibers arise from the cranial border of the proximal surface of the 3rd metacarpus.

INSERTION: By way of a short tendon to the craniodorsal edge of the proximal extremity of the 1st phalanx of the 2nd digit.

ACTION: Extension of the 2nd digit; may tend to elevate the 2nd digit slightly.

RELATIONS: Superficially the skin; deeply the 2nd metacarpus.

BLOOD SUPPLY: Metacarpal artery.

NERVE SUPPLY: Radialis profundus nerve.

Adductor of Digit 2 (Fig. 4.16)
(Adductor Digiti Secundi)
(Adductor Pollicis—Fisher)

LOCATION: A small, triangular muscle lying on the caudal border of the 2nd digit with its origin on the 3rd metacarpus just distal to the distal extremity of the 2nd metacarpus.

ORIGIN: Fleshy origin from the cranial border of the 3rd metacarpus just distal to the distal extremity of the 2nd metacarpus.

INSERTION: Mainly fleshy along the caudal aspect of the 1st phalanx of the 2nd digit.

ACTION: Adduction of the 2nd digit.

RELATIONS: Superficially the skin and the 1st phalanx of the 2nd digit.

BLOOD SUPPLY: Metacarpal artery.

NERVE SUPPLY: Median nerve.

Flexor Metacarpi—Fisher (Fig. 4.14)
(Ulnometacarpalis Dorsalis—Hudson)

LOCATION: A small muscle located on the caudodorsal aspect of the carpus.

ORIGIN: By a wide, strong tendon on the dorsal aspect of the distal extremity of the ulna.

INSERTION: Mainly fleshy on the caudal aspect of the proximal extremity of the 4th metacarpus near its fusion with the 3rd metacarpus.

ACTION: Flexion of the carpus.

RELATIONS: Superficially the skin; deeply the ulna and carpometacarpus.

BLOOD SUPPLY: Cubital artery.

NERVE SUPPLY: Median nerve.

Flexor of Digit 3 (Fig. 4.15)
(Flexor Digiti Tertii)
(Flexor Digiti Quarti—Chamberlain)

LOCATION: A long, thin muscle located along the caudal border of the 4th metacarpus.

ORIGIN: The fibers start just distal to the insertion of the flexor metacarpi.

INSERTION: Both fleshy and tendinous

on the caudoproximal aspect of the 1st phalanx of the 4th digit.

ACTION: Since the 4th digit is closely bound to the 3rd digit by ligament and fascia, this muscle flexes the distal extremity of the wing.

RELATIONS: Superficially the skin; deeply the 4th metacarpus and the 4th digit.

BLOOD SUPPLY: Metacarpal artery.

NERVE SUPPLY: Radial nerve.

Interosseous Dorsalis (Fig. 4.14)

LOCATION: In the oval interosseous space between the 3rd and 4th metacarpals, lying adjacent and superficial to the interosseous volaris (palmaris).

ORIGIN: Along the border of the interosseous space; the caudodorsal aspect of the 3rd metacarpus and the craniodorsal border of the 4th metacarpus.

INSERTION: The muscle fibers converge on a median raphe that leads into a long tendon at the distal extremity of the carpometacarpus. This tendon passes distad along the craniodorsal border of the 1st phalanx of the 3rd digit to its point of insertion on the craniodorsal border of the distal half of the 2nd phalanx of the 3rd digit.

ACTION: Extension and slight elevation of the 3rd digit.

RELATIONS: Adjacent and superficial to the interosseous volaris.

BLOOD SUPPLY: Metacarpal artery.

NERVE SUPPLY: Median nerve.

Interosseous Volaris (Fig. 4.14) (Interosseous Ventralis—Chamberlain)

LOCATION: In the interosseous space formed by the 3rd and 4th metacarpals deep to the interosseous dorsalis muscle.

ORIGIN: Along the caudoventral border of the proximal three-fourths of the

4th metacarpus, which forms the interosseous space. The origin of this muscle is deep to the interosseous dorsalis muscle.

INSERTION: The tendon of this muscle passes to the dorsal surface of the manus, angling caudodistad to the caudal border of the 1st phalanx of the 3rd digit. Passing distad along the caudal border of the 1st and 2nd phalanges of the 3rd digit, it inserts on the caudal border of the distal extremity of the 2nd phalanx of the 3rd digit.

ACTION: Opposite to that of the interosseous dorsalis in that it flexes the 3rd digit, but it also aids in its elevation.

RELATIONS: In the interosseous space formed by the 3rd and 4th metacarpals deep to the interosseous dorsalis muscle.

BLOOD SUPPLY: Metacarpal artery.

NERVE SUPPLY: Radialis profundus nerve.

Abductor Indicis (Fig. 4.17)

LOCATION: A long, narrow muscle located along the cranioventral border of the 3rd metacarpus.

ORIGIN: Fleshy origin from the cranioventral border of the 3rd metacarpus, at a point opposite the distal extremity of the 2nd metacarpus and extending distally the entire length of the 3rd metacarpus.

INSERTION: Mainly tendinous on the cranioproximal extremity of the 1st phalanx of the 3rd digit.

ACTION: Flexes the 3rd digit.

RELATIONS: The tendons of the deep digital flexor and superficial digital flexor muscles pass over and partially conceal this muscle for its entire length.

BLOOD SUPPLY: Median artery.

NERVE SUPPLY: Radialis profundus nerve.

Abductor of Digit 2 (Fig. 4.16)
(Abductor Digiti Secundi)
(Abductor Pollicis—Hudson)

LOCATION: A small, triangular muscle located on the cranioventral aspect of the 2nd metacarpus and the 2nd digit.

ORIGIN: Arises from the ventrodistal extremity of the tendon of the extensor carpi radialis muscle and from the cranioventral aspect of the 2nd metacarpus.

INSERTION: Fleshy and tendinous along the cranioventral aspect of the 2nd digit.

ACTION: Depresses and abducts the 2nd digit; extends the digit. Because of its origin on the extensor carpi radialis this muscle may serve as a tendon and extend and abduct the 2nd digit when the extensor carpi radialis contracts.

RELATIONS: Superficially the skin; deeply the 2nd metacarpus and the 2nd digit.

BLOOD SUPPLY: Metacarpal artery.

NERVE SUPPLY: Radial nerve.

MUSCLES OF THE TRUNK

External Abdominal Oblique (Fig. 4.11)
(Obliquus Externus Abdominis)

LOCATION: This muscle is superficial and the most extensive of the abdominal group. It has a narrow belly and the fibers are directed ventrolaterally.

ORIGIN: From the lateral surfaces of the last three or four ribs, the lateral border of the preacetabular ilium, and the ventral border of the pubis.

INSERTION: Caudolateral process of the sternum and by means of the interosseous sternal ligaments to the linea alba and the xiphoid process.

ACTION: Compresses the abdomen.

RELATIONS: Superficially the skin and thigh; deeply the internal, rectus, and transverse abdominal muscles.

BLOOD SUPPLY: Intercostal and lumbar arteries.

NERVE SUPPLY: Second thoracic to the last lumbar spinal nerves.

Internal Abdominal Oblique (Fig. 4.12)
(Obliquus Internus Abdominis)

LOCATION: A mostly fleshy muscle which occupies the angle formed by the ilium and pubis dorsally and the last rib cranially.

ORIGIN: Vertebral and sternal parts of the ventral border of the last rib. Its fibers are directed downward and forward at right angles to those of the external abdominal oblique muscle.

INSERTION: Abdominal fascia and the linea alba.

ACTION: Compresses the abdomen.

RELATIONS: Superficially the external abdominal oblique muscle; deeply the transversus abdominis muscle.

BLOOD SUPPLY: Intercostal and femoral arteries.

NERVE SUPPLY: Intercostal and lumbar nerves.

Rectus Abdominis (Fig. 4.12)

LOCATION: Ventrolateral region of the abdomen.

ORIGIN: Medial and lateral processes of the sternum and the ventral border of the last sternal rib. The fibers are nearly parallel to the long axis of the body.

INSERTION: On the caudal extremity of the pubis and the linea alba.

ACTION: Compresses the abdomen.

RELATIONS: Superficially the abdominal oblique muscles; deeply the transversus abdominis muscle.

BLOOD SUPPLY: Intercostal and femoral arteries.

NERVE SUPPLY: Intercostal and lumbar nerves.

Transversus Abdominis (Fig. 4.12)

LOCATION: An extensive, thin sheet forming the deepest layer of the abdominal muscles; it is fleshy at its origin and has an extensive aponeurotic insertion. Its fibers lie at right angles to the long axis of the body.

ORIGIN: Medial surface of the last three sternal ribs, the lateral border of the preacetabular ilium, and the free border of the pubis.

INSERTION: Caudolateral process of the sternum and the linea alba.

ACTION: Compresses the abdomen.

RELATIONS: Superficially the internal abdominal oblique and rectus abdominis muscles; deeply the peritoneum.

BLOOD SUPPLY: Intercostal and femoral arteries.

NERVE SUPPLY: Intercostal nerves.

Sphincter Ani (Fig. 4.18)

LOCATION: A circular muscle of the anus.

ORIGIN: Anal fascia.

INSERTION: Anal fascia.

ACTION: Closes the anus.

RELATIONS: Superficially the skin; deeply the anal mucosa and the bursa of Fabricius; cranially the levator ani muscle.

BLOOD SUPPLY: Hemorrhoidal artery.

NERVE SUPPLY: Synsacral spinal nerves 8, 9, and 10.

Levator Ani (Fig. 4.18)

LOCATION: Caudolateral region of the pelvis.

ORIGIN: Caudal tuberosity of the ilium and the transverse process of the 3rd coccygeal vertebra.

INSERTION: Into the sphincter ani muscle.

ACTION: Elevates the anus.

RELATIONS: Superficially the skin; deeply the semitendinosus and caudofemoralis muscles.

BLOOD SUPPLY: Caudal hemorrhoidal artery.

NERVE SUPPLY: Synsacral spinal nerves 8, 9, and 10.

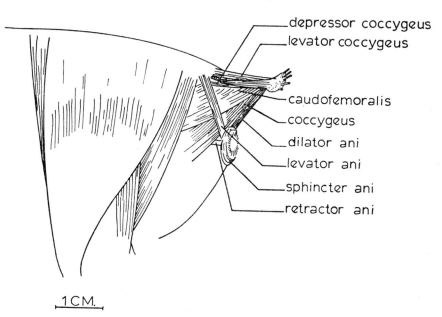

depressor coccygeus
levator coccygeus
caudofemoralis
coccygeus
dilator ani
levator ani
sphincter ani
retractor ani

1CM.

FIG. 4.18—Muscles of the tail region, lateral view.

External Intercostals (Fig. 4.12)

LOCATION: There are five in number located in the lateral thoracic region with fibers slanting sternally and ventrally.

ORIGIN: Caudal borders of the 2nd to 6th ribs.

INSERTION: Cranial border of each succeeding vertebral rib from the 3rd to the 7th.

ACTION: Aids in fixing the ribs in respiration and inspiration.

RELATIONS: Superficially the pectoralis, metapatagialis, serratus dorsalis, serratus ventralis, and latissimus dorsi muscles; deeply the internal intercostal muscles.

BLOOD SUPPLY: Intercostal arteries.

NERVE SUPPLY: Intercostal nerves.

Internal Intercostals (Fig. 4.13)

LOCATION: Five in number in the lateral thoracic region.

ORIGIN: Cranial borders of the 3rd to 7th ribs, inclusive. The fibers of these muscles slant cranially and ventrally.

INSERTION: Caudal border of each preceding vertebral rib 2nd to 6th inclusive.

ACTION: Helps fix the ribs in respiration (expiration).

RELATIONS: Superficially the external intercostal muscles; deeply the diaphragmatic and abdominal air sacs.

BLOOD SUPPLY: Intercostal arteries.

NERVE SUPPLY: Intercostal nerves.

Scalenus (Fig. 4.13)

LOCATION: A rather large muscle with two parts in the craniodorsal thoracic region adjacent dorsally to the roots of the nerves of the brachial plexus.

ORIGIN: Medial portion: from the transverse process of the 14th cervical vertebra. Dorsal portion: from the transverse process of the 1st thoracic vertebra.

INSERTION: Medial portion: on the lateral surface of the 1st thoracic rib. Dorsal portion: on the 2nd vertebral rib and its uncinate process.

ACTION: Aids in respiration.

RELATIONS: Dorsally the rhomboideus muscle; ventrally the brachial plexus.

BLOOD SUPPLY: Vertebral artery.

NERVE SUPPLY: Branch from the brachial plexus.

Levatores Costarum (Fig. 4.12)

LOCATION: Four in number in the dorsal thoracic region with fibers directed craniodorsally.

ORIGIN: From the transverse processes of the 2nd through the 5th thoracic vertebrae.

INSERTION: Craniolateral surface of the 3rd through the 6th vertebral ribs.

ACTION: Draws the ribs cranially during respiration.

RELATIONS: Laterally the serratus muscles; medially the pleura and lungs.

BLOOD SUPPLY: Intercostal arteries.

NERVE SUPPLY: Intercostal nerves.

Subcostalis (Fig. 4.12)

LOCATION: The ventrolateral thoracic region; the fibers are parallel to the long axis of the body.

ORIGIN: The caudal border of the lateral cranial sternal process of the sternum and borders of the 2nd to 6th sternal ribs.

INSERTION: Cranial borders of the 2nd to 7th sternal ribs.

ACTION: Aids in respiration.

RELATIONS: Superficially the pectoralis muscle; deeply the abdominal and diaphragmatic air sacs.

BLOOD SUPPLY: Intercostal arteries.

NERVE SUPPLY: Intercostal nerves.

Levator Coccygeus (Fig. 4.18)

LOCATION: The caudal region, from the dorsal sacrum and ischium to the pygostyle.

ORIGIN: Dorsal surface of the sacrum and ischium.

INSERTION: Dorsal surface of the pygostyle.

ACTION: Elevates the pygostyle.

RELATIONS: Dorsally the skin; deeply the sacrum and ischium and the semitendinosus muscles.

BLOOD SUPPLY: Sacral artery.

NERVE SUPPLY: Coccygeal and synsacral spinal nerves.

Coccygeus (Fig. 4.18)

LOCATION: Caudal region with the muscle fibers proceeding dorsoventrad. Note: No distinct separation is seen in the quail, the lateral part is either absent or has become fused with the very prominent medial part.

ORIGIN: Caudal process of the pubis.

INSERTION: Cranioventral surface of the pygostyle.

ACTION: Depresses the cauda.

RELATIONS: Laterally the skin; deeply the fold of skin between this muscle and the sphincter ani muscle.

BLOOD SUPPLY: Branches from the internal pudic and middle sacral arteries.

NERVE SUPPLY: Synsacral spinal nerves 8, 9, and 10.

Retractor Ani (Fig. 4.18)

LOCATION: The pelvic region with fibers running parallel to the long axis of the body.

ORIGIN: The caudal pelvic region near the caudal process of the pubis.

INSERTION: The sphincter ani muscle laterally.

ACTION: Retracts the anus and the cloaca.

RELATIONS: Laterally the skin, levator ani, and lateral part of the coccygeus muscle; deeply the medial part of the coccygeus muscle and the cloaca.

BLOOD SUPPLY: Branches of the internal pudic artery.

NERVE SUPPLY: Synsacral spinal nerves 8 and 9.

Dilator Ani (Fig. 4.18)

LOCATION: Ischiorectal fossa between the tail and the cloaca.

ORIGIN: Caudolateral feather follicles and fibrous connective tissue of the caudal feather tract in common with the small dorsal branch of the coccygeus muscle.

INSERTION: This long, cylindrical muscle passes ventrad over the coccygeus muscle and under the sphincter ani muscle to the corner of the anus, from where it continues around the ventral border of the cloaca to join with the same muscle of the opposite side.

ACTION: Copulatory action.

RELATIONS: Superficially the skin and sphincter ani muscle; deeply the caudofemoralis and coccygeus muscles.

BLOOD SUPPLY: Median sacral artery.

NERVE SUPPLY: Synsacral spinal nerves.

Depressor Coccygeus (Fig. 4.18)

LOCATION: Caudal region on the ventral surface of the coccygeal vertebrae.

ORIGIN: Caudoventral surface of the pygostyle.

INSERTION: Ventral surface of the pygostyle.

ACTION: Depresses the coccygeal vertebrae.

RELATIONS: Dorsally the coccygeal vertebrae; ventrally the cloaca; laterally the coccygeus, caudofemoralis, and semitendinosus muscles.

BLOOD SUPPLY: Median sacral artery.

NERVE SUPPLY: Synsacral and coccygeal spinal nerves.

Longissimus Dorsi (Fig. 4.19)

LOCATION: One of the longest and most powerful muscles of the body, it makes up the bulk of the muscle in the dorsal region. It may be divided into a dorsal and a ventral division.

ORIGIN: The dorsal division, semispinalis dorsi, fills in the triangular space formed by the iliosacral junction and the spinous processes of the synsacrum. It passes forward adjacent to the spinous processes and overlies the transverse processes of the thoracic and cervical vertebrae to the 1st segment. The ventral division, longissimus cervicis, arises under the cranial part of the ilium and passes forward to the 2nd cervical vertebrae.

INSERTION: Both divisions have diffuse insertions on the lateral surfaces of the ribs and transverse processes.

ACTION: Acting with its fellow, it produces a powerful extension of the back; acting singly it would flex the spine laterally.

RELATIONS: Superficially the ilium, scapula, and muscles of the shoulder; deeply the sacrum, the transverse processes of the thoracic vertebrae, the vertical portion of the ribs, and the external intercostal muscles.

BLOOD SUPPLY: Dorsal branches of the intercostal arteries.

NERVE SUPPLY: Dorsal branches of the intercostal nerves and the thoracic spinal nerves.

MUSCLES OF THE PELVIC GIRDLE AND CRURA

Sartorius (Figs. 4.10, 4.20, 4.21)

LOCATION: A long, triangular muscle at the craniomedial surface of the limb in the pelvic and crural region. The fibers form a thin band extending caudally and ventrally.

ORIGIN: Lumbosacral dorsal spinous proc-

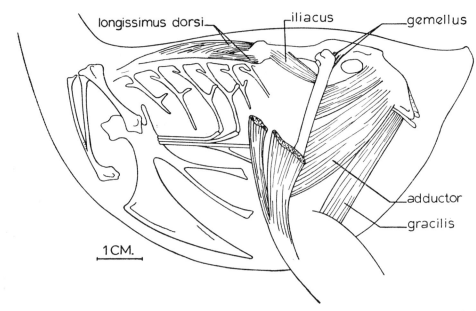

FIG. 4.19—Muscles of the pelvic girdle and crura, lateral view.

esses and the dorsal surface of the craniolateral border of the wing of the ilium.

INSERTION: By a wide aponeurosis to the tibial crest.

ACTION: Flexes the hip; extends the stifle and adducts the limb.

RELATIONS: Superficially the skin, a considerable mass of fatty tissue, and a valley-like depression formed by this muscle and the craniolateral surface of the tensor fasciae latae muscle; deeply the medial surface of the quadriceps femoris muscle and the distal edge of the fleshy large part of the pectineus muscle.

BLOOD SUPPLY: Femoral, circumflex femoral, and genu suprema arteries.

NERVE SUPPLY: Femoral nerve.

Tensor Fasciae Latae (Figs. 4.10, 4.20) (Gluteus Primus—Shufeldt; Iliotibialis—Gadow and Selenka; Hudson)

LOCATION: A rather broad, thin muscle which is triangular in shape; its base is attached to an aponeurotic sheet over the cranial portion of the pelvis; the apex of the triangle, which is also aponeurotic, extends to the region of the stifle.

ORIGIN: Dorsolateral fascia, spines of the lumbar and sacral vertebrae, and lateral ridge on the crest of the ilium superficial to the caudal division of the gluteus superficialis muscle.

INSERTION: Tibial aponeurosis at its attachment to the tibial crest and to the lateral patellofemoral ligament.

ACTION: Flexes the hip and extends the knee.

RELATIONS: Superficially the skin and the sartorius muscle; deeply the quadriceps femoris, gluteus superficialis, gluteus medius, and the greater trochanter of the femur. The muscle is distinctly aponeurotic both at its origin and insertion. The aponeurotic part is designated fascia lata, and the muscular portion is a thin, right triangle with its base posi-

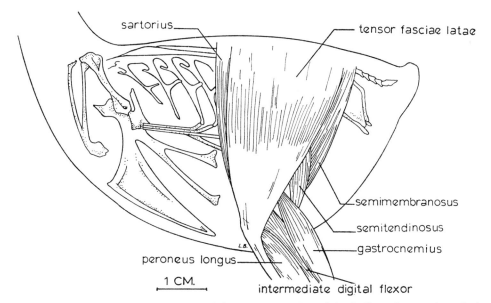

FIG. 4.20—Superficial muscles of the pelvic girdle and crura, lateral view.

tioned at the greater trochanter and the hypotenuse at the vastus lateralis.

BLOOD SUPPLY: Circumflex femoral artery.

NERVES SUPPLY: Cranial gluteal and femoral nerves.

Gluteus Superficialis (Fig. 4.22)

LOCATION: This muscle consists of two parts: the cranial head, which extends craniodorsally from the greater trochanter to the crest of the ilium, and the smaller caudal head, which extends dorsally from

the trochanter to the dorsal border of the ilium.

CRANIAL HEAD

ORIGIN: The tuber coxae and the adjacent part of the lateral border of the wing of the ilium.

INSERTION: The 3rd trochanter of the femur on the proximal lateral surface of the femur below the greater trochanter.

ACTION: Flexes the hip.

RELATIONS: Superficially the sartorius and tensor fasciae latae muscles; deeply the gluteus medius, quadri-

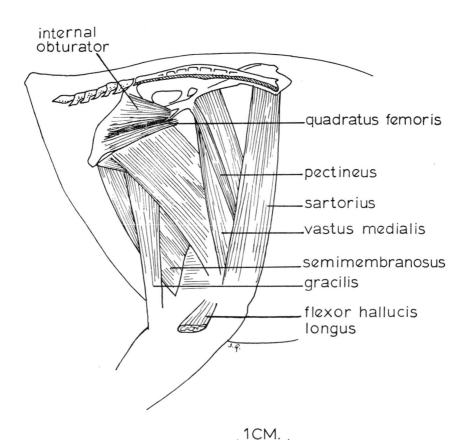

internal obturator

quadratus femoris

pectineus

sartorius

vastus medialis

semimembranosus

gracilis

flexor hallucis longus

1CM.

FIG. 4.21—Deep muscles of the pelvic girdle and crura, medial view.

ceps femoris, and external abdominal oblique muscles.

BLOOD SUPPLY: Cranial gluteal artery; circumflex femoral (cranial head).

NERVE SUPPLY: Cranial gluteal, lumbalis, and femoral nerves.

CAUDAL HEAD

ORIGIN: The caudal part of the gluteal fossa of the ilium.

INSERTION: Caudolateral surface of the proximal extremity of the femur just below the greater trochanter and above and caudal to the 3rd trochanter.

ACTION: To extend and abduct the hip.

RELATIONS: Superficially the aponeurosis between the tensor fasciae latae and the biceps femoris, the gluteus medius; deeply the fibrous layer of the joint capsule of the hip joint and the greater trochanter of the femur and adjacent areas to the trochanter.

BLOOD SUPPLY: Caudal gluteal and femoral arteries.

NERVE SUPPLY: Caudal gluteal and lumbalis nerves.

Gluteus Medius (Fig. 4.22)

LOCATION: This muscle is very large and covers the dorsal surface of the wing of the ilium.

ORIGIN: A deep concave depression on the dorsal surface of the wing of the ilium called the gluteal fossa.

INSERTION: To the greater part of the lateral surface of the greater trochanter of the femur. Interposed between the tendon of insertion of this muscle and the lateral surface of the greater trochanter of the femur is a large bursa termed the bursa trochanteris (trochanteric bursa).

ACTION: To extend the hip articulation and abduct the limb.

RELATIONS: Superficially the sartorius, tensor fasciae latae, biceps femoris, and gluteus superficialis (caudal head) muscles; deeply the dorsal

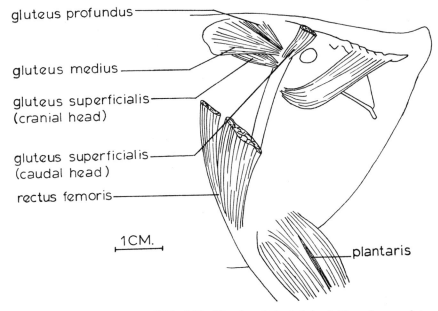

gluteus profundus

gluteus medius

gluteus superficialis
(cranial head)

gluteus superficialis
(caudal head)

rectus femoris

1CM.

plantaris

FIG. 4.22—Muscles of the pelvic girdle and crura, lateral view.

surface of the wing of the ilium, the cranial head of the gluteus superficialis, and the gluteus profundus.

BLOOD SUPPLY: Femoral and cranial gluteal arteries.

NERVE SUPPLY: Lumbalis nerve.

Gluteus Profundus (Fig. 4.22)

LOCATION: This is a small, quadrilateral muscle which lies just beneath the caudal part of the preceding muscle. It passes around the cranial border of the hip articulation.

ORIGIN: From the caudolateral edge of the wing of the ilium and the caudoventral surface of the acetabulum.

INSERTION: Trochanter major of the femur between the insertion of the cranial head and that of the caudal head of the gluteus superficialis.

ACTION: To flex the hip and rotate and abduct the thigh.

RELATIONS: Superficially the gluteus medius covers this muscle entirely; deeply the ilium, iliacus muscle, rectus femoris, gluteus superficialis (cranial head), and the hip articulation.

BLOOD SUPPLY: Cranial gluteal and femoral arteries.

NERVE SUPPLY: Lumbar nerves.

Biceps Femoris (Fig. 4.10)

LOCATION: This muscle is the largest in the pelvic and crural region and constitutes the greater part of the muscular mass of the lateral thigh.

ORIGIN: Lumbodorsal fascia, the dorsal surface of the ischium at the proximal extremity of the origin. This muscle blends with the aponeurotic origin of the tensor fasciae latae muscle. Both of these muscles form an aponeurosis that extends over the greater trochanter of the femur at the hip joint.

INSERTION: Lateral surface of the patella, the tendons of insertion of the rectus femoris and vastus lateralis, and the tibial crest and crural fascia.

ACTION: Extends the hip, flexes the knee, and rotates the leg inward.

RELATIONS: Superficially the skin and fascia; deeply the semimembranosus, semitendinosus, and vastus lateralis of the quadriceps femoris group, the lateral head of the gastrocnemius, the coccygeal fascia, and the caudal head of the gluteus superficialis muscle.

BLOOD SUPPLY: Caudal gluteal, superior nutrient, and femoral arteries.

NERVE SUPPLY: Caudal gluteal and ischiatic nerves.

Semimembranosus (Figs. 4.10, 4.20, 4.21, 4.24)

LOCATION: This is a large, three-sided muscle lying on the medial surface of the semitendinosus and biceps femoris muscles and it is composed of a cranial and a caudal portion.

ORIGIN: Both parts have a common origin: the ventrolateral area of the caudal part of the ischium and the 1st and 2nd coccygeal vertebrae.

INSERTION: The fibers of the cranial portion extend downward and forward to wind around the caudal and ventral areas of the femur. The caudal part descends in a vertical direction and expands to form a wide sheet that inserts on the tibiotarsus at an aponeurosis between the internal and medial heads of the gastrocnemius.

ACTION: To extend the hip, flex the knee, rotate the leg outward and adduct the limb, extend the hock, and flex the digits.

RELATIONS: Superficially the skin on the caudal thigh and the caudofemoralis muscles; laterally the biceps femoris and semitendinosus muscles; deeply the adductor, quadratus femoris, and caudofemoralis muscles.

BLOOD SUPPLY: Caudal gluteal, deep femoral, caudal tibial, and caudal femoral arteries.

NERVE SUPPLY: Ischiatic nerve.

Semitendinosus (Figs. 4.20, 4.24)

LOCATION: This long muscle lies behind and beneath the biceps femoris muscle.

ORIGIN: The crest and lateral surface of the ischium.

INSERTION: Two (three) prominent tendons of insertion are found on the caudal surface of the upper one-fourth of the tibia. Many tendinous fibers also end in the crural fascia.

Circulus tendinosus (Figs. 4.38, 4.39): A tendinous loop exists near the caudolateral aspect of the knee that aids markedly in the action of the semitendinosus. Passing through the loop are tendons of insertion of the above muscle and the peroneal nerve, one of the major branches of the sciatic nerve. The loop begins from the deep surface of the tendon of origin of the intermediate digital flexor and the lateral head of the gastrocnemius. It then passes over the lateral surface of the semitendinosus just at the point where the muscular part of the muscle becomes tendinous. The loop then folds medially over the caudal aspect of the semitendinosus and passes up the leg to attach to the craniolateral aspect of the distal extremity of the femur just above the articular surface of the patella.

ACTION: To extend the hip, flex the knee, and aid in extension of the hock articulation.

RELATIONS: Superficially the biceps femoris muscle, which almost entirely covers it, and the skin; deeply the semimembranosus, quadratus femoris, and caudofemoralis muscles and the aponeurotic insertion of the gluteal muscles; the sciatic, peroneal, and tibial nerves and branches of the femoral artery and vein. The tendons of insertion of this muscle to the tibiotarsus are in relationship with the lateral sides of the principal flexor muscles of the hock and digits.

BLOOD SUPPLY: Caudal gluteal, caudal tibial, and deep femoral arteries.

NERVE SUPPLY: Ischiatic nerve.

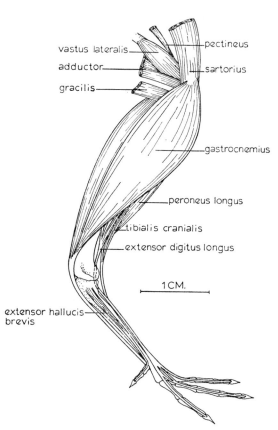

vastus lateralis
pectineus
adductor
sartorius
gracilis
gastrocnemius
peroneus longus
tibialis cranialis
extensor digitus longus
1 CM.
extensor hallucis brevis

FIG. 4.23—Muscles of the pelvic limb, medial view.

Quadriceps Femoris

LOCATION: This composes the large muscle that surrounds the femur except on its caudal surface. It has four muscular parts: *rectus femoris* (Fig. 4.22), *vastus lateralis* (Figs. 4.23, 4.24), *vastus medialis* (Fig. 4.21), and *vastus intermedialis*. All have their origin on the proximal extremity of the femur.

ORIGIN: The medial and lateral vasti and the rectus femoris originate from the medial, caudolateral, and proximocranial aspects of the femur,

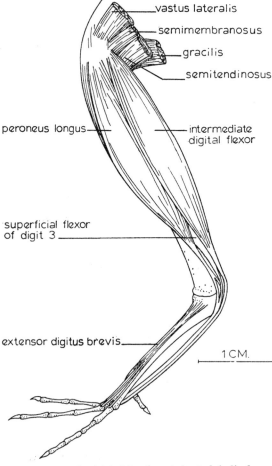

FIG. 4.24—Muscles of the pelvic limb, lateral view.

respectively. The vastus intermedius of the quadriceps femoris originates deeply on the cranial surface of the femur and is completely covered by the above three heads. All of the four parts are fused tightly, and it is not possible to separate them completely.

INSERTION: The primary insertions of the four components are to the respective proximal surfaces of the patella. The vastus lateralis also exhibits an aponeurotic insertion to the tibial crest by its incorporation into the broad patellotibial ligament.

ACTION: This large muscular mass acts solely to extend the knee.

RELATIONS: Superficially the sartorius, biceps femoris, and tensor fasciae latae muscles. At the proximal extremity of the femur the gluteus medius overlaps the attachment of the adductor semimembranosus, quadratus femoris, and caudofemoralis muscles and the cranial border of the semitendinosus.

BLOOD SUPPLY: Circumflex femoral, femoral, genu suprema, and superior nutrient arteries.

NERVE SUPPLY: Femoral and ischiatic nerves.

Quadratus Femoris (Fig. 4.21) (Ischiofemoralis—Hudson)

LOCATION: This is a three-sided muscle that spreads out in a fanlike manner behind the hip articulation.

ORIGIN: From the ventrolateral surface of the ischium below, and caudal to the tuber ischii.

INSERTION: Caudolateral surface of the femur below the greater trochanter.

ACTION: To extend the hip articulation, adduct the limb, and rotate the the thigh outward.

RELATIONS: Superficially the semimembranosus, semitendinosus, vastus lateralis, and biceps femoris muscles, the deep femoral vessels, and the great sciatic nerve; deeply the external obturator and the adductor muscles.

BLOOD SUPPLY: Deep femoral and caudal gluteal arteries.

NERVE SUPPLY: Ischiatic nerve.

Caudofemoralis (Fig. 4.18) (Piriformis—Hudson; Cruratus Caudalis —Chamberlain)

LOCATION: This bandlike muscle is positioned just below and behind the quadratus femoris, and its fibers extend caudodorsally to the cranioventral extremity of the pygostyle and to the adjacent three coccygeal vertebrae.

ORIGIN: From the ventral surface of the pygostyle and the adjacent three coccygeal vertebrae.

INSERTION: Proximocaudal surface of the femur just below the insertion of the quadratus femoris muscle.

ACTION: To extend the hip when the pygostyle is fixed and to depress the tail when the limb is stationary.

RELATIONS: Superficially the biceps femoris, semimembranosus, semitendinosus, and vastus lateralis muscles and the ischiatic nerve and deep femoral vessels; deeply the external obturator and the gracilis muscles and the skin on the medial surface of the thigh.

BLOOD SUPPLY: Deep femoral, internal pudic, umbilical, and caudal gluteal arteries.

NERVE SUPPLY: Ischiatic nerve.

Iliacus (Fig. 4.19)

LOCATION: A thin, somewhat triangular sheet composed primarily of fibers which extend ventrolaterally from the fossa and lateral border of the ilium to the craniolateral surface of the proximal extremity of the fe-

mur. Most of the fibers insert on the trochanter minor.

ORIGIN: Fossa and lateral border of the ilium cranial to the acetabulum.

INSERTION: Trochanter minor of the femur.

ACTION: To flex the hip joint and rotate the thigh outward.

RELATIONS: Dorsally the ilium, gluteus medius muscle, and branches of the iliac arteries; ventrally the inguinal ligament, the sartorius and abdominal muscles; laterally the rectus femoris; cranially the abdominal muscles; caudally the hip joint.

BLOOD SUPPLY: Femoral artery.

NERVE SUPPLY: Femoral nerve.

Gemellus (Fig. 4.19)

LOCATION: A thin, triangular muscle that is partially separated into two parts by the tendon of the internal obturator muscle.

ORIGIN: Lateral border of the ischium below the ischiatic foramen.

INSERTION: Caudal aspect of the trochanter, medial to the insertion of the internal obturator muscle.

ACTION: Rotation of the femur outward.

RELATIONS: Superficially the biceps femoris and gluteus medium muscles and the ischiatic blood vessels and nerves; deeply the internal obturator and the hip joint.

BLOOD SUPPLY: Femoral artery and branches of the obturator artery.

NERVE SUPPLY: Obturator nerve.

External Obturator (Fig. 4.11) (Obturator Externus)

LOCATION: A pyramid-shaped muscle that extends from the lateral and ventral region of the pelvis laterally across the surface of the hip joint to the lower region of the trochanter.

ORIGIN: Lateral surface of the ischium caudal to the ischiatic foramen and ventral to the origin of the quadratus femoris.

INSERTION: Lower portion of the trochanteric ridge distal to the insertion of the internal obturator.

ACTION: To adduct the thigh and rotate the femur outward.

RELATIONS: Medially the adductor muscle, the quadratus femoris muscle, and the femoral vessels; laterally the gemellus, internal obturator, and biceps femoris muscles; cranially the pectineus muscle and the hip joint.

BLOOD SUPPLY: Caudal gluteal and deep femoral arteries.

NERVE SUPPLY: Obturator nerve.

Internal Obturator (Fig. 4.21) (Obturator Internus)

LOCATION: This extensive, triangular muscle arises from the pelvic surface of the ischium and pubis. The tendon emerges through the obturator foramen and extends laterally to the caudolateral region of the trochanter major of the femur.

ORIGIN: Ventral concavity of the ilium and the pelvic surface of the ischium and pubis.

INSERTION: Trochanter major proximal to the insertion of the internal obturator and distal to the insertion of the gluteus medius.

ACTION: To rotate the femur outward and extend the hip.

RELATIONS: Pelvic fascia, covered in part by peritoneum, obturator vessels, and nerves, lie between two partially separated heads; laterally the ischium and pubis, external obturator, and gemellus muscles.

BLOOD SUPPLY: Obturator, internal pudic, and umbilical arteries.

NERVE SUPPLY: Obturator nerve.

Gracilis (Figs. 4.19, 4.21, 4.23–4.25)

LOCATION: One of the muscles which make up the first layer of the medial muscles of the thigh. It is situated behind the sartorius and in front of the adductor.

ORIGIN: Caudolateral surface of the ischium.

INSERTION. Crural fascia and medial tuberosity of the proximal extremity of the tibia.

ACTION: To extend the hip, flex the knee, and adduct the limb.

RELATIONS: Superficially the skin and fascia; cranially the sartorius muscle; caudally the adductor; laterally the femoral vessels.

BLOOD SUPPLY: Deep femoral and caudal tibial arteries.

NERVE SUPPLY: Obturator nerve.

Adductor (Figs. 4.19, 4.23, 4.26)

LOCATION: May be divided into two parts: lateral (cranial) and medial (caudal). The division, however, is difficult and the terminology is confusing.

ORIGIN: Adductor lateralis (cranial): the lateral border of the surface of the ilium cranial to the origin of the gracilis muscle.

INSERTION: Caudal surface of the distal extremity of the femur.

ORIGIN: Adductor medialis (caudal): lateral border of the pubis and ischiopubic membrane.

INSERTION: Medial surface of the distal extremity of the femur.

ACTION: To adduct the thigh and extend the hip.

RELATIONS: Medially the skin and fascia; caudally the gracilis and semimembranosus muscles; laterally the semitendinosus.

BLOOD SUPPLY: Femoral, deep femoral, and superior nutrient femoral arteries.

NERVE SUPPLY: Obturator nerve.

Pectineus (Figs. 4.21, 4.23)
(Ambiens—Gadow and Selenka; Fisher,
Hudson, and Shufeldt)

LOCATION: This muscle is highly developed only in reptiles and birds and is represented as the pectineus muscle in mammals.

ORIGIN: The lateral side of the pectineal process of the pubis and the prepubic tendon.

INSERTION: The small tendon winds around the knee from the medial to the lateral surface; penetrates the fascia above the tibiopatellar ligament and continues distad in its course to the lateral surface of the fibula and under the tendon of insertion of the semimembranosus muscle. It joins the fibers of the flexors of digits 2 and 3.

ACTION: Aids in flexion of the 2nd and 3rd digits (perching muscle); also flexes the hip and extends the knee.

RELATIONS: Laterally the fleshy part of the muscle is related to the quadriceps femoris muscle (rectus femoris and vastus medialis); medially the external abdominal oblique muscles, the sartorius muscle, and the skin on the medial surface of the thigh.

BLOOD SUPPLY: Femoral artery.

NERVE SUPPLY: Femoral nerve.

MUSCLES OF THE PELVIC LIMB

Gastrocnemius
(Figs. 4.20, 4.23, 4.25, 4.27)

LOCATION: This is the largest muscle of the true leg segment of the pelvic limb. It covers the caudolateral surface of the leg and arises from two heads.

ORIGIN: The lateral head is from the lateral epicondyle of the femur just cranial to the distal margin of the femoral insertion of the semimembranosus muscle; it is also connected with the distal portion of the tendinous loop for the semimembranosus muscle. It continues distad on the caudolateral border of the leg and fuses with the common tendon of the gastrocnemius. The medial head has its origin from an area just proximal to the medial condyle of the femur from the tibial crest and the patellar ligament.

INSERTION: Both heads of the gastrocnemius partially compose the tendon of Achilles and do not insert on the hypotarsal sesamoid bone, but plantar to it. Below the hock the tendon of the gastrocnemius fuses with the digital flexor tendon.

ACTION: To flex the knee (stifle) and extend the tarsus.

RELATIONS: Superficially the skin; deeply the tibialis cranialis, extensor digitus longus, quadriceps femoris, sartorius, adductor, semitendinosus, gracilis, and biceps femoris muscles.

BLOOD SUPPLY: Caudal tibial, lateral tibial, genu suprema, peroneal, and ramus tibialis arteries.

NERVE SUPPLY: Tibial nerve.

Plantaris (Fig. 4.22)
(Soleus)

LOCATION: This is a small, slender muscle that lies along the lateral border of the gastrocnemius. Its fleshy, short belly continues distad under the common, deep fascia of the proximal half of the lateral surface of the leg. Its thin tendon fuses with that of the gastrocnemius at the lower one-third of the leg. Due to its small size it is difficult to separate from the medial and internal parts of the gastrocnemius, between which its tendons lie.

ORIGIN: Craniomedial region of the proximal extremity of the tibia distal to the articulation with the femur.

INSERTION: Tendon of the gastrocnemius.

ACTION: To assist the gastrocnemius.

RELATIONS: Superficially the gastrocnemius, skin and fascia, and peroneal nerve; deeply the superficial flexor of digit 2 and the flexor hallucis longus. **Note:** The flexor muscle of the digits of birds in general appear to be developed mostly as a component mass in the fleshy or contractile portions of the muscle. The tendons, however, are entirely independent; therefore, various divisional categories have been used in naming partially separated muscles. For this reason the problem will be simplified as much as possible by using the terminology of Chamberlain and others who have not considered all the tendinous divisions as separable muscles.

BLOOD SUPPLY: Medial tibial artery.

NERVE SUPPLY: Tibial nerve.

Median Intermediate Digital Flexor (Fig. 4.26)
(Flexor Digitus Perforatus et Perforans Digiti Secundi)

LOCATION: This long flexor muscle of digit 2 is chiefly tendinous in its structure. It passes distad on the caudal surface of the tibia and extends through a canal of the hypotarsus, continuing distad on the plantar surface of the tarsometatarsus. The tendon is bound down by an annular ligament.

ORIGIN: Deep fascia of the surface of the knee joint.

INSERTION: Two small medial and lateral areas of the proximal extremity of the plantar surface of the 2nd phalanx of the 2nd digit.

ACTION: Flexes the 2nd digit.

RELATIONS: Superficially the superficial flexor of digit 3, and the gastro-

cnemius muscle; deeply the flexor hallucis brevis muscle.

BLOOD SUPPLY: Caudal tibial artery.

NERVE SUPPLY: Lateral tibial nerve.

Intermediate Digital Flexor (Figs. 4.20, 4.24, 4.26–4.28)
Flexor Digitus Perforatus et Perforans Digiti Tertii

LOCATION: This flexor of the 3rd digit lies parallel to the preceding muscle,

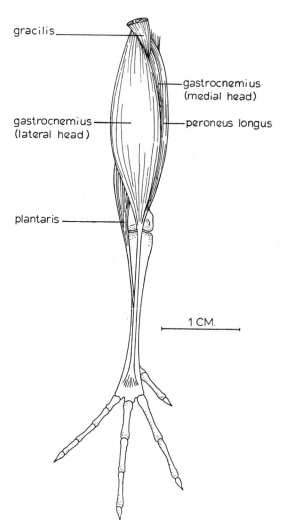

FIG. 4.25—Superficial muscles of the pelvic limb, caudal view.

and their fleshy portions are partially fused.

ORIGIN: Lateral epicondyle of the femur, the lateral surface of the proximal extremity of the fibula, and the tibiopatellar ligament.

INSERTION: Dorsal extremity of the 2nd phalanx of the 3rd digit.

ACTION: Flexes the 3rd digit.

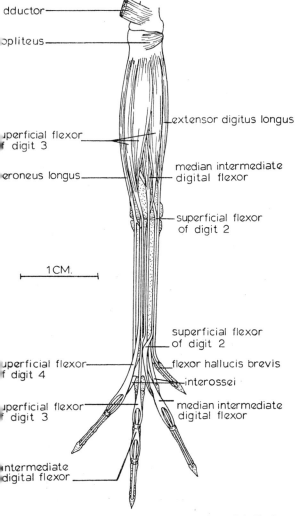

FIG. 4.26—Deep muscles of the pelvic limb, caudal view.

RELATIONS: Superficially the gastrocnemius, superficial flexors of digits 2 and 3; deeply the superficial flexor of digit 4 and the deep digital flexor.

BLOOD SUPPLY: Caudal tibial artery.

NERVE SUPPLY: Lateral tibial nerve.

Superficial Flexor of Digit 4 (Fig. 4.26) (Flexor Digitus Perforatus Digiti Quarti)

LOCATION: This flexor of digit 4 is closely associated in its course with the other flexors of digits 3 and 4.

ORIGIN: The intercondyloid fossa of the femur beside the tendon of origin of the flexor of digit 3, and the caudal head of the flexor hallucis longus. It also has an extensive origin from the caudal surface of the belly of the flexor hallucis longus.

INSERTION: Plantar surface of the distal extremities of the 1st, 2nd, and 3rd phalanges of the 4th digit. The tendon passes through the tibial cartilage ensheathed by the flattened tendon of the superficial flexor of digit 3. It accompanies the tendon of this muscle to the proximal extremity of the 1st phalanx of the 4th digit; at this point it divides into a medial and a lateral branch. The lateral branch inserts on the caudolateral surface of the 1st phalanx. At the proximal extremity of the 2nd phalanx the medial tendon encloses a branch of the long digital flexor tendon. It inserts on the proximal extremity of the 3rd phalanx.

ACTION: To flex the 4th digit.

RELATIONS: Superficially the semitendinosus and intermediate digital flexor muscles; deeply the superficial flexor of digit 3.

BLOOD SUPPLY: Caudal tibial artery.
NERVE SUPPLY: Lateral tibial nerve.

Superficial Flexor of Digit 3
(Figs. 4.24, 4.26)
(Flexor Digitus Perforatus
Digiti Tertii)

LOCATION: Superficial flexor of digit 3.
ORIGIN: From the intercondyloid fossa region with the superficial flexor of digit 4 and the caudal head of the flexor hallucis longus. It is also fused with the caudomedial surface of the superficial flexor of digit 4 which may also be considered as an origin of the muscle. The distal fleshy junction is at the lower third of the leg. The tendon continues laterad and pierces the tibial cartilage. At the tarsus the tendon widens and ensheathes the tendon of the superficial flexor of digit 4. The two tendons continue this relationship throughout the tarsal canal and distal to the middle of the tarsometatarsus. Just distal to the tarsal canal the tendon of the peroneus longus muscle joins the other two to continue distad. The tendon continues mediodistad to the medial side of the intermediate digital flexor.
INSERTION: Arises from the tendon of the peroneus longus muscle, on the plantar surfaces of the proximal end of the 1st (proximal) and 2nd phalanges of the 3rd digit, diverging into medial and lateral branches.
ACTION: Flexes the 3rd digit.
RELATIONS: Superficially the intermediate flexor of digit 3, the superficial flexor of digit 4, and the gastrocnemius muscle; deeply the flexor hallucis longus, deep digital flexor, and the superficial flexor of digit 3.
BLOOD SUPPLY: Caudal tibial and peroneal arteries.
NERVE SUPPLY: Ischiatic nerve.

Superficial Flexor of Digit 2
(Fig. 4.26)
(Flexor Digitus Perforatus
Digiti Secundi)

LOCATION: This long, slender flexor of the 2nd digit is primarily tendinous. It winds from the lateral surface of the leg caudally to the tarsus and continues distad on the caudomedial surface of the tarsometatarsus.
ORIGIN: Its tendinous fibers of origin arise from a small area just proximal to the lateral condyle and below the area of origin of the lateral head of the gastrocnemius. These fibers are associated with the tendon of insertion of the pectineus muscle and to the fibers of origin of the two intermediate digital flexors and to the cranial head of the flexor hallucis longus as well as to the tendinous loop for the biceps femoris. Its tendon of insertion pierces the tibial cartilage caudally to the tendon of the flexor hallucis longus muscle.
INSERTION: Two rather large areas flanking the plantar surface at the proximal extremity of the 1st phalanx of the 2nd digit.
ACTION: Flexes the 2nd digit.
RELATIONS: Superficially the fleshy belly is related by the gastrocnemius, the superficial flexor of digit 3, and the flexor hallucis longus; deeply the intermediate digital flexor and the extensor digitus longus; laterally the skin and fascia of the leg.
BLOOD SUPPLY: Caudal tibial artery and peroneal artery.
NERVE SUPPLY: Ischiatic nerve.

Flexor Hallucis Longus (Fig. 4.21)

LOCATION: One of the longest and most powerful flexor muscles of the leg situated between the lateral head of the gastrocnemius and the extensor digitus longus.
ORIGIN: Arises from two heads separated

by the tendons of the biceps femoris; the smaller head arises from an area of the lateral condyle of the femur in company with the two intermediate digital flexors and the superficial flexor of digit 2. The larger of the two tendons of origin arises from the intercondyloid fossa beside the origins of superficial flexors of digits 3 and 4. The two tendons of origin fuse to form a single round belly. The long tendon of insertion is formed just proximal to the tibial cartilage which is pierced, forming an osseous canal throughout its length. The tendon progresses distad and crosses over the surface of the extensor digitus longus. On reaching the proximal extremity of the first metatarsal bone, it passes between the 1st and 2nd metatarsals and pierces the large flattened tendon of the flexor hallucis brevis.

INSERTION: A small branch at the plantar surface of the distal extremity of the 1st phalanx, and in addition by its main branch to the plantar surface of the unguinal phalanx.

ACTION: Flexes the 1st digit.

RELATIONS: Medially the superficial flexors of digits 3 and 4; cranially the extensor digitus longus; caudally the lateral head of the gastrocnemius; and laterally the median intermediate digital flexor.

BLOOD SUPPLY: Ramus tibialis artery.

NERVE SUPPLY: Ischiatic nerve.

Deep Digital Flexor (Fig. 4.28) (Flexor Digitus Perforans)

LOCATION: This is the most deeply situated muscle on the plantar surface of the leg. It is the powerful flexor of digits 2, 3, and 4 and arises by two distinct heads.

ORIGIN: The femoral head arises from an area proximal to the lateral condyle and directly between the two heads

of origin of the flexor hallucis longus; this head fuses with the much larger tibiofibular head that arises from an extensive area of attachment of at least one-half the length of the plantar surface of the tibia and fibula. The fleshy portion of this muscle extends downward in a pennate fashion to join a centrally positioned tendon.

INSERTION: At the distal one-fourth of the tibia the fleshy fibers discontinue,

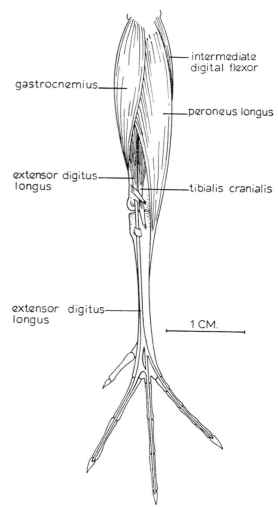

gastrocnemius

intermediate digital flexor

peroneus longus

extensor digitus longus

tibialis cranialis

extensor digitus longus

1 CM.

FIG. 4.27—Superficial muscles of the pelvic limb, cranial view.

and the powerful tendon of insertion penetrates the tibial cartilages just medial to the penetration of the flexor hallucis longus. From the sulcus of the tarsometatarsus the tendon deviates to the lateral side, so that the tendon comes to lie between the 1st and 2nd metatarsal bones. At the tarsometatarsal phalangeal articulations the tendon is divided into three branches, one of

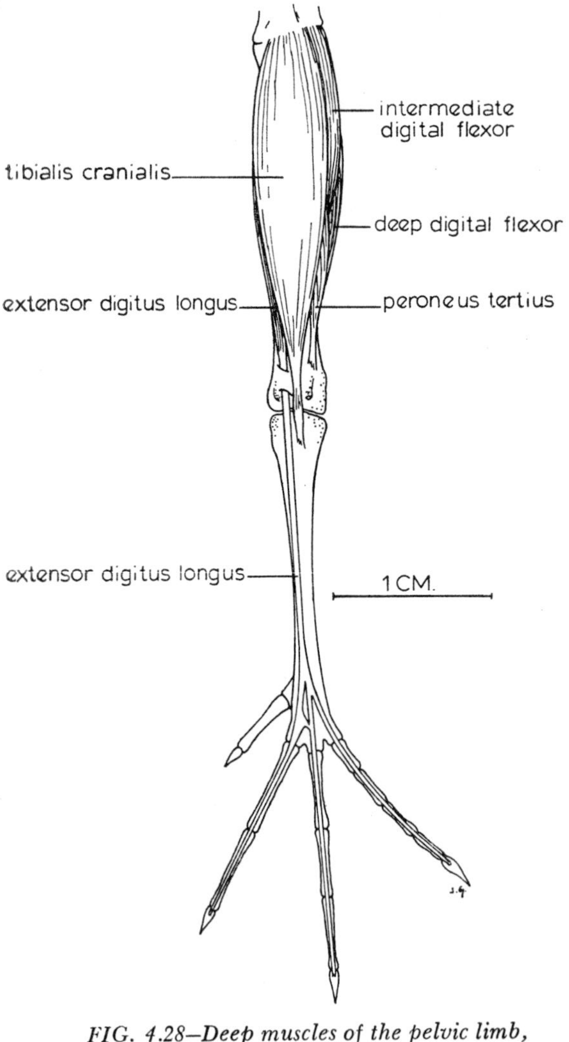

which passes distad to the plantar surfaces of each of the 2nd, 3rd, and 4th digits. The tendons of the other flexors of the digits are perforated in its course. The insertion of each digit is double; one attaches to the plantar surface of the distal extremity of the next to the last phalanx, and the primary branch to the plantar surface of the proximal extremity of the unguinal phalanx.

ACTION: To flex the toes of the 2nd, 3rd, and 4th digits.

RELATIONS: Cranially the tibia and fibula; medially the plantaris; caudally the flexor hallucis longus; laterally the tendons of the biceps femoris and the intermediate digital flexor.

BLOOD SUPPLY: Cranial tibial and ramus tibialis arteries.

NERVE SUPPLY: Tibial nerve.

Flexor Hallucis Brevis (Fig. 4.26)

LOCATION: On the caudomedial surface of the tarsometatarsus. Its fleshy part is in the shape of a small spindle at its proximal extremity. Its tendon extends distally just beneath the skin and fascia and caudal to the bone on the medial side of the pes. At the distal extremity of the pes it continues into the space between the 1st and 2nd metatarsal bones, becomes greatly enlarged and flattened, and curves around the tendon of the flexor hallucis longus.

ORIGIN: Plantar surface of the proximal extremity of the tarsometatarsus.

INSERTION: Proximal extremity of the 1st phalanx of the 2nd digit.

ACTION: Flexes the 2nd digit.

RELATIONS: Superficially the flexor hallucis longus and the deep digital flexor muscles; deeply the plantar interossei muscles.

BLOOD SUPPLY: Cranial tibial artery.

NERVE SUPPLY: Tibial nerve.

FIG. 4.28—Deep muscles of the pelvic limb, cranial view.

tibialis cranialis

intermediate digital flexor

deep digital flexor

extensor digitus longus

peroneus tertius

extensor digitus longus

1 CM.

Interossei (Fig. 4.26)

LOCATION: Two muscles are present which extend from the plantar surface of the tarsometatarsus to the lateral surface of the proximal extremities of the 1st phalanx.

ORIGIN: Plantar surface of the tarsometatarsus.

INSERTION: Proximal extremity of the lateral surface of the 1st phalanx.

ACTION: To adduct the 2nd and 4th digits.

RELATIONS: Superficially the deep digital flexor.

BLOOD SUPPLY: Dorsal pedal artery.

NERVE SUPPLY: Tibial nerve.

Peroneus Longus (Figs. 4.20, 4.23–4.27)

LOCATION: This is a rather large flexor that is situated in the craniomedial region of the leg. It is for the most part subcutaneous.

ORIGIN: Medial and lateral aspects of the dorsal surface of the proximal extremity of the tibia and from the tibiopatellar ligament. The wide belly of the muscle curves around to cover the tibialis cranialis and the peroneus brevis.

INSERTION: A strong tendon extends caudally and distally on the lateral side of the leg. Just above the tarsus a short tendinous branch extends to the lateral margin of the tibial cartilage. The main tendon continues distad on the lateral side of the tarsometatarsus. In its course it unites with the superficial flexor of digit 3.

ACTION: Helps to extend the tarsometatarsus and aids the superficial flexor of digit 3 in flexion.

RELATIONS: Superficially the skin and fascia; deeply the tibialis cranialis and peroneus tertius.

BLOOD SUPPLY: Cranial tibial, medial tibial, lateral tibial, and cranial recurrent tibial arteries.

NERVE SUPPLY: Common peroneal nerve.

Tibialis Cranialis (Figs. 4.23, 4.27, 4.28)

LOCATION: This rather large muscle lies on the dorsal surface of the leg partly covered by the peroneus longus.

ORIGIN: There are two distinct tendons of origin: one on the tibial crest near that of the extensor digitus longus, the other a caudal or femoral head that arises from the distal extremity of the condyle of the femur. The femoral and tibial heads fuse into a round, fleshy belly that is situated superficially and makes up the cranial portion of the leg. Just above the tarsus it forms a strong tendon that is bound down by an annular ligament. It is accompanied by the extensor digitus longus.

INSERTION: The tendon widens somewhat before inserting on the craniomedial aspect of the proximal extremity of the tarsometatarsus.

ACTION: Flexes the tarsal articulation.

RELATIONS: Cranially the peroneus longus muscle and the skin and fascia; caudally the peroneus tertius muscle, the tibia, and the extensor digitus longus muscle.

BLOOD SUPPLY: Cranial tibial and peroneal arteries.

NERVE SUPPLY: Common peroneal nerve.

Extensor Digitus Longus (Figs. 4.23, 4.26–4.28)

LOCATION: This muscle composes the largest part of the muscular mass on the immediate cranial surface of the tibia. Its tendon is bound very tightly in the intercondyloid groove of the tibia at the hock joint. About halfway down the tarsometatarsus the tendon trifurcates in the direction of the digits.

ORIGIN: From the tibial crest and the

dorsal surface of the shaft of the tibia.

INSERTION: On the proximodorsal surface of the distal phalanges of the 2nd, 3rd, and 4th digits. These tendons are firmly bound to the phalangeal articulations in these digits; these might be considered secondary insertions for they do aid in movement at these points.

ACTION: Extends the digits and flexes the tarsus.

RELATIONS: Superficially the skin and tibialis cranialis muscle; deeply the tibiotarsus, the extensor hallucis brevis muscle, and the tarsus.

BLOOD SUPPLY: Cranial tibial, peroneal, and cranial recurrent tibial arteries.

NERVE SUPPLY: Common peroneal nerve.

Peroneus Tertius (Fig. 4.28)

LOCATION: This muscle composes a large part of the musculature on the immediate lateral surface of the tibiotarsus (tibia).

ORIGIN: From the dorsolateral surface of the fibula, the interosseous ligament, and the adjacent surface of the tibiotarsus.

INSERTION: The tendon of this muscle crosses the tarsal articulation obliquely along the caudolateral aspect of the tendon, then inserts on the proximal aspect of the plantar tarsometatarsal tuberosity of the tarsometatarsus.

ACTION: Rotates the tarsometatarsus inward.

RELATIONS: Superficially the tibialis cranialis and peroneus longus muscles; deeply the fibula, the interosseous ligament, and the tibiotarsus.

BLOOD SUPPLY: Cranial tibial artery.

NERVE SUPPLY: Common peroneal nerve.

Extensor Hallucis Brevis (Fig. 4.23)

LOCATION: This small muscle lies on the dorsomedial aspect of the tarsometatarsus.

ORIGIN: Dorsomedial aspect of the tarsometatarsus.

INSERTION: On the proximodorsal surface of the distal phalanx of the 1st digit.

ACTION: Extends and abducts the 1st digit.

RELATIONS: Superficially the tendons of the extensor digitus longus muscle; deeply the tarsometatarsus.

BLOOD SUPPLY: Craniomedial metatarsal artery.

NERVE SUPPLY: Common peroneal nerve.

Extensor Digitus Brevis (Fig. 4.24)

LOCATION: This muscle occupies the greater part of the immediate dorsal surface of the tarsometatarsus. It lies within the lateral limits of the bone and has been termed the interossei dorsalis.

ORIGIN: Dorsomedial surface of the tarsometatarsus.

INSERTION: The dorsoproximal aspect of the 1st phalanx of the 3rd digit and the median aspect of the 1st phalanx of the 2nd and 4th digits.

ACTION: Extends and abducts the 2nd and 4th digits and extends the 3rd digit.

RELATIONS: Superficially the tendons of the extensor digitus longus muscles; deeply the tarsometatarsus and the 1st phalanges of the 2nd, 3rd, and 4th digits.

BLOOD SUPPLY: Craniolateral metatarsal artery.

NERVE SUPPLY: Deep dorsal proper digital nerve (off the common peroneal).

Popliteus (Fig. 4.26)

LOCATION: In the caudal proximity of the knee.

ORIGIN: From the caudoproximal surface of the tibia.

INSERTION: To the caudomedial surface of the head of the fibula.

ACTION: Rotates the leg inward.

RELATIONS: Superficially the median intermediate digital flexors of digits 2, 3, and 4; deeply the tibia.

BLOOD SUPPLY: Popliteal artery.

NERVE SUPPLY: Deep peroneal nerve.

CHAPTER FIVE

Neurology

THE nervous system of birds has become highly developed and specialized in keeping with the complex problems of locomotion. The reflex mechanisms are so highly developed that the bird can to a large degree depend upon its involuntary responses not only for protection and for obtaining food but for competence in the control of its habitual activities and everyday behavior. The common structural plan of the brain of both birds and mammals is quite similar; however, each varies considerably in the size and position of its various parts and in the location of the connecting neural pathways. Those parts of the brain which are associated with a very acute sense of sight have become highly specialized, while certain other parts such as those associated with the poor sense of smell or taste have become decidedly atrophic. This is exemplified by the poorly developed olfactory lobes of the brain.

MENINGES

The meninges are fibrous membranes which surround and protect the brain and spinal cord. They include three membranes: the dura mater (pachymenix), the arachnoid, and the pia mater (the latter two are collectively called the leptomenix).

The *dura mater* of the cranial cavity serves a dual function and consists of two layers: external (endosteal) and internal (meningeal). These layers are closely united except where venous sinuses are situated between them. The endosteal layer is closely adherent to the bones of the cranial cavity for which it acts as an internal periosteum. The cranial meningeal layer is very similar to the spinal dura and serves a similar function. It supplies sheaths for the cranial nerves and protects the brain itself. It differs from the spinal dura in that it forms three distinct processes which separate the different parts of the brain. These processes are: the falx cerebri, the tentorium cerebelli, and the diaphragma sellae. The falx cerebri is a midsagittal sickle-shaped fold of dura (meningeal layer) extending ventrally between the cerebral hemispheres. It fuses caudally with the tentorium cerebelli. The latter is the meningeal partition which runs transversely between the cerebellum and the cerebral hemispheres. The diaphragma sellae is a circular diaphragm that bridges the sella turcica forming a foramen through which the infundibulum of the pituitary gland passes. The cranial dura mater is continuous with the spinal dura mater at the foramen magnum.

The spinal dura mater resembles the meningeal layer of the cranial dura mater. It is not regularly attached to the spinal canal and thus leaves a space between it and the periosteum of the canal. This space is called the epidural space. It is filled with a variable amount of semisolid fatty material. The spinal dura is in the form of a long tubular envelope surrounding the spinal cord. Lateral tubular extensions of the dura cover the spinal nerve roots and accompany them to the intervertebral foramina. They terminate by becoming continuous with the epineurium of the spinal nerves.

Caudally the spinal dura tapers to a point and fuses with the pia mater to form the filum terminale, which then extends caudally for a very short distance to attach to the periosteum of the spinal canal at the 6th or 7th coccygeal vertebra.

The *arachnoid membranes* of both the cranial cavity and spinal canal are very delicate transparent membranes which are avascular. These membranes are situated between the dura and pia mater and are separated from them by the subdural and subarachnoid cavities, respectively. The subdural cavity is a very narrow space which contains a small amount of clear yellow fluid. Since the cranial and spinal arachnoid membranes are continuous at the foramen magnum, so are the arachnoid cavities. They communicate with the ventricular system of the brain by way of the 4th ventricle. The arachnoid membrane has tubular extensions which surround the origin of the cranial nerves as well as the dorsal and ventral spinal nerve roots. It ends caudally in the formation of the filum terminale. The arachnoid membrane is attached to the underlying pia mater by connective tissue trabeculae which pass through the subarachnoid space.

The *pia mater* is a delicate and very vascular membrane which adheres very closely to the surfaces of the brain and spinal cord. The cranial pia mater follows all the fissures of the brain very closely. The trabeculae thus formed penetrate the brain substance and support the blood vessels which enter the brain. The spinal pia mater (Fig. 5.11), although continuous with the cranial pia mater, is much thicker and denser than that of the cranium. In addition to supplying processes into the spinal cord proper, the pia also has attachments to the spinal dura by strong denticulate ligaments. These serve to anchor the spinal cord in the center of the subarachnoid cavity. The spinal pia mater attaches caudally at the 6th or 7th coccygeal vertebra along with the arachnoid and dura.

BRAIN

The general form and structure of the avian brain (Figs. 5.1–5.4) resembles that of its reptilian ancestors, but it is much larger and more highly developed. As in mammals the brain of birds conforms in great part in shape and size to the cavity in which it lies. However, there is a marked variation in these dimensions of the brains in different species. This was shown by Marshall (1961) who reported that among five unrelated species of birds with approximately the same body weight (80–90 gm) the brain weight ranged from .73 gm in the coturnix quail to 2.7 gm in the great spotted woodpecker. The average weight of the coturnix brain is approximately 0.75% of the body weight. The average width measured through the cerebral hemispheres just rostral to the optic chiasma is 14 mm.

The length of the brain when measured from the rostral tip of the olfactory bulb to the caudal tip of the medulla oblongata (in the region of the foramen magnum) is 16 mm. The general shape and position of the brain in the skull is determined by a number of factors. These are: the large size of the cerebral hemisphere, the cerebellum, and the optic lobes. In addition the narrowness of the cranial cavity and the large size and position of the eyes cause the cerebellum and the cerebral hemispheres to displace the greatly enlarged optic lobes into a ventrolateral position

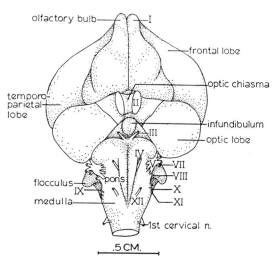

FIG. 5.1—Brain, ventral view.

between the eyes and the cranial portion of the medullary bulb. The size and position of the eyes produce a large concavity on the cranioventral surface of the cerebral hemispheres and a resultant diminution of the rostral portion of the brain. All these factors influence the axis of the brain, which is determined by measuring the angle between the longitudinal axis of the skull and the base line of the brain (the base line is a line extending from the caudal extremity of the medulla to the dorsal surface of the optic chiasma). In coturnix the axis of the brain and that of the skull form an angle of approximately 40°.

With the meninges and vessels removed, the ventral surface presents the brain stem which is a rostral continuation of the spinal cord. The brain stem is short and very broad and consists of three parts. The medulla oblongata (Figs. 5.1, 5.4, 5.8) forms the caudal part. The pons (Fig. 5.1, 5.4), which appears as a continuation of the medulla, is a transversely elongated mass which sends fiber tracts on either side into the cerebullum (Figs. 5.2–5.4) through the cerebellar

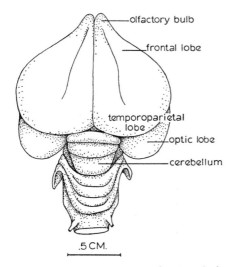

FIG. 5.2—Brain, dorsal view.

peduncles. The corpora quadrigemina (anterior and posterior colliculi) (Fig. 5.4) are not peduncular, but are represented by small fiber tracts extending from the cranial end of the pons toward the cerebral hemispheres. They appear to blend into the large optic tracts. Situated between the rudimentary cerebral peduncles is the hypophysis cerebri, or pituitary body. It is suspended by a very delicate pars tuberalis. Its infundibulum, or stalk (Fig. 5.1), continues from the tuber cinereum under the 3rd ventricle (Fig. 5.4). The mammillary bodies, as they appear in mammals, have not been found. Immediately caudolateral to the pituitary body are the bodies of the extremely large optic lobes (Figs. 5.1–5.3). Projecting from the craniomedial surface of the lobes are very large bands of white matter, the optic tracts. These cross obliquely cranial to the pituitary body to unite and form the optic chiasma (Figs. 5.1, 5.3). Dorsal and rostral to the chiasma the median longitudinal fissure separates the cerebral hemispheres. At the rostral extremity of each hemisphere are the small olfactory bulbs (Figs. 5.1–5.3) from

which the olfactory nerve fibers continue. The superficial origin of the cranial nerves, with the exception of the 4th, or trochlear, are visible on the base of the brain.

When the dorsal surface of the brain is viewed, the cerebral hemispheres, the cerebellum, the optic lobes, and part of the medulla oblongata are visible. The cerebral hemispheres form an ovoid mass and are separated from each other by the median longitudinal fissure. Their surfaces, unlike those in mammals, do not possess prominent gyri and sulci, but are smooth except for minor valleculae and elevations (sagittal). It is possible to distinguish the frontal and temporoparietal lobes (Figs. 5.1–5.3) corresponding to those of mammals. The caudal extremity of the hemispheres overlies the cranial part of the cerebellum. The transverse fissure containing the tentorium cerebelli separates the cerebrum and cerebellum.

The ventricular system of the avian brain is similar to that of mammals, consisting of two lateral ventricles, and the 3rd and 4th ventricles connected by the cerebral aqueduct (Fig. 5.4).

The great development of the somatic striatum completely fills the interior of the caudal part of the cerebral hemisphere and is largely responsible for its size. The small undeveloped olfactory nerve and bulb are associated with a poorly developed hippocampal formation in the dorsal and medial walls of the hemisphere. The thalamus (Fig. 5.4) is small and completely hidden from view ventrally by the large, flat optic tracts. In coturnix the cerebellum is composed chiefly of the central body and the flocculi (Fig. 5.1). The central body rising above the brain stem is well developed and is separated from the medulla oblongata by the 4th ventricle. The degree of development is correlated with the complexity of body movements

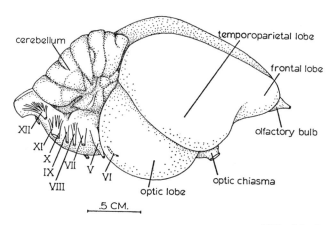

FIG. 5.3—Brain, lateral view.

and the maintenance of the posture of the bird.

The structure of the medulla oblongata compares favorably with the cranial portion of the spinal cord. The central canal (Fig. 5.11) of the cord is a direct continuation of the widened 4th ventricle; within the medulla it is separated from the overlying cerebellum by a thin membranous roof that is modified to form the choroid plexus of the ventricle.

The two lobes of hypothalamus lie lateral to the 3rd ventricle, attached by a slender tract that passes through it.

CRANIAL NERVES

The 12 pairs of cranial nerves (Figs. 5.1, 5.3, 5.5–5.9, 5.21) are numbered according to their rostral to caudal origins from the brain. Their numbers, names, and functional classifications are given in the following table.

Olfactory Nerve

The *olfactory nerve* (Figs. 5.1, 5.5) is an extension of the semitransparent olfactory lobe. The nerve is of the same appearance and extends from the rostral tip of the olfactory lobe to the dorsal turbinate. It is accompanied by the eth-

moid artery. The nerve and artery and a satellite vein are enclosed in a long groove formed in the ethmoidal and frontal bones. Laterally they are bounded by the connective tissue orbital lining. Just before the nerve reaches the dorsal turbinate, a branch of the trigeminal, the ophthalmic, crosses its laterorostral surface. The olfactory nerve divides into many fine branches and terminates in the turbinates.

Optic Nerve

From the medioventral surface of each tectum a large nerve emerges. These nerves merge to form the *optic chiasma* (Figs. 5.1, 5.3, 5.6) rostral to the pituitary gland. They bifurcate and one

Number	Name	Function
I	Olfactory	Sensory (smell)
II	Optic	Sensory (sight)
III	Oculomotor	Motor
IV	Trochlear	Motor
V	Trigeminal	Mixed
VI	Abducens	Motor
VII	Facial	Mixed
VIII	Acoustic	Sensory (hearing)
IX	Glossopharyngeal	Mixed
X	Vagus	Mixed
XI	Spinal accessory	Motor
XII	Hypoglossal	Motor

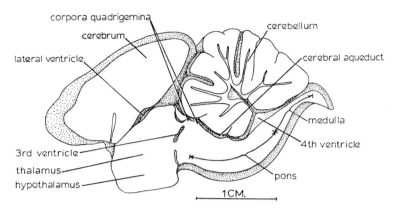

FIG. 5.4—Brain, median section.

branch terminates in the caudomedial surface of each globe. Under the dissecting microscope the optic chiasma in cross section shows a series of slits in its surface.

Oculomotor Nerve

The *oculomotor nerve* (Figs. 5.1, 5.6, 5.7) emerges from the medulla immediately caudal to the pituitary gland. It progresses rostrad lateral to the pituitary, then on to the optic foramen. It comes through the foramen medial to the ophthalmic nerve and lateroventral to the

optic nerve. The oculomotor nerve progresses rostrad for a few millimeters and bifurcates into a dorsal and a ventral branch.

The dorsal branch progresses dorsad, splits into many fine branches, and terminates in the dorsal rectus muscle.

The ventral branch progresses ventrad around the caudal surface of the optic nerve and gives off numerous small branches to the ventral rectus muscle. A branch leaves the main nerve ventral to the optic nerve and progresses rostrad across the lateral surface of Harder's

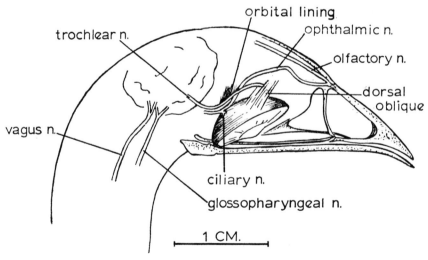

FIG. 5.5—Nerves of the head, lateral view.

gland (Fig. 5.7) to terminate in the ventral oblique muscle. The main portion of the ventral branch, after picking up a small branch from the abducens, gives off another branch, the ciliary nerve (Fig. 5.5), which progresses laterad and enters the globe from its caudolateral aspect. The ventral branch of the nerve continues on around the optic nerve to its rostral surface and there supplies the large medial rectus muscle near its origin.

Trochlear Nerve

The *trochlear nerve* (Figs. 5.1, 5.5, 5.7) originates from the dorsal surface of the medulla. It emerges from the brain stem caudal to the tectum (Fig. 5.6) and between the cerebellum and cerebrum. The nerve curves first dorsally, then ventrally, and finally rostrally along the ventromedial surface of the tectum to the optic foramen. From the foramen it courses dorsad in the orbital lining, then leaves the lining and curves rostromedially to terminate in the global surface of the dorsal oblique muscle.

Trigeminal Nerve

After leaving its bulbar origin and forming the semilunar (gasserian or maxillomandibular) ganglion, the *trigeminal nerve* (Figs. 5.1, 5.3, 5.7, 5.8) emerges from the brain stem caudoventral to the origin of the trochlear nerve, at the caudomedial aspect of the tectum. It bifurcates into a medial and a lateral branch as it crosses the ventral surface of the tectum.

Ophthalmic Nerve

The medial branch of the trigeminal, the *ophthalmic nerve* (Figs. 5.5–5.7), is composed chiefly of fibers of the somatic sensory system. It courses along with, but ventral to, the trochlear nerve and passes into the orbital cavity lateral to the optic nerve. The ophthalmic nerve then courses dorsorostrad, curving up over the dorsomedial surface of the globe to the medial canthus of the eye. Here it divides into three branches. A fine frontal branch progresses laterad to the subcutaneous tissues and skin of the medial canthus of the eye. A larger

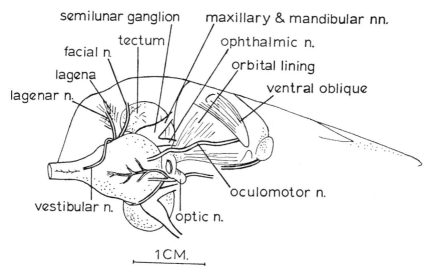

FIG. 5.6—*Nerves of the ventral region of the head.*

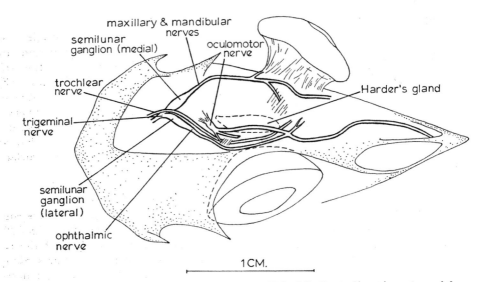

FIG. 5.7—*Deep dissection of cranial nerves.*

lacrimal branch accompanies a tubelike extension from Harder's gland and terminates in an arterial rete and the glandular structure at the medial canthus. The third branch, the nasociliary, gives off the ethmoidal nerve which is the main continuation of the ophthalmic nerve. It progresses rostromediad over the dorsal turbinate and continues rostrad close to the ethmoidal nerve of the opposite side. Midway along the dorsal turbinate the two ethmoidal nerves curve sharply ventrad and then continue rostrad between the two plates forming the nasal septum. They continue rostrad to the caudal extremity of the beak where they split into many fine branches. Another nerve, a composite branch of the facial and glossopharyngeal nerves, progresses caudad along the dorsal border of Harder's gland and continues rostrad from the medial canthus of the eye to terminate in the dorsal turbinate and skin of that area. This can easily be identified mistakenly as a branch of the ophthalmic nerve in the quail.

Maxillary Nerve

The lateral branch of the trigeminal nerve splits indistinctly into dorsal and ventral groups of fibers. These are also classified chiefly as somatic sensory components. The dorsal group may be termed the *maxillary nerve* (Figs. 5.6, 5.7, 5.9). As it emerges from its foramen in the skull, it is surrounded by a complete rete of arteries. A large branch progresses dorsad, bifurcates, and terminates in the temporalis muscle. A small branch progresses laterorostrad to the conjunctival tissue in the area of the lower eyelid and nictitating membrane. A small nerve leaves the main trunk deep to the lateral canthus of the eye and progresses medioventrad in the orbital lining. This nerve enters the orbital lining ventral to the dorsal turbinate. It then penetrates a rete of arteries, progresses ventrad, then rostrad to enter the hard palate. In the hard palate it continues to the tip of the beak and terminates. As the maxillary nerve progresses rostrad, a number of branches comparable to those of mammals are found. The names, however, are not appropriate because of the differences of the development of the side of the face, the lack of teeth, and the large size of the eyes. These branches are distributed to the lacrimal glands and the caudal angle of the mouth and cheeks.

Mandibular Nerve

A lateral branch of the trigeminal, the *mandibular nerve* (Figs. 5.6, 5.7, 5.9), a branch of the main lateral complex, progresses first laterad, then rostrad, and finally ventrad to the mandibular foramen. Just before the nerve enters the foramen, it gives off a small branch which progresses rostrad to the caudal angle of the beak. The mandibular nerve enters the mandibular foramen and progresses rostrad in the bony canal to the tip of the mandible, where it appears to join the mandibular nerve from the opposite side.

Abducens Nerve

The *abducens nerve* emerges from the ventromedial surface of the medulla on a transverse plane with the caudal border of the tectum. This nerve progresses ventrorostrad in a bony canal and reaches the optic foramen. It passes through this foramen lateral to the oculomotor nerve. As it emerges, it gives off a large branch to the lateral rectus muscle. A smaller branch progresses mediad to join the large ciliary nerve which enters the globe. The nerve terminates in supplying the retractor bulbi muscles.

Facial Nerve

The *facial nerve* (Figs. 5.1, 5.3, 5.6) emerges from the lateral surface of the medulla just caudal to the tectum. The cranial roots of the nerves are located very close to those of the acoustic nerve. The facial and the acoustic nerves thus

formed progress laterad and enter the internal acoustic meatus of the temporal bone. The facial nerve enters the cranioventral portion of the meatus, traverses the facial canal through the temporal bone, and leaves the canal by way of the foramen lacerum. The first part of the canal runs around the cochlea to the tympanic recess which lodges the geniculate ganglion. From the ganglion the facial canal continues in company with the maxillary canal, from which it is only partially separated, to its external orifice at the foramen lacerum.

The geniculate ganglion is situated in the ampulla of the facial canal; from this ganglion the greater superficial petrosal nerve and the facial root of the lesser superficial petrosal nerve arise. The cranial continuance of the facial nerve gives off the chorda tympani and a communicating branch to the cranial cervical ganglion of the sympathetic nerve. The chorda tympani accompanies the facial nerve a short distance and then leaves the facial canal and continues ventrolaterad in the maxillary canal to join the facial root of the lesser superficial petrosal nerve. At the external acoustic meatus it passes through a foramen and continues cranioventrad over the quadratopterygoid joint and the superficial temporal and facial veins and penetrates the pterygoquadratosphenoideus muscle. After giving off anastomotic branches to the pterygoid nerve, it continues forward and enters the inferior alveolar canal in company with the inferior alveolar nerve (so named because of the similar structure of a nerve that is distributed to the alveoli of the teeth of mammals).

Acoustic Nerve

The *acoustic nerve* (Figs. 5.1, 5.3), leaves the lateral aspect of the medulla just caudal to the facial nerve. It is easily separable into two distinct parts:

the lagenar part for the registering of sound vibrations, and the vestibular part which functions in maintaining the position of the body and the mechanism of equilibration. The lagenar (Fig. 5.6), or larger of the two divisions, curves ventrad in the lagena to supply the organ of Corti. The vestibular branch (Fig. 5.6) continues into the vestibule caudal to the lagenar branch to supply the hair cells of the maculae of the utriculus, sacculus, and lagena and the cristae ampullaris. The macula of the lagena is a cup-shaped neuroepithelial structure peculiar to birds.

Glossopharyngeal Nerve

The *glossopharyngeal nerve* (Figs. 5.1, 5.3, 5.5, 5.9) emerges from the caudolateral surface of the medulla caudal and ventral to the acoustic nerve. It penetrates the cranial wall by progressing caudolaterad in a bony canal. As it emerges from the skull, it is joined by the large heart-shaped jugular ganglion. The apex of this ganglion also joins the vagus nerve and receives fibers from

the facial nerve. After its emergence from the skull the glossopharyngeal nerve courses caudad, then ventrad, and gives off muscular branches to the hyoglossal muscles in the region of the angle of the greater cornua of the hyoid bone.

Just before the glossopharyngeal nerve leaves the skull, it sends a large branch rostromediad with the internal carotid artery in its bony canal. It receives a branch from the facial nerve just rostral to the ventral aspect of the lagena and progresses rostrad to the choanae. Here a branch is given off to the hard palate. The continuing trunk progresses on to the orbit and passes along the dorsal border of Harder's gland. It joins the ophthalmic nerve near the dorsal turbinate and terminates in the mucous membrane of the turbinates and the skin of the area.

A small branch leaves the parent trunk and progresses rostrad with an artery to ramify in the lateral wall of the pharynx on a level with the caudal extremity of the orbit. Just caudal to the above branch the glossopharyngeal nerve

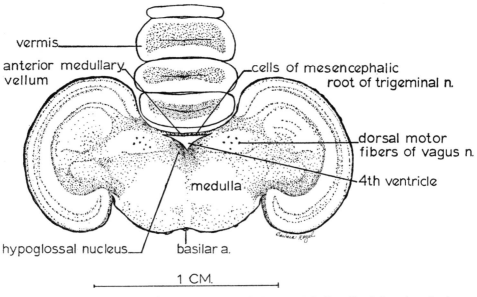

vermis

anterior medullary vellum

cells of mesencephalic root of trigeminal n.

dorsal motor fibers of vagus n.

4th ventricle

medulla

hypoglossal nucleus   basilar a.

1 CM.

FIG. 5.8—*Mesencephalic cells of the trigeminal nerve.*

splits into a complex maze of branches intertwining in an arterial rete. It gives off some fine branches to the hypoglossal nerve. A branch appears to progress caudad through this maze and to continue down the neck with an artery midway to the thoracic inlet; in its course it ramifies on the dorsolateral wall of the trachea and the ventrolateral wall of the esophagus. Another branch leaves the maze and progresses ventrolaterad with the main trunk of the hypoglossal nerve to which it is adhered with fine connective tissue. This nerve continues ventrorostrad to the midline and then rostrad to ramify in the ventral wall of the pharynx, where the trachea blends into the pharynx.

Vagus Nerve

The *vagus nerve* (Figs. 5.1, 5.3, 5.5, 5.9) emerges from the medulla very close to the caudolateral region of the glossopharyngeal nerve. It progresses directly through its own bony canal to emerge via the vagal foramen. As it emerges from the skull, it is joined by fibers from the large ganglion of the glossopharyngeal nerve. A small branch leaves the vagus as it emerges from the skull. This branch receives a few fibers from the glossopharyngeal nerve and progresses laterodorsad to terminate in the cutaneous colli lateralis muscle. This is thought to be the termination of the spinal accessory nerve. The vagus nerve progresses caudad in the jugular groove as the intestinal branch and is joined by a large branch from the cranial cervical ganglion. Its caudal continuation will be described under the autonomic nervous system.

Spinal Accessory Nerve

The *spinal accessory nerve* (Figs. 5.1, 5.3, 5.9) is a composite of fibers from the 1st, 2nd, and 3rd cervical nerves. As nearly as one can tell with a dissecting microscope, the nerve begins at cervical nerve 3. It progresses rostrad, receives fibers from cervical nerves 2 and 1, and then continues rostrad in the meninges into the cranium, where it curves laterally for 1 mm and bifurcates. One branch penetrates the skull and progresses caudad, emerges from the skull, and joins the hypoglossal nerve. The other small branch progresses ventrad to the vagus nerve, which it joins and with which it emerges from the

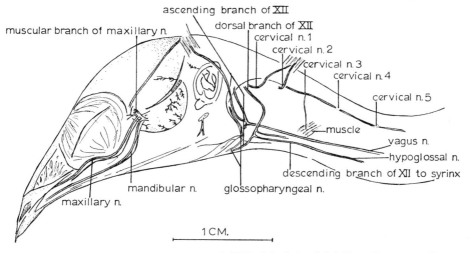

FIG. 5.9—Superficial dissection of cranial nerves.

vagal foramen. It then receives some fibers from the glossopharyngeal nerve and progresses to the caudal portion of the auditory meatus, where most of the fibers terminate. A few fibers continue on to the cutaneous colli lateralis muscle.

Hypoglossal Nerve

The *hypoglossal nerve* (Figs. 5.1, 5.3, 5.8, 5.9) emerges from the caudoventral portion of the medulla. It progresses caudad through its bony canal to emerge from the hypoglossal foramen. It immediately divides into a large dorsal branch and a smaller ventral branch. As the dorsal branch progresses, it gives off a fine branch to the 1st cervical nerve and then continues to supply the muscles of the dorsum of the neck near the skull. The ventral branch progresses at first ventrad, then lateroventrad, and soon crosses the vagus nerve. At this point it gives off a small branch which continues caudad down the neck in close proximity to the lateral surface of the jugular vein to the syrinx. Here another small branch is given off, which turns rostrad to accompany the vagus nerve and enter the skull. The main continuation of the ventral branch of the hypoglossal then begins a rostromedial course to the ventral pharyngeal area. In this area six small branches are given off at 2–4 mm intervals. These fibers progress through the sternothyrohyoideus and sternotrachealis muscles and then disappear in the tracheal wall. The rostral continuation of this nerve ramifies in and supplies the poorly developed muscles of the tongue.

SPINAL CORD

The *spinal cord* (Figs. 5.10–5.14) is that part of the nervous system which lies in the vertebral canal. It extends from the level of the foramen magnum

cranially to the last free vertebra (pygostyle) caudally. It is white in color and generally cylindrical in form. The cord shows marked enlargements at the cervicothoracic and synsacral regions. Its caudal extremity is tapered. The enlargements are formed by the convergence of nerve roots which form the large brachial and synsacral plexuses. The cervicothoracic enlargement is very similar to the corresponding enlargement of the same region in other vertebrates; however, the caudal enlargement is much more complicated. It is formed not only by a mass development of the gray matter but also by a unique dorsal transformation of other spinal cord tissues.

At the level of the ischiatic nerve the dorsal funicular tracts separate along a zone of four segments which represent the 4th to 7th synsacral nerves and leave a cleft (rhomboid sinus) filled with a mass of large cells that are rich in glycogen. The details of the development of the rhomboid sinus have been reported by Ganfenni (1930) and De Gennaro (1959) as observed in the chicken embryo during the 7th to 13th days of incubation.

The spinal cord may be divided into segments, each segment being that portion from which the rootlets arise to form a pair of spinal nerves. A spinal cord segment is identified by the same name and number as the pair of spinal nerves which attach to it. The coturnix quail has 40 spinal cord segments: 15 cervical, 7 thoracic, 12 synsacral, and 6 coccygeal. The segments are longest in the midcervical region and shortest in the coccygeal region, thus corresponding with the lengths of the vertebrae of the same region. The segments with the largest diameter are found in the cervicothoracic and synsacral regions. Due to the rapid development and growth of coturnix, the spinal cord and vertebral

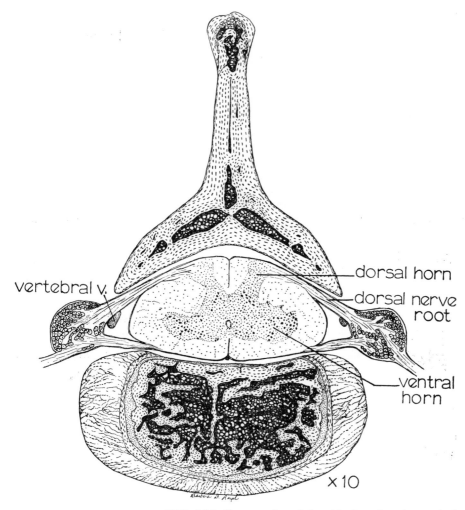

×10

FIG. 5.10—Cross section of the spinal cord at the cervical area.

column have only a difference of one vertebra in their lengths. Therefore, the external structure of the caudal section of the cord in relation to the vertebrae is distinctive. The spinal nerve roots emerge from the spinal canal almost perpendicular to the cord. (In most vertebrates the roots are directed caudally due to an extended growth of the vertebral column; therefore, the conus medullaris and filum terminale are very short and a cauda equina is absent.)

The external landmarks such as the different sulci and fissures, except for the rhomboid sinus, are similar to those found in other vertebrates. The internal structure is also the same, showing the **H**-shaped area of gray matter surrounded by the white matter. The central canal is in the gray commissure of the **H**, and the dorsal and ventral horns are present as in other vertebrates. The cellular arrangement has a distinct resemblance to the mammalian plan although somewhat more primitive. The spinal nerves exit via dorsal and ventral rami from

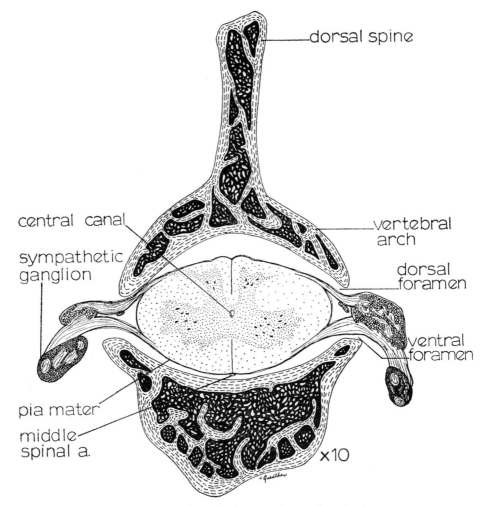

FIG. 5.11—Cross section of the spinal cord at the thoracic area.

their respective horns, join as in mammals, and at this point the dorsal root, or spinal ganglion, is attached.

CERVICAL NERVES

There are 15 pairs of *cervical nerves* (Figs. 5.13–5.15), which accompany correspondingly the 14 cervical vertebrae. The 1st cervical nerve emerges between the skull and atlas, while the remaining 14 nerves pass from the spinal cord through the intervertebral foramina

formed by the spaces between their adjacent vertebrae. The last, or 15th, cervical nerve leaves the vertebral canal through the intervertebral foramen between the last cervical and 1st thoracic vertebrae. Therefore, the cervical nerves are named according to the cervical number in front of which they emerge, with the exception of the last pair.

The 1st cervical nerve arises within the cranial cavity, passes through the foramen magnum, and emerges between the skull and atlas. The large medial

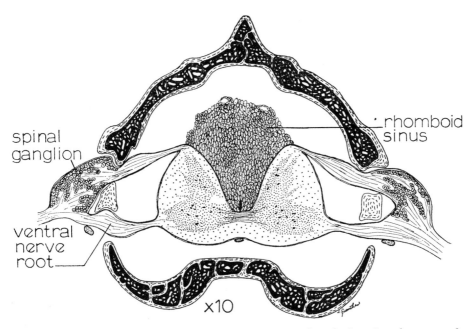

spinal
ganglion

ventral
nerve
root

rhomboid
sinus

x10

FIG. 5.12—Cross section of the spinal cord at the synsacral area.

and lateral parts of the dorsal branch supply most of the musculature adjacent to the caudal portion of the skull, namely the complexus, obliquus capitis cranialis, biventer cervicis, and the fused rectus capitis dorsalis major and rectus capitis ventralis lateralis muscles. The medial twig of the ventral branch supplies the obliquus capitis caudalis, rectus capitis ventralis medialis, and the trachelomastoideus muscles; while the lateral twig anastomoses and courses with the 12th cervical nerve, the hypoglossal.

The 2nd cervical nerve's ventral and dorsal branches aid in supplying basically the same muscles as the 1st cervical nerve; however, they send small branches which anastomose with the 1st cervical nerve in the formation of the cranial and caudal cervical plexuses.

The cranial cervical plexus is formed by the anastomoses of small branches of the 1st, 2nd, and 3rd cervical nerves which act as communicating twigs between the dorsal branches of the

named spinal nerves. The caudal cervical plexus is also formed by communicating twigs from the ventral branches of the first three cervical nerves along with the ventral branch of the hypoglossal nerve. The 3rd through the 12th cervical nerves are typical spinal nerves. The ventral and dorsal branches divide into medial and lateral twigs. The medial twigs supply only the adjacent cervical muscles, while the lateral twigs supply a few muscles but principally give rise to the large ventral and dorsal cutaneous nerves which supply the skin and cutaneous muscles of the neck. The ventral cutaneous branch of the 12th nerve supplies the cutaneous region related to the ingluvies.

The ventral branches of the 13th, 14th, and 15th cervical nerves enter into the formation of the brachial plexus; while the very small dorsal branches supply the overlying muscles of the caudal neck region as well as the scalenus.

vertebral
segments

spinal cord
segments

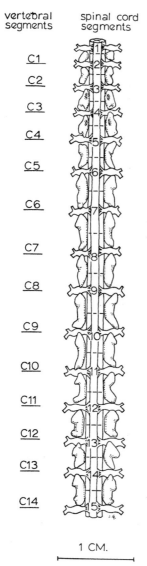

C1

C2

C3

C4

C5

C6

C7

C8

C9

C10

C11

C12

C13

C14

1 CM.

FIG. 5.13—Schematic drawing of the origins of the spinal nerves, including the brachial plexus.

THORACIC NERVES

There are 7 pairs of *thoracic nerves* (Figs. 5.14, 5.15, 5.18, 5.19). They emerge from the spinal cord through the intervertebral foramina caudal to the vertebra with the same name. For example, the 1st thoracic nerve emerges through the foramen formed between the 1st and 2nd thoracic vertebrae. A typical thoracic spinal nerve has a dorsal and a ventral branch.

The dorsal branches of the thoracic nerves are much smaller than the ventral ones. They immediately divide into medial and lateral twigs. The medial twig supplies the back muscles, namely the longissimus dorsi and multifidus cervicis, while the lateral branches partially supply the levatores costarum and serratus dorsalis muscles and terminate as very fine cutaneous nerves supplying the skin of the back region.

The ventral branches are the largest branches of the thoracic spinal nerve and, with the exception of the 1st and 7th, are commonly known as the intercostal nerves. The greater portion of the ventral branch of the first thoracic nerve turns craniad and helps to form the brachial plexus; however, a small twig which may be considered its lateral branch leaves the upper portion to supply the musculature of the first intercostal space. The ventral branches of thoracic nerves 2–6 are basically the same. In a few instances the ventral branch of the 2nd thoracic nerve sends a small twig to the brachial plexus. They appear above the sympathetic ganglion (Fig. 5.11) and pass downward in the intercostal spaces about 2 mm caudal to the border of the rib of the same name. Near their proximal extremities a small muscular twig leaves and supplies the levatores costarum and serratus dorsalis muscles. Approximately halfway down the intercostal spaces the nerves leave their subpleural relationships and pass between the intercostal muscles, where they divide into two branches of almost equal size. The cranial branches supply small twigs to the adjacent muscles, as they reach the junction of the vertebral and sternal ribs, and terminate by sup-

vertebral
segments

spinal cord
segments

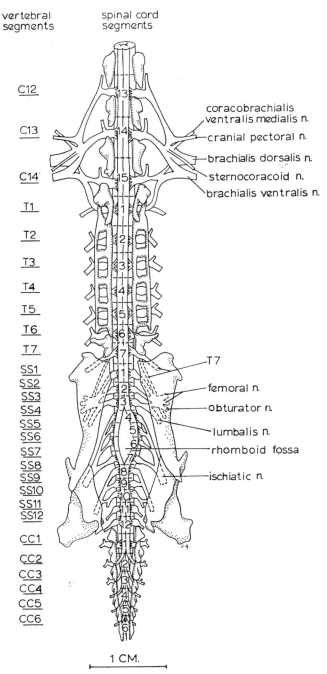

C12

C13

C14

T1

T2

T3

T4

T5

T6

T7

SS1
SS2
SS3
SS4
SS5
SS6
SS7
SS8
SS9
SS10
SS11
SS12

CC1

CC2

CC3

CC4

CC5

CC6

coracobrachialis
ventralis medialis n.

cranial pectoral n.

brachialis dorsalis n.

sternocoracoid n.

brachialis ventralis n.

T7

femoral n.

obturator n.

lumbalis n.

rhomboid fossa

ischiatic n.

1 CM.

FIG. 5.14—Schematic drawing of the origins of the spinal nerves, including the
synsacral plexus.

plying the skin of the lateral and ventral thoracic and abdominal regions.

The caudal branches supply the intercostal muscles and part of the abdominal muscles and terminate in the rectus abdominis muscle. The ventral branch of the 7th thoracic nerve gives off a large lateral twig which courses caudoventrad and becomes associated with the cranial portion of the synsacral plexus. The nerve then continues along the ventral border of the internal obturator muscle between the attachments of the internal abdominal oblique medially and the external abdominal oblique laterally, both of which it supplies, and terminates at their caudal extremities. The medial twig of the ventral branch of the 7th thoracic nerve courses caudoventrad for a short distance and divides into cutaneous and muscular branches.

SYNSACRAL NERVES

There are 12 pairs of *synsacral nerves* (Figs. 5.14, 5.18, 5.19). Each member of a pair has the same number as the vertebral segment preceding it. The nerves are formed by the anastomosis of the dorsal and ventral spinal nerve roots at a point just outside the intervertebral foramen. The resulting spinal nerve is extremely short due to its immediate division into very small dorsal and much larger and longer ventral branches.

The dorsal branches of the synsacral spinal nerves are directed dorsally to terminate by supplying the musculature on the dorsal surface of this region, namely the longissimus dorsi and cranial part of the levator coccygeus muscle. The cutaneous nerves of the dorsal synsacral region are derived from the dorsal branches of the synsacral spinal nerves.

The ventral branches of the synsacral spinal nerves are much larger than the dorsal ones and have a more complex distribution. The ventral branches of

the first 7 synsacral spinal nerves are discussed in the text under the description of the synsacral plexus and nerve supply of the pelvic limb. The ventral branches of synsacral nerves 8 and 9 anastomose shortly after emerging from their respective foramina and pass caudad through the caudal lobe of the kidney as a nerve trunk. This nerve trunk continues caudad passing medial to the dorsal border of the internal obturator and the semimembranosus muscles. It then perforates the peritoneum into the ischiorectal fossa to pass between the caudofemoralis laterally and the coccygeus muscle medially. The nerve then becomes related to the cranioventral surface of the levator ani muscle, which it follows to the sphincter ani muscle. The nerve supplies the above muscle and the skin on the lateral, caudal, and ventral surfaces of the cloaca and the caudal region of the torso.

The 10th synsacral nerve (ventral branch) leaves the synsacrum and passes caudoventrad over the semimembranosus, at which point it gives off an anastomotic branch to join the common trunk of synsacral nerves 8 and 9, which continues through the ischiorectal fossa. The nerve then passes between the caudofemoralis medially and the levator ani muscle laterally and becomes subcutaneous on the craniodorsolateral portion of the cloaca. This nerve supplies the sphincter ani and coccygeus muscles in addition to the cutaneous area mentioned above.

Synsacral spinal nerves 11 and 12 are closely related in direction to the 10th nerve, but do not anastomose with the common trunk of the 8th and 9th synsacral nerves. The 11th and 12th do, however, anastomose with the 10th synsacral nerve. The distribution of the last two synsacral nerves is mostly cutaneous to the dorsum of the cloaca.

There are some minute branches which supply the coccygeal muscles.

COCCYGEAL NERVES

There are 6 pairs of *coccygeal nerves* (Fig. 5.14). The spinal cord is continued to the 6th coccygeal vertebra, and there is no caudal vertebral canal beyond this point. The coccygeal spinal nerves are typical spinal nerves. They are very short due to their immediate branching into dorsal and ventral branches, which join adjacent coccygeal spinal nerves to form a network of nerves that supply the musculature on the dorsal and lateral surface of the tail as well as the skin of the same region.

The ventral branches have a similar distribution on the ventral and lateral surface of the tail. These nerves supply the coccygeus and depressor coccygeus muscles. They also supply the skin on the dorsum of the cloaca and ventral surface of the tail.

NERVES OF THE BRACHIAL PLEXUS

The *brachial plexus* (Figs. 5.15–5.17) is a network of nerves formed by the anastomoses established between the ventral branches of the last 3 cervical and 1st thoracic nerves. Occasionally the ventral branch of the 12th cervical nerve contributes a small twig to the plexus. The 13th, 14th, and 15th cervical nerves along with the 1st thoracic nerve are the major consistent roots forming the plexus. A small branch from the 2nd thoracic nerve may also help in its formation, but it is very inconsistent. The nerves arising from the plexus supply the muscles, skin, and other structures of the shoulder region and pectoral limb. The plexus is bounded dorsally by the scalenus, serratus ventralis (cranial portion), and subscapularis muscles, later-

ally by the teres major muscle, and ventrally by the coracobrachialis ventralis medialis muscle. The nerves are described as they lie cranial to caudal in the plexus.

Long Thoracic Nerve

The *long thoracic nerve* (Fig. 5.15) is the most dorsal of the brachial plexus. It consists of two small nerves which arise from twigs off the 13th and 14th cervical nerves before they branch to aid in the formation of the plexus. After anastomosing, one twig turns ventrad and supplies the serratus ventralis muscle, while the other branch courses dorsad over the caudal neck muscles to supply the serratus dorsalis, rhomboideus, and trapezius muscles.

Cranial Pectoral Nerve

The *cranial pectoral nerve* (Fig. 5.15) from the cranial portion of the plexus arises from the 13th and 14th cervical nerves. It courses cranioventrad between the coracobrachialis ventralis medialis and subscapularis muscles, through the substance of the supracoracoideus muscle, and enters the deep pectoral muscle. The nerve supplies the latter two muscles.

Coracobrachialis Ventralis Medialis Nerve

The *coracobrachialis ventralis medialis nerve* (Fig. 5.15) courses with, and is smaller than, the cranial pectoral nerve and lies along its caudal border. It arises entirely from the 13th cervical nerve and passes craniad on the ventral surface of the subscapularis muscle for a short distance before perforating the thick coracobrachialis ventralis medialis muscle which it supplies.

Subscapular Nerve

The *subscapular nerve* (Fig. 5.15) arises from the 13th cervical nerve and

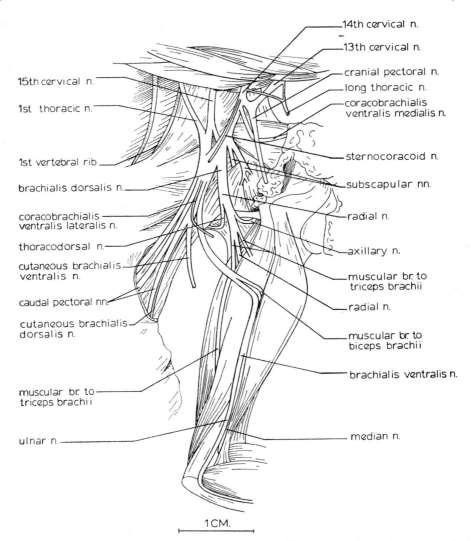

FIG. 5.15—*Nerves of the brachial plexus and brachium, ventral view.*

is situated on the craniodorsal border of the very prominent brachialis muscle. It is usually single but occasionally may be double. This nerve is short and lies ventral to a small groove formed by the caudal border of the subscapularis muscle and the insertion of the serratus ventralis (cranial portion) muscle. Initially, it courses dorsolaterad over the head of the coracobrachialis ventralis medialis muscle for a short distance be-

fore several small twigs leave to supply the subscapularis muscle. It then becomes related to the cranial portion of the teres major muscle, which it supplies. Several branches innervate the small teres minor muscle also.

Sternocoracoid Nerve

The *sternocoracoid nerve* (Fig. 5.15) arises from the 13th cervical nerve immediately caudal to the origin of the subscapular nerve. It is very small and courses caudoventrad obliquely across the ventral surface of the entire plexus. It then passes through an arterial plexus and terminates by supplying the sterno-coracoideus muscle.

Brachialis Dorsalis Nerve

The *brachialis dorsalis nerve* (Fig. 5.15) is the largest nerve of the brachial plexus. It arises from the 14th and 15th cervical and 1st thoracic nerves. This large, short nerve acts as a common trunk for the radial, axillary, and thoracodorsal nerves. It initially courses ventrolaterad, dorsal to the coracobrachialis ventralis medialis muscle; and as it reaches the cranioventral border of the teres major and the caudal border of the cranial portion of the long head of the triceps brachii, it turns dorsad and divides into three major branches.

Axillary Nerve

The *axillary nerve* (Fig. 5.15) arises from the cranial border of the brachialis dorsalis nerve trunk and immediately turns to course craniodorsad into the axillary region. It then becomes related to the ventral surface of the teres major muscle, passes between the two large portions of the triceps, and reaches the ventral surface of the deltoideus muscle, where a small twig leaves the nerve and perforates the head of the triceps medialis muscle. A very short distance farther small branches enter the long head of the triceps and deltoideus muscles. The main portion of the axillary then passes up over the shoulder joint region and becomes related to the caudal border of the coracobrachialis dorsalis muscle, to which it contributes several small branches. The nerve then courses dorsad over the coracobrachialis dorsalis muscle and terminates by innervating the patagialis brevis and patagialis longus muscles.

Radial Nerve

The *radial nerve* (Figs. 5.15–5.17) is the main continuation and the largest branch of the brachialis dorsalis nerve trunk. This nerve will be described more fully later.

Thoracodorsal Nerve

The *thoracodorsal nerve* (Fig. 5.15) arises from the caudal border of the brachialis dorsalis nerve, higher up toward the plexus than the radial or axillary nerves. It turns backward then upward over the teres major muscle and splits into caudal and cranial branches which innervate respectively the caudal and cranial portions of the latissimus dorsi muscle.

Cutaneous Brachialis Dorsalis Nerve

The *cutaneous brachialis dorsalis nerve* (Fig. 5.15) proceeds caudad in the brachial plexus and lies caudal to the small thoracodorsal nerve. It is approximately the same size as the thoracodorsal nerve and arises from the 15th cervical and 1st thoracic nerves. It courses ventrad to the ventral border of the teres major muscle and then turns dorsolaterad to become related to the ventral surface of the latissimus dorsi muscle near its insertion on the humerus. Here a small twig leaves the nerve and courses up over the long head of the triceps brachii and the deltoideus muscle to supply the skin and feather follicles in the proximodorsal portion of the brachium. The small main trunk continues distad along the caudodorsal border of the long head of the triceps brachii and ramifies in the skin of the dorsal portion of the brachium.

Brachialis Ventralis Nerve

The *brachialis ventralis nerve* (Fig. 5.15) arises primarily from the 15th cervical and 1st thoracic nerves. It passes ventrolaterad between the teres major and superficial pectoral muscles and becomes related to the caudoventral portion of the brachium. Here it courses between the medial head of the triceps and the biceps brachii and continues its course down the brachium on the caudodorsal surface of the belly of the biceps brachii, to which it sends a muscular branch which also innervates the patagialis accessorius muscle. Approximately halfway down the arm the nerve divides into the median and ulnar nerves.

Cutaneous Brachialis Ventralis Nerve

The *cutaneous brachialis ventralis nerve* (Fig. 5.15) arises primarily from the 1st thoracic nerve and lies along the caudal border of the brachialis ventralis nerve. It passes through the axillary region and becomes related to the ventral surface of the biceps brachii muscle. It terminates by ramifying in the skin of the ventral brachium and elbow region.

Caudal Pectoral Nerves

The *caudal pectoral nerves* (Fig. 5.15) consist of the most caudal two or three nerves in the plexus. They arise from the 15th cervical and 1st thoracic nerves and are approximately the same size as the brachialis ventralis nerve. They course caudoventrad to the superficial pectoral muscle and terminate by branching into numerous ramifications which supply the largest muscle of the body.

NERVES OF THE PECTORAL LIMB

Radial Nerve

The *radial nerve* (Figs. 5.15–5.17) is the main continuation and the largest branch of the brachialis dorsalis nerve. As it passes through the axillary region and reaches the craniodorsal surface of

the superficial pectoral muscle, it immediately gives off from its caudal border a large muscular branch to the triceps brachii. A short distance farther distad a somewhat larger branch leaves to perforate and partially supply the long head of the triceps. The nerve then continues distad, lying in the groove formed by the two large portions of the triceps, until it reaches the caudal aspect of the elbow region, where it gives off a small branch that perforates the distal extremity of the fused heads of the triceps. The nerve then terminates by ramifying in the muscular portion of the expansor secundariorum muscle located on the caudoventral portion of the antebrachium just distal to the elbow.

After the origin of the large muscular branch to the triceps, the main continuation of the radial nerve courses down the brachium between the two large portions of the triceps, turns slightly craniodorsad, and passes over the humerus near its distal third portion, where it gives off a small branch to the cranial patagium and becomes associated with the cranial aspect of the elbow joint. Here a small cutaneous branch arises and courses over the dorsal surface of the extensor carpi radialis muscle to supply the heavy fascia and skin in the proximodorsal antebrachial region.

The radial nerve then gives off a small muscular branch which enters and supplies the cranial extremity of the powerful extensor carpi radialis muscle (also innervated by a muscular branch of the median nerve). A few millimeters distad a small superficial nerve arises from the radial nerve and courses distad along the caudodorsal border of the extensor carpi radialis muscle. It supplies the skin over the distal portion of the antebrachium, and near the distal extremity of the preceding muscle the

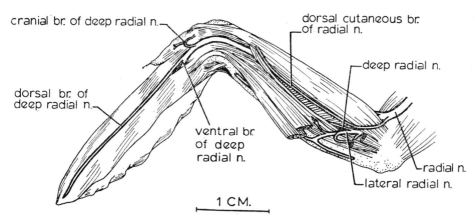

FIG. 5.16—Nerves of the dorsal forearm and manus.

nerve terminates by supplying the skin over the carpal joint. The main continuation of the radial nerve then courses deep to the heads of the extensor carpi radialis and supinator medialis muscles, furnishing the latter with a small twig. Directly ventral to the supinator medialis muscle and dorsal to the proximal extremity of the radius, the radial nerve divides into the lateral radial and deep radial nerves.

Lateral Radial Nerve

The *lateral radial nerve* (Fig. 5.16) is the caudal branch of the radial nerve. It courses caudolaterad between the supinator lateralis ventrally and the common digital extensor and extensor carpi ulnaris muscles dorsally and supplies all three with small muscular branches. As the nerve reaches the caudal aspect of the antebrachium, it divides into cranial and caudal branches which course cutaneously up and down the dorsal surface of the ulna, supplying the large feather follicles of the caudal forearm.

Deep Radial Nerve

The *deep radial nerve* (Fig. 5.16) is the cranial branch of the radial nerve. It courses ventrad, deep between the

radial and ulnar heads of the extensor pollicis longus muscle, supplying both with a small muscular branch, and comes to lie immediately dorsal to the median nerve. It passes distad approximately 12–15 mm with the median nerve before it turns slightly dorsad to course along the dorsal surface of the extensor of the 3rd digit to which it sends several small muscular branches. It then passes over the carpal joint under the annular ligament lying adjacent cranially to the tendon of the extensor of the 3rd digit and becomes associated with the cranial portion of the manus, where it divides into three branches. The very small, most cranial branch supplies the extensor of the 2nd digit. The dorsal branch courses distad for 1–2 mm and divides into cranial and caudal twigs. The cranial twig courses along the dorsal border of the abductor indicis muscle, which is located along the cranioventral border of the 3rd metacarpal, innervating it and the adjacent skin. The caudal twig courses distad along the dorsal surface of the 3rd metacarpal, adjacent caudally to the tendon of the extensor of the 3rd digit, and supplies the large feather follicles of the dorsal manus with a small branch to each follicle.

The ventral, or deep, branch of the radialis profundus nerve supplies the flexor metacarpi muscle with a small muscular branch before it turns ventrad into the interosseous space formed by the fusion of the 3rd and 4th metacarpal bones. Here it courses distad between the interosseous volaris and interosseous dorsalis muscles, innervating both. The nerve terminates by supplying the skin of the caudal surface of the 3rd digit.

Ulnar Nerve

The *ulnar nerve* (Fig. 5.17) is the caudal branch of the brachialis ventralis nerve. It lies on the caudoventral border of the biceps brachii muscle and accompanies the median nerve to the cranial portion of the elbow region where it courses obliquely across the ventral surface of the proximal extremities of the ventral antebrachial muscles. As it reaches the caudal border of the forearm it gives off two branches. The small muscular branch turns forward and upward into the caudal part of the expansor secundariorum muscle, while the larger branch courses distad along the ventral surface of the flexor carpi radialis muscle and terminates by innervating this muscle. The ulnar nerve then

courses distad along the caudal border of the ulna, sends off a muscular branch to the anconeus medialis muscle, and continues distad until it reaches the caudal portion of the carpal joint, where it becomes related to the caudal border of the manus. It sends a small branch to the flexor metacarpi muscle, then continues distad along the caudal surface of the 4th metacarpal, supplying the flexor of the 3rd digit.

Median Nerve

The *median nerve* (Fig. 5.17) is the cranial branch of the brachialis ventralis nerve. It courses distad with the ulnar nerve along the caudoventral border of the biceps brachii muscle until it reaches the cranioventral portion of the elbow joint. Here it enters the forearm and passes between the pronator brevis muscle ventrally and the brachialis muscle dorsally and gives rise to five muscular branches. Four of these supply the brachialis, pronator brevis, pronator longus, and extensor carpi radialis (partially) muscles respectively, while the fifth passes ventrad between the two pronator muscles to innervate the extensor and adductor of the 2nd and 3rd digits. The main continuation of the

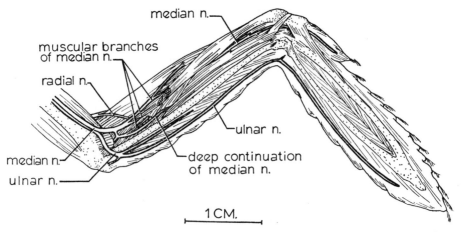

FIG. 5.17—Nerves of the ventral forearm and manus.

median nerve courses distad deep to the pronator longus and the extensor and adductor of the 2nd and 3rd digits and becomes closely associated with the deep radial nerve. Before it enters the manus, the median nerve sends small muscular branches to the extensor carpi obliquus and flexor digitorum sublimis muscles. In the manus region the median nerve supplies the adductor of the 2nd digit.

NERVES OF THE SYNSACRAL PLEXUS

The *synsacral plexus* (Figs. 5.14, 5.18–5.20) is a large anastomotic complex of nerves which gives rise to nerves distributed to the pelvis and pelvic limb. It is derived from the ventral branches of the first 7 synsacral segments. The plexus is composed of two major groups of nerves which are divided anatomically by the ventral border of the ilium. The cranial group which originates from the 1st, 2nd, 3rd, and occasionally the 4th synsacral nerves passes laterally in a caudoventral direction to the ventral border of the ilium and dorsal to the cranial lobe of the kidney. This group gives origin to the obturator, lumbalis, and femoral nerves. The caudal group is derived from the 4th, 5th, 6th, and 7th synsacral nerves. These synsacral nerves anastomose and pass through the substance of the caudal lobe of the kidney to continue caudoventrad toward the ischiatic foramen, through which they disappear before turning ventrad into the thigh.

Obturator Nerve

The *obturator nerve* (Figs. 5.14, 5.18, 5.19) arises from the 1st, 2nd, and 3rd synsacral nerves. It runs caudolaterad from the vertebral column parallel to the ventral border of the ilium to the obturator foramen, through which it disappears. Immediately before pass-

ing through the obturator foramen, it gives off branches which supply the internal obturator muscle. After passing through the foramen, other branches extend laterally and caudally to supply the external obturator and gemellus muscles. The main continuation of the obturator nerve then turns ventrad and supplies the adductor muscle.

Lumbalis Nerve

The *lumbalis nerve* (Figs. 5.14, 5.19) originates from the plexus as an anastomosis of the first three synsacral spinal nerves; the main contribution coming from the 2nd and 3rd of the series. The distribution of the lumbalis nerve is similar to that of the gluteal nerve in mammals. Following its origin it deviates laterally in a cranioventral direction for a short distance, then turns dorsad perforating the gluteus profundus muscle, to which it sends smaller branches, and continues dorsad to supply the cranial gluteus superficialis and the gluteus medius muscles.

Femoral Nerve

The *femoral nerve* (Figs. 5.14, 5.19) is derived from the same portion of the synsacral plexus that supplies the obturator and lumbalis nerves. It differs

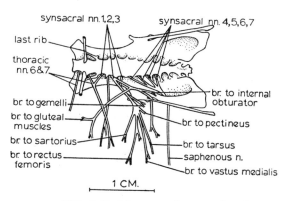

FIG. *5.18—Nerves of the ventral region of the pelvis.*

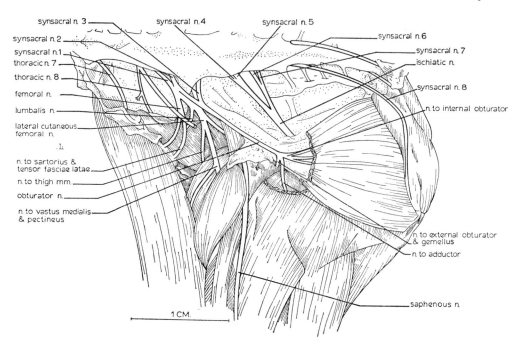

FIG. 5.19—Nerves of the pelvis.

from the femoral nerve in mammals in that it is composed of three major branches instead of only one. Usually the 1st branch of the femoral nerve complex is derived mainly from that part of the plexus supplied by the 1st synsacral spinal nerve. It has one large anastomotic branch with the trunk of the 2nd and 3rd branches of the femoral nerve. Ventrolateral to the ilium the 1st major branch of the femoral nerve extends craniolaterally, perforating the abdominal muscles and continuing into the craniomedial portion of the thigh to supply the sartorius and tensor fasciae latae muscles. This nerve continues as a cutaneous branch (lateral cutaneous femoral) between the above muscles to supply the skin on the craniolateral surface of the thigh. The 2nd and 3rd branches of the femoral nerve arise as a common trunk formed from that portion of the plexus supplied by the 2nd and 3rd synsacral nerves. As men-

tioned above, the trunk anastomoses with the 1st femoral branch. Just distal to the ventral border of the ilium the trunk continues through the lateral abdominal musculature. Upon entering the space between the torso and thigh, the trunk divides. One division extends ventrolaterally into the femoral triangle and supplies the pectineus and vastus medialis muscles. The other supplies the iliacus muscle.

Saphenous Nerve

The *saphenous nerve* (Figs. 5.18, 5.19) arises usually from the anastomotic complex of the femoral nerves immediately proximal to the abdominal wall. It runs caudad in close proximity with the iliacus muscle which it encircles, passing from its medial side around its dorsal border, and continues ventrad over its lateral side. It then courses under the pectineal process of the pubis and continues distad on the medial surface of the thigh in the muscular groove between the adductor muscle caudally and the vastus medialis muscle cranially. At the point where the saphenous nerve becomes associated with the muscular groove, it divides into deep muscular and superficial cutaneous branches. The muscular branch is very small, contributes nerve fibers to the above muscles, and terminates a few millimeters proximal to the stifle joint. The cutaneous branch runs parallel to the muscular branch and continues past the stifle on the medial side of the leg. It then deviates to the craniomedial surface of the tarsometatarsus and terminates about the level of the 1st digit. It supplies the skin on the medial side of the thigh and the craniomedial surface of the leg and tarsometatarsus.

Ischiatic Nerve

The ischiatic nerve (Figs. 5.14, 5.19) is formed by the confluence of the ventral branches of synsacral nerves 4, 5, 6, and 7. These nerves anastomose in the substance of the caudal lobe of the kidney prior to going through the ischiatic foramen. They are directed caudoventrally until reaching the foramen; they then turn ventrad as the ischiatic nerve which enters the thigh between the quadratus femoris muscle deeply and the semitendinosus muscle superficially. Immediately after passing through the foramen, the ischiatic contributes small nerves which supply the caudal gluteus superficialis, vastus intermedius and lateralis, quadratus femoris, and caudofemoralis muscles. There are also very small branches to the adductor muscles.

Arising near the same point as the above nerves, from the caudal surface of the ischiatic, is a large fascicular branch that passes caudoventrad to supply the hamstring muscles, namely the biceps femoris, semitendinosus, semimembra-

nosus, and gracilis. Arising in conjunction with the fascicular branch of the ischiatic is a rather large nerve that extends caudally between the adductor and semimembranosus medially and the semitendinosus and biceps femoris laterally. The nerve becomes subcutaneous on the caudal surface between the semimembranosus and the biceps in the middle of the thigh. It supplies the skin in that region and extends down toward the leg.

In addition to this nerve there is a much smaller nerve, the caudal cutaneous crural, which arises (distal to the fasciculus) from the caudal side of the ischiatic and continues in close proximity with the parent trunk to the distal one-third of the thigh; here it deviates caudally between the semimembranosus and semitendinosus and emerges subcutaneously in the popliteal region to supply the skin in that area and the proximal end of the leg.

As the ischiatic continues down the thigh, it runs medial and parallel to the cranial border of the semitendinosus. In its course it crosses the lateral surface of the caudofemoralis, adductor, and semimembranosus muscles in that order. It perforates the biceps in the distal third of the thigh to supply the skin on the lateral surface of the distal end of the thigh and proximal end of the leg. The ischiatic terminates by giving rise to the common peroneal and tibial (cranial and caudal nerve groups) nerves about midway between the hip and stifle joint. These nerves continue in a common sheath to a point immediately above the stifle joint. Here the nerves separate to innervate different muscle groups.

Common Peroneal Nerve

A few millimeters proximal to the stifle the *common peroneal nerve* (Fig. 5.20) separates from the tibial and de-

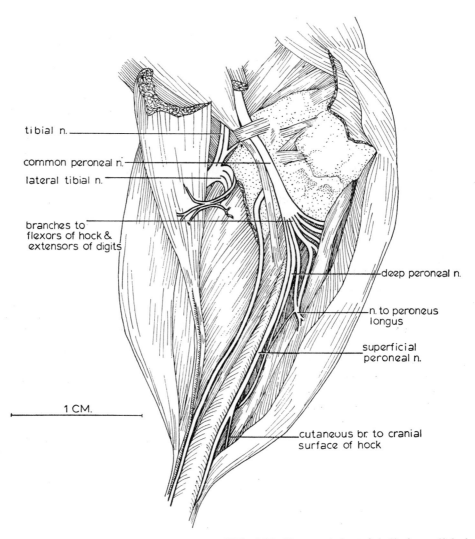

tibial n.

common peroneal n.

lateral tibial n.

branches to
flexors of hock &
extensors of digits

deep peroneal n.

n. to peroneus
longus

superficial
peroneal n.

1 CM.

cutaneous br. to cranial
surface of hock

FIG. 5.20—Nerves of the pelvic limb, medial view.

viates craniolaterally to pass through
the circulus tendinosus with the tendon
of the semitendinosus muscle. It then
continues toward the craniolateral portion of the leg by passing obliquely between the tibial and lateral heads of the
gastrocnemius. As the nerve passes between the muscular portion of the intermediate digital flexors laterally and
the deep digital flexor medially, it gives
rise to a complex of nerve branches

which spread out over the craniolateral
portion of the leg to supply the tibialis
cranialis, peroneus longus, peroneus
brevis, and extensor digitus longus
muscles.

The common peroneal nerve continues cranioventrad and becomes associated with the ventral surface of the
peroneus longus muscle. Here the nerve
terminates into the superficial and
deep peroneal nerves. These terminal

branches continue down the leg related cranially to the peroneus longus and caudally to the cranial border of the deep digital flexor muscles.

About halfway down the leg the nerves cross the muscular mass of the peroneus tertius and at this point become associated with the cranial tibial artery. Here the superficial peroneal nerve contributes a cutaneous branch which perforates the fascia on the lateral surface of the peroneus longus to supply the skin in that region. The superficial peroneal nerve continues on the lateral side of the cranial tibial artery, while the deep peroneal lies on the medial side of it. The nerves continue ventrad to the distal third of the leg, where they become subfascial. The superficial peroneal continues over the cranial surface of the hock joint under the fascia.

At the level of the joint a cutaneous branch arises to supply the skin on the craniolateral surface of the articulation and the tarsometatarsus. It also continues ventrad to supply the skin of the 3rd and 4th digits. The superficial peroneal nerve continues past the joint where it goes under the lateral border of the extensor digitus longus. As it continues down the tarsometatarsus, it gives origin to small nerves which innervate the extensors of the 3rd and 4th digits. At the end of the tarsometatarsus the nerve terminates into the dorsal proper digital nerves 3 and 4 to supply the 3rd and 4th digits.

The deep peroneal nerve runs parallel to the superficial peroneal nerve to a point some 5 cm proximal to the hock joint, where it deviates slightly ventrad to pass through the proximal annular ligament of the hock with the cranial tibial artery and tendon of the tibialis cranialis muscle. After passing the joint, the nerve crosses the cranial surface of the extensor digitus longus

tendon to its medial side and goes under the tendon to continue down the tarsometatarsus in that position. The nerve supplies small branches which innervate the extensor hallucis brevis and the flexor of digit 2. There is a small branch which passes from the deep peroneal nerve across the flexor of digit 2 to anastomose with the superficial peroneal nerve. The deep peroneal nerve terminates by dividing into the dorsal proper digital nerves 1 and 2 to supply the 1st and 2nd digits.

Tibial Nerve

The *tibial nerve* (Fig. 5.20) is the larger terminal branch of the ischiatic nerve. It is in a common sheath with the common peroneal from its origin to a point some 5 cm proximal to the caudal surface of the stifle joint, where it separates from the peroneal nerve. Close to its origin the tibial nerve gives rise to the tibialis plantaris which continues in company with the peroneal nerve until the latter goes between the superficial and deep digital flexor muscles. Shortly after the tibial nerve separates from the peroneal nerve, it turns ventrad and immediately divides into two major branches, the lateral and medial tibial. The lateral tibial nerve goes between the tibial and lateral heads of the gastrocnemius to supply the lateral head of the gastrocnemius. It continues medial to the above muscle to ramify in the intermediate and deep digital flexor muscles.

The medial tibial nerve is the larger branch of the tibial nerve. It divides into two smaller branches, one of which supplies the tibial head of the gastrocnemius, the deep digital flexor, and the popliteus. The other branch supplies the medial head of the gastrocnemius, flexor hallucis longus, and caudal tibial muscles. Arising from the medial tibial nerve is a small nerve which follows the cranial border of the tibial head of the gastrocnemius to the distal third of the leg. It then crosses medially to the cranial surface of the medial head of the gastrocnemius to become a cutaneous nerve that supplies the skin on the medial and caudal surface of the hock joint, then continues down the mediocaudal side of the tarsometatarsus, supplying the skin from the hock to and including the 1st digit.

The tibialis plantaris is the first branch of the tibial nerve. It arises shortly after the latter is formed, then follows the peroneal nerve to the superficial flexors to which it contributes small innervating branches. The nerve then follows the cranial border of the deep digital flexor to the hock. Here a cutaneous branch arises to supply the skin and fascia on the lateral and caudal surface of the hock and tarsometatarsus. It continues ventrad to supply the skin of the distal end of the tarsometatarsus and 3rd and 4th digits. The tibialis plantaris nerve perforates the deep fascia binding the Achilles tendon, passes from the lateral to the cranial surface

of the deep flexor tendons, and continues down the tarsometatarsus under the deep flexor tendons. In this course it supplies the flexor hallucis brevis, extensor digitus brevis, and the flexors of digits 2 and 4. At the distal end of the tarsometatarsus the tibialis plantaris divides into the plantar proper digital nerves 2, 3, and 4. The plantar proper digital nerve to the 1st digit is an extension of the branch that supplies the flexor hallucis brevis.

AUTONOMIC NERVOUS SYSTEM

The autonomic nervous system (Fig. 5.21) may be defined as that functional division of the nervous system responsible for the motor innervation of the viscera; namely the intestines, blood vessels, glands, and organs composed of nonstriated, or smooth, muscles. It is sometimes referred to as the involuntary, visceral, or vegetative nervous system. There is also an afferent component of this system which transmits sensory impulses from the viscera, as, for example, pain from distended bowels or from

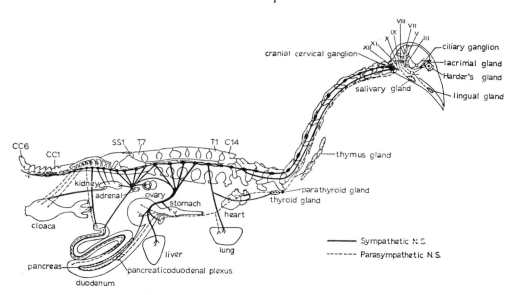

FIG. 5.21—Diagram of the spinal nerves and autonomic nervous system.

blood vessels. The autonomic nervous system is coordinated segmentally with the somatic or cerebrospinal portion of the central nervous system in the brain stem and in the spinal cord, the hypothalamus acting as the control center.

On an anatomical or physiological basis the autonomic nervous system can be subdivided into sympathetic and parasympathetic divisions. (Both divisions are arranged in a so-called two-neuron unit, as at least two types of neurons are necessary to connect the central nervous system with the structure to be innervated.) The cell body of the first type, or preganglionic neuron, is situated in the brain or spinal cord. The axons of these neurons extend from the central nervous system to a peripheral ganglion in which it will synapse with a dendrite or cell body of a postganglionic neuron. The axons of either single or chains of postganglionic neurons end by supplying either the smooth muscle or gland cells of the viscera. Autonomic ganglia are named according to their specific location in the body and are classified as vertebral, collateral, or terminal. Vertebral ganglia are those associated with the sympathetic trunk, while collateral ganglia are found further away from the vertebral column, such as the aortic and celiac ganglia of the abdominal cavity. Terminal ganglia are microscopic and are usually located in the walls of the various blood vessels or body organs.

Sympathetic Division

The sympathetic division of the autonomic nervous system originates in the lateral column of gray matter of the thoracolumbar segments of the spinal cord. Preganglionic axons or visceral efferent fibers leave the spinal cord by way of the ventral roots of the spinal nerves and immediately connect with a chain of ganglia which are joined to

each other by connecting interganglionic fibers, forming the pair of lateral sympathetic trunks on either side of the vertebral column. Some of the axons or fibers bypass the sympathetic ganglia of the trunk to continue into the collateral ganglia of the prevertebral plexus, or they may end directly in a local network of visceral organs. The postganglionic fibers from the various ganglia run with the spinal nerves to be distributed to the heart, blood vessels, smooth muscles, and glands throughout the body.

The sympathetic trunk is composed of a series of ganglia connected by intervening cords. They extend on either side of the vertebral column from the base of the skull to the region of the 5th coccygeal vertebra where they become untraceable. The large cranial cervical ganglion is situated at the cephalic end of the trunk proper.

The *ciliary ganglion* is approximately one-half as large as the cranial cervical ganglion. Its base is attached to the ventral branch of the 3rd cranial nerve and its apex gives rise to the greater ciliary nerve (Fig. 5.5). The ganglion is related somewhat ventrolaterally to the very large optic nerve. The very minute sympathetic fibers joining the ciliary ganglion arise from the dorsal branch of the vidian nerve. The greater ciliary nerve courses forward to enter the sclera. Along its curved pathway it receives a small twig from a muscular branch of the abducens nerve and from the ophthalmic portion of the trigeminal. The smaller ciliary nerves arising from the ganglion pierce the sclera adjacent to the optic nerve.

The *stapedial nerve* (internal maxillary of Hsieh, 1951) is a sympathetic nerve arising from the cranial cervical ganglion. It courses craniodorsad to enter the stapedial canal in company with the stapedial artery. Along its course it receives a small tympanic branch from the glossopharyngeal nerve and anastomotic twig from the facial nerve. The lesser superficial petrosal nerve (stapedial nerve) then enters the area of the vascular rete temporalis, where its delicate fibers ramify repeatedly to form a plexus of nerves which is entangled with the small vessels of the vascular plexus. Several of these fibers join with the maxillary and mandibular branches of the trigeminal nerve. Small fibers from the plexus accompany the arteries leaving the rete temporalis to supply the lacrimal gland and respective structures supplied by the arteries.

The *internal carotid nerve* is the major sympathetic nerve to the cephalic region. It arises from the craniomedial portion of the cranial cervical ganglion and enters the carotid canal in company with the internal carotid artery. In the cranial portion of the carotid canal the internal carotid is joined by the greater superficial petrosal nerve, a branch of the facial. The nerve thus formed by this union is the vidian nerve. The small fibers to the pituitary are too small to be observed by the unaided eye. Shortly after leaving the canal, the vidian nerve divides into dorsal and ventral branches. The ventral branch courses in company with the palatine artery along the palatine bone. It gives off small fibers to the eustachian tube, sphenopterygoid, palatine and maxillary salivary glands, and the pharynx. It then joins the sphenopalatine ganglion just cranial to the chonial notch of the palatine bone. The dorsal branch of the vidian nerve is related to the course of the sphenomaxillary artery. It gives off small twigs to the ciliary ganglion, oculomotor nerve, periorbita, Harder's gland, and an anastomotic branch to the ophthalmic nerve before it connects with the ethmoidal ganglion. Sympathetic fibers leave the cranial cervical ganglion by way of the

internal carotid nerve to supply structures of the head.

Including the cranial cervical a total of *37 pairs of sympathetic ganglia* are found in coturnix. They are: 1 cranial cervical, 14 cervical, 7 thoracic, 12 synsacral, and 3 coccygeal. The size of the ganglia vary considerably, the cranial cervical being the largest. Next in size are the thoracic ganglia, followed by the cervical and synsacral. The three coccygeal are barely visible. In the cervical region the sympathetic fibers from the cranial cervical ganglion run caudally in the cervical region and are divided into two tracts: the deeper one courses with the vertebral artery and vein in the transverse canal of the cervical vertebrae; the superficial tract accompanies the vagus nerve. At the junction of the cervical and thoracic regions the two tracts join and continue as components of the thoracolumbar trunks. Sympathetic ganglia in the thoracic and synsacral vertebral region fuse with the dorsal root ganglia. The intervening, or interganglionic, cord is single in the cervical region and in the first 7 or 8 synsacral vertebral segments. The cord is usually double between the last cervical and 1st thoracic, and between the 1st and 2nd thoracic sympathetic ganglia. The two cords in this region are approximately of equal size, and one runs dorsal to the head of the rib while the other runs ventral to it.

Grahame (1953) in his review of the work of Hsieh states that all thoracic ganglia have a double interganglionic cord in domestic fowl; however, this is not the case in quail. The caudal five interganglionic cords of the thoracic region in coturnix are usually single. In two of the birds examined a double cord was found between the 2nd and 3rd thoracic ganglia. In the coccygeal region three ganglia were found with double interganglionic cords. The sympathetic trunk appeared single after the last observable, or 3rd, coccygeal ganglion. At this point the trunk was still paired and not joined. No impar ganglion was found in the caudal coccygeal region. Sympathetic rami communications appear only in the cranial cervical ganglion area and in the caudal synsacral and cranial coccygeal regions. The general pattern found was that the ventral branch of each spinal nerve passes over the dorsal surface of its respective sympathetic ganglia and receives fibers directly from them.

The sympathetic ganglia give rise to numerous small branches which enter into the formation of various plexuses throughout the body. The sympathetic cardiac nerve arises from the first thoracic ganglia. For a short distance it lies adjacent to the caudal border of the first thoracic nerve to the brachial plexus before turning caudomediad toward the heart. As it becomes related to the ventral surface of the cranial portion of the lung, it divides into medial and lateral branches, both of which immediately divide into two or three smaller branches, thus forming the cardiac sympathetic plexus. One of these small branches joins the vagus just distal to the origin of the recurrent laryngeal nerve. Several follow the large blood vessels of this region and the remainder supply sympathetic innervation to the heart and lungs.

The *greater splanchnic nerves* arise from the 2nd, 3rd, 4th, and 5th thoracic ganglia and from the aortic plexus. They unite just dorsal to the origin of the celiac artery from the aorta to form one nerve. It courses downward along the lateral side of the celiac artery for 2–3 mm before it joins the nerve from the opposite side, thus resulting in the formation of the celiac plexus. This plexus surrounds the artery and is related directly dorsal to the mid-dorsal sur-

face of the proventriculus. A small branch from the plexus can be traced into the proventriculus. Two nerves leaving the plexus continue downward with the celiac artery to supply the following viscera: the gizzard, muscular stomach, spleen, and pancreas and their blood vessels. No connection with the vagus was observed, although a branch of the celiac plexus passes near the right recurrent branch of the vagus.

The *lesser splanchnic nerves* arise from the 5th, 6th, and 7th thoracic and the 1st and 2nd synsacral sympathetic ganglia. They all course ventrad to the dorsal surface of the aorta, where they aid in the formation of the large aortic plexus which extends nearly the entire length of a fully matured testicle or approximately 10–12 mm. From this plexus arise many divisional plexuses, namely the renal, adrenal, cranial mesenteric, and testicular or ovarian plexuses which supply the respective structures with sympathetic fibers. The ovary and oviduct of the female reproductive system receive some twigs from the majority of the above plexuses and, in addition, a few fibers from the pelvic and caudal mesenteric plexuses. Again no connection with the vagus was observed; however, several small fibers joined the aortic plexus with the celiac plexus.

The small branches arising from the caudal two-thirds of the sympathetic ganglia aid in the formation of the *pelvic and caudal mesenteric plexuses* which supply the viscera in their respective regions. The visceral efferent fibers of the parasympathetic division of the autonomic system originate from two regions of the body. Axons from the brain stem leave as part of cranial nerves III, VII, IX, and X, while corresponding preganglionic parasympathetic fibers leave the spinal cord with the ventral roots of synsacral nerves 6, 7, 8, and 9 in the majority of cases. Fibers from the first three cranial nerves named above are distributed to the head region while the 10th, or vagus, nerve sends fibers to the thoracic and abdominal viscera. Fibers from the synsacral nerves join the pelvic plexus in the caudal part of the body. This division is sometimes referred to as the craniosacral portion of the autonomic nervous system due to the origin of its fibers.

Parasympathetic Division

The *vagus nerve,* or 10th cranial (Fig. 5.21), is the major component of the parasympathetic portion of the autonomic nervous system. Approximately four to eight fine rootlets from the dorsolateral area of the medulla oblongata converge into one ganglion in forming the vagus nerve. Several rootlets forming the 9th cranial, or glossopharyngeal, nerve lie cranial to those of the vagus, while the rootlets caudal to it pass with the vagus through the vagal foramen and later give rise to the spinal accessory nerve.

The vagus emerges from the ventrolateral surface of the skull and immediately becomes related to the ventral border of the fused rectus capitis dorsalis major and ventralis lateralis muscles, and the dorsolateral surface of the rectus capitis ventralis medialis muscle. Less than 1 mm caudal to its emergence, a ramus from the cervical sympathetic trunk traverses the lateral surface of the vagus, from which it receives small fibers, and continues ventrad to the cranial cervical ganglion. Just caudal to this crossing, the fibers of the spinal accessory nerve leave the vagus and turn ventrad before coursing craniodorsad to the cranial portion of the cutaneous colli lateralis muscle. A large anastomotic branch then leaves the vagus about 1 mm distal to the origin of the spinal accessory nerve. This branch joins the glossopharyngeal and

divides into pharyngeal and laryngeal branches which course with the branches of the same name from the glossopharyngeal nerve. Approximately 3 mm distal to the anastomotic ramus the hypoglossal nerve traverses the lateral surface of the vagus, from which it receives several anastomotic twigs. The vagus nerve then continues caudad to the thoracic cavity, giving off small fibers to the different portions of the thymus gland. In the cervical region the right vagus nerve lies along the dorsal surface of the jugular vein, and the left lies along its ventral surface.

Upon entering the thoracic cavity, the vagus becomes related to the dorsolateral surface of the thyroid gland to which a few small fibers extend. The vagus continues caudad for approximately 5 mm, where it enlarges to form a small ganglion known as the ganglion nodosum. This structure is located immediately dorsal to the bifurcation of the brachiochephalic trunk into the common carotid and subclavian arteries.

Immediately caudal to the ganglion nodosum, the left vagus gives rise to a very small left superior cardiac ramus that courses along the cranioventral border of the left cranial vena cava, traverses the ventral surface of the left atrium, divides, and then ramifies generally in the region of the conus arteriosus. Approximately 1 mm distal to the ganglion the left recurrent laryngeal nerve arises from the medial surface of the left vagus. It initially courses dorsomediad for approximately 5–7 mm, adjacent cranially to the pulmonary artery, giving off from its caudal surface several small twigs which innervate the caudal thoracic portion of the esophagus. Just before the left recurrent nerve makes a 90° turn craniad, it sends three to four small twigs to supply the left bronchus and the syrinx. Along its cranial course it lies between the espohagus dorsally and the trachea ventrally and sends numerous small fibers to the esophagus, trachea, and ingluvies. Near the midcervical region it terminates by anastomosing with the pharyngeal branch of the glossopharyngeal nerve. After the origin of the recurrent laryngeal nerve the left vagus continues adjacent to the lateral surface of the pulmonary vein and through the thoracoabdominal diaphragm into the abdominal cavity. Along the latter course through the thoracic region the left vagus gives off the following branches: the inferior cardiac, bronchial, pulmonary, and vascular and a few small fibers to the thoracoabdominal and pulmonary diaphragms (obliqui septales).

Caudal to the ganglion nodosum the right vagus gives rise to two very small twigs, the right superior cardiac rami, which terminate in the wall of the aortic arch. The right recurrent laryngeal nerve arises from the vagus 2 mm caudal to the ganglion. It courses mediad cranial to the right pulmonary artery, around the caudal border of the aortic arch, and becomes related to the ventrolateral border of the caudal portion of the esophagus. It continues craniad in the same manner as the left recurrent laryngeal nerve. After giving rise to the recurrent nerve, the right vagus courses over the right cranial vena cava and

under the right pulmonary vein, where it turns mediad and crosses the midline to the left side. It then passes through the membranous thoracoabdominal diaphragm and joins the left vagus on the ventral surface of the cranial portion of the proventriculus. In the thoracic region both vagi give rise to the same branches. As the two vagi approach the cranioventral extremity of the proventriculus, they are connected by a large crossing branch which is followed by a complete anastomosis. Prior to the true junction of the vagi small fibers leave the left vagus, supplying the entire ventral portion of the proventriculus, while those of the right vagus supply the dorsal portion of the glandular stomach.

The joined vagi, now called the gastric nerve, course caudad along the midventral portion of the proventriculus and become related to the ventral portion of the isthmus, which connects the glandular and muscular portions of the stomach. Here the gastric nerve passes over the celiac artery where it divides into two branches, one of which supplies the ventral surface of the muscular extremity of the duodenum, where it supplies the pancreas, and enters into the formation of the gastroduodenal plexus. The right gastric nerve gives off a small hepatic branch and terminates on the dorsal surface of the ventriculus.

CHAPTER SIX

Splanchnology

THE splanchnology of the quail deals with the anatomy of the digestive, respiratory, and urogenital systems, which will be described from their cranial to their caudal extremities. Their topographical relationships to the divisions of other systems or organs are included. Pertinent histological features will be found grouped in a summarized portion of the description of gross anatomy.

DIGESTIVE SYSTEM

The digestive system (Figs. 6.1–6.20) consists of those structures directly concerned with the reception and assimilation of food, its passage through the body, and expulsion of the waste. These structural organs are classified under two groups: the accessory organs and the alimentary canal.

The *accessory organs* consist of the beak, tongue, salivary glands, liver, gallbladder, and pancreas. Discussion of the first three organs will follow the description of the mouth, while the latter two will be considered following the description of the cloaca. The spleen will also be discussed because of its location, although it is not functionally related to the digestive system.

The *alimentary canal* is a tube which extends from the mouth to the cloaca. Irregular dilatations such as the

207

stomach and ceca occur in certain regions along its course. It consists of the
following consecutive segments: mouth
—including the beak, tongue, and
salivary glands; pharynx; esophagus—the
cranial portion (ingluvies, or crop) and
the caudal portion; stomach—proventriculus (glandular stomach) and ventriculus or gizzard (muscular stomach);
small intestine; large intestine; and
cloaca.

HISTOLOGY OF THE ALIMENTARY CANAL

The digestive tract in coturnix is
lined with a continuous mucous membrane from the mouth to the vent. The
following layers of mucosa are recognized: the lamina epithelialis, the
lamina propria, and the lamina muscularis mucosa. Beneath the mucous
membrane there is a submucosa which
may be lacking in some areas of the
tract. The submucosa is covered by a
muscle coat which is usually composed
of an inner circular and an outer longitudinal layer of smooth muscle. The
peripheral layer is the tunica serosa, or
fibrosa. The extent of development of
the classified layers varies considerably
in certain regions of the digestive tract.

Mouth

The roof of the *mouth* is triangular
in shape and in a large portion is
formed by the hard palate which is
bounded rostrally by the beak, laterally
by the palatine ridges, and caudally by
the dorsal portion of the pharynx. The
complete absence of a soft palate in the
quail leaves no distinct demarcation between the mouth and the pharynx. In
chickens it is commonly considered that
a large transverse row of papillae at the
caudal extremity of the hard palate (Fig.
6.2) marks the caudal limit of the roof
of the mouth. This gives a convenient
landmark; and they may also be used as
a dividing line between the mouth and

pharynx in coturnix, since the papillae
are arranged in a similar manner. In
the rostral and lateral portions of the
roof of the mouth there is a wide groove
that receives the ventral beak. This
groove is divided rostrally by a short
median ridge, the caudal extremity of
which joins a pair of palatine ridges.
The palatine ridges arch laterally and
extend caudally along the lateral side of
the hard palate to its caudal border.
The two maxillary gland openings are
located just caudal to the rostral end of
the palatine ridges. Openings of the
lateral palatine glands occur lateral to
the palatine ridge, while the openings of
the medial palatine glands occur medial
to the ridge.

The caudal nares (choanae) occur as
a slitlike opening in the caudal portion
of the midline, originating approximately 2 mm caudal to the openings of the
maxillary gland and extending caudally
to the midpoint of the pharynx. Dorsally the common opening of the caudal
nares becomes divided into the right and
left choanae. The margins of the nares
are thick and are covered by longitudinal rows of filiform papillae. In addition to these papillae three groups of
filiform papillae are found in the hard
palate. The caudal transverse row separating the oral cavity from the pharynx
contains 10–11 papillae on each side of
the choanae making up the most prominent group. The middle group of
papillae is rudimentary and barely
noticeable with the unaided eye. The
papillae are arranged in a row which is
directed rostrolaterally from the margin
of the caudal nares. The cranial group
of papillae is located just rostral to the
origin of the slitlike cleft. It contains
three large papillae very close together,
with the one in the center just cranial to
the two lateral ones. Most of the
papillae are directed caudally and appear to function as a mechanical aid in

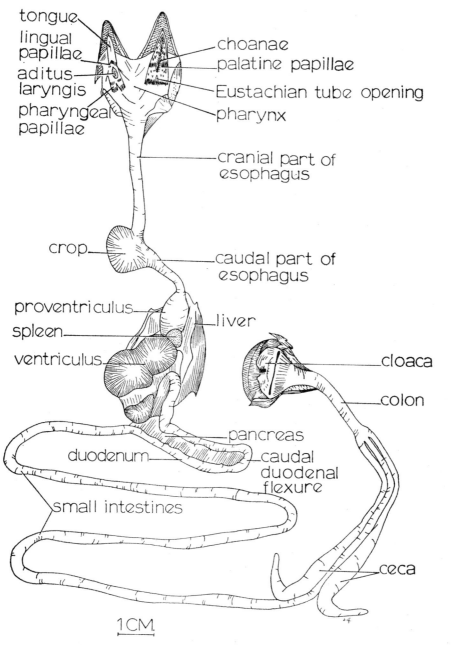

tongue
lingual papillae
aditus laryngis
pharyngeal papillae

choanae
palatine papillae
Eustachian tube opening
pharynx

cranial part of esophagus

crop
caudal part of esophagus

proventriculus
spleen
ventriculus
liver

cloaca
colon

pancreas
duodenum
caudal duodenal flexure

small intestines

ceca

1CM.

FIG. 6.1–Digestive system.

keeping the food in the mouth during swallowing.

The floor of the mouth is supported by the integument and mylohyoideus and articulohyoideus muscles. It is V-shaped and gradually becomes wider and deeper caudally. Its caudal limit is considered to be at the point of the transverse row of papillae located on the caudal border of the tongue. These papillae lie ventral to those of the transverse row of the hard palate when the mouth is closed and the tongue is at rest. Near its vertex the floor of the mouth receives many small openings from the large, paired, mandibular salivary glands. The tongue occupies the greater portion of the floor of the mouth and is attached to it by an extensive fold of mucosa, the frenum linguae. The lateral walls of the mouth are covered with horny cornified epithelium similar to that of the beak.

HISTOLOGY OF THE MOUTH

The lamina epithelialis of the mucosa of the mouth is composed of stratified squamous epithelium which forms thickenings and papillae of cornified epithelium in areas exposed to severe wear, as on the tongue and hard palate. In these areas the lamina propria at the epithelial junction forms a distinct papillary body. Rather coarse collagenous tissue bundles form the bulk of the lamina propria; however, as a rule the fibers become finer superficially. It contains a rather rich capillary bed and ducts of the submucosal glands. Due to the lack of a muscularis mucosa, the tunica propria passes without structural demarcation into the submucosa, which in turn lies in contact with the striated muscles of the head. The submucosa is composed of loose fibroelastic connective tissue and contains oral glands, lymphatic nodules, and rich deposits of adipose cells. The striated musculature is composed of those

skeletal muscles which happen to be present and form part of the orbital wall. In those areas where no skeletal muscles are developed, the submucosa passes without demarcation into that of the periosteum or perichondrium of the surrounding bone or cartilage.

The characteristics of the oral cavity may be summarized as follows: The lamina epithelialis presents a high degree of cornification at those areas which are subjected to excessive wear. This is primarily due to the fact that birds in general have no teeth. A muscularis mucosa is absent, and the only muscles present are the skeletal muscles of the skull, which are adjacent to the mouth. No distinct serosa or fibrosa is present, as the submucosa either joins the epimysium of the muscles or the periosteum of the bones of the skull. (See Figure 6.2.)

Beak

The *beak* (Fig. 6.1) is used as the main prehensile and masticatory organ of food and to some extent as a weapon and universal tool for many functions. The lips and cheeks are replaced by the beak. The ventral beak is supported by the mandible and conforms to its shape, forming an angle of approximately 30° at the sharp, pointed apex. The oral surface is concave transversely and slightly convex longitudinally, forming a groove for the tip of the tongue. The dorsal edge of the ventral beak is sharp, an anatomical feature which suggests that the quail is primarily a grain eater. The lateral borders are smooth and rounded. The dorsal beak and its oral surface are concave in both directions. Its dorsal surface is convex in both length and width with a slight ridge, the culmen, at its apex. This small projection has a calcareous portion at hatching time which is used to break the egg shell, and is called the "egg tooth." The dorsal beak is larger than the ventral

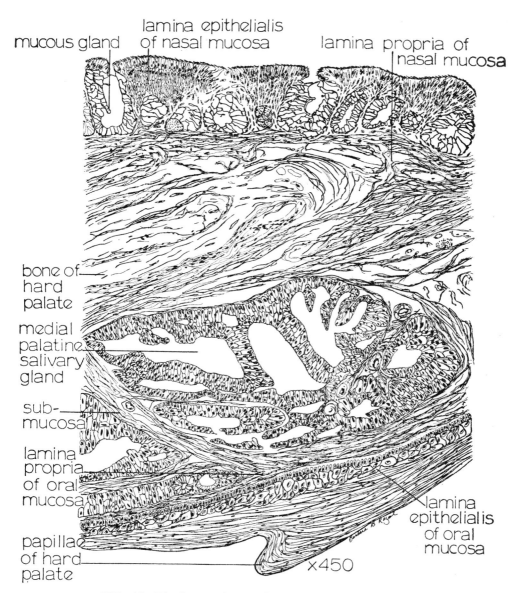

mucous gland   lamina epithelialis   lamina propria of
                of nasal mucosa   nasal mucosa

bone of
hard
palate

medial
palatine
salivary
gland

sub-
mucosa

lamina
propria
of oral
mucosa

papillae
of hard
palate

lamina
epithelialis
of oral
mucosa

×450

FIG. 6.2—Histology of the mouth, longitudinal section through the hard palate.

beak and, with the oral aperture closed, it projects about 1 mm forward over the ventral beak. The ventral border of the dorsal beak is sharp and grooved to receive the border of the lower beak, thereby producing an efficient closing mechanism for the mouth cavity. Its shape is very much like that of the lower beak and conforms to the shape of the incisive bone rostrally and the jugal arch further caudad.

Tongue

The *tongue* (Fig. 6.1) of the quail is 1 cm in length, is triangular, and conforms to the shape of the lower beak. It is very firm and almost devoid of muscle. (It may aid the beak as a prehensile organ.) It is triangular in cross section, the dorsal surface being the widest. The two lateral surfaces slant ventromedially to join at the ventral midline. The caudal portion of the dorsal border bears a transverse row of filiform papillae directed caudally. They become longer laterally and continue caudad on the lateral border for a short distance. The caudal portion of the tongue contains numerous lingual glands, the ducts of which open on the dorsal and ventrolateral surfaces. The frenum linguae is a reflected fold of mucosa connecting the ventral surfaces of the tongue to the floor of the mouth. It joins only the caudal half of the body of the tongue, leaving the apex free for movement. The entoglossum of the hyoid apparatus is embedded in the body of the tongue and is responsible for the firmness and for the greater part of the movement of the tongue.

HISTOLOGY OF THE TONGUE

The histology of the tongue of coturnix differs from that of the mammalian tongue in that the striated muscle which makes up the bulk of the structure in mammals is replaced by firm connective tissue and an abundance of mucous glands. In the apex, or tip, of the tongue a bar of hyaline cartilage supports a horny epithelial capping comparable to the horn of the beak. The horny capping is thickest on the ventral side of the tip. As the stratum corneum cells of the epithelium of the dorsum of the tongue desquamate, they do so as multicellular scales with a caudal free border. This produces a continuous layer of overlapping cornified epithelial projections which point caudally. The larger macroscopic papillae extend above the mucosal surface and have a well-developed conical lamina propria as a supporting core. Taste buds as

found in mammals have not been found on the dorsum of the tongue of coturnix.

Salivary Glands

Saliva is a clear, alkaline, seromucous, somewhat viscid digestive fluid secreted by the salivary glands. The serous portion of saliva serves to moisten and soften food and to keep the mouth moist. It contains the enzyme ptyalin, which breaks down carbohydrates. The mucous portion acts as a lubricant to aid in the passage of food through the pharynx and esophagus to the stomach.

The salivary gland tissue associated with the mouth is abundant. The salivary glands are classified as compound, branched, tubular glands with intralobular and interlobular ducts from which an excretory duct continues to the mouth cavity. These glands are: maxillary, medial and lateral palatine, sphenopterygoid, cricoarytenoid, lingual, mandibular (submaxillary), and angularis oralis. Most of these glands have numerous excretory ducts, but the maxillary and angularis oralis have but one.

The paired *maxillary glands* are located in the cranial portion of the roof of the mouth, just dorsal to the cranial group of papillae on the hard palate. These small glands are somewhat circular in shape and have single openings.

The *medial and lateral palatine glands* (Fig. 6.2) are located in the roof of the mouth and the cranial portion of the pharynx. They are named according to their medial and lateral relation to the palatine ridge. Each group is arranged in longitudinal rows composed of numerous small lobules about the size of the head of a pin. The lateral group does not continue caudally into the roof of the pharynx as does the medial group.

The small group of *sphenoptery-*

goid glands are located in the caudal portion of the dorsal pharynx around the eustachian infundibulum.

The *lingual glands* are very small and numerous; they make up the greater part of the caudal half of the basal portion of the tongue.

The *paired mandibular glands* (submaxillary) are strictly mucous and are the largest and most distinct of the group. Each gland is a slender mass approximately 1 cm long and only 2–3 mm wide, located in the apical portion of the intermandibular space just medial to the ramus of the mandible. Superficially they are covered by skin and the thin mylohyoideus muscle, and deeply by the oral mucosa and the hyomandibularis muscle. Numerous excretory ducts open into the floor of the mouth.

HISTOLOGY OF THE SALIVARY GLANDS

The end-pieces of all the salivary glands are supplied with mucous parenchymal cells. No serous cells were observed in any of the glands except the sphenopterygoid and palatine glands. The mucous cells show evidence of various stages of secretory activity. Some are very tall and markedly distended with light-staining coarse secretory granules which flatten the nucleus against the basal wall. Others are narrow and may be devoid of granules. The lumen of the end-pieces is wide and is continuous with the rather large interlobar ducts. The serous cells may in rare cases make up the entire parenchymal lining of an end-piece; more often however, they form only a part of the tubuloalveolar circumference. No well-formed demilunes or secretory capillaries were found. The basement membrane is distinct and the end-pieces are separated by generous deposits of muscular loose connective tissue. Numerous smaller intraalveolar ducts lead centrally into a single large excretory duct that is a rather wide, open central canal of the lobule. The excretory duct may join the central excretory duct of other lobules or it may continue to the lumen of the oral or pharyngeal cavities. The excretory ducts are lined with a simple cuboidal or columnar epithelium. No striated cells or excretory ducts are distinguishable in the passageways. The stratified squamous epithelium of the oral or pharyngeal cavities continues into the lamina propria for a short distance, making up a part of the extraglandular portion of the excretory duct. Numerous lymphatic infiltrations appear in the lamina propria in the vicinity of these glands. These accumulations may appear only as infiltrations of the interlobar connective tissue or complete nodules, or groups of nodules may invade the lamina propria or submucosa to such an extent that they crowd the glandular structures or replace a portion of the parenchyma within a lobular capsule. This condition is found in the region of the aditus laryngis in coturnix; therefore, the accumulation of lymphatic nodules may be called nonfollicular, or plate, tonsils of the pharynx. (See Figure 6.2.)

Pharynx

The *pharynx* (Figs. 6.1, 6.22) is a musculomembranous tube approximately 7 mm in length which connects the mouth with the esophagus. It also serves as a respiratory passage. Caudally its boundary is marked by a dorsal and a ventral transverse row of papillae. The dorsal row is just behind the caudal border of the eustachian infundibulum and contains 10–12 filiform papillae with their apexes pointing caudally. The ventral row is approximately 2 mm to the aditus laryngis and contains slightly larger papillae. There are 14–16 of these, also directed caudally. A very small secondary row occurs 1 mm caudal to the preceding row of papillae. The dorsal wall of the pharynx is sparsely covered with small filiform papillae and contains numerous openings for the sphenopterygoid and medial palatine salivary glands which are located in the lamina propria of the roof of the pharynx. The choanae, or openings of the caudal nares, are situated in the caudal portion of the roof of the pharynx. The eustachian infundibulum is continued caudally and leads into the eustachian tubes, which are air passageways to the tympanic cavity of the ear and spaces of the pneumatic bones of the cranium.

The floor of the pharynx presents a transverse row of papillae which correspond to the middle and caudal rows of the roof of the pharynx. The aditus laryngis is a slitlike opening 3–4 mm in length that occupies a large portion of the roof of the pharynx, the lateral margins of which are formed of cartilaginous ridges; adjacent to these are the openings of the paired cricoarytenoid glands. The dorsal relations of the pharynx include the mandibulomaxillaris lateralis and medialis muscles, the medial process of the mandible, the pterygoid bone, and the internal maxillary veins and arteries. Laterally and ventrally the principal relations are the hyoid bone and articulohyoideus muscle, the cricoarytenoid glands, and the cranial portion of the trachea. The openings of the pharynx are: the isthmus faucium, the aditus laryngis, aditus esophagi, and the pharyngeal openings of the eustachian tubes.

HISTOLOGY OF THE PHARYNX

The oropharynx is directly continuous with the mouth. The lamina epithelialis of the mucosa is a stratified squamous epithelium, the surface cells of which frequently become desquamated. On the conical papillae a thick stratum of highly keratinized cells is present. The lamina epithelialis of the nasopharynx bears a pseudostratified, ciliated, columnar epithelium which resembles that of the nasal cavity. The lamina propria of both the oral and the nasopharynx is composed of a fibroelastic connective tissue infiltrated with islands of the lymphatic cells and nodules. The nodules are especially thick in the regions of the border of the choanae and the eustachian infundibulum. The mucous glands which are similar in structure to those of the oral and nasal cavity continue throughout the walls of the pharynx. An incomplete muscularis mucosa is developed in the longitudinal direction. The submucosa is not structurally separable from the lamina propria mucosa. The muscle coat is of striated muscle consisting partly of longitudinal but mostly of circular fibers. Some of these are the ventral muscles of the skull and those of the neck which pass by the pharynx in their course. The pharyngeal fascia, or adventitia, is of loose connective tissue containing many large blood vessels, nerves, and lymphatics.

Esophagus

The *esophagus* (Figs. 6.1, 6.3, 6.4) is a musculomembranous tube which begins at the caudal rows of papillae of the pharynx, extends to the proventriculus, and becomes gradually smaller in diameter caudally until it measures about 3 mm when relaxed. It is approximately 7.5 cm in length in the adult quail. One of its major characteristics is its capacity of great distention to allow the passage of large particles of food. This is accomplished by arrangement of the mucosa into numerous longitudinal folds. Cranially the esophagus begins in the median plane ventral to the rectus capitis ventralis medialis muscle and dorsal to the trachea. As it courses caudoventrad, it gradually passes to the right side of the neck. At the level of the 4th or 5th cervical vertebra it lies fully to the right side. It then crosses the convexity of the neck and finally reaches its ventral surface at approximately the 12th or 13th cervical vertebra.

Since the cervical (cranial) portion of the esophagus does not follow the contour of the neck, it is somewhat shorter than the corresponding portion of the vertebral column. At this point the esophagus is related dorsally to the trachea, the sternothyrohyoideus, and sternotrachealis muscles; ventrally to the jugular vein, vagus nerve, thymus gland in the young, and the cranial and caudal cervical arteries; deeply to the skin and cutaneous muscles; and superficially to the deep cervical muscles of the neck. Just before the esophagus enters the thorax it gives origin to a large ventral diverticulum, the crop (ingluvies), which lies mostly to the right of the median plane. This is a thin, tough-walled structure with the major portion lying to the right of the midline. Its primary function is the storage of food, and its size varies in proportion to the amount of food present. Its capacity is a little larger in the female. In a number of specimens the average capacity of the full crop was 8–9 gm of ingesta. This amount varies in proportion to the size, age, and sex of the quail. When distended, the shape of the crop tends to be spherical. There is a slit approximately 7 mm long in the ventromedial portion of the esophagus to allow food to enter and leave. A contracted, empty crop presents large folds of mucosa which allow for expansion and shrinkage of the organ. The crop is related deeply to the skin, fat, and cutaneous muscles extending forward from the hypocleidium; all these structures aid in its support. It is related laterally to

the trachea and cranially to the pectoral muscles and fascia of the thoracic inlet. Its walls are richly supplied with blood vessels and nerves.

The thoracic (caudal) portion of the esophagus passes through the thoracic inlet and gradually crosses over to the left of the midline. It is related dorsally to the trachea, sternotrachealis muscle, syrinx, the base of the neck, vertebral artery and vein, thymus, right common carotid artery, cranial portion of the lungs, and the pulmonary diaphragm. Near the middle of the thoracic cavity the esophagus passes very close to the right thyroid gland, and lies between the thoracocervical and cranial thoracic air sacs. It continues caudally between the pulmonary veins and on through the esophageal hiatus of the thoracoabdominal diaphragm into the abdominal cavity, where it joins the glandular stomach (proventriculus).

HISTOLOGY OF THE ESOPHAGUS

The lamina epithelialis of the mucous membrane of the esophagus is composed of a thick layer of stratified squamous epithelium covering numerous longitudinal folds and an extensive papillary body. Many of the cells of the surface layer are keratinized and show a tendency to desquamate. The tunica propria is composed of loose connective tissue containing numerous mucous glands and lymph nodes. Sometimes these two structures are so intermingled that they occupy the same glandular capsule. The mucous glands are characterized by a wide collecting sinus into which folds of the parenchymal tissue project. The tube-shaped end-pieces of the glands are lined with a simple cuboidal epithelium and the excretory duct with a stratified squamous epithelium. The connective tissue of the lamina propria forms a capsular limitation of the gland. The muscularis mucosa forms a continuous

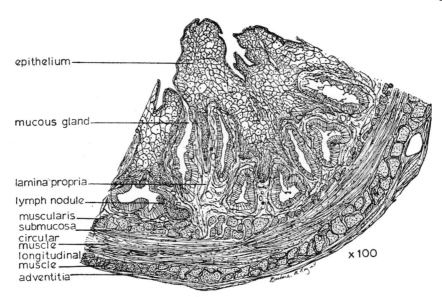

epithelium

mucous gland

lamina propria

lymph nodule

muscularis
submucosa
circular
muscle
longitudinal
muscle
adventitia

x 100

FIG. 6.3—Histology of the esophagus near the pharynx.

sheet of longitudinal fibers. The sheet follows the longitudinal folded contour of the mucosa; however, it is interrupted at many places by the rich deposition of the mucous glands and lymph nodes. The submucosa is very thin except for angular areas formed between the muscularis mucosa and the inner circular coat. It is well supplied with blood and lymph vessels and nerves.

The muscle coats of the esophagus are composed of smooth fibers throughout, which are arranged in an inner thicker, spiral, or circular layer and a peripheral longitudinal one. Rather large nerve ganglia and plexuses of blood and lymph vessels are found between the muscle layers. The fibrous coat of the esophagus is thin. Its fibers are only slightly more condensed than are those of the cervical fascia in which the organ is freely movable. (See Figure 6.3.)

HISTOLOGY OF THE CROP

The histology of the crop resembles that of the esophagus in many respects;

however the mucosal folds are not as high as those of the esophagus. The lamina epithelialis is thick and superficially cornified. The mucous glands and lymph nodes are restricted to the areas near the junction with the esophagus. In the thin, diverticular part of the organ the muscular coats are thin and are intermingled with the numerous elastic connective tissue bundles. The highly vascular adventitia is loosely attached to the cervical fascia.

Stomach

The *stomach* consists of two parts, the proventriculus or glandular portion and the ventriculus (gizzard) or muscular portion.

The *proventriculus* (Figs. 6.1, 6.4–6.6) is an ellipsoidal thick-walled organ located in the craniodorsal portion of the abdominal cavity to the left of the median plane. It is approximately 1.3–1.5 cm in length and .7–.8 cm at its greatest diameter. Its outer surface is covered with visceral peritoneum, through which its muscle can be seen.

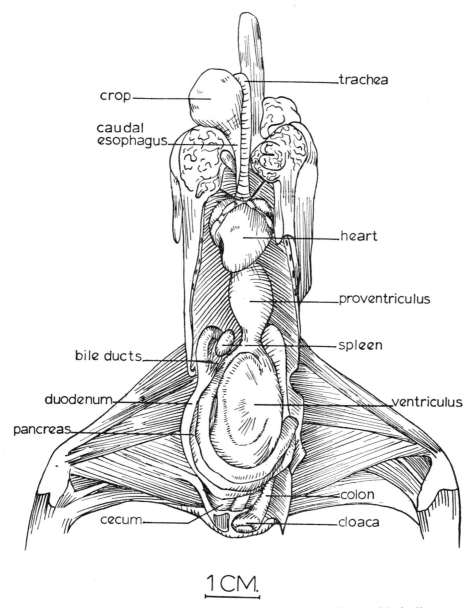

crop

caudal
esophagus

trachea

heart

proventriculus

spleen

bile ducts

duodenum

pancreas

ventriculus

colon

cecum

cloaca

1 CM.

FIG. 6.4—*Viscera with the liver removed.*

Its inner surface contains many longitudinal folds of mucosa and presents small cone-shaped prominences for the openings of the gastric glands. The lumen is continuous cranially with that of the esophagus, and caudally it be-

comes constricted before it empties into the gizzard. The diameter of the proventricular lumen is only slightly greater than that of the esophagus. The size of the proventriculus is not due to a large lumen, but to the thick muscular and glandular wall. Ventrally the entire glandular stomach lies on the dorsal surface of the left lobe of the liver; laterally it is adjacent to the body wall and the thoracoabdominal diaphragm in the region of the 3rd, 4th, and 5th vertebral intercostal spaces. It is covered dorsally by the pulmonary diaphragm and lungs and partially by the testicle (or ovary) and intestines. Dorsomedially it is related to the spleen; medially it is adjacent to the accessory lobe of the liver and the caudal vena cava.

The major function of the glandular stomach is to secrete gastric juices and enzymes. Since its lumen is relatively small, it appears that food would pass through it rather rapidly; therefore, little if any digestion would have time to occur.

The isthmus is the constricted caudal portion of the proventriculus which connects the latter with the gizzard. It is only 3–4 mm in length and its lumen is about the size of that of the esophagus.

The muscular portion of the stomach, the *ventriculus* (gizzard), (Figs. 6.1, 6.4, 6.5, 6.7) is a firm, thickened, oval, muscular organ lying mostly to the left of the median plane in the midventral portion of the abdominal cavity. It is very large, measuring approximately 2.3–2.5 cm long and 1.5 cm wide. The isthmus opens into the craniodorsal portion of the gizzard. The ingesta leaves the gizzard through the pylorus. The two openings are only 6–7 mm apart. The outer surface of the gizzard presents two pairs of muscles: two thin, pale-colored, intermediate ones and two thick, dark red ones which comprise the bulk of the organ. One of the intermediate muscles originates near the proventriculus and the other from the caudal end of the organ. The two thick, dark red muscles flank the intermediate ones and arch around the borders of the

gizzard. Both pairs of muscles have their insertions on a circular tendinous aponeurosis on the medial and lateral sides of the organ. The inner cavity of the gizzard presents a somewhat S-shaped lumen with cranioventral and caudodorsal blind sacs, or diverticula. Its mucous membrane lining is thrown into longitudinal folds or ridges and is covered by a yellow keratinized substance that is secreted by the underlying glands. This horny substance forms a thick lining in the areas covered by thick musculature and is very thin in the diverticular spaces adjacent to the thin musculature.

The gizzard, which is one of the larger organs of the body, has numerous relations. The great abdominal air sac covers much of the gizzard dorsolaterally. The left surface is related to the liver and abdominal wall and, in some birds, is covered with large amounts of subperitoneal fat. The dorsal surface is also related to the left cecum, small intestines, ovary and oviduct in the female, and the testicles in the male. The right surface is adjacent to the origin and termination of the duodenum, the cranial portion of the pancreas, and the right cecum. The ventral surface is related to the right and left lobes of the liver, the ventral abdominal wall, and some subperitoneal fat. The gizzard is also related cranially to the duodenum and pancreas.

The visceral peritoneum helps to form a serosa of the stomach and there are also several folds of it associated with the organ as omenta. The gastrosplenic omentum extends from the right caudolateral portion of the proventriculus to the ventromedial portion of the spleen. Two folds of the lesser omentum are attached to the ventriculus. The right fold of lesser omentum extends from the cranioventral portion of the gizzard dorsolaterally to the caudal border of the right lobe of the liver. It encloses the

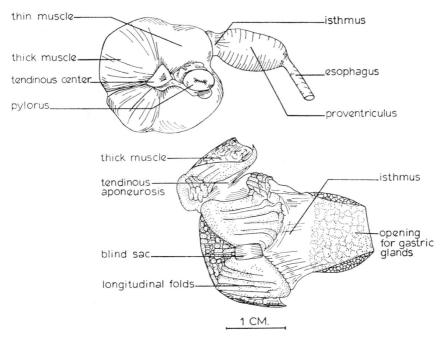

FIG. 6.5—Proventriculus and ventriculus.

gallbladder and is partially continuous with the mesentery of the intestines. The left fold of lesser omentum connects the left craniolateral portion of the gizzard with the dorsal portion of the left lobe of the liver. The ventral mesentery (called the falciform, interlobar, and principal ligament of the liver by various authors) is an extensive fold of peritoneum in the ventral portion of the peritoneal cavity that helps to maintain the position of the liver and proventriculus. The cranial attachment of the ventral mesentery is to the thoracoabdominal diaphragm; the ventral attachment is to the sternum. It extends deeply between the right and left lobes of the liver and is attached to the fibrous tissue of the organ. Caudal to the liver the mesentery attaches to the left surface of the ventriculus. In many specimens the folds of this ligament contain large amounts of fat. The function of the muscular stomach is mechanical. The strong mus-

cles of this organ are capable of remarkable force. Small fine stones and grit are invariably found in the organ.

HISTOLOGY OF THE PROVENTRICULUS

At the junction of the caudal portion of the esophagus with the proventriculus, the lamina epithelialis gradually becomes thinner and changes from a stratified squamous epithelium to a simple columnar epithelium. The lamina propria is richly supplied with closely aggregated lymphatic nodules. These have been called the esophageal tonsils in some birds. The mucous membrane of the proventriculus is characterized by the presence of macroscopic papillae, in the center of which is a large gland duct. Numerous papillae extend into the lumen of the duct. Surrounding the duct and making up its wall are concentric folds arranged in a consecutive manner. In the angular spaces between the duct systems the folds are replaced by large, blunt papillae. The lamina epithelialis covers the folds and the papillae and lines the spaces between the lamina and the papillae. Those cells nearest the surface demonstrate a mucous reaction, while those located deeper in the spaces between the folds and villi lack the mucous forming characteristics. The lamina propria and submucosa are composed of loose, highly vascular connective tissue and are separated by a thin interrupted muscularis mucosa. The muscle coats are composed of inner circular and outer longitudinal layers. Lymph nodes are present but scarce. Ganglionated nerve plexuses are observed in the submucosa and between the muscle coats. The serous layer is very thin and is composed of fairly compact fibers containing blood and lymph vessels and nerves. One layer of mesothelial cells forms the parietal layer of the serosa. (See Figure 6.6.)

HISTOLOGY OF THE VENTRICULUS

The lamina epithelialis of the mucous membrane of the gizzard is composed of simple columnar epithelium which is continued into the ducts of numerous simple, branched tubular glands. The surface epithelium is covered by a highly keratinized layer that is a secretion product of the mucosal glands. This hard keratinized strata has a rough inner surface; and close observation reveals columns of secretion which have condensed, producing a longitudinal striation perpendicular to the surface. Each of these columns has alternating light- and dark-staining strata which are

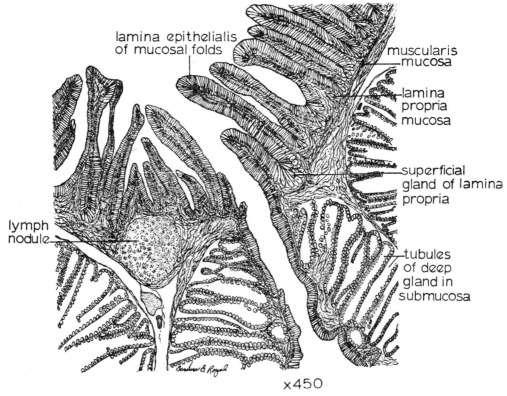

×450

FIG. 6.6—Histology of the proventriculus, mucosa, and glands.

parallel with the inner lining surface and also with those of adjacent columns. These indicate various degrees of secretory activity of the mucosal glands.

The mucosal glands are classified as a simple, branched tubular type. They are rather long and straight, and some of the end-pieces will show as many as four branches. Several glands are grouped together in the lamina propria. The mucosal connective tissue is highly vascular and presents numerous cells and fibers characteristic of those of irregular loose connective tissue. The submucosa, which is not separable from the lamina propria because of the lack of muscularis mucosa, is composed of very compact bundles of collagenous fibers. No lymphatic deposits have been found. Rather large ganglionated nerve plexuses appear just above the muscular coat and in the connective tissue septa between the muscular bundles. Two muscular coats are apparent: The inner one, which is thin, runs perpendicular to the thick muscle fiber bundles of the outer coat; the outer muscular coat is differentiated by the presence of numerous diamond-shaped bundles produced by an odd crisscrossing of rather heavy, collagenous connective tissue fibers. These fibers finally terminate in a flat, aponeurotic structure between the two paired muscular layers. They are easily seen by sectioning the organ in a longitudinal direction. The organ is covered with a thin serosa composed of compact collagenous fibers and a surface layer of mesothelium. (See Figure 6.7.)

Small Intestine

The complete intestine is a membranous tube extending from the ventriculus to the cloaca. Its total length averages 50–52 cm, which is approximately five times the length of the body. The *small intestine* (Figs. 6.1, 6.4) may arbitrarily be divided into three portions, the

duodenum, jejunum, and ileum. The duodenum may be distinguished from the other divisions of the small intestine by its fixed position and the presence of the pancreas between the limbs of its loops. There is no great size or structural differentiation between the jejunum and ileum, which are arranged in coils and suspended by the mesentery.

The *duodenum* is the first, or most fixed, portion of the small intestine. It is arranged in a long narrow loop enclosing the major portion of the pancreas and measures about 8–9 cm in length. It originates at the external opening of the gizzard, where it lies

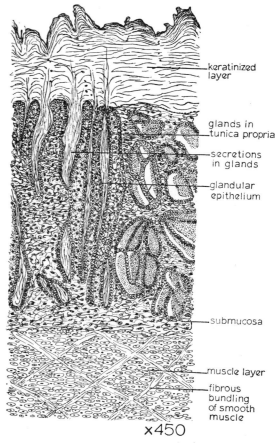

keratinized layer

glands in tunica propria

secretions in glands

glandular epithelium

submucosa

muscle layer

fibrous bundling of smooth muscle

×450

FIG. 6.7—*Histology of the ventriculus, mucosa, and muscular coats.*

slightly to the right of the median plane. It courses craniad for a distance of approximately 5 cm and then turns caudoventrad to form the cranial duodenal flexure which lies in contact with the visceral surface of the right lobe of the liver. From this flexure the ventral limb of the duodenum, commonly called the descending portion, runs caudoventrad along the midportion of the right side of the gizzard until it reaches its caudal surface. It then turns to cross the midline to the left side and courses slightly upward. At this point it lies in the ventral portion of the abdominal cavity. It continues on in a slightly caudodorsal course and reaches the apex of the loop which is located between the cloaca and the abdominal wall to the left of the midline. The apex of the loop is called the caudal duodenal flexure. The ascending limb from the flexure then courses cranially toward the gizzard and upon reaching its caudal border the duodenum turns upward over the ventral limb and terminates by joining the jejunum near the caudal extremity of the gallbladder. The junction of the duodenum with the jejunum is marked by a sudden diminution of the caliber of the gut. Three pancreatic ducts enter the ventromedial surface of the duodenum at its termination. Some authors consider this point as the division between the duodenum and jejunum in other birds.

The *jejunum* and *ileum* form the movable mesenteric portion of the small intestine. There is no clear demarcation between the two parts, but some authors state that the remnant of the yolk stalk may be taken as the dividing point. Since there are very few, if any, differences in the macroscopic structure of the jejunum and ileum and this portion of the small intestine is attached to the dorsal abdominal wall by a continuous fold of peritoneum, the mesentery,

it would seem practical to refer to it as the mesenteric portion of the small intestine. This portion is situated in the dorsal part of the abdominal cavity coiled between the two large abdominal air sacs, above the duodenum and ventricular stomach, and below the testicles, ovaries, and kidneys. In the laying female it is pushed to the right of the median plane by the follicles and oviduct. This portion originates as the continuation of the duodenum, initially courses craniodorsad above the right lobe of the liver, and lies against the lateral abdominal wall. As it reaches the ventral border of the right testicle in the male, or the ventral portion of the right cranial lobe of the kidney in the female, the intestine turns to cross the midline just caudal to the fold of the mesentery and then turns to course caudad, forming three coils in the dorsal portion of the abdominal cavity above the ventriculus.

The third coil terminates just caudal to the origin of the two ceca and is adjacent dorsally to the proventricular opening to the gizzard. The intestine then makes a turn back under itself, courses caudad, and turns to cross the median plane following the contour of the caudodorsal border of the gizzard. As it continues its cranial direction it begins a large S-shaped course in a dorsoventral direction. The lower half of the S-shaped curve becomes flanked on either side by the large ceca. The intestine then continues craniodorsad, crosses to the left of the midline just above the spleen and the caudal portion of the proventriculus, and terminates at the origin of the two ceca at the large intestine. Thus the last 7–8 cm of the small intestine are adjacent to the ceca. At approximately two-thirds of the length of the intestine and on the side opposite the attachment of the great mesentery, there is a small, rounded projection which is known as Meckel's diverticulum. In young birds it is quite large, but decreases in size as the quail matures and is rarely visible at the age of two months.

The intestine of coturnix differs from those of mammals in several respects. The fixed loops of the colon as found in mammals are lacking. This is probably due to the very short colon in the bird. The small intestines are not rotated into a permanently coiled arrangement. They are freely movable, limited only by the length of the mesentery. The duodenum is not anchored to the colon by a mesoduodenum. However, in coturnix an ileoduodenal ligament which holds these portions of the small intestines together is developed. This ligament is not present in mammals.

HISTOLOGY OF THE SMALL INTESTINE

The small intestine is composed of a mucosa, submucosa, muscle coat, and serosa. The mucosa is thrown into numerous high papillae between which the ducts of the short glands of Lieberkühn empty. The lamina epithelialis of the villi is composed of a simple columnar epithelium which displays a definite striated border. Numerous goblet cells are dispersed in the epithelial sheet and migrating leucocytes are to be found in the lamina propria and surface epithelium. The lamina propria of the villi is highly vascular and is composed of loose connective tissue with a few muscle cells running chiefly parallel with the length of the villi. Centrally located lacteals are found in the villi, the lumen of which can be followed down to the parenchymatous portion of the gland tubule. The muscularis mucosa appears as a narrow longitudinal sheet that lies close to the inner circular muscle coat. The submucosa is thin and in some places appears to be absent. The inner

circular layer of smooth muscle is much the thicker of the two muscle coats. It is composed of rather tightly arranged bundles of smooth muscle fibers. Ganglionated nerve fiber bundles are found in the submucosa and between the two muscle coats. The thinner, outer longitudinal muscle coat displays numerous large blood vessels and is covered with a thin serous coat composed of a thin layer of compact connective tissue and a surface mesothelial layer. It is attached by loose connective tissue to the capsule of the pancreas which intervenes between the loops of the duodenum. No Brunner's glands have been observed in

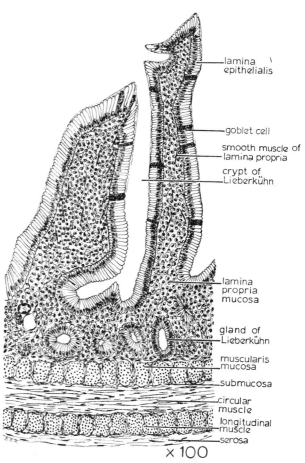

FIG. 6.8—Histology of the duodenum.

the duodenum. Numerous lymphatic infiltrations and nodules were found in the mucosa of older birds. Two bile ducts and three pancreatic ducts enter the duodenum near its termination. (See Figure 6.8.)

Large Intestine

The *large intestine* (Figs. 6.1, 6.4) consists of the two ceca and the colon.

The *ceca* are long, dilated, blind pouches which open into the colon. They have an average length of 10 cm and extend along the terminal portion of the small intestine to which they are attached by narrow peritoneal folds. The first 3 cm of the cecum has a diameter of approximately 3 cm, with a thick wall and a small lumen. The remainder of the cecum is about 6 cm in diameter, with a thin wall and a large lumen except for the blind distal extremity which may reach an average of .9–1 cm in size.

The *colon* averages 3 cm in length. It originates as the continuation of the small intestine and courses caudad along the ventral border of the cranial and middle lobes of the left kidney and then reaches the midline where it is continued by the cloaca. Its diameter is slightly larger than that of the small intestine and its walls are somewhat thicker. The mesocolon is a caudal extension of the common intestinal mesentery which attaches the colon to the dorsal abdominal wall.

HISTOLOGY OF THE LARGE INTESTINE

The histological structure of the large intestine correlates with that of the small intestine more closely in birds than it does in mammals. There are, however, certain area differential characteristics which are worthy of note.

In the ceca (Fig. 6.9) the lamina epithelialis of the mucosal lining is of the simple columnar type with striated borders. The sheet is heavily studded with goblet cells. The villi are of varying lengths and are long in the proximal portion but gradually become shorter and fade out completely in the wide lumen of the terminal area. The lamina propria is richly infiltrated with individual lymphocytes and lymph nodules. On one side of the proximal division of the ceca there is an accumulation of lymphatic nodules that might be labeled the cecal tonsils, as found in other birds. The muscularis mucosa is poorly developed and barely distinguishable, as it is in the distal thin-walled portion of the ceca. The two usual coats of the lamina muscularis are found with various thicknesses and arrangements of the fibers. Fibrous and elastic connective tissue with numerous nerves and blood and lymph plexuses make up the supporting stroma of the organ. The serosal coat is composed of surface mesothelium on which no anchoring mesenteries are found. Differential age characteristics have been noted in the young growing bird. A few lymph infiltrations were found, and the villi were like those of the small intestine. As the age of the bird increased, the lymphatic infiltrations became general throughout the lamina propria and submucosa, and the lymph nodules were found to be abundant.

More goblet cells and mucin deposits have been found in the colon than in the small intestine. The goblet cells were so numerous that they even were found to be among the glandular cells of the glands of Lieberkühn. The circular muscle coat between the colon and cloaca is thickened to form a constriction in the lumen.

Cloaca

The *cloaca* (Figs. 6.10–6.15) is the tubular structure, situated in the perineal region, which serves as the common receptacle for the products of the diges-

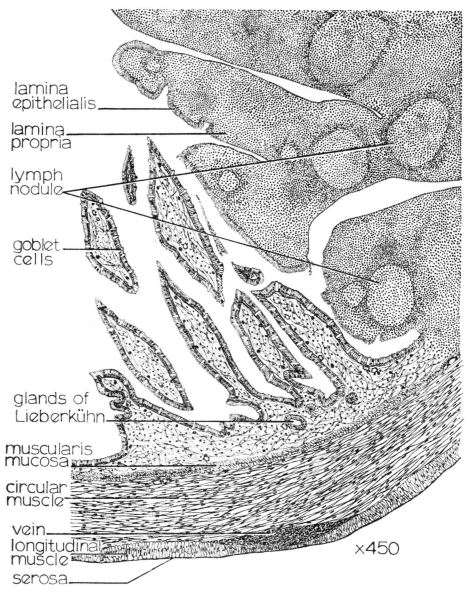

lamina
epithelialis

lamina
propria

lymph
nodule

goblet
cells

glands of
Lieberkühn

muscularis
mucosa

circular
muscle

vein

longitudinal
muscle

serosa

×450

FIG. 6.9—Histology of the cecum.

tive and urogenital systems. The cavity of the cloaca is divided by an oblique fold which is well developed dorsally but is hardly recognizable ventrally. From its dorsal attachment to the wall of the cloaca this fold extends caudoventrally and divides the cavity into func-

tional and nonfunctional portions. As in other birds the cloaca of the quail may be divided into three parts. A narrowing of the lumen of the rectum is the line of demarcation between the rectum and the *coprodeum*, which is the largest of the three divisions. The middle divi-

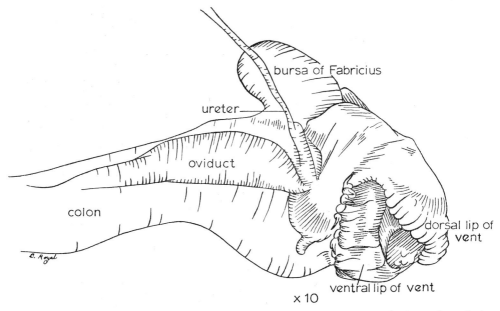

C. Royal

×10

FIG. 6.10—Female cloaca, lateral view.

sion is termed the *urodeum* and is separated from the proctodeum caudally by the oblique fold mentioned above. The last division of the cloaca is termed the *proctodeum,* from which an opening leads into a blind sac called the bursa of Fabricius. The proctodeum opens caudally at the cloacal orifice, or vent.

There is an age differentiation in the structure of the coprodeum. In young growing birds a mid-dorsal pouch in its roof extends upward beneath the well-formed bursa of Fabricius; at maturity the dorsal pouch regresses, resulting in a reduction in the size of the lumen of the coprodeum that is compensated for by the development of a secondary caudoventral pouch in the floor of this division.

Openings into the female urodeum are provided for the ureters and the vagina. The oviduct or vagina enters the urodeum by passing through the midportion of the left side of the oblique fold. In young birds the exit is

small and somewhat obscure as it opens on the ventral surface of the fold. However, during the egg-laying period the vagina is greatly enlarged, so that the oblique fold is almost obliterated due to the great size of the orifice of the female genital duct.

The ureters open nearer the proximal attachment of the oblique fold on its ventral surface. They are found on either side near the median plane. In the male the ductus deferens opens into the urodeum. Each bears a prominent papilla that originates at the lateral aspect of the oblique fold. During the breeding season these papillae protrude caudally sufficiently to open into the proctodeum just cranial to the phallus. Following the reproductive cycle they regress and open near the openings of the ureters.

The duct of the bursa of Fabricius extends caudoventrally and pierces the wall of the proctodeum just caudodorsal to the base of the oblique fold. This orifice is guarded laterally by two

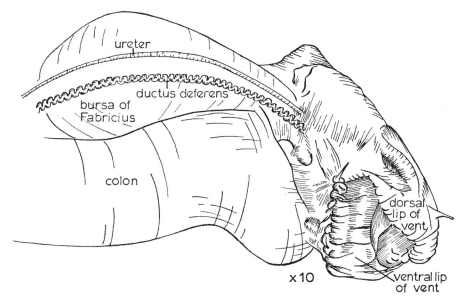

FIG. 6.11—Male cloaca, lateral view.

strong ligamentous bands, or external sphincter. The caudal opening of the cloaca to the surface is termed the vent or external cloacal orifice.

HISTOLOGY OF THE CLOACA

The three parts of the cloaca are histologically quite similar. The villi of the coprodeum appear to be a continuation of the finger-like projections of the colon. Their height is reduced, and they are more leaf shaped in the urodeum than in the coprodeum. In the proctodeum two layers of muscularis mucosa and a greatly thickened internal muscular coat are found. This formation might be considered an internal sphincter muscle.

The coprodeum, or first division of the cloaca, is a continuation of the wall of the rectum from which it is divided by a thickening of the inner circular layer of the muscle coat of the cloaca. The mucous membrane is at first composed of long narrow villi; but these soon become shorter and much broader, and their width will equal their height.

The striated border of the columnar epithelium becomes less distinct, and the goblet cells appear to outnumber the typical lining cells of the lamina epithelialis. The glands of Lieberkühn open into the depths of the rather wide spaces between the villi. The parenchymal portion of the gland is short and very tortuous. The lamina propria mucosa is composed of very delicate fibers and many connective tissue cellular elements. Lymphocytic infiltrations and nodules continue to dominate the cellular elements of the propria.

Two smooth muscle layers make up the muscularis mucosa, some of the fibers of which will penetrate into the core of the wide villi. The submucosal area is very narrow and often does not exceed the width of the perimysial bundling of the muscle layers. In the perineal region the serosa is replaced by fibrous adventitia which blends with the connective tissue sheaths of the striated muscle of the pelvis. The oblique fold which separates the coprodeum from the urodeum has a continuance of the cop-

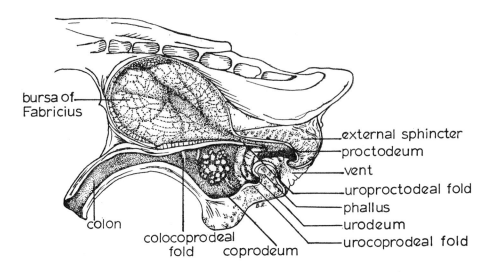

bursa of Fabricius

external sphincter
proctodeum
vent
uroproctodeal fold
phallus
urodeum
urocoprodeal fold

colon

colocoprodeal fold   coprodeum

1 CM.

FIG. 6.12—Cloaca, median section.

rodeal mucous membrane on its dorsal surface at its tip and for a short continuing distance on its ventral surface. The remainder of the mucosa of the ventral surface of the fold has a low villus arrangement covered with simple columnar epithelium. On the root of the fold stratified squamous epithelium prevails and continues into the duct of the bursa of Fabricius. The caudal portion of the urodeum and the proctodeum of the quail presents a lamina epithelialis of the stratified squamous type.

Lymphatic nodules continue in the lamina propria connective tissue. Just below the submucosa of the proctodeum a wide expanse occupied by compound tubuloalveolar glands appears. Their many lobules occupy the entire area of the perineum out to the striated musculature and integument of the body. Some of the gland ducts penetrate the proctodeal lamina epithelialis to enter its lumen. Surrounding the terminal portion of the proctodeum and extending

into the folds of the vent are two layers of striated muscle. The inner one is primarily longitudinal and the external one is arranged in a circular manner. Glands of the proctodeum extend down to the dorsal lip of the vent. The ventral lip does not contain the glands, but the muscle coats extend to the free border of the fold of the vent. A cross section of the base of the oblique fold which separates the urodeum from the proctodeum reveals a section of the penetrating ductus deferens. It is lined with a simple columnar epithelium surrounded by a wide, smooth muscle coat, the fibers of which are intermingled with delicate connective tissue fibers, blood vessels, nerves, and lymphatics. An imperfect capsule of collagenous connective tissue fibers delimit the ductus deferens from the surrounding tissues of the fold.

Liver

The *liver* (Figs. 6.1, 6.16, 6.17, 6.19), which is the largest organ of the body, is situated in the cranioventral portion

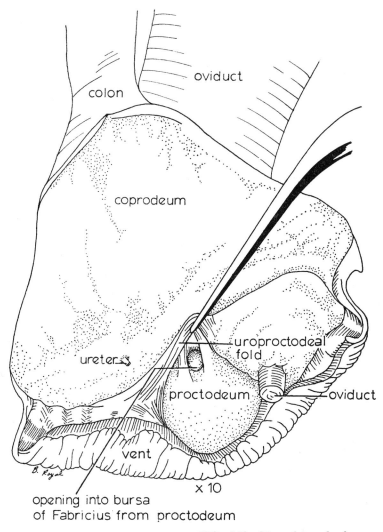

colon

oviduct

coprodeum

uroproctodeal
fold

ureters

proctodeum

oviduct

vent

B. Royal

× 10

opening into bursa
of Fabricius from proctodeum

FIG. 6.13—Opened female cloaca, ventral view.

of the abdominal cavity just caudal to the heart and and separated from it by the thoracoabdominal diaphragm. It has a characteristic reddish-brown color and is rather friable. It extends from the level of the 2nd or 3rd thoracic vertebra cranially to near the 6th or 7th lumbosacral segment caudally. It is related dorsally to the sternum and the abdominal floor; ventrally to the aorta, the caudal vena cava, the proventriculus, and the ovary and oviduct in the female, and the testicles in the male; and cranially to the spleen, ventriculus, and intestines.

The size and weight of the liver in the adult varies greatly, depending upon the sex of the quail. In the egg-producing female the liver averages approximately 4.8% of the body weight; while in the male it is 3.1%, thus in comparison by body weight the liver of the lay-

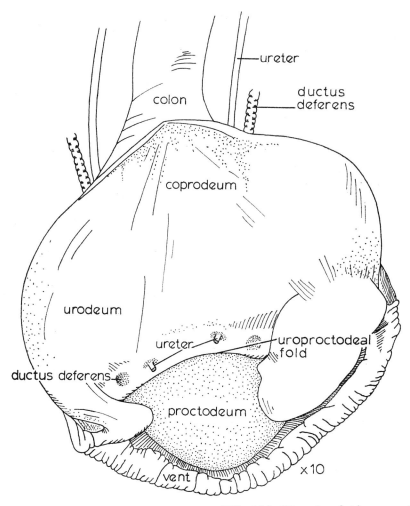

FIG. 6.14—Opened male cloaca, ventral view.

ing female is 1.57 times larger than that of the male. The average body weight of the adult male is 95 gm. while that of the laying female is 125 gm. This means that the body weight of the laying female is approximately 1.3 times greater than that of the male.

The liver is divided into two lobes, the right lobe being considerably thicker and slightly longer than the left. The average length of the right lobe of the mature male is approximately 3.3 cm, or one-third the length of the body,

while the left lobe is only 2.7 cm in length. Dorsally the left lobe is partly divided by a longitudinal fissure which begins at the caudal border of the lobe and extends approximately two-thirds of its length.

The parietal surface of the liver is highly convex and smooth, and lies mainly in contact with the great abdominal air sacs, pulmonary diaphragm, sternum, and the adjacent sternal and vertebral ribs. The diaphragmatic, or cranial, surface is deeply concave with

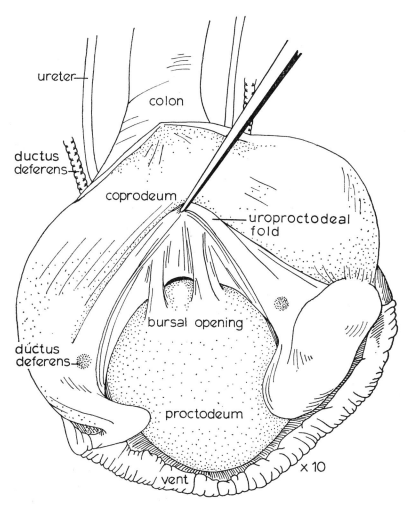

FIG. 6.15—Opened male cloaca, ventral view.

the two lobes forming a sacculation, or fossa, for the apex of the heart with the thoracoabdominal diaphragm separating the two organs. The visceral, or caudo-dorsal, surface is irregularly concave. It lies in contact with the proventriculus, the ventriculus, the spleen, the duodenum, a portion of the small intestine, the pancreas, and the abdominal air sacs. All but the latter two structures produce noticeable impressions on the liver surface hardened *in situ*. The caudal border of each lobe slopes downward

and backward from its dorsal position until it meets the ventral border forming an angle of approximately 45°. At their craniodorsal portions the two lobes are connected by a narrow isthmus of liver tissue. The dorsal portion of the right lobe encloses the caudal vena cava as it courses toward the heart.

A porta, or hilus, for the entrance of vessels and nerves and the exit of hepatic ducts to and from the liver is associated with each lobe. The larger porta is located near the center of the

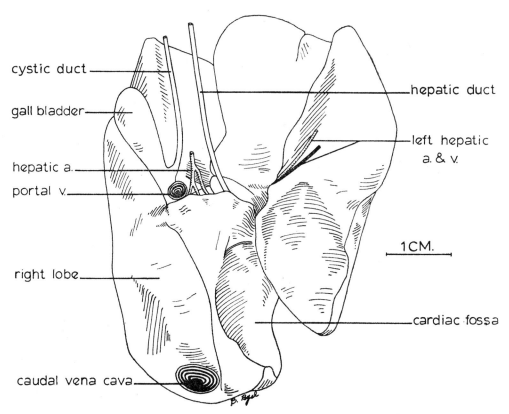

FIG. 6.16—Liver, visceral surface.

visceral surface of the right lobe, while the left porta is near the junction of the two lobes connected by the isthmus. The left porta is caudal to the proventricular fossa of the liver and dorsal to the ventricular fossa.

The cystic duct leaves the right lobe and presents a ventral dilatation, the *gallbladder,* which is a pear-shaped structure 1–1.5 cm in length when distended. Its cranial portion lies along the lateral surface of the pancreas which is enclosed by a fold of peritoneum between the loops of the duodenum. The cystic duct continues on to enter the terminal portion of the duodenum. The hepatic duct originates from the left lobe of the liver. It does not pass out through the left porta, but instead remains enclosed by a thin cover of liver tissue and

courses across to the right lobe on the caudal border of the isthmus. As the left hepatic duct approaches the right porta, it receives a tributary from the right lobe. It then turns backward and crosses the dorsal surface of the gallbladder to become parallel with the cystic duct. The two ducts then continue their course to enter the terminal portion of the duodenum. Associated with the liver are various folds of peritoneum. The ventral mesentery and the right and left folds of lesser omentum have been described in connection with the gizzard.

HISTOLOGY OF THE LIVER
AND GALLBLADDER

The liver is classified as a compound tubular gland. It is composed of two main lobes which are joined by an isthmus. Each lobe is divided into lobules which are the histological units of the liver.

The capsule of the liver is composed of an exterior serous membrane of one layer of simple mesothelial cells with a thin layer of connective tissue, the capsule of Glisson, beneath. The interlobular septa is thinner than in mammals; therefore, the lobulation is less distinct. The portal fissure of coturnix is divided into two parts, one for each of the two lobes. Each fissure is surrounded by a thickening of Glisson's capsule at the isthmus. The portal triad, composed of the portal vein, hepatic artery, and bile ducts, continue from the portal fissure to ramify in and around each liver lobule. They are supported by a delicate reticular stroma which also forms the retaining meshwork for the parenchymal liver cells and sinusoids of the lobule. The liver cells are a little larger in coturnix than in mammals; the nucleus is large and spherical and appears most often in the proximal portion. The cell membrane is less distinct than those of the mammalian liver cells, which makes the identification of bile capillaries more difficult. The liver cords form columnar or concentric layers about the intralobular bile capillaries. The sinusoids are rather wide and are lined with sinusoidal lining cells, and bridging phagocytic Kupffer's cells are present. The lymphatics form a plexus in the capsule of Glisson and internally follow the larger blood vessels and ducts. Accumulations of lymphocytes are conspicuous around the blood vessels and between the liver cords. Eosinophilic leucocytes are also found intermingled with the lymphocytes, or they may form small foci of their own. The nerves of the liver are mostly unmyelinated and are distributed along the course of the blood vessels. (See Figure 6.17.)

The gallbladder has a rather thick capsule which is continuous with that of the liver. Externally a single layer of mesothelial cells represents the peri-

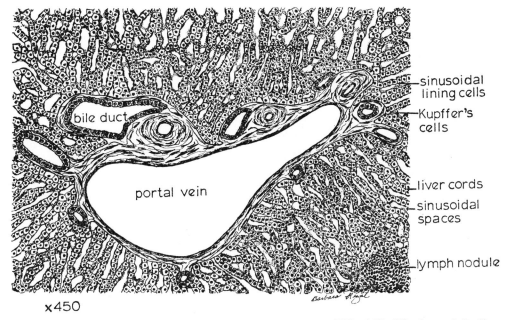

×450

FIG. 6.17—Histology of the liver.

toneal reflection. Scattered smooth muscle cells running in a longitudinal direction help to make up the thickness of the bladder capsule. The mucous membrane is thrown into numerous folds which are lined with a tall, simple columnar epithelium. (See Figure 6.18.)

Pancreas

The *pancreas* (Figs. 6.1, 6.4, 6.19) is a slender, elongated, pale yellow gland situated in the interduodenal space formed by the ascending and descending limbs of the duodenum. It may be divided into a dorsal lobe and right and left ventral lobes. The dorsal lobe extends from the region of the pylorus of the gizzard along the left dorsal surface of the descending limb of the duodenum to the apex of the duodenal loop. (A splenic lobe described as a cranial continuation of the dorsal lobe has not been found in a large number of specimens.) The left ventral lobe runs along beside the dorsal lobe, being separated from the latter by the pancreaticoduode-

nal vessels and nerves. It lies in contact with the ventral surface of the ascending limb of the duodenum along its entire length. The right ventral lobe of the pancreas is somewhat shorter than the left; it extends from the region where the pancreatic and bile ducts enter the duodenum and fuses with the left ventral lobe. The dorsal lobe and the right ventral lobe fuse for a short distance at the apex of the duodenal loop. The left ventral and dorsal lobes ultimately fuse in the region of the caudal tip of the gallbladder.

Other than the duodenum the relations of the pancreas are few. The right ventral lobe usually lies close to the floor of the abdominal cavity, while the dorsal lobe and the left ventral lobe are adjacent to the ileum and the two ceca. Along with the bile ducts, there are three pancreatic ducts which enter the duodenum near its termination. The dorsal pancreatic duct lies closest to the hepatic duct. It extends from the cranial region of the dorsal lobe backward to enter the duodenum just cranial to

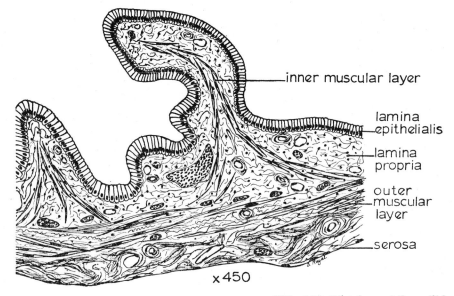

inner muscular layer

lamina epithelialis

lamina propria

outer muscular layer

serosa

×450

FIG. 6.18—Histology of the gallbladder.

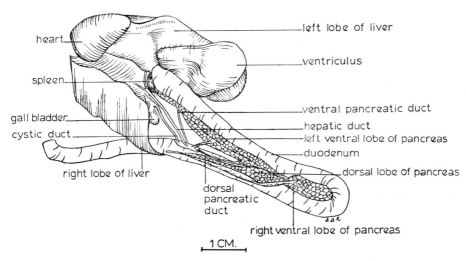

FIG. 6.19—*Pancreatic and bile ducts, ventrolateral view.*

the entrance of the two ventral ducts, which originate from the distal portion of the left and right ventral lobes of the pancreas and course forward. Along their way the pancreatic ducts receive tributaries from each of the lobules.

HISTOLOGY OF THE PANCREAS

Structurally the pancreas is a compound tubuloacinar gland. It has a very thin fibrous capsule covered by a peritoneal reflection of serous membrane. The parenchymal cells and ducts are supported in a reticular connective tissue stroma. The lobulation is not distinct as it is in the mammalian pancreas, and the perivascular connective tissue occasionally contains lymph nodules. Some of the differential structural characteristics of the pancreas which distinguish it from the salivary glands are the absence of striated tubules and basket cells and the presence of islets of Langerhans and the centroacinar cells. The conical or pyramid-shaped secretory cells are arranged in a single layer. They resemble serous cells but are distinguished by the presence of two zones. The inner zone is coarsely granular, while the outer (basal)

zone appears almost homogeneous or may present faint radial striations. The lumen of the end-piece is narrow. The centroacinar cells are the beginning lining cells of the long intercalated ducts which are lined with flat or cuboidal epithelium. The intercalated ducts are intralobular in position and pass directly into the interlobular ducts which are lined with simple columnar epithelium. The interlobular (or interacinar) connective tissue which surrounds the ducts is very fine and poorly developed. The excretory ducts of the pancreas are lined with a stratified columnar epithelium. The propria of the duct is fibroelastic connective tissue. Externally the duct is incorporated in the serous membrane of the peritoneal reflection between the two limbs of the duodenum. Smooth muscle forms a sphincter at its termination. The islets of Langerhans, its endocrine component, are numerous in coturnix. They are scattered among the lobules and appear as clusters of polyhedral cells held in the reticular stroma and supplied with a rich capillary plexus. Staining characteristics indicate the possibility of the presence of three types of cells.

The pancreas receives blood from the

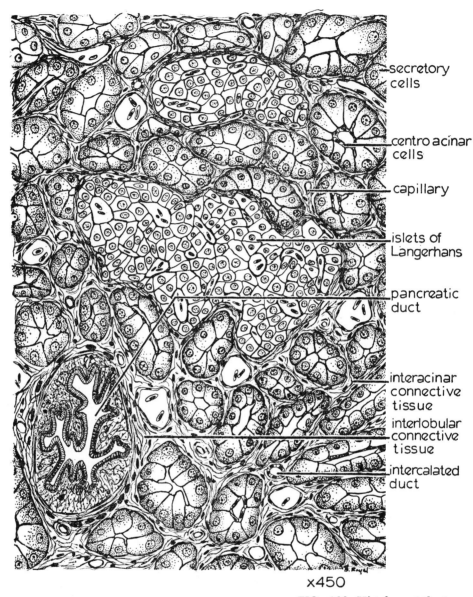

secretory cells

centro acinar cells

capillary

islets of Langerhans

pancreatic duct

interacinar connective tissue

interlobular connective tissue

intercalated duct

×450

FIG. 6.20—Histology of the pancreas.

pancreaticoduodenal arteries which are distributed to the parenchyma by way of the interlobular connective tissue. The blood leaves the pancreas by way of the pancreaticoduodenal veins, which in turn supply the portal vein. The nerves to the pancreas are from the splanchnic (sympathetic) and vagus (parasympathetic). The former are non-medullated and the latter are medullated preganglionic fibers. The terminal fibers of the nerves are distributed to the secretory acini and the walls of the blood vessels. (See Figure 6.20.)

Spleen

The *spleen* (Figs. 6.1, 6.4, 6.21) is a spherical organ which is dark reddish-brown in color. It is described with the digestive system strictly because of its location, even though it has no known digestive function. It ranges in diameter from 4–6 mm, but even though small it has numerous relations. It is situated in the cranial portion of the abdominal cavity between the two lobes of the liver and lies ventral to the testicle or ovary and just under the origin of the two ceca. To its left is the left lobe of the liver and the isthmus connecting the two portions of the stomach. On the right side is the right lobe of the liver and the origin of the duodenum. Caudally it lies against the cranial portion of the muscular stomach. It also is in contact with the greater abdominal air sac. The hilus of the spleen faces cranially and is close to the celiac artery from which the splenic arteries arise.

HISTOLOGY OF THE SPLEEN

The spleen of coturnix is similar to that of mammals in that it is a blood forming and destroying organ and is one of the largest single masses of lymphatic tissue in the body. Unlike other collections of lymphatic tissue which are interposed in the lymph stream in mammals, the spleen is intercalated in the blood stream. It has no afferent lymphatics and no lymph sinuses; its sinuses, like those of hemal nodes of mammals, are filled with blood.

The supporting framework consists of a capsule, the trabeculae, and a reticular stroma. A serous membrane of mesothelium covers its surface and lines the depression of the hilum. The rather thick capsule is composed chiefly of compact collagenous bundles; however, numerous elastic fibers and smooth muscle cells are intermingled. Nerves, lymphatics, and blood vessels form plexuses which communicate with those

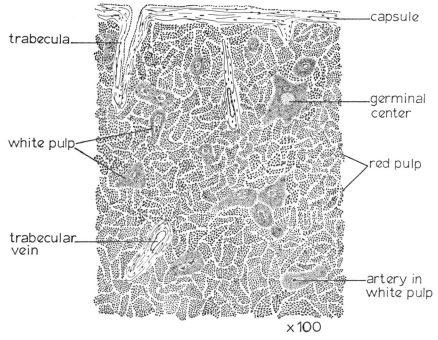

x 100

FIG. 6.21–Histology of the spleen.

of the trabeculae. The structure of the trabeculae is similar to that of the capsule. They radiate from the indentation of the capsule at the hilus out through the organ to branch and anastomose among themselves and finally join the inside of the capsule. They thus divide the organ into smaller and smaller chambers in which the reticular stroma takes over to support the rather free parenchymal cells of the organ.

The parenchyma of the spleen of coturnix is, as in mammals, divisible into the red and white pulp areas. The white pulp is composed of typical lymphatic tissue associated with the arteries which leave the trabeculae. In this area the lymphatic tissue undergoes the same changes as those described for lymphatic tissue in general. Lymphocytopoietic centers in the nodules appear and disappear in connection with the general condition of the bird. Reaction centers are common in certain infections and intoxications. The red pulp consists of the venous sinuses and the tissue filling the spaces between them, the splenic (Billroth's) cords. In the meshes of the reticular stroma between the sinuses are many lymphocytes of all sizes, free macrophages, and all the elements of circulating blood. These are all intermingled without order and the preponderance of the lymphocytic cells varies with the activity of the germinal centers of the adjacent white pulp.

The veins of the spleen begin as anastomosing venous sinuses which penetrate all the red pulp and are especially numerous outside the marginal zone surrounding the white pulp. These vessels in coturnix are not as large comparatively as they are in mammals, although they do change in size according to the amount of blood they contain. The sinus veins continue into the trabeculae and leave the organ at the hilus as the splenic veins.

Some of the differential characteristics of the spleen of coturnix are: The trabeculae are very tortuous in their course, so much so that most of the sections appear as tangential or cross sections; the trabecular arteries have an unusually thick tunica media composed mostly of smooth muscle. The white pulp seems to occupy as much space as the red pulp and there is no fine line of differentiation between them. The white pulp is not always completely surrounded by the red pulp and small areas of white pulp border the venous sinuses. The lining cells of the venous sinuses are very flat and do not appear like the high reticular lining cells of the mammalian spleen. No thick sheaths of Schweigger-Seidel were found in the walls of the smaller red-pulp arteries. (See Figure 6.21.)

PELVIC CAVITY

The pelvic cavity communicates freely with the abdominal cavity without a sharp line of demarcation. The greater part of the dorsal and lateral walls of the cavity are formed by the bony pelvis and the first three or four coccygeal vertebrae. Due to the failure of the closing of the ventral bony pelvis, and a complete lack of a symphysis in birds, the ventral wall or floor of the pelvis is formed only by the abdominal muscles.

PERITONEUM

The peritoneum is a thin, serous membrane lining the abdominal cavity and completely or partially covering the viscera contained therein. The peritoneal cavity is that portion of the abdominal space enclosed by the peritoneum. It is an entirely closed sac in the male, but in the female there is a small abdominal orifice for the fallopian tubes. The inner surface of the membrane is smooth and glistening and is moistened by peritoneal fluid, which tends to reduce friction between the visceral organs and between the viscera, organs, and abdominal wall. The outer surface of the peritoneum is related to the subserous tissue which fuses it with the fascia of the abdominal wall.

Several topographical subdivisions of the peritoneum may be differentiated. The parietal peritoneum lines the abdominal walls. The visceral peritoneum partially or completely covers the viscera. The connecting folds of peritoneum are termed mesenteries, omenta, ligaments, and folds. A *mesentery* is a fold attaching the intestines to the abdominal wall. It is a structural pathway for vessels and nerves to the intestines and in some cases contains much fat between its layers. An *omentum* is a fold of peritoneum passing from the stomach to other viscera. There are three present in the quail—the lesser, greater, and gastrosplenic omenta. A *ligament* is a fold of peritoneum passing between viscera

other than parts of the digestive tube. Simple *peritoneal folds* connect portions of the digestive tube. The pelvic peritoneum is continuous with the abdominal peritoneum. No perineum is present in the quail.

RESPIRATORY SYSTEM

The *respiratory system* (Figs. 6.22–6.30) consists of the lungs and accessory passages which provide for the exchange of gases between the air and the blood. The nasal cavity, pharynx, larynx, trachea, syrinx, bronchi, and air sacs compose the accessory passages. The ventilation apparatus of birds is unique in its structure, possessing a complete system of air sacs with interconnecting bronchi. This system provides the bird with the most efficient means of respiration known among vertebrates.

Nasal Cavity

The *nasal cavity* (Figs. 6.22–6.25) forms the most cranial, or facial, portion of the respiratory system and extends

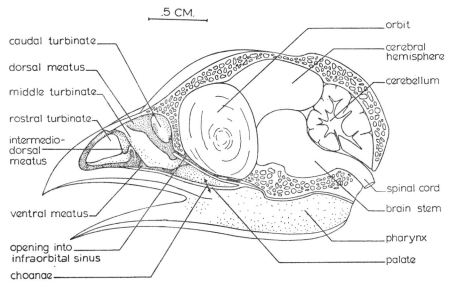

FIG. 6.22—Nasal cavity and pharynx, medial view.

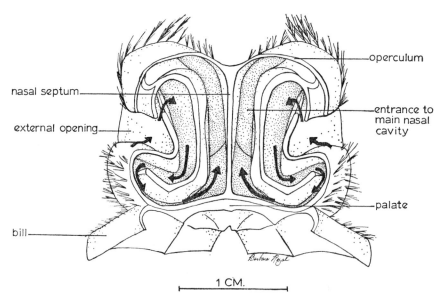

nasal septum

external opening

bill

operculum

entrance to
main nasal
cavity

palate

1 CM.

FIG. 6.23—Nasal atrium, cross section.

from the nostrils (external nares) at the base of the beak to the choanae (internal or caudal nares). The skeletal parts of the nasal cavity include laterally the premaxilla, the maxilla, and the lateral rami of the nasal bone; dorsally the nasal process of the premaxilla, the frontal bone, and the nasal bone; ventrally the maxilla and palatine bones. The cavity is divided equally by the longitudinal nasal septum which becomes continuous caudally with the interorbital septum. The right and left halves created by this septum are referred to as fossae.

The *nostrils* (external nares) are two narrow longitudinal openings into the nasal cavity located at the upper portion of the base of the beak. The nasal aperture of the skeleton is large and triangular in shape and is formed by the premaxilla, maxilla, and nasal bones. However, the size of the nostrils is greatly reduced by dorsal and ventral folds of the integument. The ventral fold of skin projects into the convex or lateral portions of the rostral turbinate and is covered externally by a number

of small feathers that aid in filtering the air.

The *nasal fossa* extends from the nostrils to the choanae, and the infraorbital sinus and the nasolacrimal duct open into it. This space is short and narrow and is occupied to a great extent by three turbinate bodies. These turbinates project from the lateral wall of the chamber and consist of a cartilaginous skeleton with a mucous membrane covering. Each is named according to its location in the fossa. Air passages, or channels, called meatuses are formed between these turbinates and the walls of the fossa. The turbinates are three in number and with their moist mucous membrane covering and rich blood supply aid in warming and filtering the inhaled air.

The *rostral turbinate* (ventral) lies opposite the nostrils and is convex medially. It is triangular to oval in outline. The caudal border of this structure attaches to the lateral wall of the nasal fossa and the dorsal border of the nostril. Its free dorsal and ventral edges are

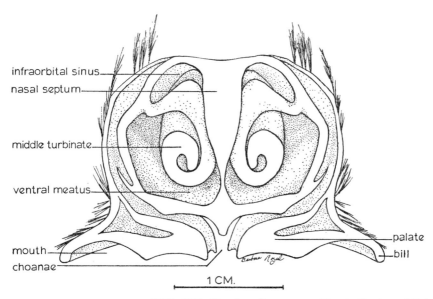

infraorbital sinus
nasal septum
middle turbinate
ventral meatus
mouth
choanae
palate
bill

1 CM.

FIG. 6.24—Nasal cavity, cross section in the preorbital region.

scrolled approximately three-fourths of a revolution laterally.

The *middle turbinate* is the largest of the three and is situated obliquely between the dorsal and ventral turbinates. This tubular structure attaches to the lateral wall of the nasal fossa with its free or unattached portion cranial to its area of attachment. On cross section it exhibits a scroll 1–1½ turns ventrolaterally.

The *caudal turbinate* is the smallest turbinate body and resembles a large blister on the caudodorsal surface of the lateral wall of the nasal fossa. It is oval in shape with its convex surface facing the nasal cavity. The rostral half of its mucous membrane covering is respiratory in function; the caudal half is olfactory. The olfactory nerve fibers originate in the olfactory epithelial areas of this turbinate structure and pass caudomediad, forming bundles which in turn join to form the olfactory nerve.

The *common meatus* is the largest of the air passages. It lies between the turbinate and the nasal septum and

communicates freely with all the other meatuses.

The *dorsal meatus* is the air channel formed between the turbinate bodies and the dorsolateral wall of the nasal cavity. Air from this meatus may pass ventrad through the two middle meatuses.

The *ventral meatus* extends laterally from the common meatus and lies ventral to the rostral and middle turbinates and dorsal to the floor of the nasal cavity.

The *intermediodorsal meatus* lies between the rostral and middle turbinates. It communicates dorsally with the dorsal meatus, ventrally with the ventral meatus, and medially with the common meatus.

The *choanae* (caudal nares) are long narrow openings from each nasal fossa into the pharynx and the caudal portion of the mouth. These openings are separated by the ventral portion of the nasal septum and rostrum of the sphenoid bone. However, these partitions do not reach the ventral limit of the

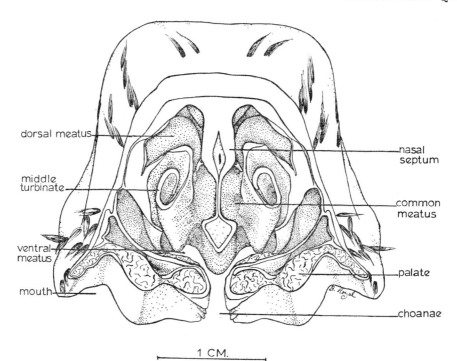

FIG. 6.25—Nasal cavity, cross section between the eyes and the nostrils.

choanae, which therefore appear as a common opening in the roof of the mouth.

The *intermediocaudal meatus* extends caudoventrally between the caudal and middle turbinates. Communications exist between it and the dorsal, ventral, and common meatuses.

The *infraorbital sinus* is a large paranasal cavity situated beneath the orbit and lateral to the choanae, nasal septum, and mouth. It extends cranially from a point midway between the nostril and the orbit and caudally to a region behind the orbit. It is roughly triangular in shape and is bounded laterally by the integument, ventrally by the roof of the pharynx and mouth, and dorsally by the floor of the orbit and the turbinates.

The *paranasal sinuses* are lined with a mucous membrane that differs somewhat from that of the nasal cavity.

Like the nasal cavity mucosa the propria is uncommonly rich in lymphocytes, but the mucous glands are more scattered and the epithelial sheet is thinner. The submucosa is dense and presents few, if any, cavernous venous sinuses.

The *lateral nasal gland* is a small atypical gland located under the frontal bone near the medial canthus of the eye. The excretory ducts empty into the dorsal meatus of the nasal cavity. The tubular end-pieces of the gland are lined with low columnar cells which have a spherical nucleus, and the cytoplasm is filled with rather fine acidophilic granules. The function of this gland in the quail is not clear; however, it has been suggested that the reason for its presence in other birds is to keep the nostrils from drying out during flight.

The arteries of the nasal cavity form deep periosteal and more superficial nets of capillaries to supply extensively developed mucous glands and the expanded surface area of the nasal epithelium. The veins arising from the capillary nets converge to form cavernous plexuses of muscular, valveless veins. The rich blood supply is necessary not only to aid the glands in supplying copious amounts of secretion but also to aid the mucous membrane in acting as an organ for controlling the temperature and humidity of inspired air. The lymphatics form a subepithelial and a deep capillary net. The entire nasal mucosa receives myelinated sensory fibers from the trigeminal nerve. Unmyelinated fibers of the olfactory region converge to form the olfactory nerve.

HISTOLOGY OF THE NASAL CAVITY
AND INFRAORBITAL SINUS

The nasal cavity is divided into the vestibular, respiratory, and olfactory regions. The mucosa of the vestibula and the rostral turbinates is composed of a thin, faintly pigmented, stratified squamous epithelium. Its basement membrane is smooth. Only six to eight cells make up the thickness of the sheet. The free surface of the sheet is atypical, since it is studded with a continuous layer of spherical projections. The stratum corneum cells of this layer stick together when desquamated, to form what appears to be an overly stretched coil spring. The lamina propria mucosa of this region is composed of fairly compact collagenous fibers with a few cells and no glands. The compact lamina propria is joined to the underlying hyaline cartilage or bone by highly vascular, loose connective tissue. At the caudal extremity of the medial surface of the rostral turbinate the mucosal epithelium abruptly changes to the pseudostratified ciliated columnar type with a few goblet cells. This respiratory type of epithelium forms the general lining of the remainder of the nasal cavity.

The lamina propria and submucosa are continuous, and no muscularis mucosa is found. In this fine-fibered connective tissue is found a continuous layer of from one to four rows of well-developed active mucous gland alveolae. Numerous lymphatic cells infiltrate the stroma, and lymphatic nodules are scattered in the rostral areas but become thickened to the proportion of tonsils in the region of the choanae. The submucosa is composed of fairly regular collagenous tissue. It is highly vascular and in certain areas sizable venous plexuses develop to form a cushion-like consistency and a red coloring of the mucous membrane. The submucosa passes directly into the perichondrium or periosteum which invests the nasal septum or turbinates.

Pharynx

The *pharynx* (Fig. 6.22) is the musculomembranous cavity located caudal to the mouth and is both respiratory and digestive in function. Rostrally it is continuous with the mouth, caudally with the cranial larynx and esophagus, and dorsally with the choanae and eustachian tubes (auditory tubes). A detailed description of the pharynx is presented in the discussion of the digestive system.

Larynx

The *larynx* is the short cartilaginous and musculomembranous tube which connects the trachea with the pharynx. It serves to regulate the flow of air to the lungs and prevents the inhalation of foreign particles. Unlike mammals the larynx of the quail has no epiglottis and has nothing to do with the production of sound. The aditus laryngis is a slitlike opening of the larynx, lying caudoventral to the choanae and just caudal to the tongue when the mouth is closed. The lateral borders of the rima glottidis are marked by two muscular lips which close the opening during deglutition. The cartilaginous skeleton of the larynx consists of the cricoid and arytenoid cartilages. No thyroid cartilage is present. Added support to the larynx is given by the two cornua of the hyoid apparatus.

The cricoid cartilage is the larger of the two cartilages and may become partly ossified early in the life of the bird. It is incomplete dorsally but resembles a tracheal ring in outline, its length being greater ventrally than dorsally. It connects dorsally with the caudal process of the body of the arytenoid cartilage to form a complete ring. The cricoid cartilage is considered by many authors to be incomplete in birds, although each primitive ramus (or half) fuses dorsally to form the body of the cartilage. After fusion the cartilage consists of a body and two rami, and resembles a horseshoe in shape. The body lies dorsally, and the two rami project forward along the cranial border of the cricoid cartilage.

Trachea

The *trachea* (Figs. 6.4, 6.26, 6.27) is a gradually narrowing cylindrical tube which extends from the cricoid cartilage of the cranial larynx to its junction with the syrinx. Approximately 6.3 cm in length, it is located in the median plane and at first lies ventral to the esophagus; then as the esophagus gradually deviates to the right, the trachea is in contact with the ventral surface of the longus colli muscle. Approximately 90 cartilaginous rings form the skeleton, or support, of the trachea. Annular ligaments, composed of elastic connective tissue, bind these rings together. The tracheal rings are complete with the exception of the first, which is incomplete dorsally. From about the fifth ring to the syrinx the rings are notched on the dorsal and ventral regions. There is a pattern of alternating overlapping of the rings at the notches which causes one lateral half of a ring to appear wide and the other half narrow. Actually the rings are more symmetrical than they appear. The changeover of overlapping of each ring occurs at the dorsal and ventral notches. This sequence of overlapping is occasionally interrupted. Another feature accompanying this pattern of overlapping is the change in shape of each half of a ring; on cross section the rings vary in shape, but most appear as an oblique triangle or rhomboid. This interlacing positioning of the rings allows for a limited shortening of the trachea. Approaching the syrinx, the tracheal rings

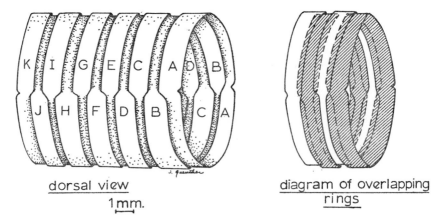

dorsal view
1mm.

diagram of overlapping rings

FIG. 6.26—Schematic illustration of the arrangement of the tracheal rings.

become narrow ventrally and lose their notches and overlapping arrangements. The last five or six rings are fused ventrally by interconnecting cartilaginous rods or extensions.

The *syrinx*, or organ of voice in the quail, is located just craniodorsal to the sternum at the division of the trachea into the two bronchi. This organ, classified as the simpler bronchotracheal type, is composed of the termination of the trachea and the beginning of the bronchi. The last three or four tracheal rings and the first two bronchial rings are modified in their structure so that they become increasingly narrow, especially on their ventral surfaces. In mature or old birds the last two or three tracheal rings may become fused dorsally. At the junction of the trachea with the syrinx the cartilaginous rings of the ventral surface present interlocking cartilaginous extensions which support the base of the osseous pessulus. The bronchial rings forming the caudal portion of the syrinx are C-shaped. The first bronchial ring is slanted caudally and attaches to the pessulus along with the tracheal rings.

The *pessulus* is a prism-shaped osseous bar situated vertically at the bifurcation of the trachea. It serves as an attachment for the last two tracheal and first bronchial rings and gives support to the syrinx. The semilunar membrane which is usually situated on the cranial aspect of the pessulus of most birds is not well developed in coturnix quail. Caudolateral to the pessulus and between the two tympanic membranes the bronchial passageway is somewhat constricted. The size of the opening is apparently controlled by two or three pairs of syringeal muscles which act upon the membrane.

The *external tympanic membrane* is a portion of the lateral wall of the bronchiotracheal junction in which no cartilage occurs. This thin membranous wall is capable of vibration and, in conjunction with the vibrations of the *internal tympanic membrane*, can be made to produce sound on expiration. The internal tympanic membrane begins on the caudal surface of the pessulus and continues caudad, covering the medial incomplete portion of the primary bronchi.

Bronchi

The primary *bronchi* extend from the bifurcation of the trachea to the lungs, where they become the mesobronchi. Sixteen to 18 C-shaped cartilaginous rings form the skeleton of the bronchi. The medial wall is membranous and continuous with the medial tympanic membrane of the syrinx.

HISTOLOGY OF THE LARYNX, TRACHEA, AND BRONCHI

The lining of the vestibule of the cranial larynx is a continuation of the mucosa of the oropharynx. The rima glottidis and the beginning of the laryngeal cavity are covered by stratified squamous epithelium and a fibroelastic propria. In the caudal remainder of the larynx the lamina epithelialis abruptly changes to the respiratory type of epithelium composed of pseudostratified, ciliated columnar cells. The supporting cartilages are joined by rather condensed fibrous membranes. No vocal cords are present. Both the cricoid and arytenoid cartilages are hyaline in nature except in the extremity of the diverging rays of the arytenoid cartilage, where elastic fibers are found in the matrix.

The respiratory type of epithelium is continuous throughout the trachea and primary bronchi in the quail. The mucous glands form a continuous layer and occupy a great deal of the space of the fibroelastic propria. Their wide, open ducts continue through the epithe-

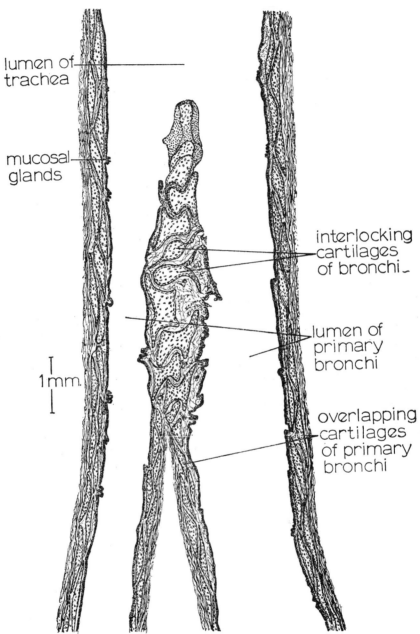

lumen of trachea

mucosal glands

interlocking cartilages of bronchi

lumen of primary bronchi

overlapping cartilages of primary bronchi

1mm.

FIG. 6.27—Tracheobronchial junction, frontal section.

lial sheet. Numerous lymphatic infiltrations and nodules crowd the cells in the proprial and epithelial sheets. For the most part the tracheal rings are complete and are composed of hyaline cartilage. On cross section the rings are in the shape of a flattened triangle. The well-developed perichondria of successive tracheal rings are connected by a fibroelastic annular ligament. Two voluntary muscles arise from the clavicle and flank the lateral ventral side of the entire length of the organ. The paired sternotrachealis muscles run from the sternum to their insertion on the lateral side of the trachea just cranial to the tracheosyringeal junction. The well-developed perichondrium is rich in capillaries and nerves. The loose connective tissue of the adventitia of the trachea contributes to the freedom of movement of the trachea in the neck.

In the syrinx the mucosal lining is somewhat modified. The epithelial sheet is thin and covers the perichondrium of the pessulus and the tympanic membranes. It is somewhat thicker over the annular ligaments between the cartilages. No glands or lymphatics occupy the propria.

The 16–18 C-shaped cartilages of the primary bronchi are oval in cross section. The medial membranous wall is composed of dense fibrous connective tissue which blends in with the perichondrium. Mucous glands and lymphatic deposits are scarce and the lamina epithelialis is of the respiratory type. At the junction of the primary bronchi and mesobronchi the C-shaped hyaline cartilages are replaced by small islands of cartilaginous plates in the mesobronchi. (See Figure 6.27.)

Lungs

The *lungs* (Figs. 6.28–6.30) are the main organ of respiration and assist in the aeration of the blood. They occupy the dorsal portion of the thorax and are closely adherent to the vertebrae and ribs. Bright red in color and of a sponge-like consistency, they are small in comparison to the size of the thorax. Unlike those of mammals, both lungs of the quail are of the same size and shape. They are not lobulated and do not collapse when the thorax is opened. The cranial extremity of the lungs lies opposite the caudal border of the first two ribs. At the costochondral junction of the 3rd rib the ventral border curves caudodorsally to the middle of the 6th rib. Three surfaces of the lungs are recognized: the costal (dorsal) surface, the diaphragmatic (ventral) surface, and the vertebral (medial) surface. The dorsal surface is convex and closely related to the ribs and intercostal muscles. Four costal furrows or impressions from the 2nd, 3rd, 4th, and 5th ribs are present. The medial surface is convex and closely related to the rudimentary diaphragm. The craniodorsal portion of the surface is slightly convex while the caudoventral half is slightly concave. The hilus of the lung is present on this surface near its center. It is here that the pulmonary artery and primary bronchi enter and the pulmonary veins leave the lungs. The pulmonary artery lies cranial to the bronchi and the pulmonary vein lies caudal to them. The structure of the lung of the quail differs from that of mammals in the branching of the bronchi and the absence of cartilages and alveolar sacs. The bronchial system in the lungs consists of the following subdivisions: the mesobronchi, secondary bronchi, tertiary bronchi, and recurrent bronchi.

The primary bronchi join the ventral surface of the lungs at the hilus and become the *mesobronchi*. The mesobronchi formed here have no cartilaginous rings; and as this S-shaped tube progresses caudad and deeper into the

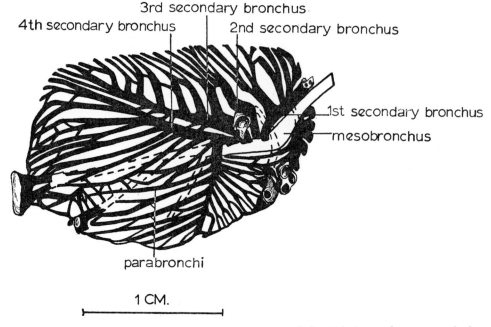

FIG. 6.28—Ventral surface of the lung.

lung tissue, it becomes increasingly smaller in diameter. Near the middle of the caudal border of the lung the mesobronchus joins the abdominal air sac. No distinct vestibule is seen near the beginning of the mesobronchi, as described in the chicken.

The *dorsal bronchi*, approximately 20 in number, are short and arise from the dorsal surface of the mesobronchi. They are distributed along the center of the dorsal surface of the lung and connect medially with the medial bronchi and laterally with the lateral bronchi of this system.

The *secondary bronchi* arise from the mesobronchus and decrease in size as they progress caudad. The terminology of McLeod *et al.* (1964) for these structures as they appear in the chicken describes them as being divided into a dorsal or a ventral group according to their distribution in the lung. The first four bronchi arise in the ventrobron-

chial system from the dorsomedial aspect of the mesobronchus and are distributed over the ventral surface of the lung. The 1st bronchus is the largest, and passes a short distance dorsad before curving ventrally to connect with the interclavicular air sac. The 2nd bronchus passes a short distance dorsad and divides into a superficial branch that extends to the medial border of the lung and a deeper one that progresses to the ventral border, where it connects with the interclavicular and cranial thoracic air sacs indirectly. The 3rd bronchus is large and superficial. Near its origin on the mesobronchus it is joined by a diverticulum from the interclavicular and cranial thoracic air sacs, and then passes caudoventrad to the junction of the medial and caudal borders of the lung, where it terminates by branching. The 4th secondary bronchus of this group passes caudomedially parallel to the 3rd, but deeper in the lung tissue. Near its origin it sends a comparatively large branch ventrally to connect with the thoracic air sacs.

The dorsal bronchial group is distributed to the dorsal surface of the lung. These bronchi arise distal to those of the ventral bronchial system and are smaller and less distinct. The three subdivisions of the dorsal bronchial system are: the dorsomedial, lateral, and intermediate bronchi, corresponding to those of the same name in the chicken. The dorsomedial bronchi are approximately eight in number and arise from the dorsomedial surface of the mesobronchus. They are directed toward the upper dorsal and medial portions of the lung. They divide a short distance from their origin into three or four branches, some of which connect medially with the ventrobronchi and some of which connect laterally with the short intermediate bronchi. The lateral bronchi are approximately eight in number and arise from the ventrolateral surface of the mesobronchi. They too branch and connect along the lateral border of the lung with the ventrobronchi and dorsally with the intermediate bronchi. The second bronchus of this group passes to the caudal portion of the lateral border of the lung and connects with the caudal thoracic air sac.

The *tertiary bronchi,* or parabronchi, are the smallest and most numerous of the bronchi. They arise from the secondary bronchi and usually join adjacent bronchi or interconnect with other parabronchi. From these tertiary bronchi arise the minute air capillaries which radiate from the lumen of the parabronchi to anastomose or join the parent bronchi. These small tubes are the homologue of the mammalian air sacs, and through their walls the exchange of gases between the air and blood takes place.

The *recurrent bronchi* convey air from the air sacs to the lungs. The largest ones connect the lower cranial portion of the abdominal air sac with the caudoventral border of the lungs, where they join the dorsal bronchial system. In addition recurrent bronchi are found passing from the cranial thoracic air sac to the ventral bronchial system on the cranioventral border of the lungs.

HISTOLOGY OF THE LUNGS

Each lobe of the lungs is rather firmly attached by fibrous tissue to the ribs and intercostal muscles and the pulmonary diaphragm. The flat medial surface is related to the ventral spine and bodies of the thoracic vertebrae and is the only surface of the lung covered with a serous membrane or pulmonary pleura. The hilus of the medial surface admits the passage of the bronchi and the pulmonary and bronchial arteries, veins, nerves, and lymphatics. The parietal capsule is very thin and composed chiefly of a few fibroblasts and compact collagenous fibers. No elastic fibers or smooth muscles were found in its structure. The lungs are made up of lobules which are not separated from each other by any noticeable connective tissue. At the hilus, loose connective tissue surrounds the larger vessels and intrapulmonary part of the mesobronchi. The lamina epithelialis is of the pseudostratified, ciliated, columnar type. Goblet cells, scattered mucous glands, islands of hyaline cartilage, and smooth muscle bands are present.

The respiratory type of epithelium with goblet cells continues in the secondary bronchi which branch from the mesobronchi. No cartilaginous islands or mucous glands are present; and the muscle bundles, although present, are quite delinquent in their structure. At this division the pulmonary artery accompanies the secondary bronchi, but no small bronchial arteries or nerves have been found. The parabronchi are the terminal portions of the conducting tubules and are open at either end, connecting with other secondary bronchi or anastomosing among themselves at variable intervals. The lamina epithelialis is of the simple cuboidal or squamous type, and no cilia were found. The lamina propria is very thin, and the smooth muscle which passes around the tubules produces noticeable constrictions in the lumen of the parabronchi. The respiratory tubules arise at right angles from each parabronchus and are supported by the intralobular connective tissue of the reticular type. The tubules branch repeatedly, becoming smaller and smaller before they terminate. The walls of the respiratory tubules resemble the alveoli of the mammalian lung, as they are richly supplied with a capillary plexus. In the respiratory region the pulmonary arteries and veins are found midway between the lobules. The para-

bronchi occupy the axis of the lobule. Both pulmonary arteries and veins display a rather thick fibrous connective tissue adventitia. Since the parabronchus is the last tubule of the conducting portion of the lung of coturnix, and the respiratory tubules are comparable to the alveoli of the mammalian lung, we would naturally expect to find that the continuation of the pulmonary and bronchial arteries and the bronchial nerve accompanies the parabronchus into the axis of the lung lobule. This is not the case, however, as both the pulmonary arteries and veins are found only at the areas of the junction of two or more lobules, and the bronchial artery and nerves are so finely branched that their lobular distribution becomes diffuse. Structurally the air sacs are composed of an internal simple squamous epithelial lining and a simple squamous mesothelial serosa with just enough loose connective tissue to anchor the epithelial sheets and support the

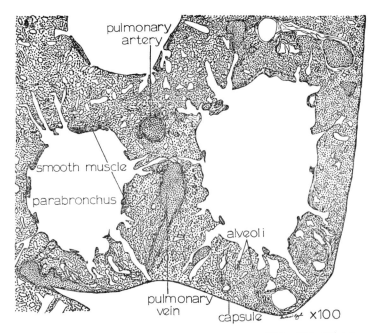

FIG. 6.29—Histology of the lung.

vessels and nerves between them. (See Figure 6.29.)

Air Sacs

The *air sacs* (Fig. 6.30) are extra-pulmonary extensions of the bronchi. These thin-walled mucoserous sacs extend around many of the visceral organs and into many of the bones of the body. The nomenclature used to describe the air sacs varies from author to author but is based on the location or position (Table 6.1). The nomenclature used in

this discussion is mainly in accordance with that used by Lucas and Stettenheim (1965) and Bradley and Grahame (1950). The exact function of the air sacs is unknown and will not be dealt with in this description.

The *interclavicular air sac* is the only single sac of the body. It occupies the cranial portion of the thoracic cavity and is closely related to the sternum, coracoid, and clavicular bones and to the various muscles and vessels of this region. The esophagus and trachea lie

TABLE 6.1

NOMENCLATURE OF THE AIR SACS (CHICKEN)

	Single	Paired	Paired
Sisson and Grossman	Clavicular	Cervical	Anterior thoracic
McLeod *et al.*	Cranial thoracic	Thoracocervical	Caudal thoracic
Locy and Larsell	Cranial thoracic	Cervical	Cranial intermediate
Kaupp	Cranial thoracic	Cervical	Cranial diaphragmatic
Bradley and Grahame	Clavicular, or axillary	Cervical	Cranial thoracic
Lucas and Stettenheim	Interclavicular	Cervical	Cranial thoracic
Fitzgerald (proposed for quail)	Interclavicular	Cervical	Cranial thoracic

	Paired	Paired	Paired
Sisson and Grossman	Posterior thoracic	Abdominal	Axillary
McLeod *et al.*	Lesser abdominal	Greater abdominal	
Locy and Larsell	Caudal diaphragmatic	Abdominal	
Kaupp	Caudal diaphragmatic	Abdominal	
Bradley and Grahame	Caudal thoracic	Abdominal	
Lucas and Stettenheim	Caudal thoracic	Abdominal	
Fitzgerald (proposed for quail)	Caudal thoracic	Abdominal	

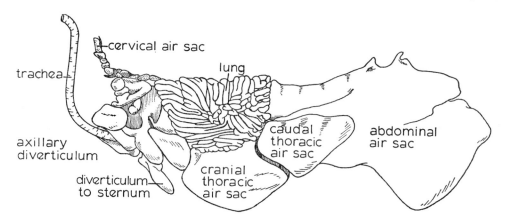

FIG. 6.30—*Latex cast of the lung and air sacs, lateral view.*

dorsal and medial to it. The interclavicular sac communicates with each lung by two separate connections. The caudolateral portions connect with the craniolateral border of the lungs. At this region the sac communicates directly with the 1st ventral bronchus and indirectly, by recurrent bronchi, with the ventral bronchial system. The caudomedial portions of the interclavicular sac communicate directly with the 3rd ventral bronchus and the cranial thoracic air sacs and indirectly, by recurrent bronchi, with the central bronchial system. This air sac is **V**-shaped on cross section with several secondary outpocketings or diverticula, of which the axillary diverticulum is the most extensive. It extends out from the main sac between the first rib and the coracoid bone to surround the shoulder joint, where it is covered in part by the superficial pectoral and teres major muscles. Subdiverticula, or extensions, project from the axillary diverticulum into the humerus and between the various muscles of this region. The extension into the humerus has been named the humeral diverticulum, or pouch. McLeod *et al.* (1964) names the other extensions from the axillary diverticulum as the pectoral and subscapular pouches according to

their associated muscles. Other diverticula extend into the keel of the sternum, the clavicle, and the coracoid bones.

The *cervical air sac* is the most cranial and dorsal of the air sacs. The main portion of the sac lies medial to the lungs and interclavicular sac from the level of the 3rd or 4th thoracic vertebra to the 8th cervical vertebra. The caudal chambers of each side fuse below the ventral spines of the thoracic vertebrae. The cranial half of the sac gives rise to small, thin projections which extend dorsally and forward to penetrate the cervical vertebrae as far forward as the 1st cervical vertebra. The projections of each side fuse between the vertebrae. The cervical air sacs communicate with the 1st ventral bronchus at the craniomedial border of the lungs. No diverticula are present.

The *caudal thoracic air sac* is a triangle-shaped sac which lies caudoventral to the lungs and medial to the last few ribs. It communicates with the large 2nd lateral secondary bronchus on the caudolateral border of the lungs. A few recurrent bronchi connect this sac with the dorsal bronchial system.

The *abdominal air sac* is the largest and most extensive sac of the body. It arises from the mesobronchus at the caudal border of the lungs and encircles most of the viscera of the abdominal cavity. It is limited ventrally and laterally by the abdominal wall, and dorsally by the roof of the pelvis and the kidney. Two small diverticula extend from this air sac to surround the femur at the hip joint (femoral diverticulum by McLeod *et al.,* 1964) but do not enter the femur. Air from the abdominal air sac leaves through the recurrent bronchi which connect it with the dorsal bronchial system.

URINARY ORGANS

The urinary organs (Figs. 6.10, 6.31, 6.32) of coturnix consist of two metanephric kidneys and their excretory ducts, the ureters. The urodeal portion of the cloaca has a limited function in the storage of the semisolid uric acid and crystals, as well as serving the digestive and reproductive systems. Contrary to that of mammals the urinary system of the quail does not possess the following structures: a urinary bladder, urethra, renal sinus, or renal pelvis or hilus.

Kidneys

The *kidneys* are glands which secrete waste products. The paired organs are reddish-brown in color, are highly friable, and consist of three distinguishable but fused lobes. They are located on either side of the vertebral column and the aorta as it courses caudad. The cranial extent of the kidneys lies caudal to the lungs, from which they are separated by a portion of the thoracoabdominal diaphragm. This is in the region of the border of the 7th vertebral rib. Its caudal extent reaches to the 12th or last synsacral segment, or the most caudal extent of the renal fossa. A sacral diverticulum from the abdominal air sac projects up over the greater portion of the kidney and surrounds the hip joint.

It serves as a cushion between the kidney and the overlying bony structures and nerve plexus and replaces the perirenal fat normally found in mammals. The ventral surface of the kidney is also adjacent to a portion of the abdominal air sac.

The average length of the mature kidney is 3.1–3.2 cm. The cranial lobe is the larger, approximately 1.4 cm in length, and is differentiated from the middle lobe dorsally by the common iliac artery and ventrally by a junction of the afferent renal and common ilac veins. The middle lobe, which measures .7–.8 cm, is the smallest one. The caudal lobe occupies the entire renal fossa and is separated from the middle lobe by the ischiatic artery. On the midventral surface of the middle and cranial portions of the caudal lobe there is a prominent efferent renal vein. The afferent renal vein courses longitudinally under the ventrolateral surface of the middle and caudal lobes. The synsacral plexus of nerves lies just above the cranial lobe while the larger sciatic nerve courses downward through the substance of the middle lobe and a portion of the caudal lobe toward the hip region.

Ureters

The paired *ureters* (Figs. 6.10, 6.11, 6.13–6.15) convey the waste products from the kidneys to the urodeal portion of the cloaca. Both the kidneys and ureters are retroperitoneal in position. The visible portion of the ureter measures approximately 3.5 cm and has a dull grayish-white appearance. It is located on the ventral surface of the kidney, medial to the ductus deferens in the male, and is visible extending from the caudal border of the cranial lobe, caudally to the tip of the caudal lobe. Here it turns slightly mediad and continues on to empty into the urodeum. Approximately six or seven main collecting tubules converge to form the ureter in the substance of the cranial lobe of the kidney. The ureter then emerges from the cranial lobe, passes above the junction of the common iliac and efferent renal veins, and becomes related to the midportion of the middle lobe. As it courses caudad along this lobe it receives five or six collecting tubules and lies between the large efferent renal vein medially and the ductus deferens in the male. In the female the left ureter is hidden or covered by the very prominent dorsal ligament of the oviduct. The ureter then leaves the middle lobe, crosses under the ischiatic artery, and becomes related to the caudal lobe from which it receives one, sometimes two, major collecting tubules. It then continues caudad dorsolateral to the colon and the bursa of Fabricius and terminates by emptying into the urodeal portion of the cloaca medial and cranial to the opening of the ductus deferens.

HISTOLOGY OF THE URINARY SYSTEM

The kidneys of coturnix are classified as compound tubular glands. They consist mainly of excreting and conducting tubules and blood vessels. The capsule is composed of a thin, dense, fibrous connective tissue that is rather intimate-

ly fused with a subpelvic connective tissue. Subcapsular connective tissue septa divide the parenchyma into lobules which correspond to the cortical lobules of mammals. The intraparenchymal stroma is formed of a delicate reticular connective tissue network that surrounds and supports the many renal tubules and blood vessels.

The ventral portion of each lobule contains a short renal pyramid surrounded by the cortical substance. As in mammals, the parenchymal tubules make up the nephrons, which begin as a small renal corpuscle composed of a tuft of capillaries, the glomerulus, and Bowman's capsule. These structures form the renal (malpighian) corpuscle. The second component of the nephron is composed of convoluted tubules which are joined to the renal corpuscle by a slightly constricted neck. The medullary portion of the proximal convoluted tubule forms a loop and is continued by the distal convoluted segment which in turn joins the collecting tubules or the first portion of the conducting tubules of the gland. Numerous collecting tubules join the larger collecting ducts, which in turn empty into the beginning tributaries of the ureter.

The lining cells of Bowman's cap-

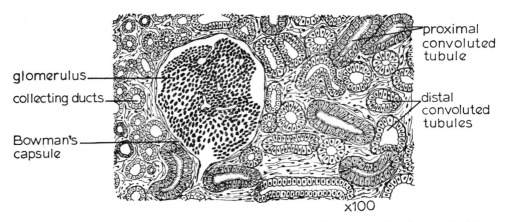

FIG. 6.31—Histology of the kidney.

sule are simple squamous cells, and those of the proximal convoluted tubule are a tall pyramidal form of simple columnar cells bearing a brush border. Their cytoplasm is striated with granules; the nucleus is centrally located. The limits of joining cells are difficult to locate because of the granular cytoplasm; the brush borders and cell membranes are very thin. The thin segment of Henle's loop stains lightly, and the cells are of the simple squamous variety. The thick segment of the loop has an epithelium resembling that of the proximal convoluted tubule except that the cells and their basal striations are shorter and the brush borders are absent. The distal convoluted tubules are somewhat smaller than the proximal ones. The nuclei are large and evenly distributed; basal striations appear in their proximal portions. The collecting ducts display much higher cells of the simple columnar type. In the fresh state they contain urate

granules which combine into larger pellets in the lumen. The papillary ducts are lined with a two-layered columnar epithelium. (See Figure 6.31.)

HISTOLOGY OF THE ADRENAL GLAND

The adrenal glands are yellow oval bodies lying just cranial to each kidney. Each gland is encased in a connective tissue capsule which contains numerous blood vessels and accompanies them into the glandular substance as trabeculae, dividing the gland into lobules. The adrenal contains both cortical and medullary tissue, but these elements are intermingled in birds, not divided into an inner and an outer layer as in mammals. The tissue corresponding to the mammalian medulla is termed chromaffin tissue, as its cells have an affinity for chromic acid. While the chromaffin cells are random in arrangement, the cells of the cortical tissue form cords. Numerous sympathetic ganglion cells

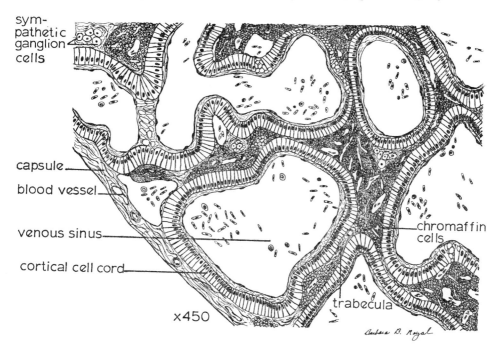

FIG. 6.32—Histology of the adrenal.

are scattered throughout the adrenal. (See Figure 6.32.)

MALE REPRODUCTIVE SYSTEM

The male reproductive system (Figs. 6.11, 6.12, 6.33) consists of paired testes, ducti deferentia, a seminal vesicle (ejaculatory duct) at the distal end of each ductus deferens, the papillae of the ductus deferens in the cloaca, and the rudimentary penis (phallus).

Testis

The *testes* are white and ovoid to elliptical in shape, somewhat similar to that of a kidney bean. They are located craniomedial to the cranial pole of each kidney and caudal to the lungs and ab-

dominal air sacs. They are attached to the dorsal body wall by a peritoneal fold called the mesorchium. The size of the testes increases tremendously during the breeding season. This increase in volume may be as much as 20-fold. In the quail the tunica albuginea is present as well as intertubular connective tissue, but the penetrating septa characteristic of the mammalian species are absent. The seminiferous tubules appear to have a greater diameter in birds than in mammals.

HISTOLOGY OF THE TESTIS

The seminiferous tubules are lined with a simple cuboidal epithelium comparable to the modified sustentacular (Sertoli) cells of the mammalian region.

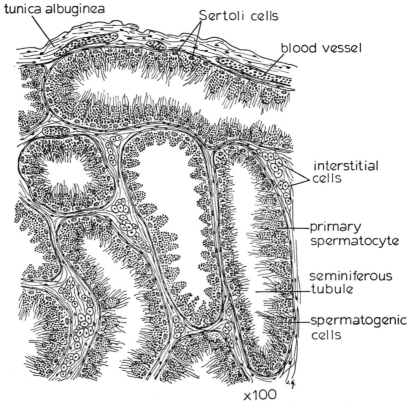

×100

FIG. 6.33—Histology of the testis.

The majority of the cells in the tubules are the spermatogenic cells, which undergo meiosis to form the sperm. Between the tubules are groups of interstitial cells, which resemble connective tissue cells but are modified to perform an endocrine function, production of the hormone testosterone. (See Figure 6.33.)

Accessory Ducts

The *vasa efferentia* of quail are very short and most of their length is extra-testicular. Their lining cells exhibit holocrine secretions and stereocilia. The *ductus epididymis* is very short and lies chiefly to the side of the testicle at the hilum. The epithelial lining is of the pseudostratified columnar type. There is no indication of secretion from the cells, and the characteristic stereo-cilia of mammals are not found.

The epididymis is continued by the *ductus deferens*, which is identified by a slightly folded mucosa and the appearance of large vacuoles in the free surface of the epithelial cells. The distal extremity of the ductus deferens is characterized by a thickening of the smooth muscle coat. At its termination, the lumen widens to provide a small storage space for the spermatozoa. It is apparent, however, that the greater number of these cells are to be found in the lumen of the ductus deferens. No glandular epithelium comparable to the glandular ampullar region of mammals is to be found. These genital ducts terminate as the ejaculatory ducts which protrude into the urodeum of the cloacal cavity lateral to the openings of the ureters.

The ductus deferens is a tubular structure which serves to transport sperm from the testes to the cloaca. The breeding season initiates characteristic changes in the ductus deferens. There is an increase in the diameter, in the degree of convolution, and a change in color. At the height of the breeding season the ductus deferens is distinctly white, has a large diameter, and is highly convoluted. The ductus deferens and the vesicle store the sperm and convey them to the cloaca, where a papilla opens into the lumen. Flanking the cranial border of the termination of the ductus deferens of the sexually mature bird, there is a voluminous gland corresponding to what is described as the seminal vesicle of other birds. It has an imperfect collagenous connective tissue capsule. The parenchyma of the vesicle is composed of convolutions or folds arranged in such a manner that labyrinthine spaces will flank the sides of the epithelial folds and cords. In the supporting core of the convolutions or folds is found supporting connective tissue, with numerous large thick-walled arteries and plexuses of nonmedullated nerve fibers.

The phallus is a rudimentary copulatory structure located on the dorsal edge of the ventral lip of the external cloacal orifice of the male. It is composed of two opposing epithelial surfaces which are different in character. The one facing the cloacal lumen is of mucous membrane which blends with and is similar to that which lines the proctodeum. The outer surface of the phallus is of a highly cornified stratified epithelium, giving the phallus a somewhat pale appearance when viewed from the outside. This outer surface of the phallus unites with the stratified epithelium of the ventral lip of the external cloacal orifice. There is a constant half-moon–shaped area of pigmentation that partially surrounds the cornified projection of the phallus. This pigment is black and is present on the caudal and lateral sides of the horny process.

The shape of the phallus most closely resembles that of a low pyramid. The height varies from bird to bird, as does the width, but the average is about

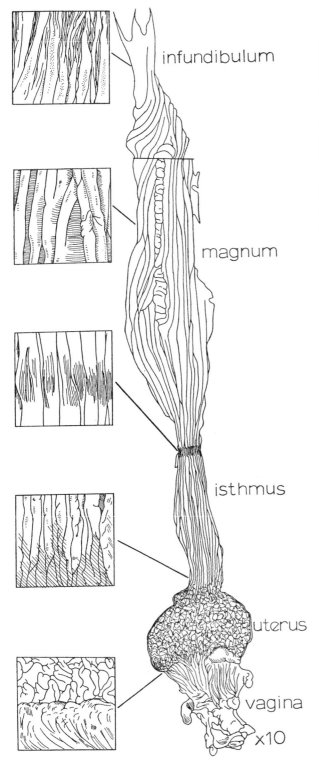

infundibulum

magnum

isthmus

uterus

vagina

×10

FIG. 6.34—Longitudinal rugae in the opened oviduct.

2–3 mm high and 6–7 mm wide. The most dorsal edge of the phallus forms a rounded mound-shaped prominence of cornified epithelium. In accordance with the tremendous hypertrophy of the male genital structures during the breeding season there is a pronounced increase in the size and thickness of the musculature of the dorsal cloacal wall. This hypertrophy sharply parallels the enlargement of the testes, the ductus deferens, and their terminal papillae into the cloaca. Undoubtedly this massive wall of muscle is essential in the manipulation of the phallus during coitus. The papillae of the ductus deferens are appropriately positioned just cranial to the lateral edges of the phallus. Its cornified layer is especially prominent near the papillae to ensure the passage of sperm into the proctodeum.

FEMALE REPRODUCTIVE SYSTEM

The location and description of the female genitalia of coturnix (Figs. 6.34, 6.35) is very similar to that described in the literature for the avian species in general. A few minor variations are noted. The dorsocranial attachment of the dorsal oviducal ligament in coturnix extends to the 6th rib instead of the 4th rib as it does in the domestic hen (Bradley and Grahame, 1950; and McLeod *et al.*, 1964). Ligaments suspending the oviduct are called dorsal and ventral ligaments of the oviduct instead of mesosalpinx and mesometrium as used by Lucas and Stettenheim (1965) for the domestic chicken, since the former terms are felt to be more accurately descriptive.

Curtis (1910) and Bradley and Grahame (1950) described an "ovarian pocket" for the hen which is essentially the same in coturnix, as well as the general topography of the oviduct. In comparing the length of the oviduct (18–24 cm) with that given by Hafez (1962) for the

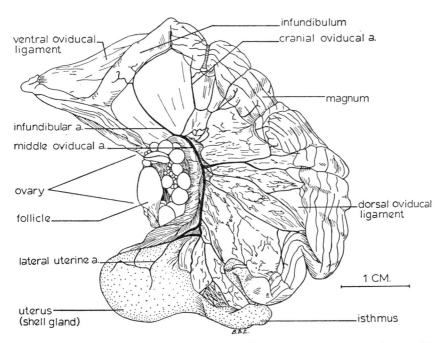

ventral oviducal ligament

infundibulum

cranial oviducal a.

magnum

infundibular a.

middle oviducal a.

ovary

follicle

dorsal oviducal ligament

lateral uterine a.

1 CM.

uterus (shell gland)

isthmus

FIG. 6.35—Female reproductive tract and its arterial supply.

hen (70–80 cm) and turkey (90–115 cm), it appears that the former is relatively longer on a total-bird weight basis. Welty (1962) indicated a weight increase of 10–50 times between the oviduct of a laying and nonlaying bird. The inactive ovary of coturnix examined in one instance weighed about .1 gm, that of the producing bird 5–7 gm or a 50–70-fold increase, which is close to the range given by Welty.

A morphological description of the external appearance of the coturnix oviduct is similar to that of the domestic hen except that the shell gland is pigmented and dark brown in color. The lengths of the various portions of the oviduct are, infundibulum 5 ± 2 cm, magnum 13 ± 1 cm, isthmus 6 ± 2 cm, shell gland, or uterus, 2 ± 1 cm, and vagina 1 cm. Internally, longitudinal rugae are observed in each segment of the oviduct. In the infundibulum there are 8 to 14, in the magnum 10 to 15

(slightly spiralled), in the isthmus 22 to 26, in the shell gland 40 to 60, and in the vagina 22 to 28. According to Sturkie (1965) the rugae of the isthmus of the domestic hen's oviduct are fewer in number than those of the magnum, which is different from that observed in coturnix. The longitudinal rugae of the shell gland of coturnix were continuous but highly convoluted, giving a floral appearance, and were not transverse as in the chicken (Surface, 1912; Romanoff and Romanoff, 1949; and Bradley and Grahame, 1950).

Histologically there are also a few minor variations between the female genitalia of coturnix and the domestic hen. The granules found in the tubular glands of the isthmus of the quail are smaller than those found in the tubular glands of the magnum. Just the opposite is reported for the hen (Bradley and Grahame, 1950).

Due to the early maturity of the

quail the genitalia undergo rapid development. Between 28 and 43 days of age the ovary weight increases 15–29 times over its 28-day weight. No increase in growth and development of the ovary have been noted in specimens over 49 days of age. The muscle layers of the oviduct reach maturity in the infundibulum and magnum in 34 days, the isthmus in 28 days, and the vagina in 21 days. By these ages the longitudinal and circular muscle layers are well differentiated. Maximum development of the longitudinal rugae of the oviduct is reached by 2 months, with the majority of the growth taking place the last 23 days. The tubular glands of the infundibulum, magnum, and isthmus also begin to develop at 37 days and reach peak development by 2 months, while these structures start to develop at 34 days in the shell gland and reach maximum development as early as 40 days. In all areas of the oviduct the epithelium shows marked change at about 34 days and functional maturity by 40 days.

As involution of the oviduct takes place at the end of a laying period, an overall shrinkage of the oviduct results. The glands disappear and the epithelial cells take on a palisade arrangement due to the concentration of nuclear material and loss of cytoplasm.

Ovary

Only the left ovary is significant in birds, the right one being vestigial if present at all. It is located just ventral to the cranial lobe of the left kidney, extending about halfway down the middle lobe. The ovarian surface appears rough, due to the early development of large egg follicles.

HISTOLOGY OF THE OVARY

The ovary of the quail contains from 10 to 1,000 ova, which vary in size according to their state of maturity. Follicles make up most of the ovarian tissue, surrounded by a limited amount of stroma and some smooth muscle. The larger follicles protrude from the ovary, attached by a narrow stalk of connective tissue, and are quite similar to those of other birds. The actual ovum consists of a nucleus and a thin ring of cytoplasm that encloses the yolk. Around this are the vitelline membrane and the zona radiata, a zona granulosa made up of cuboidal to columnar cells, and a connective tissue theca folliculi. Since the ovum and its yolk occupy the entire cavity of the follicle, there is no liquor folliculi as there is in mammals. The first maturation division of the ovum occurs at ovulation, and the second one after the ovum is penetrated by a sperm cell, usually just inside the oviduct. Albumen, shell membranes, and shell are added farther down the oviduct, as the egg passes toward the cloaca.

CHAPTER SEVEN

Esthesiology

THE special senses include organs of vision, hearing, taste, smell, and touch. These are the chief organs which receive stimuli from the outside and keep the bird aware of the changing environment.

EYE

The eyes of birds in general contain all the important structures that occur in their reptilian ancestors. They are comparatively large in coturnix and are located rostrolaterally in the orbital cavity of the skull; the optic axis deviates from the median axis approximately 60°. Because of its large size the movement of the globe in its cavity is limited. Little or no retraction movement is possible because the globes almost come into contact medially. The large size of the coturnix eye is not apparent, as most of the eye is covered by the lids, and only a small portion of the cornea is visible. The shapes of the eyes of birds are classified by Walls (1942) as being either the commonest flat type, the global type, or the tubular type. The eye of coturnix has a central retina-corneal axis length of 9 mm and a diameter at its greatest circumference of 12 mm. Thus it is properly classified as the flat type.

The eyes of birds converge nasolaterally and are a tight fit. Due to the fact that the index of optical axis diversion of coturnix is quite close to that

261

of the pigeon, it might be assumed that the overlapping of the two eye fields would also be quite the same. As the bird walks, moving objects are usually focused by corresponding movements of the head. Focus fixation is probably brought about by the use of the central fovea of one eye, and binocular field accommodation is used for recording distance perception.

The structures included in the broad description of the eye of coturnix (Figs. 7.1–7.6) are the bulbus oculi (eyeball), the lids, the lacrimal apparatus, and the eye muscles. The description of the eye muscles is included in the section on muscles of the head.

HISTOLOGY OF THE EYEBALL

The *bulbus oculi* (eyeball) is composed of the usual three coats: outer fibrous, middle vascular, and inner nervous. The outer coat is divided into a larger sclera and a much smaller cornea. The surface area ratio is approximately 50 to 1.

The sclera is superficially covered with a very compact collagenous connective tissue; the fibers are directed equatorially and longitudinally. Embedded under the superficial fibrous layer is a hyaline cartilage cup that extends forward to the ossicular ring. Its average thickness is 122μ, 70 of which are accounted for by the cartilaginous layer. At the entrance of the optic nerve (Fig. 7.4) the cartilage is interrupted to form one large free opening, 140μ in diameter, for the optic nerve, blood, and lymph vessels. The bony plate (Gemminger's ossicle) found in the eyes of some birds at the area of the entrance of the optic nerve was not found in coturnix. There are 14 or 15 scleral ring bones embedded in the fibrous layer at the corneal-scleral junction. The scleral bones are quadrilateral plates with thin margins. These plates overlap or underlap in a fairly regular fashion and help to support and maintain the shape of the sclera and choroid coats.

The cornea forms the small trans-

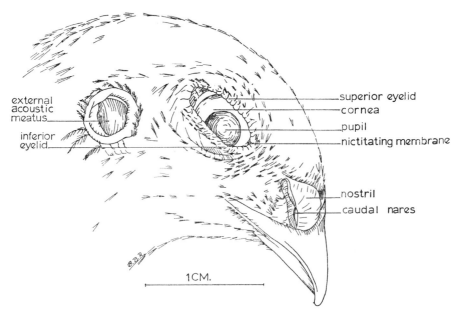

external acoustic meatus

inferior eyelid

superior eyelid

cornea

pupil

nictitating membrane

nostril

caudal nares

1CM.

FIG. 7.1—*Surface view of the eye, ear, and nostrils.*

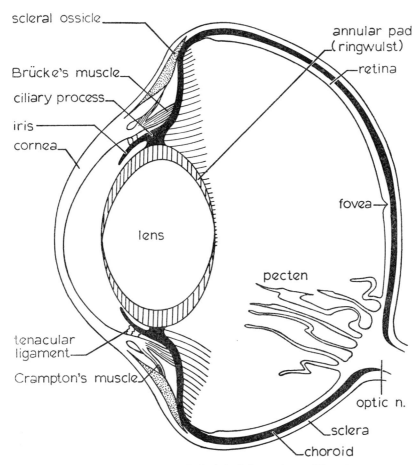

scleral ossicle

annular pad
(ringwulst)

retina

Brücke's muscle

ciliary process

iris

cornea

fovea

lens

pecten

tenacular
ligament

Crampton's muscle

optic n.

sclera

choroid

FIG. 7.2—Schematic meridional section of the eyeball.

parent part of the fibrous coat. It is nearly circular in outline and is continuous at the limbus with the sclera. It measures 123μ in thickness. The cornea is thicker toward the nasal area. Within this joining border is the circular canal of Schlemm. The surface layer of the cornea is composed of a stratified squamous epithelium with an average thickness of 123μ. The surface cells are soft and nucleated. No Bowman's membrane was found between the epithelium and the substantia propria. The principal supporting layer of the cornea is the substantia propria. It is 105μ thick and is composed of collagenous fibers which run parallel to the corneal surface. Corneal corpuscles or cells are seen in the narrow spaces between the fibers. Additional spaces appear which are nonvascular and are filled with tissue fluid. On the deep surface is a single layer of simple squamous mesenchymal epithelium (postcorneal epithelium) which forms part of the lining of the anterior chamber of the eye. This membrane is separated from the substantia propria by a well-defined Descemet's membrane. (See Figure 7.5.)

The middle coat of the bulbus (tunica vasculosa, or uveal coat), is a highly vascular pigmented layer con-

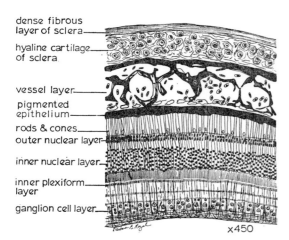

dense fibrous
layer of sclera———
hyaline cartilage——
of sclera

vessel layer——
pigmented
epithelium———
rods & cones——
outer nuclear layer—
inner nuclear layer—
inner plexiform——
layer
ganglion cell layer—

x450

FIG. 7.3—Histology of the retina.

sisting of the usual three parts: the choroid, ciliary process, and iris (Fig. 7.2).

The vascular layer of the eye measures up to 160μ and is composed chiefly of very closely arranged thin-walled blood vessels (Figs. 7.3, 7.4). These vessels lie so close together that on cross section they appear like a string of beads. Very little intervascular supporting tissue intervenes. The large vessels lie very close to the lamina choriocapillaris which they supply. Both the fibrous and cellular tapetum lucidum are absent in the quail. The capillary layer measures 35μ in thickness and is closely attached to the basement membrane.

The anterior portion of the choroid thins down to less than half the thickness of the fundus, becomes less vascular, and forms a basal rim to support the ciliary body. It continues forward beneath the scleral cartilage and then the scleral ossicle to fuse with the ciliary process. On its outer surface it gives rise to Crampton's muscle and the tenacular and pectinate ligaments. Its inner surface is attached to the ciliary processes which occupy the entire ciliary zone. (See Figure 7.2.)

The iris is formed from a double origin: a combination of parts of the ectodermal retina and the mesodermal choroid. The striated muscle is ectodermal. The iris has a triangular base that fits snugly between the ciliary process, the pectinate ligament, and the tendons of Crampton's muscle and the annular pad, or ringwulst. Its free extremity is very thin. The ectodermal striated muscles throughout the iris are arranged as sphincter and dilator fibers which act very rapidly. Both of the two retinal epithelial cell layers on the posterior surface of the iris are pigmented.

The pecten of the quail measures 35μ from its base at the entrance area of the optic nerve to its apex and 126μ across at its widest portion. It is of the corrugated type. The surface cells compare favorably with the retinal pigmented epithelial cells in form and origin. The majority of the blood vessels are larger than ordinary capillaries. The supporting stroma is not of ordinary connective tissue, but appears to be a scanty glial framework.

The retina (Figs. 7.3, 7.4) of coturnix is outstanding because of the precise arrangement of its layers and uniformity of its cellular structure. It measures from 245μ at its thickest portion to 132μ at its thinnest area. None of the retinal fibers seem to enter the thin layers of the organ. The average number of folds counted is 14:

Pigment layer	26.5μ
Visual cell layer	44.0μ
Outer nuclear layer	17.5μ
Inner nuclear layer	3.0μ
Bipolar elements +	
Müller's-fibers nuclei +	
Amacrine layer	52.5μ
Inner plexiform layer	70.0μ
Ganglion layer	17.5μ
Nerve fiber layer	26.5μ

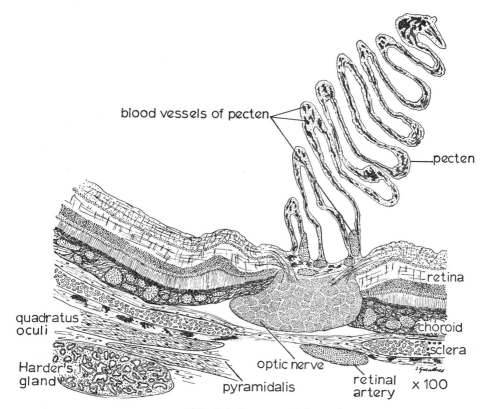

blood vessels of pecten

pecten

retina

choroid

sclera

quadratus oculi

Harder's gland

optic nerve

pyramidalis

retinal artery

× 100

FIG. 7.4—Entrance of the optic nerve into the sectioned eye.

The sublayers or divisions of the inner nuclear and inner plexiform layers are easily differentiated. The nuclei of Müller's-fibers cells are elongated and found in the center of the inner nuclear layer. The inner plexiform layer is characterized by faint cross bands which run parallel to the inner surface of the retina.

The diameter of the crystalline lens measures 4 mm at its widest circumference and has a maximum thickness of 3.5 mm. It is supported by the annular pad (ringwulst), and has a slightly greater convexity in its posterior surface than in the anterior. The process of changing of the shape and position of the lens during accommodation in the bird's eye is similar to that of reptiles. The periphery of the lens is covered with a ringlike annular pad which exerts pressure on the lens and causes it to round out during the contraction of the circular muscles. This action facilitates near-vision accommodation. The structures found in the quail that may be responsible for accommodation are: the sclerotic rings, Brücke's muscle, and the annular pad (Fig. 7.2).

Eyelids

There are two major lids of the eye, the *inferior eyelid* and the *superior eyelid* (Figs. 7.1, 7.5). Of these the lower is the more maneuverable. It is more extensive and will cover the palpebral

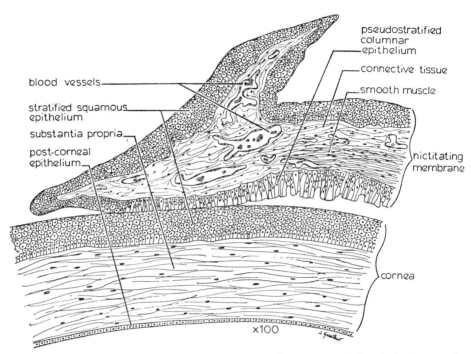

FIG. 7.5—Histology of the cornea and the nictitating membrane.

fissure when the quail is sleeping. The only structures that can be compared to the eyelashes in mammals are tiny feathers without barbs. The lids of coturnix are very thin, and there is no meibomian gland embedded in the palpebral tarsi. The *third eyelid* (nictitating membrane) (Fig. 7.5), which is used for blinking, is a very thin, highly elastic membrane which can be stretched across the entire corneal surface by the long tendon of the pyramidalis muscle. This tendon extends to the rear of the eye and passes through a pulley-like structure of the quadratus oculi muscle. This apparatus prevents the tendon of the pyramidalis muscle from coming in contact with the optic nerve during contraction. The epithelial cells at the free margin of the nictitating membrane are developed into a triangular scraping process that distributes the tears during contraction

and wipes the cornea clean during relaxation.

Glands of the Eye

The glands associated with the eye are the lacrimal and harderian (Fig. 7.6). The *lacrimal glands* of birds are situated ventral to the temporal bone and have a single duct which opens on the deep surface of the lower lid. They are not as well developed as the lacrimal glands of mammals. Histologically the lacrimal gland is of the tubuloalveolar type, distinctly lobulated, and invested in a thin capsule of connective tissue. It is a mixed gland, with both mucous and serous cells appearing in the endpieces. The secretorial cells are surrounded by a well-developed basement membrane except at intervals where basket cells intervene. Elongated intercalated portions are continuous with the excretorial ducts which are lined with a single layer of cuboidal epithelium. The larger lacrimal duct is lined with stratified columnar epithelium.

The *harderian gland* of coturnix is situated deep in the orbit in the region of the optic nerve entrance to the globe. The secretion is of a thick oily consistency that offers protection to the exposed surface of the eye. Its capsule is not surrounded by a distinct blood sinus as it is in mammals. The gland assumes a flattened oval shape as it fits snugly between the sclera and the bony structure of the orbital cavity. Trabecula-like septa divide the gland into lobules. These are usually five-sided in cross section. The septa between them are composed chiefly of collagenous bundles. There are no excretorial ducts in the interlobular septa. All the ducts of the lobule converge to the central position where they join larger central ducts which run parallel to the axis of the lobule. Therefore, no secreting alveoli are present in the central core of the lobules. In this region a few muscle and collagenous fibers surround and support the duct system. The central ducts of

each of the long lobules converge and join others to form a large excretory duct that leaves the rostral extremity of the gland and enters the space between the base of the third eyelid and the globe. This peculiar duct arrangement presents an outstanding differential characteristic of a true harderian gland. (See Figure 7.4.)

In coturnix the nasolacrimal duct has a comparatively large slitlike opening that is located cranial to the caudal portion of the middle turbinate and dorsal to the lateral margin of the caudal nares (choanae). The opening of the infraorbital sinus into the nasal cavity is not as distinct or large as the nasolacrimal duct opening. This opening is located between the caudal portion of the middle turbinate and the ventral part of the dorsal turbinate. A thin flap of mucosa covers the opening and makes it indistinct.

EAR

In coturnix the ear (Figs. 7.1, 7.7–7.10) does not form an external appendage as it does in mammals. There is, how-

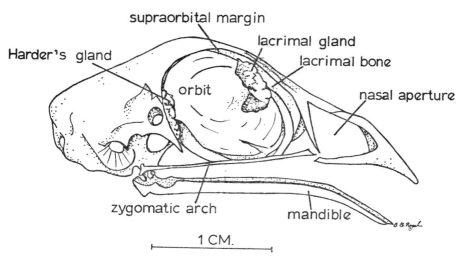

FIG. 7.6—*Glands of the orbital cavity.*

ever, a circular fold of pendulous skin which may be called an ear lobe. Above the lobe there is a small patch of skin that is thickly feathered, so that the external orifice is covered and invisible. The external acoustic meatus is located in the caudodorsal region of the temporal fossa. It is surrounded by the external auditory process which is formed by parts of the occipital, temporal, and sphenoid bones. The external canal extends caudoventrally at first and then turns caudodorsad for a short distance before it terminates at the tympanic membrane. At the bend in the canal a prominent ridge from the dorsal wall extends ventrally. A condensation of the ceruminous glands of the mucosa is found in this fold. Stratified squamous epithelium lines the canal and also forms the lining of the ducts of the glands.

The tympanic membrane is obliquely placed across the canal and is covered by a thin continuation of the epithelium of the canal. Its fibrous stroma is composed of annular and radiating fibers

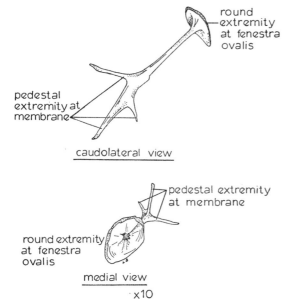

round extremity at fenestra ovalis

pedestal extremity at membrane

caudolateral view

pedestal extremity at membrane

round extremity at fenestra ovalis

medial view

x10

FIG. 7.7—Columella of the middle ear.

which anchor three or four pedestal-like cartilaginous extensions of the columella (Fig. 7.7). The tympanic surface of the membrane is covered with a very thin epithelium of the respiratory type. The tympanic cavity is situated primarily between the tympanic membrane laterally and the internal ear medially. It is flattened and presents three recesses, the central one of which leads toward the vestibule, is occupied by the columella bone, and terminates at the vestibular membrane. The round, flattened basal portion of the columella is embedded in the oval membrane, which in turn covers the fenestra ovalis. The fenestra rotunda occupies the caudal portion of this recess. The second, or rostrodorsal, recess leads to the air spaces of the cancellous bones of the head. The third, or rostroventral, recess leads to the channel of the eustachian tube.

Internal Ear

The *internal ear* (Figs. 7.8, 7.9) extends from the tympanic cavity toward the cranial vault in the substance of the temporal bone, which remains cancellous in birds. The osseous labyrinth is a thin, compact shell which is easily separated from the surrounding spongy bone. It is composed of three semicircular canals, a scala vestibuli, or vestibule, and the lagena, which takes the place of the mammalian cochlea. The central vestibule is large and is constricted at the position of the rostral utriculus and the caudal sacculus. The utricular space is continuous with the lumen of the semicircular canals. The bony lagena is not spirally curved as the cochlea is in mammals; it is a short, slightly twisted tubular structure, the terminal portion of which is slightly bent and enlarged.

The membranous labyrinth of the inner ear is composed of the utriculus and sacculus, the membranous semicircular canals, and the lagenar duct.

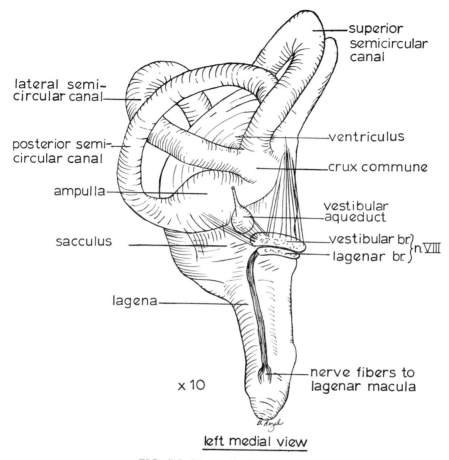

superior
semicircular
canal

lateral semi-
circular canal

posterior semi-
circular canal

ampulla

sacculus

lagena

× 10

ventriculus

crux commune

vestibular
aqueduct

vestibular br.⎱
lagenar br. ⎰ n. VIII

nerve fibers to
lagenar macula

left medial view

FIG. 7.8—Nerve distribution to the internal ear, left medial view.

The duct passes through a canal in the bone, the vestibular aqueduct, and widens into the endolymphatic sac just outside the dura mater. From the membranous sacculus a short ductus reuniens leads into the lagenar duct. Three membranous semicircular canals leave the utriculus. Their initial portions are enlarged into the ampullae which house the cristae ampullaris. The lagenar duct is a membranous tube lying in the bony lagenar canal. As all other membranous portions of the inner ear, it contains endolymph. The perilymph partially or completely surrounds all the divisions of the membranous labyrinth, thus separating it from the surrounding osseous walls. The two lymph spaces do not communicate. The lining of the perilymph spaces is a flattened mesenchymal epithelium that is confluent with the periosteum of the bone. The endolymphatic spaces are lined with epithelium which, in specific areas, is specialized to form the neuroepithelial areas of the inner ear. Maculae and cristae function to maintain both equilibrium and the organ of Corti for hearing.

Some of the differential characteristics of the ear of the quail and those of mammals are: The auricle of the external ear in mammals is replaced by the

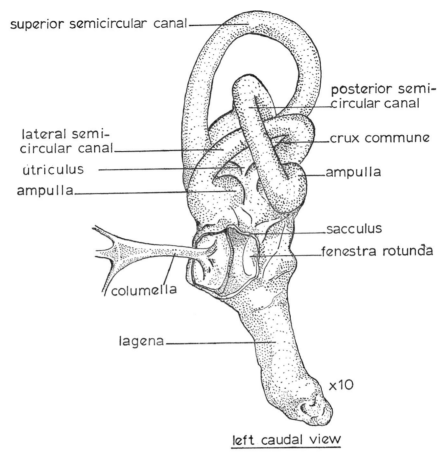

superior semicircular canal

posterior semi-circular canal

lateral semi-circular canal

crux commune

utriculus

ampulla

ampulla

sacculus

fenestra rotunda

columella

lagena

x10

left caudal view

FIG. 7.9—*Bony labyrinth of the internal ear, left caudal view.*

small semicircular ear lobe; the ossicles are replaced by the columella which traverses the tympanic cavity; the tectorial membrane is a flattened sheet of tissue which covers the hair cells of the organ of Corti and is attached at both ends. The lagenar duct is not coiled; it is held in position by two cartilaginous shelves which support the basilar membrane ventrally. The Reissner's membrane is replaced by a thick, vascular, tegmental membrane that is lined on the lagenar duct surface by an inconstant striated epithelium. Numerous blood vessels come very close to the endolymph of the lagenar duct. At the

terminal extremity of the lagenar duct the scala vestibuli and the scala tympani do not communicate by the perilymphatic opening known as helicotrema in mammals. At this position the lagenar macula is developed and is adherent to cartilage, which in turn is supported by trabeculae attached to the blind end of the bony lagena. The function of the lagenar macula is not known in birds. The basilar membrane between the inner and outer cartilaginous shells separating the lagenar duct from the scala tympani is relatively much shorter than in mammals. The shortness of the membrane is paralleled by a smaller number of transverse fibers that may have something to do with the frequency ranges that are audible to the bird. There is, however, a much larger number of hair cells in the organ of Corti. The spiral ganglion cells are more numerous, and the number of hair cells supplied by one single nerve fiber appears to be considerably less in coturnix than is apparent in the ear of mammals. In fact, the nerve fibers are so numerous that each and every hair cell may have its own. (See Figure 7.10.)

SENSE OF SMELL

Due to the small size and poor development of the olfactory lobe of the brain in coturnix it is believed that the sense of smell is of relatively little importance. On the other hand, dissection of the posterior turbinates at the termination of the olfactory nerve displays a rather thick epithelium that, when sec-

tioned and examined microscopically, proved to be of the olfactory type. The remainder of the nasal epithelium was of the respiratory type, and no structure comparable to the vomeronasal organ, or organ of Jacobson, as found in mammals could be demonstrated. Sturkie (1954) reported that, for most birds, the presence of neuroanatomical structures suggests that the olfactory sense can be transmitted, even though it is not noted in the activities of the bird.

HISTOLOGY OF THE OLFACTORY REGION

The olfactory mucosa differs from that of the respiratory region in that it is thicker and has a dull color caused by the pigment granules of the epithelium. The area is restricted to the mucosa of the caudal turbinate near the entrance area of the olfactory nerve in the nasal cavity. The three usual differentiating types of cells are found: the supporting (sustentacular), the basal, and the ol-

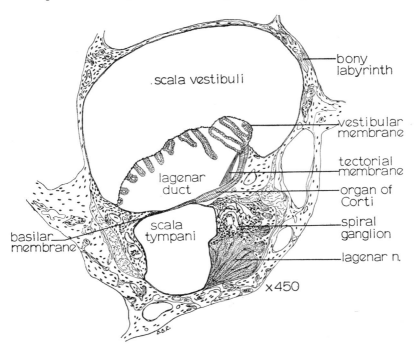

FIG. 7.10—Histology of the lagena, cross section near its base.

factory cells. The supporting cells are tall columnar, their lateral borders indented with the nuclear impressions of the olfactory cells; their cytoplasm is finely granular and faintly pigmented. The nucleus is large, oval in shape, and situated in the distal portion of the cell. The olfactory cells are tall and slender, extending through the entire width of the epithelial sheet. The nucleus is oval and occupies the greater part of the central body portion of the cell. The location of the body portion of the cell and nucleus may be at any level of the deeper half of the epithelial sheet. Peripheral and basal processes extend from the body of the cell. The peripheral one is slender and bears a short delicate olfactory hair that extends beyond the surface of the epithelial sheet. The proximal, or basal, process extends from the body of the cell through the basement membrane as an unmyelinated fiber of the olfactory nerve. This neuroepithelial cell process continues as the peripheral nerve cellular element to the glomeruli of the olfactory bulb, which is situated in the rostral extremity of the cranial cavity.

A third type of cell is recognized; it is angular in shape and is located at the basement membrane. The angular processes are joined to form a network around the proximal portions of the supporting cells. The collagenous propria mucosa is highly cellular superficially; centrally it is occupied by many olfactory nerve bundles, venous sinuses, and tubular olfactory (Bowman's) glands. Deeply the propria becomes more compact and joins the periosteum or perichondrium of the supporting turbinate structures. The cells of the olfactory glands of Bowman are cylindrical or pyramidal; they have a dark-staining spherical nucleus and display yellow to gray pigmented cytoplasmic granules. The mucoserous secretion is discharged through a rather large duct lined with squamous or cuboidal epithelium. The secretion covers the surface of the olfactory area and surrounds the nonmotile short hair processes which project beyond the surface of the sheet.

SENSE OF TASTE

The sense of taste, like that of smell, seems to be poorly developed in the quail. In observing the eating habits of the bird, it was noticed that no signs of either favorable or unfavorable taste reaction were shown. Crickets and other insects which had been killed with poisonous insecticides were readily accepted and eaten in large quantities.

Serial sections of both the upper and lower portions of the beak revealed quite a number of Herbst's corpuscles in the lamina propria of the oral mucosa. Such corpuscles are generally considered to have a tactile function rather than a recording of specific taste. According to Kare and Medway (1959) coturnix, along with a number of other birds tested, was indifferent to the taste of the common sugars.

SENSE OF TOUCH AND THERMAL CONTROL

The sense of touch in birds is rather highly developed; some land birds are able to register the vibrations of distant earthquakes or explosions. This ability is thought to be possible through the presence of pacinian corpuscles which are advantageously placed in the substance of the digital pads and fibrous layers of the synovial bursa beneath the tendons of the pelvic limb.

Most birds, like mammals, are homeothermic, or in other words are warm-blooded animals. This indicates that a remarkable evolutionary change has taken place from their reptilian ancestors, which were of the poikilothermic or cold-blooded classification. As in mammals the temperature of such deep-seated organs as the heart, liver, stomach, and brain is maintained at a rather narrow range, more so in larger birds than in smaller ones. This thermal balance is to a large degree controlled by the common integument of the bird.

When the heat production of the quail's body exceeds the heat lost, the temperature control is brought about primarily by spreading of the wings, which allows an increased radiation of heat from those areas of the body that are not covered by feathers. On the other hand, heat of the body is conserved very effectively in a cold environment by the layer of dead air space which is produced by the confluence of the air cavities of the quills of the feathers. In other words, the animal's body is enclosed by a dead air space and the transmission of heat is controlled much as it is in a thermos bottle.

Heat lost by evaporation is negligible in birds, inasmuch as they do not possess sweat glands. They are, however, able to lose some heat by vaporization of moisture from the skin. Vaporization of moisture is brought about by panting, which increases the evaporating-cooling mechanism of the moist mucous membrane lining of the respiratory tract.

It is reported by Sturkie (1965) that some types of birds habitually lay their eggs in a heap of compost that supplies the optimum temperature environment for incubation of their eggs. The optimum temperature of the compost heap can be registered accurately by thrusting the beak into the depth of the pile. It is assumed that the temperature of the nest can thus be determined by the tactile corpuscles of the beak and can be controlled by varying the depth at which the eggs are deposited.

CHAPTER EIGHT

Endocrinology

In coturnix those organs, or parts of organs, which produce hormones are known as endocrine glands and are quite similar in form and structure to those in mammals. A review of the literature of the endocrinology of birds reveals a vast amount of detailed research, the magnitude of which makes it impractical to mention in this presentation. The endocrine glands (Figs. 8.1–8.3) are: the ectodermal hypophysis, pineal body, endodermal thyroid, parathyroids, islets of Langerhans of the pancreas, thymus, mesodermal adrenal cortex, corpus luteum of the ovary, and interstitial cells of the testicle and ovary. The adrenal body is described in the section of splanchnology devoted to the kidney. The interstitial cells of the testicle and ovary appear with the description of the genitalia and the islets of Langerhans appear in the description of the pancreas.

HYPOPHYSIS

The *hypophysis* lies in the median sella turcica of the body of the sphenoid bone. It is in the form of a somewhat flattened oval disc in coturnix and measures 3.5 mm in length, 2.0 mm in breadth, and 2.0 mm in thickness. It is

275

suspended by a pedunculated outpouch-
ing of the floor of the diencephalon and
is covered by a thick capsule, the dorsal
portion of which is confluent with the
dura mater. The hypophysis is composed of two divisions differing in origin,
structure, and function. One of ectodermal origin, the neurohypophysis,
arises from the infundibulum of the
diencephalon. The other, the adeno-
hypophysis, also of ectodermal origin,
comes from the dorsal evagination of
the stomodeum of the embryo. All of
the parts except the pars nervosa are
derived from the stomodeal division in
coturnix and, as in many other birds,
only the infundibular cavity persists in
the mature gland. The hypophyseal cavity and the pars intermedia are not
found.

HISTOLOGY OF THE HYPOPHYSIS

The capsule of connective tissue
is thick and is composed of a compact
layer of predominantly collagenous
fibers. Trabeculae divide the gland into
lobes and lobules and support a reticular
stroma, in the meshes of which are
found the parenchymal cells. A rich
supply of nerves, lymphatics, and blood
vessels are conducted from the capsule
through the trabeculae to the parenchyma. The blood vessels form a rich network of wide, thin-walled sinuses
around the cords and layers of parenchymal cells of the lobules. There are
three kinds of cells; their names and
classification are designated according to
their staining reactions, which are quite
comparable to those of mammals. Those
cells with a clear cytoplasm and a vesicular nucleus are known as chief, or
chromophobe, cells. Those with a
granular cytoplasm are known as chromophil cells which are either eosin-
staining (acidophils), or basic-staining
(basophils). The acidophil cell nucleus
is vesicular while that of the basophil
is solider and stains darker. Other in-

frequent structures found in the pars
distalis of birds according to Lucas and
Stettenheim (1965) are pigment granules,
colloid-filled follicles, hypoplastic epithelial tissue, and nodules of lymphatic
tissue. Sturkie (1965) relates that the
pars distalis of the bird produces all the
known hormones found in the pituitaries of mammals and lists over a hundred
references of physiological experimen-
tation related to the hypophysis of birds.

The pars nervosa (infundibular
part) of the coturnix hypophysis is small
and is separated from the adenohypoph-
ysis by a complete septum of connective
tissue. The infundibular cavity is wide
and is lined with ependymal cells. Two
hormones which have at least a tempo-
rary existence in the pars nervosa of
birds are oxytocin and argine vasotrocin.
The presence of vasopressin is uncertain.
According to Sturkie (1965) the neurosecretory mechanism plays an important part in the control and regulation
of the pituitary function of birds, as well
as in lower and higher vertebrates. This
mechanism has been reviewed thorough-
ly by Farner and Oksche (1962) and by
Benoit (1962).

The pars distalis is clearly separable
into two regions: a caudal region composed chiefly of "A1" acidophils, which
stain orange to red with Orange G or
Acid Fuchsine, and the cephalic region
which harbors more of the "A2" acidophils. These cells are smaller and stain
scarlet with Acid Fuchsine. The basophils of the cephalic region are smaller
still and are found to be numerous in
the caudal region.

According to Marshall (1962) it is
believed that the basophils secrete the
gonadotrophic hormone and that the
acidophils secrete prolactin and perhaps
a growth hormone, and probably the
thyroid-stimulating hormone and the
adrenocorticotrophic hormone also. He
also states that the following hormones
have been isolated from avian pituitaries.

The gonadotrophins are: FSH, the follicular-stimulating hormone which stimulates the ovarian follicles in the female and spermatogenesis in the male; LH, the luteinizing hormone which aids in the formation of the corpora lutea; ICSH, the interstitial-cell-stimulating hormone; ACTH, the adrenocorticotrophic hormone which stimulates the adrenal cortex; and TSH, the thyroid-stimulating hormone. Those pituitary hormones which have not been proven to exist in the domestic fowl are: the pancreatic islet-cell-stimulating, the para-thyroid-stimulating, and the growth hormones.

The pars tuberalis is composed primarily of the chromophobe cells; however, a few of the acidophils may be found in some species.

For a more complete explanation of the physiology of the hypothalamo-hypophyseal complex, Sturkie recommends a review of the works of Farner and Oksche (1962), Benoit (1962), Wingstrand (1951, Grignon (1956), Legait (1959), Mosier (1955), Duncan (1956), Oksche (1962), Oksche *et al.* (1959, 1964), and others.

THYROID GLANDS

The *thyroid glands* of coturnix are situated at the thoracic inlet at the base

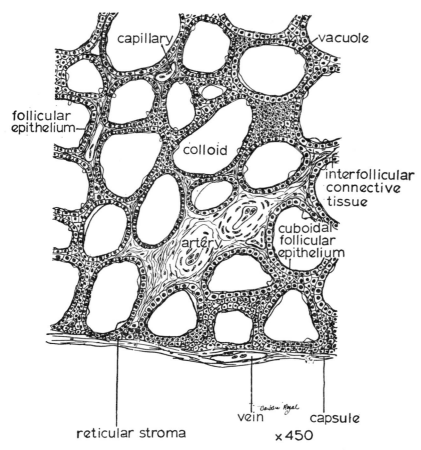

FIG. 8.1—Histology of the thyroid.

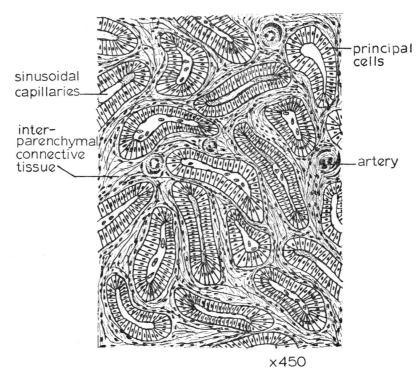

sinusoidal capillaries

inter-parenchymal connective tissue

principal cells

artery

×450

FIG. 8.2—Histology of the parathyroid.

of the neck. Each of the pair is superficially located in close association to the jugular veins, first rib, and caudal lobe of the thymus. As in the domestic fowl they do not touch the trachea and are not joined by an isthmus, as they are in domestic animals. They have an average length of 2 mm and a breadth of .5 mm.

HISTOLOGY OF THE THYROID GLAND

A thin capsule separates the gland from the surrounding loose connective tissue. A few very delicate trabeculae from the inner surface of the capsule divide the gland into connected lobules. They carry the larger blood vessels which enter and leave the gland at various places, since no hilus is formed. Depending on how they are sectioned, the saclike follicles appear as round or oval cavities lined with either a low or a high simple cuboidal epithelium and

containing the thyroid hormone, which is stored as a hyaline-appearing colloid. The cytoplasm, which stains in a variable manner according to its secretorial activity, contains numerous vacuoles. The nuclei are spherical and are centrally placed. As in mammals the follicular epithelium is supported by a reticular stroma, a well-developed basement membrane is lacking, and the blood capillaries form a dense plexus around each and every one of the follicles. Numerous groups of cells which resemble those of the parathyroid occur in the angular spaces between the follicles. The hormones of the thyroid are triiodothyronine and thyroxine (Wentworth and Mellen, 1961b). (See Figure 8.1.)

PARATHYROID GLANDS

The *parathyroid glands* of coturnix are represented by a pair of oval lobes on each side of the caudal region of the neck in close proximity to the base of the thyroids, ventral to the jugular veins and dorsal to the common carotid artery. They are easily distinguished by their dull white color in contrast to the dark red color of the thyroid. They are usually very much smaller than the thyroid; however, it is reported that sometimes in the female they may reach half the size of the thyroid.

HISTOLOGY OF THE PARATHYROID

The parenchyma is enclosed by the connective tissue capsule and is composed of branching coils, or cords, of the epithelial cells or principal cells. The cytoplasm of most of the cells is chromophil and stains intensely with eosin. The oxophil cells as found in mammals are

absent. It is reported that the parathyroid hormone aids in regulating the calcium content of the blood and the excretion of phosphorus. Total removal of the parathyroids causes death from tetany. Aberrant parathyroids are not rare and they are usually designated as the third or fourth parathyroids. (See Figure 8.2.)

THYMUS

The *thymus* appears as a series of longitudinally connected lobes in the jugular furrow from which the thoracic inlet extends to the pharynx. None of the lobules appear in the mediastinum. Each lobe is divided into lobules by a connective tissue interlobular stroma, which is an extension of the outer capsule.

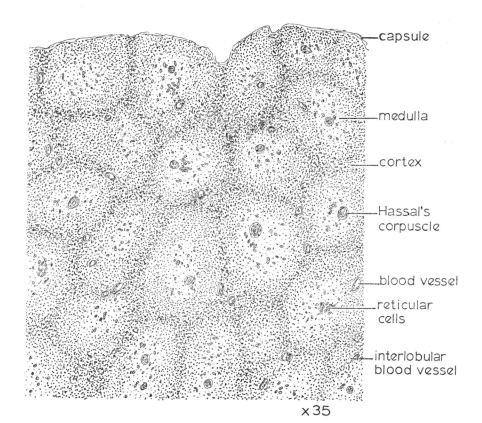

×35

FIG. 8.3—Histology of the thymus.

HISTOLOGY OF THE THYMUS

The stroma consists of a stellate reticulum derived from the entodermal lining of the embryonic pharynx. Each lobule has a cortex in which the stroma is infiltrated with small cells that are not distinguishable from the small-sized lymphocytes. These are called thymocytes. No germinal, or reaction, centers of lymph sinuses are present. The medulla of each lobule is made up chiefly of epithelial reticular cells which are not phagocytic and are not considered a part of the reticuloendothelial system. Numerous thymic bodies, or Hassal's corpuscles, occur in the medulla which measures from $12–100\mu$ in diameter. It appears that they are composed of degenerative reticular cells which have formed a concentric mass, each cell being placed similarly to the arrangement of the leaves of the cabbage head. The center of the mass may be so degenerated that it has a cystic or a calcified appearance. The thymus of coturnix, as in other birds, undergoes atrophy with age. (See Figure 8.3.)

PINEAL BODY

The *pineal body* (epiphysis cerebri) is a small gland situated in the narrow space between the cerebral hemispheres and the cerebellum. Within the 3rd ventricle the choroid plexus extends from the foramen of Monroe along the roof of the 3rd ventricle to the stalk of the pineal body.

HISTOLOGY OF THE PINEAL BODY

The stalk and body of the gland are hollow, and their lining is of the ependymal cells. The cerebral fluid of the 3rd ventricle is thus free to flow through the stalk and into the lumen of the body of the gland. From the body raylike lobules extend to its capsule, which is formed by a reflection of the pia mater. As in mammals the sand bodies or calcareous inclusions are found in old birds. Although much has been written about the anatomy and physiology of the pineal gland, conclusive evidence of the presence of a hormone is lacking. Kitay and Altschule (1954) and Kelly (1962) report evidence which seems to indicate that the pineal gland produces a substance which has an antigonadotrophic effect in birds and mammals. Additional research is necessary to substantiate the belief that the pineal gland and the thymus are endocrine in function.

CHAPTER NINE

Integument

THE integument of an animal includes the skin and its appendages, those structures on or near the surface of an animal's body that come into contact with the environment. The integumentary system of the quail is composed primarily of: skin, claws, beak, nasal folds, scales, oil gland, metatarsal and digital pads, ear rims, and feathers.

SKIN

The *skin* is soft and pliable, and is for the most part loosely attached to the deep musculature beneath. A firm attachment of skin to the underlying structures is found on the elbow, the caudodorsal surface of the forearm, the cranial surface of the manus or wing, the lumbosacral region, and from the hocks distally to the ends of the digits. Many of the superficial muscles are tightly attached to the deep surface of the skin. This arrangement facilitates movements of the feathers and is readily seen when the feathers are raised—when the bird becomes excited, for instance. The skin is pale due to the absence of pigmentation and the lack of a well-developed dermal blood-capillary plexus. In the thinner parts of the skin such as the region of the keel, thigh, and foreleg the skin is transparent and the red musculature beneath may be seen.

281

CLAWS

The *claws* are pointed horny caps located on the distal phalanges of the 2nd digit of the pectoral limb and the distal phalanges of each digit of the pelvic limb. Thus the quail has ten claws, one on each of the wings and four on each foot. The claws on the feet are sharp, with the tips in a plantar position. Their primary function is for support and in scratching for food. The claws of the pectoral limb, or wing, are rudimentary, have no function, and are often absent. When present, they are located on the 2nd and last phalanges of the 2nd digit.

BEAK

The *beak,* or bill, is composed of two **V**-shaped sections which cover the upper and lower bony jaws. The upper or dorsal part covers the premaxilla and its nasal and maxillary processes. The lower or ventral part covers the rostral half of the mandible. The dorsal part is by far the larger and in caged animals may grow to extend far over the tip of the lower part and become directed ventrally. The dorsal part bears grooves on its ventral surface which fit snugly in place beneath and partially inside the dorsal portion when the mouth is closed. Prehension and mastication of food is the primary function of the beak.

NASAL FOLDS

Paired *nasal folds,* composed of less highly cornified horn than that of the beak, are situated dorsomedially to the external nares. These folds are thin and pliable and serve to protect the external nares.

SCALES

Scales, or overlapping plaquelike formations of horny epithelium, are found on the plantar surface of the hock. These scales completely surround the tar-

sometatarsus and the dorsal and lateral surfaces of the digits. They overlap with the free ends directed distally, and serve as protective shields for the underlying structures.

OIL GLAND

The *oil gland,* or preen gland, is positioned just beneath the skin, dorsal to the 1st coccygeal vertebra. In well-fed quail the gland is embedded in a cushion of fat. It has two distinct lobes positioned side by side, with their long axis parallel to the median plane. The lobes are oblong in shape and each is about 12 mm long and 4 mm wide. There is a single duct in a central papilla which extends from the caudal border of the gland. It extends through the surface of the skin and about 3 mm above it. The bird obtains the oil through this papilla, which is on the midline and is cranial to the pygostyle. There are no other oil or sebaceous glands in the skin. The oil is used by the bird to groom the feathers and to keep the beak from becoming brittle.

METATARSAL AND DIGITAL PADS

There are *metatarsal and digital pads* located on the plantar surface of the foot. They are moundlike elevations of the skin and subcutaneous fascia and are located at the articulations. The metatarsal pad is the largest and is located at the base of the foot beneath the three tarsometatarsal-phalangeal articulations. The number of the digital pads on each digit corresponds to the number of the digit. The largest of the digital pads is the most distal one on each digit, and it may extend beyond the articulation along the plantar surface of the claws.

EAR RIM

An *ear rim* of specialized epithelium surrounds the opening of the external ear and is positioned rostrodorsally to the external acoustic meatus. The rim is round or elliptical in shape, and the opening it encircles is protected by a dozen or more tiny feathers which span it caudodorsally. The epidermis of the ear rim becomes the least cornified of any of the horny structures of the integument.

FEATHERS

The *feathers* are the largest and most important component of the integumentary system of the bird. They are distinctive structures which provide a lightweight, resistant, and very flexible body covering. They have various functions which are vital to the health of the bird. They protect the skin from abra-

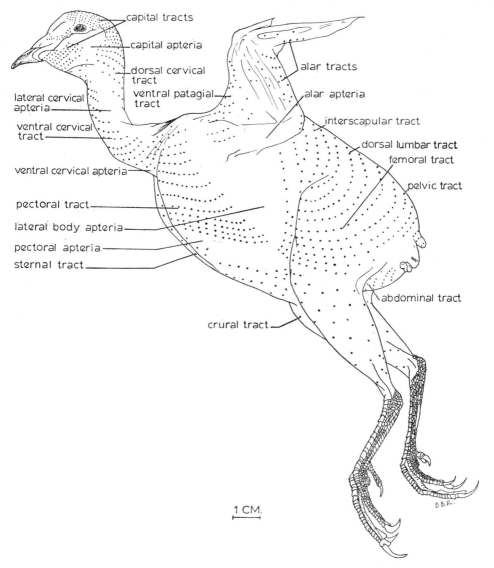

capital tracts
capital apteria
dorsal cervical tract
ventral patagial tract
lateral cervical apteria
ventral cervical tract
ventral cervical apteria
pectoral tract
lateral body apteria
pectoral apteria
sternal tract
crural tract
alar tracts
alar apteria
interscapular tract
dorsal lumbar tract
femoral tract
pelvic tract
abdominal tract

1 CM.

FIG. 9.1—Feather tracts, lateral view.

sions and wear and contain many dead-air spaces which act to insulate the body. Their paramount importance is that they aid in flight, since their shape and direction offer minimum resistance to air and a maximum of support. Various types of feathers are classified as contour, down, filoplumes, and bristles. The contour feathers are not positioned in the skin in a haphazard manner but are found in definite, bilateral, symmetrically arranged tracts called pterylae. The bare skin between these tracts is called apteria.

The pterylae (Fig. 9.1) are named according to the area of the body they cover:

1. *Capital tract* (cephalic)—covers the entire head.
2. *Dorsal cervical tract*—extends along the dorsal surface of the neck and blends with the capital tract cranially.
3. *Ventral cervical tract*—extends from the ventral surface of the capital tract to the ventrolateral surface of the neck. It bifurcates at the caudal third of the neck, and the two extensions continue caudad to the pectoral tracts.
4. *Interscapular tract* (dorsal thoracic) —the extension of the dorsal cervical tract between the scapulae. This tract bifurcates at the midthoracic region.
5. *Dorsal lumbar and pelvic tracts*—the extension of the dorsal thoracic tracts over the lumbosacral and pelvic areas.
6. *Pectoral tract*—**V**-shaped and on the cranial and ventrolateral surface of the breast.
7. *Lateral body tract*—on the lateral surface of the pectoral muscle, dorsal to the pectoral tract and ventral to the axillary fossa.
8. *Sternal tract*—long narrow tract which extends parallel to and on either side of the keel from the clavicle to the caudal tip of the keel.
9. *Humeral tract*—the dorsal surface of the upper arm just below the shoulder parallel to the midline.
10. *Abdominal tract*—along the ventral abdominal floor from the tip of the keel to the cloaca.
11. *Alar tract*—the dorsal and ventral surface of the wing in some birds; subdivisions are present.
12. *Femoral tract*—the craniolateral surface of the thigh.
13. *Crural tract*—completely surrounds the crural or foreleg area.

Bibliography

ABPLANALP, H., WOODWARD, A. E., and WILSON, W. O. "The Effects of Unnatural Day Lengths Upon Maturation and Egg Production of Japanese Quail, *Coturnix coturnix japonica.*" *Poultry Sci.* 41 (1962):1963–68.

AITKEN, R. N. C., and JOHNSTON, H. S. "Observation on the Fine Structure of the Infundibulum of the Avian (Fowl) Oviduct." *J. Anat.* 97 (1963):87–99.

ALBRIGHT, J. T., and KHAIRALLAH, L. H. "Ultrastructional Studies of Intracosternal Granules in the Chicken Oviduct." *Anat. Rec.* 148 (1964):356.

ALLEN, G. M. *Birds and Their Attributes.* Boston: Marshal Jones Co., 1925.

AMOROSO, E. C., and FIN, C. A. "Ovarian Activity During Gestation, Ovum Transport and Implantation." In *The Ovary,* edited by S. Zuckerman. New York: Academic Press, 1962.

AREY, L. B. *Developmental Anatomy.* 7th ed. Philadelphia and London: W. B. Saunders Co., 1965.

ASDELL, S. A. "Mechanism of Ovulation." In *The Ovary,* edited by S. Zuckerman. New York: Academic Press, 1962.

ASMUNSON, V. S., and BURMESTER, B. R. "The Secretory Activity of the Parts of the Hen's Oviduct." *J. Exp. Zool.* 72 (1936):225–46.

BAILEY, R. E. "Accessory Reproductive Organs of the Male Frigillid Birds, Seasonal Variations and Response to Various Sex Hormones." *Anat. Rec.* 115 (1953):1–20.

BANG, B. G. "Anatomical Evidence for Olfactory Function in Some Species of Birds." *Nature* 188 (1960):547.

————. "The Surface Pattern of the Nasal Mucosa and Its Relation to Mucous Flow—A Study of Chicken and Herring Gull Nasal Mucosae." *J. Morphol.* 109 (1961):57.

BANG, B. G., and BANG, F. B. "Effect of Water Deprivation on Nasal Mucous Flow." *Proc. Soc. Exp. Biol. Med.* 106 (1961):516.

BARNET, C. H., and LEWIS, O. J. "The Evolution of Some Traction Epiphyses in Birds and Mammals." *J. Anat.* 92 (1958):593.

BENOIT, J. "Hypothalamo-hypophyseal Control of the Sexual Activity in Birds." *Gen. Comp. Endocrinol.,* Suppl. 1 (1962):254.

BICKFORD, A. A. "Fully Formed and Functional Right Oviduct in a Single-Comb White Leghorn Pullet." *Avian Diseases* 9 (1965):464–70.

BISSONETTE, T. H., and ZUJKO, A. J. "Normal Progressive Changes in the Ovary of the Starling *(Sturnus vulgaris)* From December to April." *Auk* 53 (1936): 31–50.

BISWAL, G. "Additional Histological Findings in the Chicken Reproductive Tract." *Poultry Sci.* 33 (1954):843–51.

BLIVAISS, B. B. "Interrelations of Thyroid and Gonad in the Development of Plumage and Other Sex Characters in Brown Leghorn Roosters." *Physiol. Zool.* 20 (1947):67.

BLOOM, M. A., DOMM, L. V., NALBANDOV, A. V., and BLOOM, W. "Medullary Bone of Laying Chickens." *Am. J. Anat.* 102 (1958):411–54.

BLOUNT, W. P. "Thrombocyte Formation in the Domestic Hen." *Vet. J.* 95 (1939):195.

BOBR, L. W., LORENZ, F. W., and OGASAWARA, F. X. "Role of Uterovaginal Junction in Storage of Cock Spermatozoa." *Poultry Sci.* 41 (1962):1628.

————. "Distribution of Spermatozoa in the Oviduct and Fertility in Domestic Birds (Transport of Spermatozoa in the Fowl Oviduct)." *J. Reprod. Fertility* 8 (1964):39–48, 49–58.

BOSCH, R. A., and ANGULO, E. "Cytological and Cytochemical Features of the Albumen Secreting Part of the Fowl's Oviduct." *Rec. Med. Vet.* 139 (1963): 927–32.

BOSS, J. H., SCULLY, E. E., WEGNER, K. H., and COHEN, R. B. "Structural Variations in the Adult Ovary, Clinical Significance." *Obstet. Gynecol.* 25 (1965): 747–64.

BOURNE, G. H., ed. *Structural Aspects of Aging.* New York: Hafner Publishing Co., 1961.

BRADLEY, O. C., and GRAHAME, T. *The Structure of the Fowl.* Edinburgh and London: Oliver and Boyd, 1950.

BRANT, J. W. A., and NALBANDOV, A. V. "Role of Sex Hormones in Albumen Secretion by the Oviduct of Chickens." *Poultry Sci.* 35 (1956):692–700.

BROWNE, M. M. "A Study of the Sacral Autonomic Nerves in a Chick and a Human Embryo." *Anat. Rec.* 116 (1953):189–203.

BURROWS, W. H., and QUINN, J. P. "The Collection of Spermatozoa From the Domestic Fowl and Turkey." *Poultry Sci.* 16 (1937):19–24.

CARD, L. E. *Poultry Production.* 9th ed. Philadelphia: Lea & Febiger, 1962.

CHAISSON, R. B. *Laboratory Anatomy of the Pigeon.* Dubuque, Iowa: W. C. Brown Co., 1958.

CHAKRAVORTI, K. P., and SADHU, D. P. "Some Aspects of the Histological and Histochemical Studies on the Oviduct of the Hen." *Proc. Zool. Soc. London* 14 (1961):27–32.

————. "Histological and Histochemical Studies of the Hormone-Stimulated Oviduct of the Pigeon." *Acta Histochem.* (Jena) 16 (1963):343–56.

CHAMBERLAIN, F. W. *Atlas of Avian Anatomy.* Michigan State College Bull. No. 5, Lansing, 1943.

————. "Female Genital Tract of the Domestic Chicken." Michigan State Univ. Agr. Exp. Sta., unpublished, approx. 1943.

CHAUVEAU, A. *The Comparative Anatomy of the Domesticated Animals.* New York: Appleton and Co., 1891.

COBB, S. "Observations on the Comparative Anatomy of the Avian Brain." *Perspectives Biol. Med.* 3 (1960):383.

COHEN, H., and DAVIES, S. "The Development of the Cerebrospinal Fluid Spaces and Choroid Plexuses in the Chick." *J. Anat.* 72 (1937):23.

COLE, R. K. "Histology of the Oviduct of the Fowl in Relation to Variations of the Firm Egg Albumen." *Anat. Rec.* 71 (1938):349–62.

CONRAD, R. M., and PHILLIPS, R. E. "The Formation of the Chalazae and the Inner White of the Hen's Egg." *Poultry Sci.* 17 (1938):143–46.

CONRAD, R. M., and WARREN, D. C. "The Alternate White and Yellow Layers of Yolk in Hen's Ova." *Poultry Sci.* 18 (1939):220–24.

COVER, M. S. "The Gross and Microscopic Anatomy of the Respiratory System of the Turkey. I. The Nasal Cavity and Infraorbital Sinus." *Am. J. Vet. Res.* 14 (1953a):113.

————. "Gross and Microscopic Anatomy of the Respiratory System of the Turkey. II. The Larynx, Trachea, Syrinx, Bronchi, and Lungs." *Am. J. Vet. Res.* 14 (1953b):230.

————. "Gross and Microscopic Anatomy of the Respiratory System of the Turkey. III. The Air Sacs." *Am. J. Vet. Res.* 14 (1953c):239.

CUNNINGHAM, J. T., and SMART, W. A. M. "Structure and Origin of the Corpus Luteum in Lower Vertebrates." *Proc. Roy. Soc.* 116 (1934):258–81.

CURTIS, M. R. *The Ligaments of the Oviduct in the Domestic Fowl.* Maine Agr. Exp. Sta. Ann. Rept. 176 (1910):1–20.

DAVIS, D. E. "The Bursting of Avian Follicles at the Beginning of Atresia." *Anat. Rec.* 82 (1942a):153–65.

————. "The Regression of the Avian Post-ovulatory Follicle." *Anat. Rec.* 82 (1942b):297–307.

DENNINGTON, E. M., and LUCAS, A. M. "Influence of Heat Treatment on the Number of Ectopic Lymphoid Foci in Chickens." *Am. J. Vet. Res.* 21 (1960):734.

DICKSON, A. D., and MILLEN, J. W. "The Meningeal Relationships of the Glycogen Body in the Chick." *J. Anat.* 91 (1957):47.

DRANSFIELD, J. W. "The Lymphatic System of the Domestic Fowl." *Vet. J.* 101 (1945):171–79.

DRIGGERS, J. C., and COMAR, C. L. "The Secretion of Radioactive Calcium (Ca45) in the Hen's Egg." *Poultry Sci.* 28 (1949):420–24.

DUNCAN, D. "An Electron Microscope Study of the Neurohypophysis of a Bird, *Gallus domesticus*." *Anat. Rec.* 125 (1956):457.

DUKES, H. H. *The Physiology of Domestic Animals.* 7th ed. Ithaca, N.Y.: Comstock Publishing Co., 1955.

ECKSTEIN, P., and ZUCKERMAN, S. "Morphology of the Reproductive Tract." In A. J. Marshall, *Physiology of Reproduction*, 3rd ed. New York: Longmans, Green Co., 1956.

EGLITIS, I., and KNOUFF, R. A. "A Histological and Histochemical Analysis of the Inner Lining and Glandular Epithelium of the Chicken Gizzard." *Am. J. Anat.* 3 (1962):49.

ELLIS, C. J., and GETTY, R. A Guide to the Dissection of the Common Fowl *(Gallus domesticus)*. 2nd ed. Copyright, authors. Ames, Iowa. 1964.

FARNER, D. S., and OKSCHE, A. "Neurosecretion in Birds." *Gen. Comp. Endocrinol.* 2 (1962):113.

FISHER, H. K. "Adaptations and Comparative Anatomy of the Locomotor Apparatus of New World Vultures." *Am. Midland Naturalist* 35 (1946):545–729.

FLEMING, R. E. "The Origin of the Vertebral and External Carotid Arteries in Birds." *Anat. Rec.* 33 (1926):183.

FLOQUET, A., and GRIGNON, G. "Morphological Study of the Development of the Post-ovulatory Follicle in the Fowl." *Gen. Comp. Endocrinol.* 3 (1963):699.

FORSYTH, D. "The Comparative Anatomy, Gross and Minute, of the Thyroid and Parathyroid Glands in Mammals and Birds." *J. Anat. Physiol.* 42 (1908):141, 302.

FRANCHI, L. L. "The Structure of the Ovary." In *The Ovary*, edited by S. Zuckerman. New York: Academic Press, 1962.

FRANCHI, L. L., MANDL, A. M., and ZUCKERMAN, S. "The Development of the Ovary and the Process of Oogenesis." In *The Ovary*, edited by S. Zuckerman. New York: Academic Press, 1962.

FREEDMAN, S. L., and STURKIE, P. D. "Extrinsic Nerves of the Chicken Uterus (Shell Gland)." *Anat. Rec.* 147 (1963):431–37.

————. "Blood Vessels of the Chicken's Uterus (Shell Gland)." *Am. J. Anat.* 113 (1963):1–7.

FURBINGER, M. "Zur Vergleichenden Anatomie des Brutschulterapparates und der Schultermuskeln." *Z. Natuurw.* (Jena) 36 (1902):289–736.

GADOW, H., and SELENKA, E. "Vögel." In *Bronn's Klassen und Ordnungen des Thier-Reiches.* Leipzig: Anatomischer Theil, 1891.

GIBBS, O. S. "The Function of the Fowl's Ureters." *Am. J. Physiol.* 87 (1929):594.

GLENNY, F. H. "Modifications of Pattern in the Aortic Arch System of Birds and Their Phylogenetic Significance." *Proc. U.S. Nat. Museum* 104 (1955):525.

GOMORI, G. *Microscopic Histochemistry, Principles and Practice.* Chicago: University of Chicago Press, 1952.

GRAHAME, T. "The Sympathetic and Parasympathetic Nervous Systems of the Fowl." Notes on a Ph.D. thesis. *Brit. Vet. J.* 109 (1953):481.

GRASSE, P. P. "Organization des Societes d'Oiseaux. Traite de Zoologie." Tome 15. *Oiseaux.* Paris: Masson et Cie, 1950.

GRAY, J. C. "The Anatomy of the Male Genital Ducts in the Fowl." *J. Morphol.* 60 (1937):393–405.

GREEN, J. D. "The Comparative Anatomy of the Hypophysis With Special Reference to Its Blood Supply and Innervation." *Am. J. Anat.* 88 (1951):225.

GRIGG, G. W. "The Structure of Stored Sperm in the Hen and the Nature of the Release Mechanism." *Poultry Sci.* 36 (1957):450–51.

GRIGNON, G. *Développement du Complexe Hypothalamo-hypophysaire Chez l'Embryon de Poulet.* Nancy: Société d'Impressions Typographiques, 1956.

GURAYA, S. S. "Structure and Function of So-called Yolk Nucleus in the Oogenesis of Birds." *Quart. J. Microscop. Sci.* 103 (1962):411–15.

HADEK, R., and GETTY, R. "Age-Change Studies of the Ovary of the Domesticated Pig." *Am. J. Vet. Res.* 20 (1959):578–84.

HAFEZ, E. S. S. *Reproduction in Farm Animals.* Philadelphia: Lea & Febiger, 1962.

HARTMAN, F. A., and ALBERTIN, R. H. "A Preliminary Study of the Avian Adrenal." *Auk* 68 (1951):202.

HARTMAN, F. A., KNOUFF, R. A., McNUTT, A. W., and CARVER, J. E. "Chromaffin Patterns in Bird Adrenals." *Anat. Rec.* 97 (1947):211.

HEINROTH, O., and HEINROTH, K. *The Birds.* Ann Arbor: University of Michigan Press, 1958.

HEWETT, E. A. "Physiology of the Reproductive System of the Fowl." *J. Am. Vet. Med. Assoc.* 95 (1939):201–10.

HILL, R. T. *Prologue to Neuroendocrinology Symposium From Advances in Neuroendocrinology.* Edited by A. V. Nalbandov. Urbana: University of Illinois Press, 1963.

HODGES, R. E. "Blood Supply to the Avian Oviduct With Special Reference to the Shell Gland." *J. Anat.* 99 (1965):485–506.

HOHN, E. O. "Action of Certain Hormones on the Thymus of the Domestic Hen." *J. Endocrinol.* 19 (1959):282.

————. "Endocrine Glands, Thymus, and Pineal Body." In A. J. Marshall, *Biology and Comparative Physiology of Birds.* New York: Academic Press, 1961.

HOLMES, A. "The Pattern and Symmetry of Adult Plumage Units in Relation to the Order and Locus of Origin of the Embryonic Feather Papillae." *Am. J. Anat.* 56 (1935):243.

Howes, J. R. "Environmental Factors Affecting Ovulation in Coturnix Quail." *J. Alabama Acad. Sci.* 35 (1964):20–21.

———. "Japanese Quail as Found in Japan." *Quail Quart.* 1 (1964):19–30.

Hseih, T. M. "The Sympathetic and Parasympathetic Nervous Systems of the Fowl." Ph.D. dissertation, University of Edinburgh, 1951.

Hudson, G. E. "Studies on the Muscles of the Pelvic Appendage in Birds." *Am. Midland Naturalist* 18 (1937):1.

Hudson, G. E., and Lanzillotti, P. J. "Gross Anatomy of the Wing Muscles in the Family Corvidae." *Am. Midland Naturalist* 53 (1955):1.

———. "Muscles of the Pectoral Limb in Galliform Birds." *Am. Midland Naturalist* 71 (1964):1.

Hudson, G. E., Lanzillotti, P. J., and Edwards, G. D. "Muscles of the Pelvic Limb in Galliform Birds." *Am. Midland Naturalist* 61 (1959):1.

Ivey, W. D. "The Histogenesis of the Esophagus and Crop of the Chicken, Turkey, Game Bird, and Pigeon." M.S. thesis, Auburn University, 1948.

Johnson, J. S. "The Innervation of the Female Genitalia in the Hen." *Anat. Rec.* 29 (1925):387.

Johnston, H. S. R., and Aitken, R. N. C. "The Fine Structure of the Uterus of the Domestic Fowl." *J. Anat.* 97 (1963):333–44.

Jollie, M. T. "The Head Skeleton of the Chicken and Remarks on the Anatomy of This Region in Other Birds." *J. Morphol.* 100 (1957):389–436.

Jones, D. S. "The Origin of the Vagi and the Parasympathetic Ganglion Cells of the Viscera of the Chick." *Anat. Rec.* 82 (1942):185–97.

Kannankeril, J., and Domm, L. V. "The Development of the Ovary in the Japanese Quail *(Coturnix coturnix japonica)*." *Anat. Rec.* 148 (1964):297.

Kar, A. B. "Studies on the Ligaments of the Oviduct in the Domestic Fowl." *Anat. Rec.* 97 (1947):175–95.

Kare, M. R., and Medway, W. "Discrimination Between Carbohydrates in the Fowl." *Poultry Sci.* 38 (1959):1119.

Kaupp, B. F. *The Anatomy of the Domestic Fowl.* Philadelphia and London: W. B. Saunders Co., 1918.

Kelly, D. E. "Pineal Organs: Photoreception, Secretion, and Development." *Am. Scientist* 50 (1962):597.

Kirkpatrick, C. M., and Leopold, A. C. "The Role of Darkness in Sexual Activity of the Quail." *Science* 116 (1952):280–81.

Kitay, J. I., and Altschule, M. D. *The Pineal Gland—A Review of the Physiologic Literature.* Cambridge: Harvard University Press, 1954.

Kitoh, J. "Comparative and Topographical Anatomy of the Fowl. XII. Observation on the Arteries With Their Anastomoses in and Around the Brain in the Fowl." *Japan. J. Vet. Sci.* 24 (1962):141.

Kretzschmar, W. A., and Stoddard, F. J. "Physiological Changes in the Aging Female Including the Reproductive System." *Clin. Obstet. Gynecol.* 7 (1964):451–63.

Lake, P. E. The Male Reproductive Tract of the Fowl. *J. Anat.* 91 (1957):116.

———. "The Relationship Between Morphology and Function in Fowl Spermatozoa." *Proc. 10th World's Poultry Congr.*, Sect. A, 1954.

LANGLEY, J. N. "On the Sympathetic System of Birds, and on the Muscles Which Move the Feathers." *J. Physiol.* 30 (1904):221.

LARSELL, O. "The Development and Subdivisions of the Cerebellum of Birds." *J. Comp. Neurol.* 89 (1948):123.

LARSELL, O., and WHITLOCK, D. G. "Further Observations on the Cerebellum of Birds." *J. Comp. Neurol.* 97 (1952):545.

LEATHEM, J. H. "The Effects of Aging on Reproduction." In *The Endocrinology of Reproduction,* edited by T. J. Velordo. New York: Oxford University Press, 1958.

LEGAIT, H. "Contribution à l'Étude Morphologique et Expérimentale du Système Hypothalamoneuro-hypophysaire de la Poule Rhode-Island." Thèse D, Agrégation de l'Enseignement Supérieur, Louvain, 1959.

LILLIE, F. R. *The Development of the Chick.* 2nd ed. New York: Holt Publishing Co., 1930.

LINDENMAIER, P., and KARE, M. "The Taste End-Organs of the Chicken." *Poultry Sci.* 38 (1959):545.

LOCY, W. A., and LARSELL, O. "Embryology of the Bird's Lung. Based on Observations of the Domestic Fowl." Part I, *Am. J. Anat.* 19 (1916):447. Part II, *Am. J. Anat.* 20 (1916):1.

LORENZ, F. W. "Onset and Duration of Fertility in Turkeys." *Poultry Sci.* 29 (1950):20.

LUCAS, A. M. "A Discussion of Synonymy in Avian and Mammalian Hematological Nomenclature." *Am. J. Vet. Res.* 20 (1959):887.

LUCAS, A. M., and JAMROZ, C. *Atlas of Avian Hematology.* USDA, 1961.

LUCAS, A. M., and STETTENHEIM, P. R. "Avian Anatomy." In *Diseases of Poultry,* 5th ed., edited by H. E. Biester and L. H. Schwarte. Ames, Iowa: Iowa State University Press, 1965.

MACHLIN, L. J. "Studies on the Forced Involution of the Ovary and Oviduct of Hens." *Poultry Sci.* 43 (1964):1336.

MALEWITZ, T. D., and CALHOUN, M. L. "The Gross and Microscopic Anatomy of the Digestive Tract, Spleen, Kidney, Lungs, and Heart of the Turkey." *Poultry Sci.* 37 (1958):388.

MARSHALL, A. J. *Biology and Comparative Physiology of Birds,* Vol. 2. New York: Academic Press, 1961.

MARSHALL, A. J., and COOMBS, C. J. F. "Lipoid Changes in the Gonads of Wild Birds—Their Possible Bearing on Hormone Production." *Nature* (London) 1952.

MAUGER, H. H. "The Autonomic Innervation of the Genitalia of the Domestic Fowl and Its Correlation With Aortic Branchings. *Am. J. Vet. Res.* 1, 2 (1941):447–52.

MAXIMOW, A. A., and BLOOM, W. *A Textbook of Histology.* 7th ed. Philadelphia and London: W. B. Saunders Co., 1957.

MAYER, D. T., and LASLEY, J. F. "The Factor in Egg Yolk Affecting Resistance and Storage Potentialities of Mammalian Spermatozoa. *J. Animal Sci.* 3 (1944):433.

McCLUNG, R. *Handbook of Microscopical Technique.* London: Cassel and Co. Ltd., 1950.

McLEOD, W. M., TROTTER, D. M., and LUMB, J. W. *Avian Anatomy.* Minneapolis: Burgess Publishing Co., 1964.

McNALLY, E. H. "The Origin and Structure of the Vitelline Membrane of the Domestic Fowl's Egg." *Poultry Sci.* 22 (1943):40–43.

MIVART, G. "The Skeleton of *Lorius flavopalliatus* Compared With That of *Psittacus erithacus.*" Part I. *Proc. Zool. Soc. London,* 1895.

MONTAGNA, W. "Some Cytochemical Observations on Human Testes and Epididymides." *Acad. Sci.* 55 (1952):629–42.

MOORE, C. A., and ELLIOTT, R. E. Numerical and Regional Distribution of Taste Buds of the Bird." *J. Comp. Neurol.* 84 (1946):119.

MOSIER, H. D. "The Development of the Hypothalamo-neurohypophyseal Secretory System in the Chick Embryo." *Endocrinology* 57 (1955):661.

MUNRO, S. S. "The Effect of Dilution and Density on the Fertilizing Capacity of Fowl Sperm Suspensions." *Can. J. Res. D.* 16 (1938):281–99.

MYERS, J. A. "Studies on the Syrinx of *Gallus domesticus.*" *J. Morphol.* 29 (1917):165.

NALBANDOV, A. V. *Reproductive Physiology.* San Francisco: Freeman and Co., 1958.

NALBANDOV, A. V., and JAMES, M. F. "The Blood Vascular System of the Chicken Ovary. *Am. J. Anat.* 85 (1949):347–48.

NEWTON, A. *A Dictionary of Birds.* London: Adam and Charles Black, 1896.

NISHIDA, T. "Comparative and Topographical Anatomy of the Fowl. II. On the Blood Vascular System of the Thoracic Limb in the Fowl. Part I. The Artery." *Japan. J. Vet. Sci.* 22 (1960):223.

————. "Comparative and Topographical Anatomy of the Fowl. II. On the Blood Vascular System of the Hind Limb in the Fowl. Part I. The Artery." *Japan. J. Vet. Sci.* 25 (1963):93.

NISHIYAMA, H. *Studies on the Physiology of Reproduction in the Male Fowl. II. On the Erection of the Rudimentary Copulatory Organ.* Sci. Bull. Fac. Agr. Kyushu 12 (1950b):37–46.

————. *Studies on the Physiology of Reproduction in the Male Fowl. On the Accessory Organs of the Phallus.* Sci. Bull. Fac. Agr. Kyushu 12 (1950c):27–36.

————. *Studies on the Physiology of Reproduction in the Male Fowl. III. On the Addition of Transparent Fluid to the Cock's Semen.* Sci. Bull. Fac. Agr. Kyushu 13 (1951):377–87.

————. *Studies on the Physiology of Reproduction in the Male Fowl. IV. On the Mechanism of the Ejection of Transparent Fluid.* Sci. Bull. Fac. Agr. Kyushu 13 (1952a):283–92.

————. *On the Hydrogen-Ion Concentration of the Transparent Semen in the Fowl.* Sci. Bull. Fac. Agr. Kyushu 12 (1952b):277–81.

————. "Studies on the Reproductive Physiology of the Cock. V. The Influence of Androgen on the Accessory Organs of the Phallus." *Proc. 10th World's Poultry Congr.,* Sect. A, 1954.

OKSCHE, A. "The Fine Nervous Neurosecretory and Glial Structure of Median Eminence in the White-crowned Sparrow." *Proc. 3rd Intern. Conf. Neurosecretion,* Bristol, 1962.

OKSCHE, A., LAWS, D. F., KAMEMOTO, F. I., and FARNER, D. S. "The Hypothalamo-hypophyseal Neurosecretory System of the White-crowned Sparrow." *Z. Zellforsch.* 51 (1959):1.

OKSCHE, A., WILSON, W. O., and FARNER, D. S. "The Hypothalamic Neurosecretory System in Japanese Quail." *Poultry Sci.* 40 (1961):1438.

————. "The Hypothalamic Neurosecretory System of *Coturnix japonica.*" *Z. Zellforsch.* 61 (1964):688.

OLSEN, M. W., and NEHER, B. H. "The Site of Fertilization in the Domestic Fowl." *J. Exp. Zool.* 109 (1948):355–66.

OLSON, C. "Variations in the Cells and Hemoglobin Content in the Blood of the Normal Chicken." *Cornell Vet.* 24 (1937):235.

OOTA, Y., and KOBAYASHI, H. "Fine Structures of the Median Eminence and Pars Nervosa of the Pigeon." *Annot. Zool. Jap.* 35 (1962):128.

OSTMANN, O. W., RINGER, R. K., and TETZLAFF, M. "The Anatomy of the Feather Follicle and Its Immediate Surroundings." *Poultry Sci.* 42 (1963):958.

PADGETT, C. A. "Embryology and Gonadal Development of Coturnix Quail." M.S. thesis, Auburn University, 1958.

PADGETT, C. A., and IVEY, W. D. "Coturnix Quail as a Laboratory Research Animal." *Science* 129 (1959):267–68.

————. "Gonadal Histogenesis in the Coturnix Quail." *J. Alabama Acad. Sci.* 31 (1960):1–11.

PALMIERI, G. "Structure of the Oviduct of Hens at Different Functional Stages." *Nuova Vet.* 41 (1965):169–82.

PARKER, G. H. "The Ciliary Systems in the Oviduct of the Pigeon." *Proc. Soc. Exp. Biol. Med.* 27 (1930):704–6.

PARKER, J. E. "Reproductive Physiology in Poultry." In *Reproduction in Farm Animals,* edited by E. S. E. Hafez. Philadelphia: Lea & Febiger, 1962.

PAYNE, F. "The Cytology of the Anterior Pituitary of the Fowl." *Biol. Bull.* 82 (1942):79.

————. "A Cytological Study of the Thyroid Glands of Normal and Experimental Fowl, Including Interrelationships With the Pituitary, Gonads, and Adrenals." *J. Morphol.* 101 (1957):89.

————. Cytologic Evidence of Secretory Activity in the Neurohypophysis of the Fowl." *Anat. Rec.* 134 (1959):433.

PAYNE, F., and BRENEMAN, W. R. "Lymphoid Areas in Endocrine Glands of Fowl." *Poultry Sci.* 31 (1952):155.

PEARL, R., and BORING, A. M. "The Corpus Luteum in the Ovary of the Domestic Fowl. *Am. J. Anat.* 23 (1918):1–35.

PEARL, R., and SCHOPE, W. R. "Studies on the Physiology of Reproduction in the Domestic Fowl." *J. Exp. Zool.* 34 (1921):101–18.

PERRY, J. S., and ROLANDO, I. W. "The Ovarian Cycle in Vertebrates." In *The Ovary,* edited by S. Zuckerman. New York: Academic Press, 1962.

PORTMANN, A. "Sensory Organs: Equilibration." In A. J. Marshall, *Biology and and Comparative Physiology of Birds.* New York: Academic Press, 1961b.

PUMPHREY, R. "Sensory Organs: Vision." In A. J. Marshall, *Biology and Comparative Physiology of Birds.* New York: Academic Press, 1961a.

RAHN, H., and PAINTER, B. T. "A Comparative Histology of the Bird Pituitary." *Anat. Rec.* 79 (1941):297.

RENZONI, A., and ZUAY, W. B. "Comparative Studies of Pineal Structure and Composition in Birds." *Am. Zool.* 3 (1963):554.

REYNOLDS, S. H. *The Vertebrate Skeleton.* Vol. 16. New York: Cambridge University Press, 1913.

RIDDLE, O. "The Cyclical Growth of the Vesicula Seminalis in Birds Is Hormone Controlled." *Anat. Rec.* 37 (1927):1.

RINGER, A. "Thyroids." In P. D. Sturkie, *Avian Physiology,* 2nd ed. Ithaca, N.Y.: Comstock Publishing Co., 1965.

ROMANOFF, A. L. "Growth of the Avian Ovum." *Anat. Rec.* 85 (1943):261–67.

ROMANOFF, A. L., and ROMANOFF, A. J. *The Avian Egg*. New York: John Wiley and Sons, 1949.

ROMER, A. S. "The Development of the Thigh Musculature of the Chick." *J. Morphol. Physiol.* 43 (1927):347.

SCOTHORNE, R. J. "The Nasal Glands of Birds: A Histological and Histochemical Study of the Inactive Gland in the Domestic Duck." *J. Anat.* 93 (1959):246.

SHUFELDT, R. W. *Osteology of Birds*. Bull. New York State Museum, No. 130 (1909):5–381.

SISSON, S., and GROSSMAN, J. D. *Anatomy of the Domestic Animals*. 4th ed. Philadelphia and London: W. B. Saunders Co., 1960.

SITTMAN, K., and ABPLANALP, H. "Duration and Recovery of Fertility in Japanese Quail *(Coturnix coturnix japonica)*." *Poultry Sci.* 6 (1965):245–50.

STOTT, G. G. "Anatomy and Histology of the Female Genitalia of Coturnix Quail." M.S. thesis, Auburn University, 1967.

SKALLER, F. "Artificial Insemination Applied on a Large Scale to Poultry Breeding Research." *Proc. 11th World's Poultry Congr.* 3, (1951):124–29.

SMITH, M. L. *Anatomy of the Brain and Cranial Nerves of the Turkey*. Univ. Colo. Stud., Ser. A, 26 (1941):135.

STURKIE, P. D. *Avian Physiology*. Ithaca, N.Y.: Comstock Publishing Co. (1st ed. 1954), 1965.

STURKIE, P. D., and FREEDMAN, S. L. "Effects of Transection of Pelvic and Lumbosacral Nerves on Ovulation and Oviposition in Fowl." *J. Reprod. Fertility* 4 (1962):81.

SURFACE, F. M. *Histology of the Oviduct in the Hen*. Maine Agr. Exp. Sta. Bull. 206 (1912):395–435.

SUTTON-VANE, S. *The Story of Eyes*. New York: The Viking Press, 1959.

TABER, E., TABER, J., KNIGHT, S. S., AYERS, C., and FISHBURN, J. F., JR. "Factors Controlling Growth and Differentiation of the Right Gonad in the Female Domestic Fowl." *Gen. Comp. Endocrinol.* 4 (1964):343–52.

TANAKA, K., MATHER, F. B., and WILSON, W. O. "The Effect of Photoperiods on Early Growth of Gonads and on Anterior Pituitary in Coturnix Quail." *Poultry Sci.* 43 (1964a):1368.

TANAKA, K., WILSON, W. O., and MATHER, F. B. "Diurnal Variation in Gonadotrophic Potency of Anterior Pituitaries in Coturnix Quail." *Poultry Sci.* 43 (1964b):1369.

TANAKA, K., MATHER, F. B., WILSON, W. O., and McFARLAND, L. Z. "Effect of Photoperiods on Early Growth of Gonads and on Potency of Gonadotrophins of the Anterior Pituitary in Coturnix Quail. *Poultry Sci.* 44 (1965):662–65.

TRAUTMANN, A., and FIEBIGER, J. *Fundamentals of Histology of Domestic Animals*. Ithaca, N.Y.: Comstock Publishing Co., 1957.

VAN KREY, H. P., OGASAWARA, F. X., and LORENZ, F. W. "Relative Storage Potential of the Uterovaginal and Infundibular Sperm Glands of Poultry." *Poultry Sci.* 43 (1964):1373.

VAN TEINHOVEN, A. "Further Study of Neurogenic Blockade of L. H. Release in the Hen." *Anat. Rec.* 115 (1953):374.

————. "The Physiology of Reproduction in Birds." In *Reproduction in Domestic Animals*. Vol. 2, edited by H. H. Cole and P. T. Cupps. New York: Academic Press, 1959.

VERMA, O. P., and CHERMS, F. L. "Observations on the Oviduct of Turkeys." *Avian Diseases* 8 (1964):19–20.

WALLACE, G. J. *An Introduction to Ornithology*. New York: Macmillan, 1955.

WALLS, G. L. *The Vertebrate Eye and Its Adaptive Radiation*. Bloomfield Hills, Mich.: Cranbrook Institute of Science, 1942.

WARREN, D. C., and SCOTT, H. M. "Ovulation in the Domestic Hen." *Science* 80 (1934):461.

WATABE, M. "Comparative Anatomy of the Bony Labyrinth of *Gallus gallus domesticus*." *Hirosaki Med. J.* 11 (1960):320.

WATANABE, T. "Comparative and Topographical Anatomy of the Fowl. VII. On the Peripheral Course of the Vagus Nerve in the Fowl." *Japan J. Vet. Sci.* 22 (1960):145.

WELTY, J. C. *The Life of Birds*. Philadelphia and London: W. B. Saunders Co., 1962.

WENTWORTH, B. C., and MELLEN, W. J. "Circulating Thyroid Hormones in Domestic Birds." *Poultry Sci.* 40 (1961b):1275.

WETHERBEE, D. K. *Natal Plumages and Downy Pterylases of Passerine Birds of North America*. Bull. Am. Museum Nat. Hist. 113 (1957):339.

WILCOX, F. H., and CLOUD, W. S. "Alkaline Phosphatase in the Reproductive System of the Hen." *J. Reprod. Fertility* 10 (1965):321–28.

WILLIAMS, J. L. "The Development of Cervical Vertebrae in the Chick Under Normal and Experimental Conditions." *Am. J. Anat.* 71 (1942):153.

WILLIAMSON, J. H. "Studies of Cystic Right Oviducts in Two Strains of White Leghorns." *Poultry Sci.* 43 (1964g):1170–77.

————. "Cystic Remnant of the Right Mullerian Duct and Egg Production in Two Strains of White Leghorns." *Poultry Sci.* 43 (1964b):1375–76.

WILSON, W. O., URSULA, K. A., and ABPLANALP, H. "Evaluation of Coturnix as a Pilot Animal for Poultry." *Poultry Sci.* 40 (1961):651–57.

WILSON, W. O., SIOPES, T. D., and MATHER, F. B. "Effect of Frequent Photoperiods and Light Intensity on Reproduction in Quail." *Quail Quart.* 2 (1965):23–24.

WINGSTRAND, K. G. *The Structure and Development of the Avian Pituitary*. Lund, Sweden: C. W. K. Gleerup, 1951.

WOOD-GUSH, D. G. M., and GILBURG, A. B. "Relationship Between the Ovary and Oviduct in the Domestic Hen." *Nature* (London) 207 (1965):1210–11.

WOODWARD, A. E., and MATHER, F. B. "The Timing of Ovulation, Movement of the Ovum Through the Oviduct, Pigmentation, and Shell Deposition in Japanese Quail." *Poultry Sci.* 43 (1964):1427–32.

Index

Tenacular ligament of eye, 264
Tentorium cerebellae, 172
Tertiary bronchi, 247, 249
Testis, 256
Thalamus, 174
Thermal control, 272, 273
Thymus, 279, 280
Thyroid, 277, 278
Tongue, 210, 211, 212
Tonsil
  cecal, 224
  esophageal, 219
Touch, sense of, 172, 273
Trabeculae, of spleen, 238
Trachea, 244, 245, 246
Tracheal rings, 244
Transverse canal, 16
Transverse process of vertebrae, 16, 17, 18, 19
Tricuspid valve, 60
Trochanter, major of femur, 27, 28
Trochlea
  of femur, 27, 29
  of ulna, 25
Tuber cinereum, 174
Tuberosity
  of humerus (lateral, medial, deltoid), 23–24
  of radius, 25
  of rib, 20
  of scapula, 22
  of ulna, 25
Turbinates
  caudal, 10, 241
  middle, 10, 241
  rostral, 240
Tympanic cavity, 10
Tympanic membrane, 268

Uncinate ligament, 35
Ungual phalanx, 31
Ureter, 253, 254
Urodeum, 226
Uropygeal gland (oil, preen), 282
Uterus (shell gland), 259
Utriculus, 269
Uveal coat of eye, 263, 264

Vagina, 257
Valleculae, 174
Valve
  atrioventricular, 60, 61
  bicuspid, 61
  mitral, 61
  pulmonary, 61
  semilunar, 61, 62
  tricuspid, 60
Vasa efferentia, 257
Vascular coat of eye, 263, 264
Vas deferens (ductus deferens), 257
Vein
  afferent renal, 105
  anastomotic (of pes), 84
  auricular, 97
  auris interna, 96

axillary, 68, 74
brachialis (vena comitans, satellite), 75
cardiac, 62, 63
carotid, 96
caudal anastomotic, 96
caudal cephalic, 95
caudal external thoracic, 68
caudal femoral, 82
caudal hemorrhoidal, 104
caudal mesenteric (coccygeomesenteric), 104
caudal tibial, 83
caudal vena cava, 60, 61
circumflex femoral, 82
coccygeomesenteric (caudal mesenteric), 104
common iliac (external iliac), 102, 104
communicating, 104
coracoid, 68
coronary, 62, 63
cranial cephalic, 96
cranial choroid plexus, 102
cranial external thoracic, 68
cranial hemorrhoidal, 105
cranial mesenteric, 107
cranial renal, 102
cranial tibial, 84
cranial vena cava, 68
cutaneous, of neck, 94
deep brachial, 75
deep humeral, 75
digital, 84
dorsal, 94
dorsal digital, 74
dorsal metacarpal, 74
dorsal metatarsal, 84
dorsal pedal, 84
dorsal thoracic, 68
efferent renal, 106
esophageal, 94
ethmoidal, 98
external facial, 97
external iliac (common iliac), 82, 103
external occipital, 96
femoral, 82
floccular, 96
great coronary, 60
hepatic, 102
hepatic portal, 107
hyoid, 98
hypogastric (internal iliac), 104
inferior alveolar, 97
infraorbital, 97
infrapalatine, 96
ingluvies, 94
internal iliac (hypogastric), 104
internal pudic (pudendal), 104
internal thoracic, 68
ischiatic, 82, 104
jugular, 94
laryngeal, 98
lateral digital, 84
lateral occipital, 94
lateral tarsal, 84
left cardiac, 62
lumbar, 102
maxillary, 96